OXFORD WORLD'S CLASSICS

EMINENT VICTORIANS

LYTTON STRACHEY (1880–1932) is best known to posterity as a leading member of the Bloomsbury Group (among whose other luminaries were Virginia Woolf, Maynard Keynes, E. M. Forster, and Roger Fry) and as the author of the scandalous and influential book *Eminent Victorians*. The son of an Indian Service general, Strachey was from childhood chronically frail and, in later life, an unapologetic homosexual. After a largely unhappy time at school he found his milieu, and his vocation, at Cambridge. Here he was elected an 'Apostle', one of a select group of refined students, many of whom would remain his closest friends for life. After an undistinguished performance in his final examinations and a failed attempt at academic life, Strachey drifted into the world of higher London journalism. During the First World War, although medically unfit for any military service, he was courageously pacifist, aligning himself with conscientious objectors such as Bertrand Russell. He gained fame and notoriety with his second book, *Eminent Victorians* (1918), whose wit and irreverence delighted the younger and infuriated the older generation of readers. He consolidated his success with the mellower (and even better selling) *Queen Victoria* (1921). Poor health, and vexed personal relationships, made it difficult for him to sustain his career with books of equal merit. He produced *Elizabeth and Essex*, a historical life study, in 1928, and *Portraits in Miniature* a year before his death, from stomach cancer, in 1932. On his deathbed he expressed the wish that he had married Dora Carrington, with whom he had cohabited for several years. She committed suicide a few weeks later.

JOHN SUTHERLAND is Emeritus Lord Northcliffe Professor of Modern English Literature at University College London, and is the author of a number of books, including *Thackeray at Work*, *Victorian Novelists and Publishers*, and *Mrs Humphry Ward*. He has also edited *Vanity Fair*, *The Woman in White*, and *The Way We Live Now*, and has written *Is Heathcliff a Murderer?*, *Can Jane Eyre Be Happy?*, *Who Betrays Elizabeth Bennet?*, and (with Cedric Watts) *Henry V, War Criminal?* for Oxford World's Classics.

OXFORD WORLD'S CLASSICS

*For over 100 years Oxford World's Classics have brought
readers closer to the world's great literature. Now with over 700
titles—from the 4,000-year-old myths of Mesopotamia to the
twentieth century's greatest novels—the series makes available
lesser-known as well as celebrated writing.*

*The pocket-sized hardbacks of the early years contained
introductions by Virginia Woolf, T. S. Eliot, Graham Greene,
and other literary figures which enriched the experience of reading.
Today the series is recognized for its fine scholarship and
reliability in texts that span world literature, drama and poetry,
religion, philosophy and politics. Each edition includes perceptive
commentary and essential background information to meet the
changing needs of readers.*

OXFORD WORLD'S CLASSICS

LYTTON STRACHEY

Eminent Victorians

Edited with an Introduction and Notes by
JOHN SUTHERLAND

OXFORD
UNIVERSITY PRESS

OXFORD

UNIVERSITY PRESS

Great Clarendon Street, Oxford OX2 6DP

Oxford University Press is a department of the University of Oxford.
It furthers the University's objective of excellence in research, scholarship,
and education by publishing worldwide in

Oxford New York

Auckland Bangkok Buenos Aires Cape Town Chennai
Dar es Salaam Delhi Hong Kong Istanbul Karachi Kolkata
Kuala Lumpur Madrid Melbourne Mexico City Mumbai Nairobi
São Paulo Shanghai Taipei Tokyo Toronto

Oxford is a registered trade mark of Oxford University Press
in the UK and in certain other countries

Published in the United States
by Oxford University Press Inc., New York

First published as an Oxford World's Classics paperback 2003
Reissued 2009

British Library Cataloguing in Publication Data

Data available

Library of Congress Cataloging in Publication Data

Data available

ISBN 978-0-19-955501-7

13

Typeset in Ehrhardt
by RefineCatch Limited, Bungay, Suffolk
Printed and bound in Great Britain by Clays Ltd, Elcograf S.p.A.

CONTENTS

INTRODUCTION

Eminent Victorians is among that small corpus of books which have wholly changed the genre to which they belong. Michael Holroyd, the most distinguished of modern British biographers, perceives it as the baseline from which modern British biography begins. Strachey would have concurred. As he declares—with typical effrontery—in his Preface:

With us, the most delicate and humane of all the branches of the art of writing has been relegated to the journeymen of letters; we do not reflect that it is perhaps as difficult to write a good life as to live one. Those two fat volumes, with which it is our custom to commemorate the dead—who does not know them, with their ill-digested masses of material, their slip-shod style, their tone of tedious panegyric, their lamentable lack of selection, of detachment, of design? They are as familiar as the *cortège* of the undertaker, and wear the same air of slow, funereal barbarism. One is tempted to suppose, of some of them, that they were composed by that functionary, as the final item of his job. (p. 6)

Strachey, to misquote (as he himself is rarely averse to doing), comes not to bury the Victorians but to dispraise them to extinction: with the full apparatus of the 'art of writing' and, above all, 'becoming brevity'. He will—he proposes—do for biography what his *confrère* Henry James did with his 'art of fiction' for the 'great baggy monsters' of Victorian fiction. Refine, shape, and raise it from the elephantine tedium of obituary to the ranks of worthwhile (slim-volumed) literature.

Eminent Victorians came, in a sense, out of nowhere; yet it was, as Strachey maintains, historically inevitable. Before the book's publication (Giles) Lytton Strachey (1880–1932) was known, if at all, as a belletrist of relatively minor achievement: a sharp journalist and a connoisseur of the French literature that the English have never much liked to read.

He was, for those who frequented the salons of literary London, one of the ultra-fine poseurs who made up what was gradually becoming known as the Bloomsbury Group. This connection would not have recommended him to the public at large in 1912, still recoiling from the Oscar Wilde scandal. It was not a good time to be in any sense 'queer'. At 38 years old, Strachey had still to make his mark. As Michael Holroyd pictures him, in 1912:

In the fashionable phoney world of the upper classes he was a complete nonentity. People who, a mere half-dozen years later, would entreat him to lunch or dine with them, now viewed him with unconcealed distaste or overlooked him altogether. And he returned their air of contemptuous, empty-headed superiority with scathing disdain.[1]

The composition of *Eminent Victorians* and the preparation of its text for press (1912–18) coincided with the First World War: a fitting, if Wagnerian, background for a work which spectacularly subverted the certainties on which the Victorian age was founded. Some might argue that the spurious ideals of the earlier century (Queen, God, Country, Empire) were a main cause of the most terrible holocaust to afflict Europe since the Black Death. Strachey (the son of a Victorian general, a lifelong invalid, a conscientious objector, a defiant homosexual) was indubitably of that mind. His parents' generation had much to answer for.

Strachey's physical appearance, as he was writing *Eminent Victorians*, was itself a potent anti-war protest. This is how his publisher, the dandiacal Frank Swinnerton, recorded his first impression of the author, in January 1917:

He was fairly tall but his excessive thinness, almost emaciation, caused him to appear endless. He had a rather bulbous nose, the spectacles of a British Museum bookworm, a large and straggly dark beard (with a curious rufous tinge); no voice at all. He drooped if he stood upright and sagged if he sat down. He seemed entirely without vitality; and most people would have mistaken him for an elderly professor of languages who was trying to remember some grammatical rule which he had forgotten about. Sad merriment was in his eye, and about him a perpetual air of sickness and debility.[2]

Nothing there to frighten the Kaiser.

Michael Holroyd insists—against the received view that Strachey airily ignored the war—that 'it filled the horizon wherever he went, blighting his days and troubling his nights'.[3] And, of course, it dis-

---

[1] Michael Holroyd, *Lytton Strachey: A Critical Biography*, 2 vols. (1967–8), ii. 102. As citations in this introduction indicate I am immensely grateful for, and reliant on, Holroyd's pioneering scholarship.

[2] Ibid. 251.

[3] Ibid. 116.

turbed his work in progress in interesting ways. Like George Bernard Shaw's *Heartbreak House*, or D. H. Lawrence's *Women in Love*, Eminent Victorians was conditioned by the historical cataclysm against whose incessant rumbling it took shape. It is not a work easily detached from its historical moment. Nor should it be.

With hindsight, we can see the four chapters as forming distinct chronological layers, with moods corresponding to the current state of hostilities. 'Cardinal Manning' (1912–14) was written in the jingoistic and least troubled phase of the Great War. 'At this stage,' Holroyd writes, 'Bloomsbury was less resolutely pacifist than is popularly supposed.'[4] 'Florence Nightingale' was written in 1915. To paraphrase Thackeray, Strachey did not number himself among the military biographers. But it is logical to see pointed contemporary allusion in the description of Scutari, and the pervasive Whitehall maladministration which, in 1854–5, killed almost as many men in British Army hospitals as did the Russians at the front. The Arnold portrait was done over the years 1915–16. In 1916, Strachey himself was called to justify his conscientious objection before the Hampstead Tribunal. The episode is emblematic—the pacifist at bay, with only his rapier wit to defend himself. In the course of the examination (at which members of his family were present):

the military representative attempted to cause him some embarrassment by firing a volley of awkward questions from the bench.

'I understand, Mr Strachey, that you have a conscientious objection to all wars?'

'Oh no,' came the piercing, high-pitched reply, 'not at all. Only this one.'

'Then tell me, Mr Strachey, what would you do if you saw a German soldier attempting to rape your sister?'

Lytton turned and forlornly regarded each of his sisters in turn. Then he confronted the Board once more and answered with gravity: 'I should try and interpose my own body.'[5]

'The End of General Gordon', bleakest of the portraits (and another indictment of British military blimpishness and government bungling), was written in the darkest year of the war, 1917. *Eminent Victorians* itself was published in May 1918, 'interposing' itself five months before Armistice day.

---

[4] Ibid. 118.   [5] Ibid. 116.

One of *Eminent Victorians*' first readers, Frank Swinnerton (the editor at Chatto who accepted it for publication), recalls it as an experience strangely mixed with the turmoil of wartime London. He picked up the typescript in his Piccadilly office. His initial intention (busy publisher that he was) was merely to get a feel of the book. But 'the pages were so enchanting', he later wrote:

that I continued, and when night fell I could not leave the book, but took it carefully home . . . I had hardly taken the typescript up again after dinner when . . . there was an air raid by Germans. The whirring of aeroplanes overhead, the rattle of machine-gun fire, and finally the frightful thunder of a gun in the field at the bottom of our garden, would all have served do distract a mind less happily engaged; but as it was, with curtains closely drawn to prevent the escape of light, I consorted that evening with Cardinal Manning, Thomas Arnold, Florence Nightingale, and General Gordon. The nineteenth century had come alive again.[6]

Had the Great War's thunderous soundtrack not accompanied *Eminent Victorians* (had it, for example, been published in 1912), the book would—probably—have expired largely unnoticed, like most books. As it was, *Eminent Victorians* not only hit its mark: it helped change the sensibility of its time, shaking off what Leonard Woolf called the 'mortmain' (dead hand) of the last century, once and for all. Strachey was no modernist: his closest stylistic affinities are with Gibbon and Voltaire. But like those other destroyers of Victorianism —Ibsen, Shaw, and Samuel Butler—he made modernism possible. As Cyril Connolly observed, *Eminent Victorians* was 'the first book of the twenties . . . the light at the end of the tunnel'. It was not merely General Gordon who had ended.

As his manuscripts reveal, Strachey took particular care with the openings of his four portraits. In the second sentence of 'Cardinal Manning' he lays down a significant marker: 'His life was extraordinary in many ways, but its interest for the modern inquirer depends mainly upon two considerations—the light which his career throws upon the spirit of his age, and the psychological problems suggested by his inner history' (p. 9). 'Spirit of the age' refers the 'modern inquirer' back to Hazlitt. 'Psychological problems' and 'inner history' refer him to Freud. Strachey was steeped in the theories of psychoanalysis. His brother James had been Freud's pupil and

---

[6] Ibid. 250.

translator. It is not far-fetched to see *Eminent Victorians* as Oedipal biography, a striking of the father dead (an act Virginia Woolf would later do, with Mr Ramsay, in *To the Lighthouse*). Strachey was, for the first fifteen years of his life, himself a Victorian. That paternal inheritance must be exorcized.

All four of Strachey's subjects are portrayed as 'neurotics'—victims of their 'psychological problems' (problems wholly invisible to their admiring contemporaries, to themselves, and to the first generation of benighted biographers). When, in his Preface, Strachey talks of dropping his 'little bucket' into the oceanic Victorian depths the image is elegant, but not entirely apt. He was more like the potholer, headlamp glimmering, examining the dark and dirty labyrinth of the Victorian unconscious. He presents his finds with devastating understatement, contriving to hint terrible things in such apparently innocent observations as that on Gordon: 'he was particularly fond of boys' (p. 179).

It is significant that the eminent quartet comprise two lifelong virgins (Nightingale and Gordon), one celibate (Manning), and an uxorious, sex-driven monogamist (Arnold). All were excessively devout. Sex and Christianity (the second repressing the first) are, one infers, the energies driving these monsters of rectitude, virtue, public service, and heroism. Sex somehow gone wrong was the source of Manning's insatiable 'careerism', Nightingale's 'demon', Arnold's manic 'militancy', and Gordon's suicidal 'fatalism'.

It is only fair to his luckless victims to add that Strachey tendentiously overlooks the sexual, when it suits his book. In his portrait of Nightingale—generally conceded to be his friendliest—he omits to mention her work with venereal disease ('vice') among the armed forces or her promotion of midwifery. To do so would be to allow that the Lady with the Lamp probably knew more about the genital activities of her countrymen and women than did the Bloomsbury homosexual looking back and down on her.

Strachey hit on the idea for *Eminent Victorians* in 1912—two years after 'human character changed', as Virginia Woolf put it, and the world changed for ever; and two years before old Europe would go up in flames. Strachey's original scheme was more ambitious than the quartet which finally saw print in May 1918. He would, he initially thought, have a baker's dozen—a Victorian panorama. In addition to the quartet who survived, he thought he might 'do'

Henry Sidgwick, G. F. Watts, Ellen Terry, Lord Hartington, Charles Darwin, J. S. Mill, Benjamin Jowett, Thomas Carlyle, and Lord Dalhousie. Later, as he was well into the project, he toyed with the idea of Mandell Creighton.[7]

Aside from Carlyle and Darwin, these are not the usual suspects. Many will be unfamiliar, even by name, to modern readers. It is odd that no man or woman of letters suggested themselves; there is no Dickens, Trollope, Thackeray, George Eliot, Brontë, Meredith, or Hardy. Why not? 'Literary distinction', one deduces, is different from 'social eminence'. The great writers of the age were—in Strachey's analysis—immune from the ridicule with which he spatters churchmen, educators, soldiers, philanthropists, and politicians. Reading between the lines, there were even some in these target groups whom he admired sufficiently not to satirize (at least, not excessively): Newman, Gladstone, and Disraeli, for example. One cannot imagine them ever coming under the Stracheyan lash.

At the outset, Strachey foresaw a bundle of briskly 'brief lives'—on the John Aubrey model. A nearer influence was probably J. A. Froude's *Short Studies in Great Subjects* (4 vols., 1867–83), which he was reading aloud with the philosopher G. E. Moore (patron sage of Bloomsbury) in the evenings of 1912. Had Strachey taken on the whole thirteen, the portraits of his subjects would have been short indeed. The first title he came up with, 'Victorian Silhouettes', suggests something deliberately flimsy—flitting shadows on history's great wall.

The 'silhouette' plan was altered with the years-long execution of the project. Strachey chose to begin with Henry Manning as a literal 'eminence', in his office of Cardinal (or, as the ignorant Irishwoman called him, an 'Immense'[8]). The bucket had to plunge deep into the complexities of Victorian religious controversy and factionalism to pluck the heart of this complex cleric. Strachey was sucked down. The silhouette became a fully-fleshed, cap-à-pie portrait. A few more months' work on Manning and he would probably have been left with a monograph entitled 'Eminent Victorian'.

Strachey did not make the mistake in the ensuing three portraits of attempting to miniaturize a whole life. The Nightingale piece is

[7] An excellent account of the genesis of Strachey's book is given in *Eminent Victorians: The Definitive Edition* ed. Paul Levy (2002). See particularly pp. xv–xvi.
[8] See p. 50 and note.

organized round the three Crimean years: everything else is prologue and epilogue to that crisis. With Arnold it is only the fourteen years of headship which are covered. And, as 'The End of General Gordon' indicates, that study concentrates on the last dramatic days at Khartoum.

One can deduce much about *Eminent Victorians'* biographical method, and Strachey's professional standards, from his Preface (probably the last thing he wrote). It climaxes with a majestic protestation: 'That is what I have aimed at in this book—to lay bare the facts of some cases, as I understand, dispassionately, impartially, and without ulterior intentions. To quote the words of a Master—"Je n'impose rien; je ne propose rien: j'expose" ' (p. 6). Who, the reader will wonder, is this *maître*? Voltaire, perhaps (Strachey was working on him, at the time)? No. Voltairean as it sounds, the quotation is fabricated. The 'Master' is none other than Lytton Strachey himself. There follows the first sentence of the Manning section: 'Henry Edward Manning was born in 1807 and died in 1892.' But he wasn't. Henry Manning was born in 1808. As Strachey's manuscript notes record, he was himself unsure of the date but could not, apparently, be bothered to check.

Eminent Victorians is not, we deduce, the work of a stickler for historical fact, documentary trustworthiness, or modern standards of scholarly citation. Art, yes. Any amount of effort was lavished in that department. But accuracy was something else. Like English law, Strachey's motto, as a researcher, was *de minimis non curat*. Nor, to Latinize further, did he have an oppressive sense of *meum* and *tuum* where literary property was concerned. Compare, for example, the opening of the Nightingale section with the opening paragraph of Edward Cook's 1913 biography of her. This is Strachey:

Every one knows the *popular conception of Florence Nightingale*. The saintly, self-sacrificing woman, the delicate *maiden of high degree* who *threw aside the pleasures of a life of ease* to succour the afflicted, the *Lady with the Lamp, gliding through the horrors of the hospital at Scutari*, and consecrating with the radiance of her goodness the dying soldier's couch— the vision is familiar to all. *But the truth was different. . . .* And so it happens that in the real Miss Nightingale there was more that was interesting than in the *legendary* one; there was also less that was agreeable. (p. 97)

And this is Cook's first paragraph:

The *popular imagination of Miss Nightingale* is of a *girl of high degree* who, moved by a wave of pity, *forsook the pleasures of fashionable life* for the horrors of the Crimean War; who went about *the hospitals of Scutari with a lamp*, scattering flowers of comfort and ministration; who retired at the close of the war into private life, and lived thenceforth in the seclusion of an invalid room—a seclusion varied only by good deeds to hospitals and nurses and by gracious and sentimental pieties . . . *The real Florence Nightingale was very different* from *the legendary*, but also greater.[9]

Direct echoes are italicized—but manifestly everything echoes. Can anyone reasonably doubt that, had Cook not published what he did, Strachey would not have written what he did? There is nothing that a modern scholar would recognize as due citation of Strachey's plundered source. Of course, Cook's rather stodgy prose is leavened by Strachey's finer touches. And there is that sting in the tail (later to be extended at venomous length), 'there was also less that was agreeable'. But any student doing this in a Ph.D. thesis (and doing it as comprehensively as Strachey does throughout *Eminent Victorians*) would be flunked for plagiarism.

Strachey has always been an easy target for scrupulous (nitpicking, he might think) scholars (in the Notes I have included some of their trenchant denunciations). There is, I think, no modern biographer of Manning, Nightingale, Arnold, or Gordon who trusts Strachey as a reliable source, or has any other good word for him than that he writes brilliantly (that, of course, might have been praise enough for Strachey).

For his contemporaries, it was the unfairness of the portraits which hit home most hurtfully. Many, with friendlier recollections of their immediate ancestors, were enraged by Strachey's 'irresponsibility'. Edmund Gosse wrote to the *Times Literary Supplement* on 27 June to protest against the virulently sarcastic depiction of Lord Cromer in the General Gordon section. 'Even what is sparkling should be just,' Gosse declared. Mrs Humphry Ward (the most eminent of Edwardians) was reported to be beside herself at the portrait of her grandfather, Thomas Arnold (particularly the mischievously invented sarcasm, 'His legs, perhaps, were shorter than they should have been', p. 147). Mrs Ward wrote indignantly to the

---

[9] Sir Edward Cook, *The Life of Florence Nightingale*, 2 vols. (1913), vol. i, pp. xv–xvi.

Times Literary Supplement on 11 July, declaring herself (with mock humility) as 'an old literary worker and reviewer deeply displeased with "the praise—for the most part unqualified—which has been lavished on Mr. Lytton Strachey's book *Eminent Victorians*" '. That *Eminent Victorians* baited the (dying) author of *Robert Elsmere* was deliciously pleasing to Strachey. Her fury was a 'triumph', he declared.[10] There were many such triumphs. Even Strachey's most loyal apologist, Michael Holroyd, concedes that the depiction of Sir Evelyn Baring in the Gordon chapter is unfair and must have been hurtful to the statesman's surviving family.

Professional historians and biographers have, over the decades, fulminated at the bias and picked away at the pervasive wrongness of much of *Eminent Victorians*. Strachey gives hostages to these critics without even the pretence of a struggle. Take, for example, the paradox which stands as his manifesto, in the Preface's first, defiant, sentence: 'The history of the Victorian Age will never be written: we know too much about it. For ignorance is the first requisite of the historian—ignorance, which simplifies and clarifies, which selects and omits, with a placid perfection unattainable by the highest art' (p. 5). What Strachey permits himself with this brilliantly epigrammatic nonsense is the luxury of scholarly laziness. History and biography, he insinuates, are better done without research. It is art— the stylist's hand—which vivifies.

One should, however, be wary of taking Strachey—ironist that he is—at his word. This wilful pococurantism masks the scholarly effort he put into *Eminent Victorians*. The extensive notes he took in the 'Museum Notebooks' (school exercise books, which he bought from a stationer's en route to the British Museum Reading Room) witness to a creditable amount of spadework. Nor could even the most hostile critic claim that Lytton Strachey dashed off *Eminent Victorians*. It was the labour of five years, even if much of that labour did go into literary polish.

Having hit on the idea of his new book in 1912, Strachey set to work with £100 borrowed from his Cambridge friend, Harry Norton. He left London for monastic life in a cottage—first in Berkshire, then in Wiltshire—on what would turn out to be a kind of one-man, two-year reading party, interrupted only by weekend

[10] John Sutherland, *Mrs Humphry Ward* (1990), 201.

excursions to Hampstead, Bloomsbury, or Cambridge. It was at The Lacket (his Wiltshire cottage) that he wrote, from 1912–14, half of *Eminent Victorians*—breaking its back, so to speak.

Michael Holroyd describes the state of mind of Strachey at the initial period (1912–13) of the book's composition. It is strikingly different from the assured demeanour of *Eminent Victorians*' narrator, as we encounter him on the printed page. Strachey too, we apprehend, had his 'psychological problems':

At times this inactivity would profoundly depress him, but, significantly, his periodic fits of pessimism were of a different order from those that had afflicted him earlier. Then he used to wonder whether he was cut out to be a writer at all, whether he would ever be remotely capable of achieving something worth while; now he was seldom racked by such fundamental doubts, but rather weighed down in contemplation of the overwhelming difficulties, the vitality, the patience, the meticulous skill and concentration needed to bring to full fruit that talent which he recognized lying within him. 'My travail occasionally worries me horribly,' he confessed to Henry Lamb (13 April 1913), 'but I do think I'm making a little progress. I sometimes feel—I can't say what. It is disgusting to *know* that there are things in one, but to see hardly a glimmer of a way of getting them out.'[11]

The four volumes of his manuscript literary materials for *Eminent Victorians*, now housed (very appropriately) in the British Library, indicate Strachey's methods as a biographer. He would extensively mine one or two primary sources for each of his subjects. Typically they would be those 'fat-volumed' behemoths about which he is so rude in his Preface. He did not require that they be reliable sources. In fact, he did not care (so long as they provided good grist for his mill) if they were treacherously unreliable.

Strachey must have known, for example, the scandalous background to Edmund Sheridan Purcell's biography, on which he chooses to base, almost entirely, his interpretation of Manning. Purcell had stolen vast quantities of his subject's archive for the purpose of what was, effectively, a hatchet job. His two-volume *Life* has stunk in the nostrils of Manning scholars ever since it was published (despite protests and attempts to suppress it) in 1895. Strachey must have caught a whiff. None the less, he used Purcell—almost exclusively. From the nervous footnote he appended to the

---

[11] Holroyd, *Lytton Strachey*, ii. 78–9.

bibliography of the Gordon section, Lytton evidently knew that the Li Hung Chang diary, on which he relied heavily for his 'Chinese Gordon' passages, was also a corrupt (and, as it emerged, wholly forged) source. But he did not go back and rewrite once this had become known to him, although he could easily have done so. With Arnold, Strachey drew at inordinate length, and often plagiaristically, from a biographer (the pious sycophant A. P. Stanley) whom he manifestly despised. He never cites or acknowledges his borrowings (except by his appended bibliographies, which are incomplete and offhand). Strachey did no primary research. If it was not printed, for him it did not exist. And many printed resources he ignored (it is clear, for example, that he did not trouble himself to read Arnold's five volumes of sermons, or Newman's published letters). He interviewed no one; although there were many informative Victorians still alive, and only too willing to reminisce. None the less, what he read, he read with close attention and penetration. And, in the Gordon section particularly, he trawled through many files of newspapers in the London Library, assembling the intricate chronology of the hero's last days. He was, to summarize, culpably selective but—where he chose to read—laudably industrious.

From his sources, Strachey would begin by making 'topic notes'. He would jot down dates and 'curious' or illustrative anecdotes. He would try his hand with trial passages. Then he would embark on composition—which came, evidently, with great fluency. He would read, from his fair copy, to his Bloomsbury friends when the work was fit for company. This reading aloud was a useful and formative exercise. *Eminent Victorians* has a coterie feel to it—one hears, in the mind's ear, the muted applause, the chuckles, the occasional gasp. One can also, with a little effort, hear the squeaking, booming voice rolling out the sharp epigrams, delicious sarcasms, and smart cynicisms. The readings attuned Strachey to pace, nuance, and inflection. It pleased him to apply musical analogies to his quartet: Manning—*allegro vivace*; Nightingale—*andante*; Arnold—*scherzo*; Gordon—*rondo*. It was not entirely fanciful. Each of the pieces has its own stylistic mood. Once the manuscript version was perfect, the publishers, Chatto, had fair copies typed up. At this stage, and in proof, Strachey would make another series of fine-tuning verbal improvements: nothing drastic. This mode of composition and revision resulted in a work of extraordinary freshness: it reads grippingly (as Swinnerton testifies), but one also *hears* it.

It is clear that, whatever the documentary or research inadequacies, Strachey succeeded in his first and most important aim: to raise biography from the hack work of 'journeymen' to 'literary' status. He also, probably to his surprise, found himself a bestseller. The reviews were (as Mrs Humphry Ward protested) a chorus of eulogy. *Eminent Victorians* was, the *Times Literary Supplement* declared, 'masterful and subtle'. There was, the reviewer thought, something 'almost uncanny in the author's detachment'. *The Times* pronounced the book 'brilliant and extraordinarily witty'. The *Sunday Times* called it 'audaciously amusing'. J. C. Squire (a literary name to conjure with in 1918) declared *Eminent Victorians* 'a masterpiece'. The book, first published in May 1918 by Chatto at 10s. 6d., was reprinted in early June, in July, August, and September (by this point it was, as Chatto proudly declared, 'the most discussed book of the year'). *Eminent Victorians* sold strongly for the rest of Strachey's short life. It was publicly praised by, among others, the ex-Prime Minister Asquith; it was condemned by, among others, his victims' surviving families. Most importantly, it was everywhere talked about.

Strachey, buoyed up by the book's triumph, toyed with the idea of a second series but went on, instead, to the heart of Victorianism. His *Queen Victoria* came out in 1921. It was followed by *Elizabeth and Essex* (1928). There were other books and writings, until his premature death in 1932. By general agreement, *Eminent Victorians* stands alone as his masterpiece—and the biography that changed biography.

NOTE ON THE TEXT AND MANUSCRIPT

Strachey's manuscripts of the four biographical essays and his working notes for *Eminent Victorians* are held in British Library, Add. 54219–23. He evidently spent time in the British Museum Reading Room—since his notes were compiled in four quarto 'Museum Notebooks', purchased from the stationers Clarke and Davies, in Museum Street. He seems also to have used loose leaves of letter-writing paper.

The texts of the biographical essays contain instructions to the printer but do not have printers' marks on them. The final copy-texts were, presumably, the typescripts prepared by Chatto which seem not to have been preserved. Strachey evidently made minor corrections both to the typescript and to the proofs (although, once the manuscript was received by the publisher, the book seems to have been brought out in only a few months, leaving no time for major revision). Strachey was most careful about layout of the page in his Arnold essay, where he frequently instructs the printer as to breaks and two-line gaps and various typographic effects. He is least attentive in the Gordon essay in which his control of paragraph length (to take an obvious example) goes badly awry. One assumes this last essay was done under pressure of time—perhaps because, as the notebooks indicate, he was obliged to do a great amount of work among newspaper records to get the chronology of Gordon's last months straight.

The manuscript versions of the essays are relatively clean, and where Strachey does interfere with his own composition it is typically to shorten or render elliptical. He was careful not to overdo his effects (shortening, for example, his descriptions of 'hellish' Scutari). It is evident, from a characteristic kind of revision, that Strachey was composing spontaneously, not copying. The following small trip and recovery in the Arnold narrative (Add. 54222), for example, is typical of similar corrections in all four of the manuscript essays:

{Nothing was more striking than} {h} His manner of awful reverence when speaking of God or of the scriptures was particularly striking . . . [crossings out are indicated here by curly brackets]

The memoranda Strachey made for himself are attractively random. He jots down 'queries' to investigate; 'curious' passages from his reading, which have caught his imagination or amused him; chronologies; the occasional trial draft. Most interesting, perhaps, are the short-hand schemes which he laid down, before writing, such as the following for his Manning essay:

Three movements in Eng. Thought.
1. Rationalists (wanted Disestablishment) Bentham v. the Mills. Westminster Review, begun 1824.
2. Broad Churchmen (Whigs).
And [3] Archbp. Whateley and Dr Arnold. Common Sense. (Add. 54219)

In notes for Arnold, he sketched out the following large areas: 'Religion, Public Affairs, Home Life, Religion, etc.' Then, from Stanley's life of Arnold, he made a list of fifty or so 'topics' (with page references) which he followed precisely in his composition of the essay. This reading supplied the skeleton for his portraiture. Evidently he shaped his essays around such categories before filling in with finer-grained material. Shape and design were as important as texture to him. It is interesting to note that he copied out many of Manning's 'Holy Maxims'; not, apparently, because he wanted to quote them, but because they helped him get 'inside' his subject. It seems that for his Arnold essay he kept a small portrait of the Doctor in front of him as he wrote.

In his working notebook (Add. 54219) Strachey jotted down a series of provisional titles for the finished work. His final choice was, evidently, a late and happy afterthought:

Victorian Silhouettes
Some Victorian Silhouettes
Four Victorian Silhouettes
Short Lives of Eminent Victorians
Four Victorians
Four Victorian Lives
Eminent Victorians

The Explanatory Notes to this edition draw attention, where appropriate, to evidence from Strachey's manuscript material.

The text is based on the first edition, published by Chatto in 1918.

SELECT BIBLIOGRAPHY

THERE are two indispensable works for the student of *Eminent Victorians* and its author. Michael Holroyd's *Lytton Strachey: A Critical Biography*, 2 vols. (London 1967–8) and its revised edition, *Lytton Strachey: The New Biography* (1994) supply both the necessary background and an extensive account of the book's composition. The other starting-point is the commemorative 'Definitive Edition' of *Eminent Victorians* (London, 2002), with preface by Frances Partridge, introduction by Paul Levy, and afterwords to the four essays. The works which qualify the four authors of the afterwords as experts are also recommended (none of them, incidentally, approves entirely—or in some cases at all—of Strachey's effort). They are: David Newsome, *The Convert Cardinals: Newman and Manning* (1997); Terence Copley, *Black Tom—Arnold of Rugby, the Myth and the Man* (2000); John Pollock, *Gordon: The Man behind the Legend* (1993); Mark Bostridge's life of Florence Nightingale is, as I write, forthcoming. Paul Levy's *Lytton Strachey: The Really Interesting Question* (1972) and *G. E. Moore and the Cambridge Apostles* (1979) are valuable works of introduction to *Eminent Victorians*. An extremely accessible and fact-packed introduction to the author of *Eminent Victorians* is offered in John Ferns's *Lytton Strachey* (1988), a volume in Twayne's English Authors series. For those who can read French, Gabriel Merle's *Lytton Strachey (1880–1932): Biographe et critique d'un critique et biographe*, 2 vols. (1980), contains much new primary material. Michael Edmonds's *Lytton Strachey: A Bibliography* (1981) is the standard guide to the publication of the author's work and the locations of his literary remains. Serious students may also want to examine Strachey's (easily found) primary sources: E. S. Purcell, *The Life of Cardinal Manning*, 2 vols. (1895); Wilfrid Ward, *The Life and Times of Cardinal Newman*, 2 vols. (1897); Edward Cook, *The Life of Florence Nightingale*, 2 vols. (1913); A. P. Stanley, *The Life of Thomas Arnold, DD* (1844); D. C. Boulger, *The Life of General Gordon* (1896). A very scholarly examination of Strachey's readings and borrowings can be found in G. K. Simson's 'Lytton Strachey's Use of his Sources in *Eminent Victorians*', unpublished dissertation, University of Minnesota, 1963.

A CHRONOLOGY OF LYTTON STRACHEY

1880   (1 March) (Giles) Lytton Strachey born at Stowey House, Clapham Common, London, the eleventh of thirteen children, three of whom died in infancy. Lytton's mother Jane Maria Strachey (née Grant) was the second (and thirty years younger) wife of General Sir Richard Strachey (1818–1908), most of whose distinguished career was spent in India.

1884   The Strachey family moves to 69 Lancaster Gate, where Lytton is brought up. He attends the Hyde Park Kindergarten School.

1885   Death of General Gordon at Khartoum.

1887   James Strachey, last of the children (and later the translator of Freud), is born. He will be Lytton's closest sibling.

1889–93   Lytton attends boarding school at Poole in Dorset. For some months over 1892–3 he is sent on a cruise to the Middle East to recover his frail health. He will be chronically invalid throughout his life. Death of Cardinal Manning, 1892.

1893–4   Attends Abbotsholme School in Derbyshire, where he is desperately unhappy.

1894–6   Attends Leamington College. His homosexuality becomes manifest. He develops a tendency towards self-loathing.

1897–8   Attends Liverpool University, under the wing of the Professor of English, Sir Walter Raleigh. His health remains fragile.

1899–1903   Attends Trinity College Cambridge, where he forms friendships with contemporaries (Clive Bell, Leonard Woolf) who will afford him an entrée to the Bloomsbury Group. He is elected to the Apostles Society in 1902 and wins, in the same year, the Chancellor's Medal for his poem: 'Ely: An Ode'. As an 'Apostle', Strachey is brought into personal and intellectual contact with G. E. Moore, J. Maynard Keynes, Lowes Dickinson, and (indirectly) E. M. Forster. He graduates in 1903 with a disappointing second-class degree in history.

1904   Having failed to gain entry to the Civil Service, Strachey is unsuccessful in his attempt to gain a fellowship at Trinity College.

1905   Embarks on a love affair with his cousin, the artist Duncan Grant. It is complicated, in 1908, when he discovers Grant's connection with J. M. Keynes.

1907   Joins the *Spectator*, where his cousin, St Loe Strachey, is Editor. He writes widely and himself turns down the editorship of the magazine in 1908.

1909   Proposes to Virginia Stephen (later Virginia Woolf) in February. She accepts but he immediately withdraws the proposal ('a fairly honourable retreat'). Strachey's health remains poor, and requires recuperation and travel. In England he resides in London and Cambridge.

1910   Virginia Woolf's cousin, H. A. L. Fisher, invites Strachey to write a study of French literature for the Home University Library series. Deaths of Edward VII and Florence Nightingale.

1911   Strachey begins his relationship with the painter Henry Lamb, the second major love affair of his life. At this period, Strachey allows his beard to grow luxuriantly.

1912   Strachey publishes *Landmarks in French Literature*, which is well received and confirms his ambition to become (in his thirties) a book author. He has first ideas for what later becomes *Eminent Victorians*.

1913   (July) Moves to The Lacket, a country house in Wiltshire, where he remains a year, while writing the first two parts of *Eminent Victorians*.

1914   First World War begins (4 Aug.).

1915   Strachey meets the artist (Dora) Carrington, around the period (November) that he is working on the 'Dr Arnold' part of *Eminent Victorians*.

1916   At his own instigation, and as a pacifist gesture, he is examined by a Conscientious Objection board in Hampstead. He is exempted from military service, on medical grounds.

1917   (October) Moves to the Mill House, Tidmarsh, with Carrington, who has separated from Mark Gertler. In December Chatto & Windus accept *Eminent Victorians*. Strachey has tried out the work by reading chapters aloud to Bloomsbury friends. The work is adopted as one of the group's manifestos.

1918   (May) *Eminent Victorians* is published to acclaim and sales success. (August) Ralph Partridge moves into Tidmarsh where he, Strachey, and Carrington set up a *ménage à trois*. Armistice with Germany (11 Nov.).

1920 Strachey embarks on research for *Queen Victoria*. It is published in 1921. Less satirical than *Eminent Victorians*, it is even more popular.

1921 Carrington marries Ralph Partridge, 21 May. They separate in 1923, when Partridge meets Frances Marshall, whom he eventually marries.

1922 Strachey publishes *Books and Characters*.

1924 Moves from Tidmarsh into Ham Spray House, Hungerford, Berkshire.

1926 Awarded an honorary doctorate by Edinburgh University. Strachey embarks on what will be an unhappy three-year love affair with Roger Senhouse.

1928 Publishes *Elizabeth and Essex*. Sets to work on editing the Greville Memoirs—a task which will prove too much for him. (December) His mother dies (aged 87).

1931 Publishes *Portraits in Miniature*. His health begins to fail terminally.

1932 (21 January) Dies of what is posthumously diagnosed as stomach cancer. On his deathbed, he says he wishes he had married Carringon, who commits suicide on 11 March.

1933 *Characters and Commentaries* published posthumously.

EMINENT
VICTORIANS

TO

H.T. J.N.*

PREFACE

THE history of the Victorian Age will never be written: we know too much about it. For ignorance is the first requisite of the historian – ignorance, which simplifies and clarifies, which selects and omits, with a placid perfection unattainable by the highest art. Concerning the Age which has just passed, our fathers and our grandfathers have poured forth and accumulated so vast a quantity of information that the industry of a Ranke* would be submerged by it, and the perspicacity of a Gibbon* would quail before it. It is not by the direct method of a scrupulous narration that the explorer of the past can hope to depict that singular epoch. If he is wise, he will adopt a subtler strategy. He will attack his subject in unexpected places; he will fall upon the flank, or the rear; he will shoot a sudden, revealing searchlight* into obscure recesses, hitherto undivined. He will row out over that great ocean of material, and lower down into it, here and there, a little bucket, which will bring up to the light of day some characteristic specimen, from those far depths, to be examined with a careful curiosity. Guided by these considerations, I have written the ensuing studies. I have attempted, through the medium of biography, to present some Victorian visions to the modern eye. They are, in one sense, haphazard visions – that is to say, my choice of subjects has been determined by no desire to construct a system or to prove a theory, but by simple motives of convenience and of art. It has been my purpose to illustrate rather than to explain. It would have been futile to hope to tell even a *précis* of the truth about the Victorian age, for the shortest *précis* must fill innumerable volumes. But, in the lives of an ecclesiastic, an educational authority, a woman of action, and a man of adventure, I have sought to examine and elucidate certain fragments of the truth which took my fancy and lay to my hand.

I hope, however, that the following pages may prove to be of interest from the strictly biographical no less than from the historical point of view. Human beings are too important to be treated as mere symptoms of the past. They have a value which is independent of any temporal processes – which is eternal, and must be felt for its own sake. The art of biography seems to have fallen on evil times in

England. We have had, it is true, a few masterpieces, but we have never had, like the French, a great biographical tradition;* we have had no Fontenelles and Condorcets,* with their incomparable *éloges*, compressing into a few shining pages the manifold existences of men. With us, the most delicate and humane of all the branches of the art of writing has been relegated to the journeymen of letters; we do not reflect that it is perhaps as difficult to write a good life as to live one. Those two fat volumes, with which it is our custom to commemorate the dead – who does not know them, with their ill-digested masses of material, their slipshod style, their tone of tedious panegyric, their lamentable lack of selection, of detachment, of design? They are as familiar as the *cortège* of the undertaker, and wear the same air of slow, funereal barbarism. One is tempted to suppose, of some of them, that they were composed by that functionary, as the final item of his job. The studies in this book are indebted, in more ways than one, to such works – works which certainly deserve the name of Standard Biographies.* For they have provided me not only with much indispensable information, but with something even more precious – an example. How many lessons are to be learnt from them! But it is hardly necessary to particularise. To preserve, for instance, a becoming brevity – a brevity which excludes everything that is redundant and nothing that is significant – that, surely, is the first duty of the biographer. The second, no less surely, is to maintain his own freedom of spirit. It is not his business to be complimentary; it is his business to lay bare the facts of the case, as he understands them. That is what I have aimed at in this book – to lay bare the facts of some cases, as I understand them, dispassionately, impartially, and without ulterior intentions. To quote the words of a Master – 'Je n'impose rien; je ne propose rien: j'expose.'*

A list of the principal sources from which I have drawn is appended to each Biography. I would indicate, as an honourable exception to the current commodity, Sir Edward Cook's* excellent Life of Florence Nightingale, *without which my own study, though composed on a very different scale and from a decidedly different angle, could not have been written.*

CARDINAL
MANNING

CARDINAL MANNING

HENRY EDWARD MANNING was born in 1807* and died in 1892. His life was extraordinary in many ways, but its interest for the modern inquirer depends mainly upon two considerations – the light which his career throws upon the spirit of his age, and the psychological problems suggested by his inner history. He belonged to that class of eminent ecclesiastics – and it is by no means a small class – who have been distinguished less for saintliness and learning than for practical ability. Had he lived in the Middle Ages he would certainly have been neither a Francis nor an Aquinas, but he might have been an Innocent.* As it was, born in the England of the Nineteenth Century, growing up in the very seed-time of modern progress, coming to maturity with the first onrush of Liberalism, and living long enough to witness the victories of Science and Democracy, he yet, by a strange concatenation of circumstances, seemed almost to revive in his own person that long line of diplomatic and administrative clerics which, one would have thought, had come to an end for ever with Cardinal Wolsey.* In Manning, so it appeared, the Middle Ages lived again. The tall gaunt figure, with the face of smiling asceticism, the robes, and the biretta, as it passed in triumph from High Mass at the Oratory to philanthropic gatherings at Exeter Hall, from Strike Committees at the Docks* to Mayfair drawing-rooms where fashionable ladies knelt to the Prince of the Church, certainly bore witness to a singular condition of affairs. What had happened? Had a dominating character imposed itself upon a hostile environment? Or was the Nineteenth Century, after all, not so hostile? Was there something in it, scientific and progressive as it was, which went out to welcome the representative of ancient tradition and uncompromising faith? Had it, perhaps, a place in its heart for such as Manning – a soft place, one might almost say? Or, on the other hand, was it he who had been supple and yielding? he who had won by art what he would never have won by force, and who had managed, so to speak, to be one of the leaders of the procession less through merit than through a superior faculty for gliding adroitly to the front rank? And, in any case, by what odd chances, what shifts and struggles, what combinations of circumstance and character, had this old man come to be where he was? Such questions are easier to ask than to answer; but it may be instructive, and even amusing, to look a little more closely into the complexities of so curious a story.

I

UNDOUBTEDLY, what is most obviously striking in the history of Manning's career is the persistent strength of his innate character-istics. Through all the changes of his fortunes the powerful spirit of the man worked on undismayed. It was as if the Fates had laid a wager that they would daunt him; and in the end they lost their bet.

His father was a rich West India merchant, a governor of the Bank of England, a Member of Parliament, who drove into town every day from his country seat in a coach and four, and was content with nothing short of a bishop for the christening of his children. Little Henry, like the rest, had his bishop; but he was obliged to wait for him – for as long as eighteen months. In those days, and even a generation later, as Keble* bears witness, there was great laxity in regard to the early baptism of children. The delay has been noted by Manning's biographer* as the first stumbling-block in the spiritual life of the future Cardinal: but he surmounted it with success.

His father was more careful in other ways. 'His refinement and delicacy of mind were such,' wrote Manning long afterwards, 'that I never heard out of his mouth a word which might not have been spoken in the presence of the most pure and sensitive – except,' he adds, 'on one occasion. He was then forced by others to repeat a negro story which, though free from all evil *de sexu*,* was indelicate. He did it with great resistance. His example gave me a hatred of all such talk.' The family lived in an atmosphere of Evangelical piety. One day the little boy came in from the farmyard, and his mother asked him whether he had seen the peacock. 'I said yes, and the nurse said no, and my mother made me kneel down and beg God to forgive me for not speaking the truth.' At the age of four the child was told by a cousin of the age of six that 'God had a book in which He wrote down everything we did wrong. This so terrified me for days that I remember being found by my mother sitting under a kind of writ-ing-table in great fear. I never forgot this at any time in my life,' the Cardinal tells us, 'and it has been a great grace to me.' When he was

nine years old he 'devoured the Apocalypse;* and I never all through
my life forgot the "lake that burneth with fire and brimstone". That
verse has kept me like an audible voice through all my life, and
through worlds of danger in my youth.'

At Harrow the worlds of danger were already around him; but yet
he listened to the audible voice. 'At school and college I never failed
to say my prayers, so far as memory serves me, even for a day.' And
he underwent another religious experience: he read Paley's *Evidences*.* 'I took in the whole argument,' wrote Manning, when he was
over seventy, 'and I thank God that nothing has ever shaken it.' Yet
on the whole he led the unspiritual life of an ordinary schoolboy. We
have glimpses of him as a handsome lad, playing cricket, or strutting
about in tasselled Hessian top-boots.* And on one occasion at least he
gave proof of a certain dexterity of conduct which deserved to be
remembered. He went out of bounds, and a master, riding by and
seeing him on the other side of a field, tied his horse to a gate, and
ran after him. The astute youth outran the master, fetched a circle,
reached the gate, jumped on to the horse's back and rode off. For
this he was very properly chastised; but of what use was chastisement? No whipping, however severe, could have eradicated from
little Henry's mind a quality at least as firmly planted in it as his fear
of Hell and his belief in the arguments of Paley.

It had been his father's wish that Manning should go into the
Church; but the thought disgusted him; and when he reached
Oxford, his tastes, his ambitions, his successes at the Union, all
seemed to mark him out for a political career. He was a year junior to
Samuel Wilberforce, and a year senior to Gladstone.* In those days
the Union was the recruiting-ground for young politicians; Ministers came down from London to listen to the debates; and a few
years later the Duke of Newcastle gave Gladstone a pocket borough
on the strength of his speech at the Union against the Reform Bill.
To those three young men, indeed, the whole world lay open. Were
they not rich, well-connected, and endowed with an infinite capacity
for making speeches? The event justified the highest expectations of
their friends; for the least distinguished of the three died a bishop.
The only danger lay in another direction. 'Watch, my dear Samuel,'
wrote the elder Wilberforce to his son, 'watch with jealousy whether
you find yourself unduly solicitous about acquitting yourself;
whether you are too much chagrined when you fail, or are puffed up

by your success. Undue solicitude about popular estimation is a weakness against which all real Christians must guard with the utmost jealous watchfulness. The more you can retain the impression of your being surrounded by a cloud of witnesses of the invisible world, to use the scripture phrase, the more you will be armed against this besetting sin.' But suddenly it seemed as if such a warning could, after all, have very little relevance to Manning; for, on his leaving Oxford, the brimming cup was dashed from his lips. He was already beginning to dream of himself in the House of Commons, the solitary advocate of some great cause whose triumph was to be eventually brought about by his extraordinary efforts, when his father was declared a bankrupt, and all his hopes of a political career came to an end for ever.

It was at this time that Manning became intimate with a pious lady,* the sister of one of his College friends, whom he used to describe as his Spiritual Mother. He made her his confidante; and one day, as they walked together in the shrubbery, he revealed the bitterness of the disappointment into which his father's failure had plunged him. She tried to cheer him, and then she added that there were higher aims open to him which he had not considered. 'What do you mean?' he asked. 'The kingdom of Heaven,' she answered; 'heavenly ambitions are not closed against you.' The young man listened, was silent, and said at last that he did not know but she was right. She suggested reading the Bible together; and they accordingly did so during the whole of that Vacation, every morning after breakfast. Yet, in spite of these devotional exercises, and in spite of a voluminous correspondence on religious subjects with his Spiritual Mother, Manning still continued to indulge in secular hopes. He entered the Colonial Office as a supernumerary clerk, and it was only when the offer of a Merton Fellowship seemed to depend upon his taking orders that his heavenly ambitions began to assume a definite shape. Just then he fell in love with Miss Deffell, whose father would have nothing to say to a young man without prospects, and forbade him the house. It was only too true; what *were* the prospects of a supernumerary clerk in the Colonial Office? Manning went to Oxford and took orders. He was elected to the Merton Fellowship, and obtained through the influence of the Wilberforces a curacy in Sussex. At the last moment he almost drew back. 'I think the whole step has been too precipitate,' he wrote to his brother-in-law. 'I have rather allowed the instance of my friends, and the allurements of an agreeable curacy in many respects, to get the better of my sober judgment.' His vast ambitions, his dreams of public service, of honours, and of power, was all this to end in a little country curacy 'agreeable in many respects'? But there was nothing for it; the deed was done; and the Fates had apparently succeeded very effectively in getting rid of Manning.* All he could do was to make the best of a bad business. Accordingly, in the first place, he decided that he had received a call from God *'ad veritatem et ad seipsum'*;* and, in the second, forgetting Miss Deffell, he married his rector's daughter. Within a few months the rector died, and Manning stepped into his shoes: and at least it could be said that the shoes were not uncomfortable. For the next seven years he fulfilled the functions of a country clergyman. He was energetic and devout; he was polite and handsome; his fame grew in the diocese. At last he began to be spoken of as the probable successor to the old Archdeacon of Chichester. When Mrs Manning prematurely died, he was at first inconsolable, but he found relief in the distraction of redoubled work. How could he have guessed that one day he would come to number that loss among 'God's special mercies'?* Yet so it was to be. In after years, the memory of his wife seemed to be blotted from his mind; he never spoke of her; every letter, every record, of his married life he destroyed; and when word was sent to him that her grave was falling into ruin: 'It is best so,' the Cardinal answered; 'let it be. Time effaces all things.' But, when the grave was yet fresh, the young Rector would sit beside it, day after day, writing his sermons.*

II

IN the meantime a series of events was taking place in another part of England, which was to have a no less profound effect upon Manning's history than the merciful removal of his wife. In the same year in which he took up his Sussex curacy, the *Tracts for the Times** had begun to appear at Oxford. The 'Oxford Movement,' in fact, had started on its course. The phrase is still familiar; but its meaning has become somewhat obscured both by the lapse of time and the intrinsic ambiguity of the subjects connected with it. Let us borrow for a moment the wings of Historic Imagination, and, hovering lightly over the Oxford of the thirties, take a rapid bird's-eye view.

For many generations the Church of England had slept the sleep of the . . . comfortable. The sullen murmurings of dissent, the loud battle-cry of Revolution, had hardly disturbed her slumbers. Portly divines subscribed with a sigh or a smile to the Thirty-nine Articles, sank quietly into easy livings, rode gaily to hounds of a morning as gentlemen should, and, as gentlemen should, carried their two bottles of an evening. To be in the Church was in fact simply to pursue one of those professions which Nature and Society had decided were proper to gentlemen and gentlemen alone. The fervours of piety, the zeal of Apostolic charity, the enthusiasm of self-renunciation – these things were all very well in their way – and in their place; but their place was certainly not the Church of England. Gentlemen were neither fervid nor zealous, and above all they were not enthusiastic. There were, it was true, occasionally to be found within the Church some strait-laced parsons of the high Tory school who looked back with regret to the days of Laud* or talked of the Apostolical Succession; and there were groups of square-toed Evangelicals who were earnest over the Atonement, confessed to a personal love of Jesus Christ, and seemed to have arranged the whole of their lives, down to the minutest details of act and speech, with reference to Eternity. But such extremes were the rare exceptions. The great bulk of the clergy walked calmly along the smooth road of ordinary duty. They kept an eye on the poor of the parish, and they conducted the Sunday Services in a becoming manner; for the rest, they differed neither outwardly nor inwardly from the great bulk of the laity, to whom the Church was a useful organisation for the maintenance of Religion, as by law established.

The awakening came at last, however, and it was a rude one. The liberal principles of the French Revolution, checked at first in the terrors of reaction, began to make way in England. Rationalists lifted up their heads; Bentham and the Mills* propounded Utilitarianism; the Reform Bill was passed; and there were rumours abroad of disestablishment. Even Churchmen seemed to have caught the infection. Dr Whately was so bold* as to assert that, in the interpretation of Scripture, different opinions might be permitted upon matters of doubt; and Dr Arnold drew up a disquieting scheme for allowing

Dissenters into the Church, though it is true that he did not go quite so far as to contemplate the admission of Unitarians.*

At this time there was living in a country parish a young clergyman of the name of John Keble.* He had gone to Oxford at the age of fifteen, where, after a successful academic career, he had been made a Fellow of Oriel. He had then returned to his father's parish and taken up the duties of a curate. He had a thorough knowledge of the contents of the Prayer-book, the ways of a Common Room, the conjugations of the Greek Irregular Verbs, and the small jests of a country parsonage; and the defects of his experience in other directions were replaced by a zeal and a piety which were soon to prove themselves equal, and more than equal, to whatever calls might be made upon them. The superabundance of his piety overflowed into verse; and the holy simplicity of the *Christian Year* carried his name into the remotest lodging-houses of England. As for his zeal, however, it needed another outlet. Looking forth upon the doings of his fellow-men through his rectory windows in Gloucestershire, Keble felt his whole soul shaken with loathing, anger, and dread. Infidelity was stalking through the land; authority was laughed at; the hideous doctrines of Democracy were being openly preached. Worse still, if possible, the Church herself was ignorant and lukewarm; she had forgotten the mysteries of the sacraments, she had lost faith in the Apostolical Succession, she was no longer interested in the Early Fathers, and she submitted herself to the control of a secular legislature, the members of which were not even bound to profess belief in the Atonement. In the face of such enormities what could Keble do? He was ready to do anything, but he was a simple and an unambitious man, and his wrath would in all probability have consumed itself unappeased within him had he not chanced to come into contact, at the critical moment, with a spirit more excitable and daring than his own.

Hurrell Froude,* one of Keble's pupils, was a clever young man to whom had fallen a rather larger share of self-assurance and intolerance than even clever young men usually possess. What was singular about him, however, was not so much his temper as his tastes. The sort of ardour which impels more normal youths to haunt Music Halls and fall in love with actresses took the form, in Froude's case, of a romantic devotion to the Deity and an intense interest in the state of his own soul. He was obsessed by the ideals of saintliness, and convinced of the supreme importance of not eating too much. He kept a diary, in which he recorded his delinquencies, and they were many. 'I cannot say much for myself to-day,' he writes on September 29th, 1826 (he was twenty-three years old). 'I did not read the Psalms and Second Lesson after breakfast, which I had neglected to do before, though I had plenty of time on my hands. Would have liked to be thought adventurous for a scramble I had at the Devil's Bridge. Looked with greediness to see if there was a goose on the table for dinner; and though what I ate was of the plainest sort, and I took no variety, yet even this was partly the effect of accident, and I certainly rather exceeded in quantity, as I was muzzy and sleepy after dinner.' 'I allowed myself to be disgusted with ——'s pomposity,' he writes a little later; 'also smiled at an allusion in the Lessons to abstemiousness in eating. I hope not from pride or vanity, but mistrust; it certainly was unintentional.' And again, 'As to my meals, I can say that I was always careful to see that no one else would take a thing before I served myself; and I believe as to the kind of my food, a bit of cold endings of a dab at breakfast, and a scrap of mackerel at dinner, are the only things that diverged from the strict rule of simplicity.' 'I am obliged to confess,' he notes, 'that in my intercourse with the Supreme Being, I am become more and more sluggish.' And then he exclaims: 'Thine eye trieth my inward parts, and knoweth my thoughts . . . O that my ways were made so direct that I might keep Thy statutes. I will walk in Thy Commandments when Thou hast set my heart at liberty.'

Such were the preoccupations of this young man. Perhaps they would have been different if he had had a little less of what Newman describes as his 'high severe idea of the intrinsic excellence of Virginity'; but it is useless to speculate. Naturally enough the fierce and burning zeal of Keble had a profound effect upon his mind. The two became intimate friends, and Froude, eagerly seizing upon the doctrines of the elder man, saw to it that they had as full a measure of controversial notoriety as an Oxford common room could afford. He plunged the metaphysical mysteries of the Holy Catholic Church into the atmosphere of party politics. Surprised Doctors of Divinity found themselves suddenly faced with strange questions which had never entered their heads before. Was the Church of England, or was it not, a part of the Church Catholic? If it was, were not the Reformers of the sixteenth century renegades? Was not the participation of the Body and Blood of Christ essential to the maintenance of Christian life and hope in each individual? Were Timothy and Titus bishops?* Or were they not? If they were, did it not follow that the power of administering the Holy Eucharist was the attribute of a sacred order founded by Christ Himself? Did not the Fathers refer to the tradition of the Church as to something independent of the written word, and sufficient to refute heresy, even alone? Was it not therefore God's unwritten word? And did it not demand the same reverence from us as the Scriptures, and for exactly the same reason – *because it was His word?* The Doctors of Divinity were aghast at such questions, which seemed to lead they hardly knew whither; and they found it difficult to think of very apposite answers. But Hurrell Froude supplied the answers himself readily enough. All Oxford, all England, should know the truth. The time was out of joint,* and he was only too delighted to have been born to set it right.

But, after all, something more was needed than even the excitement of Froude combined with the conviction of Keble to ruffle seriously the vast calm waters of Christian thought; and it so happened that thing was not wanting: it was the genius of John Henry Newman.* If Newman had never lived, or if his father, when the gig came round on the fatal morning,* still undecided between the two Universities, had chanced to turn the horse's head in the direction of Cambridge, who can doubt that the Oxford Movement would have flickered out its little flame unobserved in the Common Room of Oriel? And how different, too, would have been the fate of Newman himself! He was a child of the Romantic Revival, a creature of emotion and of memory, a dreamer whose secret spirit dwelt apart in delectable mountains, an artist whose subtle senses caught, like a shower in the sunshine, the impalpable rainbow of the immaterial world. In other times, under other skies, his days would have been more fortunate. He might have helped to weave the garland of Meleager, or to mix the *lapis lazuli* of Fra Angelico, or to chase the delicate truth in the shade of an Athenian *palæstra*, or his hands might have fashioned those ethereal faces that smile in the niches of Chartres.* Even in his own age he might, at Cambridge, whose cloisters have ever been consecrated to poetry and common sense, have followed quietly in Gray's footsteps* and brought into flower those seeds of inspiration which now lie embedded amid the faded devotion of the *Lyra Apostolica*.* At Oxford, he was doomed.* He could not withstand the last enchantment of the Middle Age. It was in vain that he plunged into the pages of Gibbon or communed for long hours with Beethoven over his beloved violin. The air was thick with clerical sanctity, heavy with the odours of tradition and the soft warmth of spiritual authority; his friendship with Hurrell Froude did the rest. All that was weakest in him hurried him onward, and all that was strongest in him too. His curious and vaulting imagination began to construct vast philosophical fabrics out of the writings of ancient monks, and to dally with visions of angelic visitations and the efficacy of the oil of St Walburga;* his emotional nature became absorbed in the partisan passions of a University clique; and his subtle intellect concerned itself more and more exclusively with the dialectical splitting of dogmatical hairs. His future course was marked out for him all too clearly; and yet by a singular chance the true nature of the man was to emerge triumphant in the end. If Newman had died at the age of sixty, to-day he would have been already forgotten, save by a few ecclesiastical historians; but he lived to write his *Apologia*,* and to reach immortality, neither as a thinker nor as a theologian, but as an artist who has embalmed the poignant history of an intensely human spirit in the magical spices of words.

When Froude succeeded in impregnating Newman with the ideas of Keble, the Oxford Movement began. The original and remarkable characteristic of these three men was that they took the Christian Religion *au pied de la lettre*.* This had not been done in England for centuries. When they declared every Sunday that they believed in the Holy Catholic Church, they meant it. When they repeated the Athanasian Creed, they meant it. Even when they subscribed to the Thirty-nine Articles,* they meant it – or at least they thought they did. Now such a state of mind was dangerous – more dangerous, indeed, than they at first realised. They had started with the inno- cent assumption that the Christian Religion was contained in the doctrines of the Church of England; but the more they examined into this matter, the more difficult and dubious it became. The Church of England bore everywhere upon it the signs of human imperfection; it was the outcome of revolution and of compromise, of the exigencies of politicians and the caprices of princes, of the prejudices of theologians and the necessities of the State. How had it happened that this piece of patchwork had become the receptacle for the august and infinite mysteries of the Christian Faith? This was the problem with which Newman and his friends found themselves confronted. Other men might, and apparently did, see nothing very strange in such a situation; but other men saw in Christianity itself scarcely more than a convenient and respectable appendage to existence, by which a sound system of morals was inculcated, and through which one might hope to attain to everlasting bliss. To Newman and Keble it was otherwise. They saw a transcendent manifestation of Divine power, flowing down elaborate and immense through the ages; a consecrated priesthood, stretching back, through the mystic symbol of the laying on of hands, to the very Godhead; a whole universe of spiritual beings brought into communion with the Eternal by means of wafers; a great mass of metaphysical doctrines, at once incomprehensible and of incalculable import, laid down with infinite certitude; they saw the supernatural everywhere and at all times, a living force, floating invisible in angels, inspiring saints, and investing with miraculous properties the commonest material things. No wonder that they found such a spectacle hard to bring into line with the institution which had been evolved from the divorce of Henry VIII, the intrigues of Elizabethan parliaments, and the Revolution of 1688. They did, no doubt, soon satisfy themselves that they had succeeded in this apparently hopeless task; but the conclusions which they came to in order to do so were decidedly startling.

The Church of England, they declared, was indeed the one true Church, but she had been under an eclipse since the Reformation – in fact, since she had begun to exist. She had, it is true, escaped the corruptions of Rome; but she had become enslaved by the secular power, and degraded by the false doctrines of Protestantism. The Christian Religion was still preserved intact by the English priesthood, but it was preserved, as it were, unconsciously – a priceless deposit, handed down blindly from generation to generation, and subsisting less by the will of man than through the ordinance of God as expressed in the mysterious virtue of the Sacraments. Christianity, in short, had become entangled in a series of unfortunate circumstances from which it was the plain duty of Newman and his friends to rescue it forthwith. What was curious was that this task had been reserved, in so marked a manner, for them. Some of the divines of the seventeenth century had, perhaps, been vouchsafed glimpses of the truth; but they were glimpses and nothing more. No, the waters of the true Faith had dived underground at the Reformation, and they were waiting for the wand of Newman to strike the rock* before they should burst forth once more into the light of day. The whole matter, no doubt, was Providential – what other explanation could there be?

The first step, it was clear, was to purge the Church of her shames and her errors. The Reformers must be exposed; the yoke of the secular power must be thrown off; dogma must be reinstated in its old pre-eminence; and Christians must be reminded of what they had apparently forgotten – the presence of the supernatural in daily life. 'It would be a gain to this country,' Keble observed, 'were it vastly more superstitious, more bigoted, more gloomy, more fierce in its religion, than at present it shows itself to be.' 'The only good I know of Cranmer,' said Hurrell Froude,* 'was that he burnt well.' Newman preached, and soon the new views began to spread. Amongst the earliest of the converts was Dr Pusey,* a man of wealth and learning, a professor, a canon of Christ Church, who had, it was rumoured, been to Germany. Then the *Tracts for the Times* were started under Newman's editorship, and the Movement was launched upon the world.*

The Tracts were written 'with the hope of rousing members of our Church to comprehend her alarming position . . . as a man might give notice of a fire or inundation, to startle all who heard him.' They may be said to have succeeded in their object, for the sensation which they caused among clergymen throughout the country was extreme. They dealt with a great variety of questions, but the under-lying intention of all of them was to attack the accepted doctrines and practices of the Church of England. Dr Pusey wrote learnedly on Baptismal Regeneration;* he also wrote on Fasting. His treat-ment of the latter subject met with considerable disapproval, which surprised the Doctor. 'I was not prepared,' he said, 'for people questioning, even in the abstract, the duty of fasting; I thought serious-minded persons at least supposed they practised fasting in some way or other. I assumed the duty to be acknowledged and thought it only undervalued.' We live and learn, even though we have been to Germany.

Other tracts discussed the Holy Catholic Church, the Clergy, and the Liturgy. One treated of the question 'whether a clergyman of the Church of England be now bound to have morning and evening prayers daily in his parish church?' Another pointed out the

'Indications of a superintending Providence in the preservation of the Prayer-book and in the changes which it has undergone.' Another consisted of a collection of 'Advent Sermons on Antichrist.' Keble wrote a long and elaborate tract 'On the Mysticism attributed to the Early Fathers of the Church,' in which he expressed his opinions upon a large number of curious matters. 'According to men's usual way of talking,' he wrote, 'it would be called an accidental circumstance that there were *five* loaves, not more nor less, in the store of Our Lord and His disciples wherewith to provide the miraculous feast. But the ancient interpreters treat it as designed and providential, in this surely not erring: and their conjecture is that it represents the sacrifice of the whole world of sense, and especially of the Old Dispensation, which, being outward and visible, might be called the dispensation of the senses, to the FATHER of our LORD JESUS CHRIST, to be a pledge and means of communion with Him according to the terms of the new or evangelical law. This idea they arrive at by considering the number five, the number of the senses, as the mystical opponent of the visible and sensible universe: τὰ αἰσθητὰ, as distinguished from τὰ νοητὰ.* Origen* lays down the rule in express terms. "The number five," he says, "frequently, nay almost always, is taken for the five senses." ' In another passage, Keble deals with an even more recondite question. He quotes the teaching of St Barnabas* that 'Abraham, who first gave men circumcision, did thereby perform a spiritual and typical action, looking forward to the Son.' St Barnabas's argument is as follows: Abraham circumcised of his house men to the number of 318. Why 318? Observe first the 18, then the 300. Of the two letters which stand for 18, 10 is represented by ı, 8 by H. 'Thou hast here,' says St Barnabas, 'the word of Jesus.' As for the 300, 'the Cross is represented by Tau, and the letter Tau represents that number.' Unfortunately, however, St Barnabas's premise was of doubtful validity, as the Rev. Mr Maitland* pointed out, in a pamphlet impugning the conclusions of the Tract. 'The simple fact is,' he wrote, 'that when Abraham pursued Chedorlaomer "he armed his trained servants, *born in his own house*, three hundred and eighteen." When, more than thirteen (according to the common chronology, fifteen) years after, he circumcised "all the men of his house, *born in the house, and bought with money* of the stranger," and, in fact, every male who was as much as eight days old, we are not told what the number amounted to. Shall we suppose (just for the sake of the interpretation) that Abraham's family had so dwindled in the interval as that now all the males of his household, trained men, slaves, and children, equalled only and exactly the number of his warriors fifteen years before?' The question seems difficult to answer, but Keble had, as a matter of fact, forestalled the argument in the following passage, which had apparently escaped the notice of the Rev. Mr Maitland. 'Now whether the facts were really so or not (if it were, it was surely by special providence), that Abraham's household at the time of the circumcision was exactly the same number as before; still the argument of St Barnabas will stand. As thus: circumcision had from the beginning a reference to our SAVIOUR, as in other respects, so in this; that the mystical number, which is the cipher of Jesus crucified, was the number of the first circumcised household in the strength of which Abraham prevailed against the powers of the world. So St Clement of Alexandria, as cited by Fell.' And Keble supports his contention through ten pages of close print, with references to Aristeas, St Augustine, St Jerome, and Dr Whitby.

Writings of this kind could not fail of their effect. Pious youths in Oxford were carried away by them, and began to flock round the standard of Newman. Newman himself became a party chief, encouraging, organising, persuading. His long black figure, swiftly passing through the streets, was pointed at with awe; crowds flocked to his sermons; his words were repeated from mouth to mouth. 'Credo in Newmannum'* became a common catchword. Jokes were made about the Church of England, and practices, unknown for centuries, began to be revived. Young men fasted and did penance, recited the hours of the Roman Breviary, and confessed their sins to Dr Pusey. Nor was the movement confined to Oxford; it spread in widening circles through the parishes of England; the dormant devotion of the country was suddenly aroused. The new strange notion of taking Christianity literally was delightful to earnest minds; but it was also alarming. Really to mean every word you said, when you repeated the Athanasian Creed! How wonderful! And what enticing and mysterious vistas burst upon the view! But then, those vistas, where were they leading to? Supposing – oh heavens! – supposing after all they were to lead to——!

III

IN due course the Tracts made their appearance at the remote rectory in Sussex. Manning was some years younger* than Newman, and the two men had only met occasionally at the University; but now, through common friends, a closer relationship began to grow up between them. It was only to be expected that Newman should be anxious to enrol the rising young Rector among his followers; and on Manning's side there were many causes which impelled him to accept the overtures from Oxford.

He was a man of a serious and vigorous temperament, to whom it was inevitable that the bold high principles of the Movement should strongly appeal. There was also an element in his mind – that element which had terrified him in his childhood with Apocalyptic visions, and urged him in his youth to Bible-readings after breakfast – which now brought him under the spell of the Oxford theories of sacramental mysticism. And besides, the Movement offered another attraction: it imputed an extraordinary, a transcendent merit to the profession which Manning himself pursued. The cleric was not as his lay brethren; he was a creature apart, chosen by Divine will and sanctified by Divine mysteries. It was a relief to find, when one had supposed that one was nothing but a clergyman, that one might, after all, be something else – one might be a priest.

Accordingly Manning shook off his early Evangelical convictions, started an active correspondence with Newman, and was soon working for the new cause. He collected quotations, and began to translate the works of Optatus* for Dr Pusey. He wrote an article on Justin for the *British Critic*, Newman's Magazine. He published a sermon on Faith, with notes and appendices, which was condemned by an Evangelical bishop, and fiercely attacked by no less a person than the celebrated Mr Bowdler.* 'The sermon,' said Mr Bowdler, in a book which he devoted to the subject, 'was bad enough, but the appendix was abominable.' At the same time he was busy asserting the independence of the Church of England, opposing secular education, and bringing out pamphlets against the Ecclesiastical Commission,* which had been appointed by Parliament to report on Church Property. Then we find him in the role of a spiritual director of souls. Ladies met him by stealth in his church, and made their

confessions. Over one case – that of a lady, who found herself drifting towards Rome – he consulted Newman. Newman advised him to
'enlarge upon the doctrine of 1 Cor. vii';* – 'also I think you must
press on her the prospect of *benefiting* the poor Church, through
which she has her baptism, by stopping in it. Does she not care for
the souls of all around her, steeped and stifled in Protestantism? How
will she best care for them: by indulging her own feelings in the
communion of Rome, or in denying herself, and staying in sackcloth
and ashes to do them good?' Whether these arguments were successful does not appear.

For several years after his wife's death Manning was occupied
with these new activities, while his relations with Newman
developed into what was apparently a warm friendship. 'And now
vive valeque, my dear Manning,' we find Newman writing in a letter
dated 'in festo S. Car. 1838,'* 'as wishes and prays yours affectionately, John H. Newman.' But, as time went on, the situation became
more complicated. Tractarianism began to arouse the hostility, not
only of the Evangelical, but of the moderate churchmen, who could
not help perceiving, in the ever-deepening 'catholicism' of the
Oxford party, the dread approaches of Rome. The *Record* newspaper*
– an influential Evangelical journal – took up the matter and sniffed
Popery in every direction; it spoke of certain clergymen as 'tainted';
and after that, preferment seemed to pass those clergymen by. The
fact that Manning found it wise to conduct his confessional ministra-
tions in secret was in itself highly significant. It was necessary to be
careful, and Manning was very careful indeed. The neighbouring
Archdeacon, Mr Hare,* was a low churchman; Manning made
friends with him, as warmly, it seemed, as he had made friends with
Newman. He corresponded with him, asked his advice about the
books he should read, and discussed questions of Theology – 'As to
Gal. vi. 15,* *we cannot differ.* . . . With a man who reads and reasons I
can have no controversy; and you do both.' Archdeacon Hare was
pleased, but soon a rumòur reached him, which was, to say the least
of it, upsetting. Manning had been removing the high pews* from a
church in Brighton, and putting in open benches in their place.
Everyone knew what that meant; everyone knew that a high pew was
one of the bulwarks of Protestantism, and that an open bench had
upon it the taint of Rome. But Manning hastened to explain. 'My
dear friend,' he wrote, 'I did not exchange pews for open benches,

but got the pews (the same in number) moved from the nave of the church to the walls of the side aisles, so that the whole church has a regular arrangement of open benches, which (irregularly) existed before . . . I am not to-day quite well, so farewell, with much regard – Yours ever, H. E. M.' Archdeacon Hare was reassured.

It was important that he should be, for the Archdeacon of Chichester was growing very old, and Hare's influence might be exceedingly useful when a vacancy occurred. So, indeed, it fell out. A new bishop, Dr Shuttleworth,* was appointed to the See, and the old Archdeacon took the opportunity of retiring. Manning was obviously marked out as his successor, but the new bishop happened to be a low churchman, an aggressive low churchman, who went so far as to parody the Tractarian fashion of using Saints' days for the dating of letters by writing 'The Palace, washing-day,' at the beginning of his. And – what was equally serious – his views were shared by Mrs Shuttleworth, who had already decided that the pushing young Rector was 'tainted.' But at the critical moment Archdeacon Hare came to the rescue; he persuaded the Bishop that Manning was safe; and the appointment was accordingly made – behind Mrs Shuttleworth's back. She was furious, but it was too late; Manning was an Archdeacon. All the lady could do, to indicate her disapprobation, was to put a copy of Mr Bowdler's book in a conspicuous position on the drawing-room table, when he came to pay his respects at the Palace.

Among the letters of congratulation which Manning received was one from Mr Gladstone, with whom he had remained on terms of close friendship since their days together at Oxford. 'I rejoice,' Mr Gladstone wrote, 'on your account personally: but more for the sake of the Church. All my brothers-in-law are here and scarcely less delighted than I am. With great glee am I about to write your new address; but the occasion really calls for higher sentiments; and sure am I that you are one of the men to whom it is specially given to develop the solution of that great problem – how all our minor distractions are to be either abandoned, absorbed, or harmonised, through the might of the great principle of communion in the body of Christ.'

Manning was an Archdeacon; but he was not yet out of the wood. His relations with the Tractarians had leaked out, and the *Record* was beginning to be suspicious. If Mrs Shuttleworth's opinion of him were to become general, it would certainly be a grave matter. Nobody could wish to live and die a mere Archdeacon. And then, at that very moment, an event occurred which made it imperative to take a definite step, one way or the other. That event was the publication of Tract No. 90.*

For some time it had been obvious to every impartial onlooker that Newman was slipping down an inclined plane at the bottom of which lay one thing, and one thing only – the Roman Catholic Church. What was surprising was the length of time which he was taking to reach the inevitable destination. Years passed before he came to realise that his grandiose edifice of a Church Universal would crumble to pieces if one of its foundation stones was to be an amatory intrigue of Henry VIII. But at last he began to see that terrible monarch glowering at him wherever he turned his eyes. First he tried to exorcise the spectre with the rolling periods of the Caroline divines; but it only strutted the more truculently. Then in despair he plunged into the writings of the early Fathers, and sought to discover some way out of his difficulties in the complicated labyrinth of ecclesiastical history. After months spent in the study of the Monophysite heresy,* the alarming conclusion began to force itself upon him that the Church of England was perhaps in schism. Eventually he read an article by a Roman Catholic on St Augustine and the Donatists, which seemed to put the matter beyond doubt. St Augustine, in the fifth century, had pointed out that the Donatists were heretics because the Bishop of Rome had said so. The argument was crushing; it rang in Newman's ears for days and nights; and, though he continued to linger on in agony for six years more, he never could discover any reply to it. All he could hope to do was to persuade himself and any one else who liked to listen to him that the holding of Anglican orders was not inconsistent with a belief in the whole cycle of Roman doctrine, as laid down at the Council of Trent.* In this way he supposed that he could at once avoid the deadly sin of heresy and conscientiously remain a clergyman in the Church of England; and with this end in view he composed Tract No. 90.

The object of the Tract was to prove that there was nothing in the Thirty-nine Articles incompatible with the creed of the Roman Church. Newman pointed out, for instance, that it was generally supposed that the Articles condemned the doctrine of Purgatory; but they did not; they merely condemned the *Romish* doctrine of

Purgatory; and *Romish*, clearly, was not the same thing as *Roman*. Hence it followed that believers in the Roman doctrine of Purgatory might subscribe the Articles with a good conscience. Similarly, the Articles condemned 'the sacrifices of masses', but they did *not* condemn 'the sacrifice of the Mass'. Thus the Mass might be lawfully celebrated in English Churches. Newman took the trouble to examine the Articles in detail from this point of view, and the conclusion he came to in every case supported his contention in a singular manner.

The Tract produced an immense sensation, for it seemed to be a deadly and treacherous blow aimed at the very heart of the Church of England. Deadly it certainly was, but it was not so treacherous as at first sight appeared. The members of the English Church had ingenuously imagined up to that moment that it was possible to contain in a frame of words the subtle essence of their complicated doctrinal system, involving the mysteries of the Eternal and the Infinite on the one hand, and the elaborate adjustments of temporal government on the other. They did not understand that verbal definitions in such a case will only perform their functions so long as there is no dispute about the matters which they are intended to define: that is to say, so long as there is no need for them. For generations this had been the case with the Thirty-nine Articles. Their drift was clear enough; and nobody bothered over their exact meaning. But directly some one found it important to give them a new and untraditional interpretation, it appeared that they were a mass of ambiguity, and might be twisted into meaning very nearly anything that anybody liked. Steady-going churchmen were appalled and outraged when they saw Newman, in Tract No. 90, performing this operation. But, after all, he was only taking the Church of England at its word. And indeed, since Newman showed the way, the operation has become so exceedingly common that the most steady-going churchman hardly raises an eyebrow at it now.

At the time, however, Newman's treatment of the Articles seemed to display not only a perverted supersubtlety of intellect, but a temper of mind that was fundamentally dishonest. It was then that he first began to be assailed by those charges of untruthfulness which reached their culmination more than twenty years later in the celebrated controversy with Charles Kingsley, which led to the writing of the *Apologia*.* The controversy was not a very fruitful one, chiefly

because Kingsley could no more understand the nature of Newman's intelligence than a subaltern in a line regiment can understand
a Brahmin of Benares. Kingsley was a stout Protestant, whose hatred
of Popery was, at bottom, simply ethical – an honest, instinctive
horror of the practices of priestcraft and the habits of superstition;
and it was only natural that he should see in those innumerable
delicate distinctions which Newman was perpetually drawing, and
which he himself had not only never thought of, but could not even
grasp, simply another manifestation of the inherent falsehood of
Rome. But, in reality, no one, in one sense of the word, was more
truthful than Newman. The idea of deceit would have been abhorrent to him; and indeed it was owing to his very desire to explain
what he had in his mind exactly and completely, with all the refinements of which his subtle brain was capable, that persons such as
Kingsley were puzzled into thinking him dishonest. Unfortunately,
however, the possibilities of truth and falsehood depend upon other
things besides sincerity. A man may be of a scrupulous and impeccable honesty, and yet his respect for the truth – it cannot be denied
– may be insufficient. He may be, like the lunatic, the lover, and the
poet, 'of imagination all compact';* he may be blessed, or cursed, with
one of those 'seething brains', one of those 'shaping fantasies' that
'apprehend more than cool reason ever comprehends'; he may be by
nature incapable of sifting evidence, or by predilection simply
indisposed to do so. 'When we were there,' wrote Newman in a letter
to a friend after his conversion, describing a visit to Naples, and the
miraculous circumstances connected with the liquefaction of St Januarius's blood,* 'the feast of St Gennaro was coming on, and the
Jesuits were eager for us to stop – they have the utmost confidence in
the miracle – and were the more eager because many Catholics, till
they have seen it, doubt it. Our father director here tells us that
before he went to Naples he did not believe it. That is, they have
vague ideas of natural means, exaggeration, etc., not of course
imputing fraud. They say conversions often take place in consequence. It is exposed for the Octave,* and the miracle continues – it
is not simple liquefaction, but sometimes it swells, sometimes boils,
sometimes melts – no one can tell what is going to take place. They
say it is quite overcoming – and people cannot help crying to see it. I
understand that Sir H. Davy* attended every day, and it was this
extreme variety of the phenomenon which convinced him that

nothing physical would account for it. Yet there is this remarkable fact that liquefactions of blood are common at Naples – and unless it is irreverent to the Great Author of Miracles to be obstinate in the inquiry, the question certainly rises whether there is something in the air. (Mind, I don't believe there is – and, speaking humbly, and without having seen it, think it a true miracle – but I am arguing.) We *saw* the blood of St Patrizia,* half liquid; *i.e.* liquefying, on her feast day. St John Baptist's blood sometimes liquefies on the 29th of August, and did when we were at Naples, but we had not time to go to the church. We saw the liquid blood of an Oratorian Father, a good man, but not a saint, who died two centuries ago, I think; and we saw the liquid blood of Da Ponte, the great and holy Jesuit, who, I suppose, was almost a saint. But these instances do not account for liquefaction on certain days, if this is the case. But the most strange phenomenon is what happens at Ravello, a village or town above Amalfi. There is the blood of St Pantaleon.* It is in a vessel amid the stonework of the Altar – it is not touched – but on his feast in June it liquefies. And more, there is an excommunication against those who bring portions of the True Cross into the Church. Why? Because the blood liquefies, whenever it is brought. A person I know, not knowing the prohibition, brought in a portion – and the Priest suddenly said, who showed the blood, "Who has got the Holy Cross about him?" I tell you what was told me by a grave and religious man. It is a curious coincidence that in telling this to our Father Director here, he said, "Why, we have a portion of St Pantaleon's blood at the Chiesa Nuova, and it is always liquid." '*

After leaving Naples, Newman visited Loreto,* and inspected the house of the Holy Family, which, as is known to the faithful, was transported thither, in three hops, from Palestine. 'I went to Loreto,' he wrote, 'with a simple faith, believing what I still more believed when I saw it. I have no doubt now. If you ask me why I believe it, it is because *every one* believes it at Rome; cautious as they are and sceptical about some other things. *I have no antecedent difficulty in the matter.* He who floated the Ark on the surges of a world-wide sea, and enclosed in it all living things, who has hidden the terrestrial paradise, who said that faith might move mountains, who sustained thousands for forty years in a sterile wilderness, who transported Elias* and keeps him hidden till the end, could do this wonder also.'

Here, whatever else there may be, there is certainly no trace of a desire to deceive. Could a state of mind, in fact, be revealed with more absolute transparency?

When Newman was a child he 'wished that he could believe the Arabian Nights were true.'* When he came to be a man, his wish seems to have been granted.

Tract No. 90 was officially condemned by the authorities at Oxford, and in the hubbub that followed the contending parties closed their ranks; henceforward any compromise between the friends and the enemies of the Movement was impossible. Archdeacon Manning was in too conspicuous a position to be able to remain silent; he was obliged to declare himself, and he did not hesitate. In an archidiaconal charge, delivered within a few months of his appointment, he firmly repudiated the Tractarians. But the repudiation was not deemed sufficient, and a year later he repeated it with greater emphasis. Still, however, the horrid rumours were afloat. The *Record* began to investigate matters, and its vigilance was soon rewarded by an alarming discovery: the sacrament had been administered in Chichester Cathedral on a weekday, and 'Archdeacon Manning, one of the most noted and determined of the Tractarians, had acted a conspicuous part on the occasion.' It was clear that the only way of silencing these malevolent whispers was by some public demonstration whose import nobody could doubt. The annual sermon preached on Guy Fawkes Day before the University of Oxford seemed to offer the very opportunity that Manning required. He seized it; got himself appointed preacher; and delivered from the pulpit of St Mary's a virulently Protestant harangue.* This time there could indeed be no doubt about the matter: Manning had shouted 'No Popery!' in the very citadel of the Movement, and every one, including Newman, recognised that he had finally cut himself off from his old friends. Every one, that is to say, except the Archdeacon himself. On the day after the sermon, Manning walked out to the neighbouring village of Littlemore, where Newman was now living in retirement with a few chosen disciples, in the hope of being able to give a satisfactory explanation of what he had done. But he was disappointed; for when, after an awkward interval, one of the disciples appeared at the door, he was informed that Mr Newman was not at home.

With his retirement to Littlemore,* Newman had entered upon the final period of his Anglican career. Even he could no longer help perceiving that the end was now only a matter of time. His progress was hastened in an agitating manner by the indiscreet activity of one of his proselytes, W. G. Ward,* a young man who combined an extraordinary aptitude for *a priori* reasoning* with a passionate devotion to *Opéra Bouffe*.* It was difficult, in fact, to decide whether the inner nature of Ward was more truly expressing itself when he was firing off some train of scholastic paradoxes on the Eucharist or when he was trilling the airs of *Figaro* and plunging through the hilarious roulades of the *Largo al Factotum*. Even Dr Pusey could not be quite sure, though he was Ward's spiritual director. On one occasion his young penitent came to him, and confessed that a vow which he had taken to abstain from music during Lent was beginning to affect his health. Could Dr Pusey see his way to releasing him from the vow? The Doctor decided that a little sacred music would not be amiss. Ward was all gratitude, and that night a party was arranged in a friend's rooms. The concert began with the solemn harmonies of Handel, which were followed by the holy strains of the 'O Salutaris' of Cherubini. Then came the elevation and the pomp of 'Possenti Numi' from the Magic Flute. But, alas! there lies much danger in Mozart. The page was turned, and there was the delicious duet between Papageno and Papagena. Flesh and blood could not resist that; then song followed song, the music waxed faster and lighter, until at last Ward burst into the intoxicating merriment of the *Largo al Factotum*. When it was over, a faint but persistent knocking made itself heard upon the wall; and it was only then that the company remembered that the rooms next door were Dr Pusey's.*

The same *entrain** which carried Ward away when he sat down to a piano possessed him whenever he embarked on a religious discussion. 'The thing that was utterly abhorrent to him,' said one of his friends, 'was to stop short.' Given the premises, he would follow out their implications with the mercilessness of a medieval monk, and when he had reached the last limits of argument be ready to maintain whatever propositions he might find there with his dying breath. He had the extreme innocence of a child and a mathematician. Captivated by the glittering eye of Newman, he swallowed whole the supernatural conception of the universe which Newman had evolved, accepted it as a fundamental premise, and began at once to deduce from it whatsoever there might be to be deduced. His very first deductions included irrefutable proofs of (1) God's particular providence for individuals; (2) the real efficacy of intercessory prayer; (3) the reality of our communion with the saints departed; (4) the constant presence and assistance of the angels of God. Later on he explained mathematically the importance of the Ember Days. 'Who can tell,' he added, 'the degree of blessing lost to us in this land by neglecting, as we alone of Christian Churches do neglect, these holy days?' He then proceeded to convict the Reformers, not only of rebellion, but '– for my own part I see not how we can avoid adding – of perjury.' Every day his arguments became more extreme, more rigorously exact, and more distressing to his master. Newman was in the position of a cautious commander-in-chief being hurried into an engagement against his will by a dashing cavalry officer. Ward forced him forward step by step towards – no! he could not bear it; he shuddered and drew back. But it was of no avail. In vain did Keble and Pusey wring their hands and stretch forth their pleading arms to their now vanishing brother. The fatal moment was fast approaching. Ward at last published a devastating book* in which he proved conclusively by a series of syllogisms that the only proper course for the Church of England was to repent in sackcloth and ashes her separation from the Communion of Rome. The reckless author was deprived of his degree by an outraged University, and a few weeks later was received into the Catholic Church.

Newman, in a kind of despair, had flung himself into the labours of historical compilation. His views of history had changed since the days when as an undergraduate he had feasted on the worldly pages of Gibbon. 'Revealed religion,' he now thought, 'furnishes facts to other sciences, which those sciences, left to themselves, would never reach. Thus, in the science of history, the preservation of our race in Noah's Ark is an historical fact, which history never would arrive at without revelation.' With these principles to guide him, he plunged with his disciples into a prolonged study of the English Saints.* Biographies soon appeared of St Bega, St Adamnan, St Gundleus, St Guthlake, Brother Drithelm, St Amphibalus, St Wulstan, St Ebba, St Neot, St Ninian, and Cunibert the Hermit. Their austerities, their virginity, and their miraculous powers were described in detail. The public learnt with astonishment that St Ninian had turned a staff into a tree, that St German had stopped a cock from crowing, and that a child had been raised from the dead to convert St Helier. The series has subsequently been continued by a more modern writer whose relation of the history of the blessed St Maël contains, perhaps, even more matter for edification than Newman's biographies. At the time, indeed, those works caused considerable scandal. Clergymen denounced them in pamphlets. St Cuthbert was described by his biographer as having 'carried the jealousy of women, characteristic of all the saints, to an extraordinary pitch.' An example was given: whenever he held a spiritual conversation with St Ebba, he was careful to spend the ensuing hours of darkness 'in prayer, up to his neck in water.'* 'Persons who invent such tales,' wrote one indignant commentator, 'cast very grave and just suspicions on the purity of their own minds. And young persons, who talk and think in this way, are in extreme danger of falling into sinful habits. As to the volumes before us, the authors have, in their fanatical panegyrics of virginity, made use of language downright profane.'

One of the disciples at Littlemore was James Anthony Froude, the younger brother of Hurrell,* and it fell to his lot to be responsible for the biography of St Neot. While he was composing it, he began to feel some qualms.* Saints who lighted fires with icicles, changed bandits into wolves, and floated across the Irish Channel on altar-stones, produced a disturbing effect on his historical conscience. But he had promised his services to Newman, and he determined to carry through the work in the spirit in which he had begun it. He did so; but he thought it proper to add the following sentence by way of conclusion: 'This is all, and indeed rather more than all, that is known to men of the blessed St Neot; but not more than is known to the angels in heaven.'

Meanwhile the English Roman Catholics were growing impatient; was the great conversion never coming, for which they had prayed so fervently and so long? Dr Wiseman, at the head of them, was watching and waiting with special eagerness. His hand was held out under the ripening fruit; the delicious morsel seemed to be trembling on its stalk; and yet it did not fall. At last, unable to bear the suspense any longer, he dispatched to Littlemore Father Smith, an old pupil of Newman's, who had lately joined the Roman communion, with instructions that he should do his best, under cover of a simple visit of friendship, to discover how the land lay. Father Smith was received somewhat coldly, and the conversation ran entirely on topics which had nothing to do with religion. When the company separated before dinner, he was beginning to think that his errand had been useless; but on their reassembling he suddenly noticed that Newman had changed his trousers, and that the colour of the pair which he was now wearing was grey.* At the earliest moment, the emissary rushed back post-haste to Dr Wiseman. 'All is well,' he exclaimed; 'Newman no longer considers that he is in Anglican orders.' 'Praise be to God!' answered Dr Wiseman. 'But how do you know?' Father Smith described what he had seen. 'Oh, is that all? My dear father, how can you be so foolish?' But Father Smith was not to be shaken. 'I know the man,' he said, 'and I know what it means. Newman will come, and he will come soon.'

And Father Smith was right. A few weeks later, Newman suddenly slipped off to a priest, and all was over. Perhaps he would have hesitated longer still, if he could have foreseen how he was to pass the next thirty years of his unfortunate existence; but the future was hidden, and all that was certain was that the past had gone for ever, and that his eyes would rest no more upon the snapdragons of Trinity. The Oxford Movement was now ended. The University breathed such a sigh of relief as usually follows the difficult expulsion of a hard piece of matter from a living organism, and actually began to attend to education. As for the Church of England, she had tasted blood, and it was clear that she would never again be content with a vegetable diet. Her clergy, however, maintained their reputation for judicious compromise, for they followed Newman up to the very point beyond which his conclusions were logical, and, while they intoned, confessed, swung incense, and burnt candles with the exhilaration of converts, they yet managed to do so with a subtle nuance which showed that they had nothing to do with Rome. Various individuals underwent more violent changes. Several had preceded Newman into the Roman fold; among others an unhappy Mr Sibthorpe, who subsequently changed his mind, and returned to the Church of his fathers,* and then – perhaps it was only natural – changed his mind again. Many more followed Newman, and Dr Wiseman was particularly pleased by the conversion of a Mr Morris,* who, as he said, was 'the author of the essay, which won the prize, on the best method of proving Christianity to the Hindoos.' Hurrell Froude had died before Newman had read the fatal article on St Augustine; but his brother, James Anthony, together with Arthur Clough, the poet,* went through an experience which was more distressing in those days than it has since become: they lost their faith. With this difference, however, that while in Froude's case the loss of his faith turned out to be rather like the loss of a heavy portmanteau, which one afterwards discovers to have been full of old rags and brickbats, Clough was made so uneasy by the loss of his that he went on looking for it everywhere as long as he lived; but somehow he never could find it. On the other hand, Keble and Pusey continued for the rest of their lives to dance in an exemplary manner upon the tight-rope of High Anglicanism; in such an exemplary manner, indeed, that the tight-rope has its dancers still.*

IV

MANNING was now thirty-eight, and it was clear that he was the rising man in the Church of England. He had many powerful connections: he was the brother-in-law of Samuel Wilberforce, who had been lately made a bishop;* he was a close friend of Mr Gladstone, who was a Cabinet Minister; and he was becoming well known in the influential circles of society in London. His talent for affairs was recognised not only in the Church, but in the world at large, and he busied himself with matters of such varied scope as National Education, the administration of the Poor Law, and the Employment of Women. Mr Gladstone kept up an intimate correspondence with him on these and on other subjects, mingling in his letters the details of practical statesmanship with the speculations of a religious thinker. 'Sir James Graham,'* he wrote, in a discussion of the bastardy clauses of the Poor Law, 'is much pleased with the tone of your two communications. He is disposed, without putting an end to the application of the workhouse test against the mother, to make the remedy against the putative father "real and effective" for expenses incurred in the workhouse. I am not enough acquainted to know whether it would be advisable to go further. You have not proposed it; and I am disposed to believe that only with a revived and improved discipline in the Church can we hope for any generally effective check upon lawless lust.' 'I agree with you *eminently*,' he writes, in a later letter, 'in your doctrine of *filtration*. But it sometimes occurs to me, though the question may seem a strange one, how far was the Reformation, but especially the Continental

Reformation, designed by God, in the region of final causes, for that purification of the Roman Church which it has actually realised?'

In his archdeaconry, Manning lived to the full the active life of a country clergyman. His slim, athletic figure was seen everywhere – in the streets of Chichester, or on the lawns of the neighbouring rectories, or galloping over the downs in breeches and gaiters, or cutting brilliant figures on the ice. He was an excellent judge of horse-flesh, and the pair of greys which drew his hooded phaeton so swiftly through the lanes were the admiration of the county. His features were already beginning to assume their ascetic cast, but the spirit of youth had not yet fled from them, so that he seemed to combine the attractions of dignity and grace. He was a good talker, a sympathetic listener, a man who understood the difficult art of pre-serving all the vigour of a manly character and yet never giving offence. No wonder that his sermons drew crowds, no wonder that his spiritual advice was sought for eagerly by an ever-growing group of penitents, no wonder that men would say, when his name was mentioned, 'Oh, Manning! No power on earth can keep *him* from a bishopric!'*

Such was the fair outward seeming of the Archdeacon's life; but the inward reality was different. The more active, the more fortu-nate, the more full of happy promise his existence became, the more persistently was his secret imagination haunted by a dreadful vision – the lake that burneth for ever with brimstone and fire. The tempta-tions of the Evil One are many, Manning knew; and he knew also that, for him at least, the most subtle and terrible of all temptations was the temptation of worldly success. He tried to reassure himself, but it was in vain. He committed his thoughts to a diary, weighing scrupulously his every motive, examining with relentless searchings into the depths of his heart. Perhaps, after all, his longings for pre-ferment were merely legitimate hopes for 'an elevation into a sphere of higher usefulness.' But no, there was something more than that. 'I do feel pleasure,' he noted, 'in honour, precedence, elevation, the society of great people, and all this is very shameful and mean.' After Newman's conversion, he almost convinced himself that his 'visions of an ecclesiastical future' were justified by the role that he would play as a 'healer of the breach in the Church of England.' Mr Gladstone agreed with him; but there was One higher than Mr Gladstone, and did He agree? 'I am pierced by anxious thoughts.

God knows what my desires have been and are, and why they are crossed. . . . I am flattering myself with a fancy about depth and reality. . . . The great question is: Is God enough for you *now*? And if you are as now even to the end of life, will it suffice you? . . . Certainly I would rather choose to be stayed on God, than to be in the thrones of the world and the Church. Nothing else will go into Eternity.'

In a moment of ambition, he had applied for the Readership of Lincoln's Inn, but, owing chiefly to the hostile influence of the *Record*, the appointment had gone elsewhere. A little later, a more important position was offered to him – the office of sub-almoner to the Queen,* which had just been vacated by the Archbishop of York, and was almost certain to lead to a mitre. The offer threw Manning into an agony of self-examination. He drew up elaborate tables, after the manner of Robinson Crusoe, with the reasons for and against his acceptance of the post:

For	Against
1. That it comes unsought.	1. Not therefore to be accepted. Such things are trials as well as leadings.
2. That it is honourable.	2. Being what I am, ought I not therefore to decline it – (1) as humiliation; (2) as revenge on myself for Lincoln's Inn; (3) as a testimony?

And so on. He found in the end ten 'negative reasons,' with no affirmative ones to balance them, and, after a week's deliberation, he rejected the offer.

But peace of mind was as far off from him as ever. First the bitter thought came to him that 'in all this Satan tells me I am doing it to be thought mortified and holy'; and then he was obsessed by the still bitterer feelings of ineradicable disappointment and regret. He had lost a great opportunity, and it brought him small comfort to consider that 'in the region of counsels, self-chastisement, humiliation, self-discipline, penance, and of the Cross' he had perhaps done right.

The crisis passed, but it was succeeded by a fiercer one. Manning was taken seriously ill, and became convinced that he might die at any moment.* The entries in his Diary grew more elaborate than ever; his remorse for the past, his resolutions for the future, his protestations of submission to the will of God, filled page after page of parallel columns, headings and sub-headings, numbered clauses, and analytical tables. 'How do I feel about Death?' he wrote. 'Certainly great fear –

1. Because of the uncertainty of our state before God.
2. Because of the consciousness –
    (1) of great sins past,
    (2) of great sinfulness,
    (3) of most shallow repentance.
What shall I do?'

He decided to mortify himself, to read St Thomas Aquinas, and to make his 'night prayers forty instead of thirty minutes.' He determined during Lent 'to use no pleasant bread (except on Sundays and feasts) such as cake and sweetmeat'; but he added the proviso 'I do not include plain biscuits.' Opposite this entry appears the word '*kept*.' And yet his backslidings were many. Looking back over a single week, he was obliged to register 'petulance twice' and 'complacent visions.' He heard his curate being commended for bringing so many souls to God during Lent, and he 'could not bear it'; but the remorse was terrible: 'I abhorred myself on the spot, and looked upward for help.' He made out list upon list of the Almighty's special mercies towards him, and they included his creation, his regeneration, and (No. 5) 'the preservation of my life six times to my knowledge –

    (1) In illness at the age of nine.
    (2) In the water.
    (3) By a runaway horse at Oxford.
    (4) By the same.
    (5) By falling nearly through the ceiling of a church.
    (6) Again by a fall of a horse. And I know not how often in shooting, riding, etc.'

At last he became convalescent; but the spiritual experiences of those agitated weeks left an indelible mark upon his mind, and prepared the way for the great change which was to follow.

For he had other doubts besides those which held him in torment as to his own salvation; he was in doubt about the whole framework of his faith. Newman's conversion, he found, had meant something more to him than he had first realised. It had seemed to come as a call to the redoubling of his Anglican activities; but supposing, in reality, it were a call towards something very different – towards an abandonment of those activities altogether? It might be 'a trial,' or again it might be a 'leading'; how was he to judge? Already, before his illness, these doubts had begun to take possession of his mind. 'I am conscious to myself,' he wrote in his Diary, 'of an extensively changed feeling towards the Church of Rome . . . The Church of England seems to me to be diseased:* 1. *Organically* (six sub-headings). 2. *Functionally* (seven sub-headings) . . . Wherever it seems healthy it approximates the system of Rome.' Then thoughts of the Virgin Mary suddenly began to assail him –

> (1) If John the Baptist were sanctified from the womb, how much more the B. V.!
> (2) If Enoch and Elijah were exempted from death, why not the B. V. from sin?
> (3) It is a strange way of loving the Son to slight the mother!'

The arguments seemed irresistible, and a few weeks later the following entry occurs – 'Strange thoughts have visited me:

> (1) I have felt that the Episcopate of the Church of England is secularised and bound down beyond hope. . . .
> (6) I feel as if a light had fallen upon me. My feeling about the Roman Church is not intellectual. I have intellectual difficulties, but the great moral difficulties seem melting.
> (7) Something keeps rising and saying, "You will end in the Roman Church."'

He noted altogether twenty-five of these 'strange thoughts'. His mind hovered anxiously round –

> '(1) The Incarnation,
> (2) The Real Presence,
>   i Regeneration,
>   ii Eucharist, and
> (3) The Exaltation of S. M. and Saints.'

His twenty-second strange thought was as follows: 'How do I know where I may be two years hence? Where was Newman five years ago?'

It was significant, but hardly surprising, that, after his illness, Manning should have chosen to recuperate in Rome. He spent several months there, and his Diary during the whole of that period is concerned entirely with detailed descriptions of churches, ceremonies, and relics, and with minute accounts of conversations with priests and nuns. There is not a single reference either to the objects of art or to the antiquities of the place; but another omission was still more remarkable. Manning had a long interview with Pius IX, and his only record of it is contained in the bald statement: 'Audience today at the Vatican.' Precisely what passed on that occasion never transpired;* all that is known is that His Holiness expressed considerable surprise on learning from the Archdeacon that the chalice was used in the Anglican Church in the administration of Communion. 'What!' he exclaimed, 'is the same chalice made use of by every one?' 'I remember the pain I felt,' said Manning, long afterwards, 'at seeing how unknown we were to the Vicar of Jesus Christ. It made me feel our isolation.'

On his return to England, he took up once more the work in his Archdeaconry with what appetite he might. Ravaged by doubt, distracted by speculation, he yet managed to maintain an outward presence of unshaken calm. His only confidant was Robert Wilberforce, to whom, for the next two years, he poured forth in a series of letters, headed '*Under the Seal*' to indicate that they contained the secrets of the confessional, the whole history of his spiritual perturbations. The irony of his position was singular; for during the whole of this time Manning was himself holding back from the Church of Rome a host of hesitating penitents by means of arguments which he was at the very moment denouncing as fallacious to his own confessor. But what else could he do? When he received, for instance, a letter such as the following from an agitated lady,* what was he to say?

'MY DEAR FATHER IN CHRIST,

'. . . I am sure you would pity me and like to help me, if you knew the unhappy, unsettled state my mind is in, and the misery of being *entirely, wherever I am*, with those who look upon joining the Church of Rome as the most awful "fall" conceivable to any one, and are devoid of the smallest *comprehension* of how any enlightened person can do it. . . . My old Evangelical friends, with all my deep, deep love for them, do not succeed in shaking me in the least. . . .

'My brother has just published a book called *Regeneration*, which all my friends are reading and highly extolling; it has a very contrary effect to what he would desire *on my mind*. I can read and understand it all in an altogether different sense, and the facts which he quotes about the articles as drawn up in 1536, and again in 1552, and of the Irish articles of 1615 and 1634, *startle* and *shake* me about the Reformed Church in England far more than anything else, and have done ever since I first saw them in Mr Maskell's pamphlet (as quoted from Mr Dodsworth's).

'I do hope you have sometimes time and thought to pray for me still. Mr Galton's letters long ago grew into short formal notes, which hurt me and annoyed me particularly, and I never answered his last, so, literally, I have no one to say things to and get help from, which in one sense is a comfort, when my convictions seem to be leading me *on* and *on* and gaining strength in spite of all the dreariness of my lot.

'Do you know I can't help being very anxious and unhappy about poor Sister Harriet. I am afraid of her *going out of her mind*. She comforts herself by an occasional outpouring of everything to me, and I had a letter this morning. . . . She says Sister May has promised the Vicar never to talk to her or allow her to talk on the subject with her, and I doubt whether this can be good for her, because though she has lost her faith, she says, in the Church of England, yet she never thinks of what she could have faith in, and resolutely without inquiring into the question determines not to be a Roman Catholic, so that really you see she is allowing her mind to run adrift, and yet perfectly powerless.

'Forgive my troubling you with this letter, and believe me to be always your faithful, grateful and affectionate daughter,

'EMMA RYLE.

'P.S. I wish I could see you once more so very much.'

How was Manning, a director of souls, and a clergyman of the Church of England, to reply that in sober truth there was very little to choose between the state of mind of Sister Emma, or even of Sister Harriet, and his own? The dilemma was a grievous one: when a soldier finds himself fighting for a cause in which he has lost faith, it is treachery to stop, and it is treachery to go on.

At last, in the seclusion of his library, Manning turned in an agony to those old writings which had provided Newman with so much instruction and assistance; perhaps the Fathers would do something for him as well. He ransacked the pages of St Cyprian and St Cyril; he went through the complete works of St Optatus and St Leo; he explored the vast treatises of Tertullian and Justin Martyr. He had a lamp put into his phaeton, so that he might lose no time during his long winter drives. There he sat, searching St Chrysostom* for some mitigation of his anguish, while he sped along between the hedges to distant sufferers, to whom he duly administered the sacraments according to the rites of the English Church. He hurried back to commit to his Diary the analysis of his reflections, and to describe, under the mystic formula of secrecy, the intricate workings of his conscience to Robert Wilberforce. But, alas! he was no Newman; and even the fourteen folios of St Augustine himself, strange to say, gave him very little help.

The final propulsion was to come from an entirely different quarter. In November, 1847, the Reverend Mr Gorham* was presented by the Lord Chancellor to the living of Bramford Speke in the diocese of Exeter. The Bishop, Dr Phillpotts,* was a High Churchman, and he had reason to believe that Mr Gorham held evangelical opinions; he therefore subjected him to an examination on doctrine, which took the form partly of a verbal interrogatory, lasting thirty-eight hours, and partly of a series of one hundred and forty-nine written questions. At the end of the examination he came to the conclusion that Mr Gorham held heretical views on the subject of Baptismal Regeneration, and he therefore refused to institute. Mr Gorham thereupon took proceedings against the Bishop in the Court of Arches. He lost his case; and he then appealed to the Judicial Committee of the Privy Council.

The questions at issue were taken very seriously by a large number of persons. In the first place, there was the question of Baptismal Regeneration itself. This is by no means an easy one to disentangle; but it may be noted that the doctrine of Baptism includes (1) God's intention, that is to say, His purpose in electing certain persons to eternal life – an abstruse and greatly controverted subject, upon which the Church of England abstains from strict definition; (2)

God's action, whether by means of sacraments or otherwise – concerning which the Church of England maintains the efficacy of sacraments, but does not formally deny that grace may be given by other means, repentance and faith being present; and (3) the question whether sacramental grace is given instrumentally, by and at the moment of the act of baptism, or in consequence of an act of prevenient grace rendering the receiver worthy – that is to say, whether sacramental grace in baptism is given absolutely or conditionally: it was over this last question that the dispute raged hottest in the Gorham Case. The High Church party, represented by Dr Phillpotts, asserted that the mere act of baptism conferred regeneration upon the recipient and washed away his original sin. To this the Evangelicals, headed by Mr Gorham, replied that, according to the Articles, regeneration would not follow unless baptism was *rightly* received. What, then, was the meaning of 'rightly'? Clearly it implied not merely lawful administration, but worthy reception; worthiness, therefore, is the essence of the sacrament; and worthiness means faith and repentance. Now, two propositions were accepted by both parties – that all infants are born in original sin, and that original sin could be washed away by baptism. But how could both these propositions be true, argued Mr Gorham, if it was *also* true that faith and repentance were necessary before baptism could come into operation at all? How could an infant in arms be said to be in a state of faith and repentance? How, therefore, could its original sin be washed away by baptism? And yet, as every one agreed, washed away it was. The only solution of the difficulty lay in the doctrine of prevenient grace; and Mr Gorham maintained that unless God performed an act of prevenient grace by which the infant was endowed with faith and repentance, no act of baptism could be effectual; though to whom, and under what conditions, prevenient grace was given, Mr Gorham confessed himself unable to decide. The light thrown by the Bible upon the whole matter seemed somewhat dubious, for whereas the baptism of St Peter's disciples at Jerusalem and St Philip's at Samaria was followed by the gift of the Spirit, in the case of Cornelius the sacrament succeeded the gift. St Paul also was baptised; and as for the language of St John iii. 5; Rom. vi. 3, 4; 1 Peter iii. 21, it admits of more than one interpretation. There could, however, be no doubt that the Church of England assented to Dr Phillpotts' opinion; the question was whether or not she excluded Mr Gorham's. If it was decided that she did, it was clear that henceforward there would be very little peace for Evangelicals within her fold.

But there was another issue, even more fundamental than that of Baptismal Regeneration itself, involved in the Gorham trial. An Act passed in 1833 had constituted the Judicial Committee of the Privy Council the supreme court of appeal for such cases; and this Committee was a body composed entirely of laymen. It was thus obvious that the Royal Supremacy was still a fact, and that a collection of lawyers appointed by the Crown had the legal right to formulate the religious doctrine of the Church of England. In 1850 their judgment was delivered; they reversed the decision of the Court of Arches, and upheld the position of Mr Gorham. Whether his views were theologically correct or not, they said, was not their business; it was their business to decide whether the opinions under consideration were contrary or repugnant to the doctrine of the Church of England as enjoined upon the clergy by its Articles, Formularies, and Rubrics; and they had come to the conclusion that they were not. The judgment still holds good; and to this day a clergyman of the Church of England is quite at liberty to believe that Regeneration does not invariably take place when an infant is baptised.

The blow fell upon no one with greater violence than upon Manning. Not only was the supreme efficacy of the sign of the cross upon a baby's forehead one of his favourite doctrines, but up to that moment he had been convinced that the Royal Supremacy was a mere accident – a temporary usurpation – which left the spiritual dominion of the Church essentially untouched. But now the horrid reality rose up before him, crowned and triumphant; it was all too clear that an Act of Parliament, passed by Jews, Roman Catholics, and Dissenters, was the ultimate authority which decided upon the momentous niceties of the Anglican faith. Mr Gladstone, also, was deeply perturbed. It was absolutely necessary, he wrote, to 'rescue and defend the conscience of the Church from the present hideous system'. An agitation was set on foot, and several influential Anglicans, with Manning at their head, drew up and signed a formal protest against the Gorham Judgment. Mr Gladstone, however, proposed another method of procedure: precipitate action, he declared, must be avoided at all costs, and he elaborated a scheme for securing procrastination, by which a covenant was to bind all those who believed that an article of the creed had been abolished by Act of Parliament to take no steps in any direction, nor to announce their intention of doing so, until a given space of time had elapsed. Mr Gladstone was hopeful that some good might come of this – though indeed he could not be sure. 'Among others,' he wrote to Manning, 'I have consulted Robert Wilberforce and Wegg-Prosser,* and they seemed inclined to favour my proposal. It might, perhaps, have kept back Lord Feilding. But he is like a cork.'

The proposal was certainly not favoured by Manning. Protests and procrastinations, approving Wegg-Prossers and cork-like Lord Feildings – all this was feeding the wind and folly; the time for action had come. 'I can no longer continue,' he wrote to Robert Wilberforce, 'under oath and subscription binding me to the Royal Supremacy in Ecclesiastical causes, being convinced:

(1) That it is a violation of the Divine Office of the Church.
(2) That it has involved the Church of England in a separation from the universal Church, which separation I cannot clear of the character of schism.
(3) That it has thereby suspended and prevented the functions of the Church of England.'*

It was in vain that Robert Wilberforce pleaded, in vain that Mr Gladstone urged upon his mind the significance of John iii.8.[1] 'I admit,' Mr Gladstone wrote, 'that the words might in some way be satisfied by supposing our Lord simply to mean "the facts of nature are unintelligible, therefore be not afraid if revealed truths be likewise beyond the compass of the understanding"; but this seems to me a meagre meaning.'* Such considerations could hold him no longer, and Manning executed the resignation of his office and benefice before a public notary. Soon afterwards,* in the little Chapel off Buckingham Palace Road, kneeling beside Mr Gladstone, he worshipped for the last time as an Anglican. Thirty years later the Cardinal told how, just before the Communion service commenced, he turned to his friends with the words: 'I can no longer take the Communion in the Church of England.' 'I rose up, and laying my hand on Mr Gladstone's shoulder, said "Come." It was the parting

---

[1] 'The wind bloweth where it listeth, and thou hearest the sound thereof, but canst not tell whence it cometh, and whither it goeth; so is every one that is born of the Spirit.'

of the ways. Mr Gladstone remained; and I went my way. Mr Gladstone still remains where I left him.'

On April 6th, 1851, the final step was taken: Manning was
received into the Roman Catholic Church. Now at last, after the long
struggle, his mind was at rest. 'I know what you mean,' he wrote to
Robert Wilberforce, 'by saying that one sometimes feels as if all this
might turn out to be only another "Land of Shadows."* I have felt it
in time past, but not now. The θεολογία* from Nice to St Thomas
Aquinas, and the undivided unity suffused throughout the world, of
which the Cathedra Petri* is the centre – now 1800 years old, might-
ier in every power now than ever, in intellect, in science, in separation from the world; and purer too, refined by 300 years of conflict
with the modern infidel civilisation – all this is a fact more solid than
the earth.'

V

WHEN Manning joined the Church of Rome he acted under the
combined impulse of the two dominating forces in his nature. His
preoccupation with the supernatural might, alone, have been satisfied within the fold of the Anglican communion; and so might his
preoccupation with himself: the one might have found vent in the
elaborations of High Church ritual, and the other in the activities of
a bishopric. But the two together could not be quieted so easily. The
Church of England is a commodious institution; she is very anxious
to please; but, somehow or other, she has never managed to supply a
happy home to superstitious egotists. 'What an escape for my poor
soul!' Manning is said to have exclaimed when, shortly after his
conversion, a mitre was going a-begging. But, in truth, Manning's
'poor soul' had scented nobler quarry. To one of his temperament,
how was it possible, when once the choice was plainly put, to hesitate
for a moment between the respectable dignity of an English bishop,
harnessed by the secular power, with the Gorham judgment as a bit
between his teeth, and the illimitable pretensions of the humblest
priest of Rome?

For the moment, however, it seemed as if the Fates had at last
been successful in their little game of shunting Manning. The splendid career which he had so laboriously built up from the small

beginnings of his Sussex curacy was shattered – and shattered by the inevitable operation of his own essential needs. He was over forty, and he had been put back once more to the very bottom rung of the ladder – a middle-aged neophyte with, so far as could be seen, no special claim to the attention of his new superiors. The example of Newman, a far more illustrious convert, was hardly reassuring: he had been relegated to a complete obscurity, in which he was to remain until extreme old age. Why should there be anything better in store for Manning? Yet it so happened that within fourteen years of his conversion Manning was Archbishop of Westminster and the supreme ruler of the Roman Catholic community in England. This time the Fates gave up the unequal struggle; they paid over their stakes in despair, and retired from the game.

Nevertheless it is difficult to feel quite sure that Manning's plunge was as hazardous as it appeared. Certainly he was not a man who was likely to forget to look before he leaped, nor one who, if he happened to know that there was a mattress spread to receive him, would leap with less conviction. In the light of after-events, one would be glad to know what precisely passed at that mysterious interview of his with the Pope, three years before his conversion. It is at least possible that the authorities in Rome had their eye on Manning; they may well have felt that the Archdeacon of Chichester would be a great catch. What did Pio Nono say?* It is easy to imagine the persuasive innocence of his Italian voice. 'Ah, dear Signor Manning, why don't you come over to us? Do you suppose that we should not look after you?'

At any rate, when he did go over, Manning *was* looked after very thoroughly. There was, it is true, a momentary embarrassment at the outset: it was only with the greatest difficulty that he could bring himself to abandon his faith in the validity of Anglican Orders, in which he believed 'with a consciousness stronger than all reasoning.' He was convinced that he was still a priest. When the Rev. Mr Tierney,* who had received him into the Roman Catholic communion, assured him that this was not the case, he was filled with dismay and mortification. After a five hours' discussion, he started to his feet in a rage. 'Then, Mr Tierney,' he exclaimed, 'you think me insincere.' The bitter draught was swallowed at last, and, after that, all went smoothly. Manning hastened to Rome, and was immediately placed by the Pope in the highly select *Accademia Ecclesiastica*, commonly known as the 'nursery of Cardinals,' for the purpose of

completing his theological studies. When the course was finished, he
continued, by the Pope's special request, to spend six months of
every year in Rome, where he preached to the English visitors,
became acquainted with the great personages of the Papal court, and
enjoyed the privilege of constant interviews with the Holy Father. At
the same time he was able to make himself useful in London, where
Cardinal Wiseman, the newly created Archbishop of Westminster,
was seeking to reanimate the Roman Catholic community. Manning
was not only extremely popular in the pulpit and in the confessional;
he was not only highly efficient as a gleaner of souls – and of souls
who moved in the best society; he also possessed a familiarity with
official persons and official ways, which was invaluable. When
the question arose of the appointment of Catholic chaplains in the
Crimea during the war, it was Manning who approached the Minister, interviewed the Permanent Secretary, and finally succeeded in
obtaining all that was required. When a special Reformatory for
Catholic children was proposed, Manning carried through the nego-
tiation with the Government. When an attempt was made to remove
Catholic children from the Workhouses, Manning was again
indispensable. No wonder Cardinal Wiseman soon determined to
find some occupation of special importance for the energetic convert. He had long wished to establish a congregation of secular
priests in London particularly devoted to his service, and the
opportunity for the experiment had clearly now arisen. The order of
the Oblates of St Charles* was founded in Bayswater, and Manning
was put at its head. Unfortunately no portion of the body of St
Charles could be obtained for the new community, but two relics of
his blood were brought over to Bayswater from Milan. Almost at the
same time the Pope signified his appreciation of Manning's efforts
by appointing him Provost of the Chapter of Westminster – a
position which placed him at the head of the Canons of the diocese.

   This double promotion was the signal for the outbreak of an
extraordinary intestine struggle, which raged without intermission
for the next seven years, and was only to end with the accession of
Manning to the Archbishopric.* The condition of the Roman Catholic community in England was at that time a singular one. On the
one hand the old repressive laws of the seventeenth century had been
repealed by liberal legislation, and on the other a large new body of
distinguished converts had entered the Roman Church as a result of

the Oxford Movement. It was evident that there was a 'boom' in English Catholicism, and, in 1850, Pius IX recognised the fact by dividing up the whole of England into dioceses, and placing Wiseman at the head of them as Archbishop of Westminster. Wiseman's encyclical, dated 'from without the Flaminian Gate,' in which he announced the new departure, was greeted in England by a storm of indignation, culminating in the famous and furibund letter of Lord John Russell, then Prime Minister, against the insolence of the 'Papal Aggression.' Though the particular point against which the outcry was raised – the English territorial titles of the new Roman bishops – was an insignificant one, the instinct of Lord John and of the English people was in reality sound enough. Wiseman's installation did mean, in fact, a new move in the Papal game; it meant an advance, if not an aggression – a quickening in England of the long-dormant energies of the Roman Church. That Church has never had the reputation of being an institution to be trifled with; and, in those days, the Pope was still ruling as a temporal Prince over the fairest provinces of Italy. Surely, if the images of Guy Fawkes had not been garnished, on that fifth of November, with triple crowns,* it would have been a very poor compliment to His Holiness.

But it was not only the honest Protestants of England who had cause to dread the arrival of the new Cardinal Archbishop; there was a party among the Catholics themselves who viewed his installation with alarm and disgust. The families in which the Catholic tradition had been handed down uninterruptedly since the days of Elizabeth, which had known the pains of exile and of martyrdom, and which clung together, an alien and isolated group in the midst of English society, now began to feel that they were, after all, of small moment in the counsels of Rome. They had laboured through the heat of the day, but now it seemed as if the harvest was to be gathered in by a crowd of converts, who were proclaiming on every side as something new and wonderful the truths which the Old Catholics, as they came to be called, had not only known, but for which they had suffered for generations. Cardinal Wiseman, it is true, was no convert; he belonged to one of the oldest of the Catholic families; but he had spent most of his life in Rome, he was out of touch with English traditions, and his sympathy with Newman and his followers was only too apparent. One of his first acts as Archbishop was to appoint the convert W. G. Ward, who was not even in holy orders, to be

Professor of Theology at St Edmund's College – the chief seminary for young priests, in which the ancient traditions of Douay* were still flourishing. Ward was an ardent Papalist and his appointment indicated clearly enough that in Wiseman's opinion there was too little of the Italian spirit in the English community. The uneasiness of the Old Catholics was becoming intense,* when they were reassured by Wiseman's appointing as his coadjutor and successor his intimate friend, Dr Errington, who was created on the occasion Archbishop of Trebizond *in partibus infidelium*. Not only was Dr Errington* an Old Catholic of the most rigid type, he was a man of extreme energy, whose influence was certain to be great; and, in any case, Wiseman was growing old, so that before very long it seemed inevitable that the policy of the diocese would be in proper hands. Such was the position of affairs when, two years after Errington's appointment, Manning became head of the Oblates of St Charles and Provost of the Chapter of Westminster.

The Archbishop of Trebizond had been for some time growing more and more suspicious of Manning's influence, and this sudden elevation appeared to justify his worst fears. But his alarm was turned to fury when he learnt that St Edmund's College, from which he had just succeeded in removing the obnoxious W. G. Ward, was to be placed under the control of the Oblates of St Charles. The Oblates did not attempt to conceal the fact that one of their principal aims was to introduce the customs of a Roman Seminary into England. A grim perspective of espionage and tale-bearing, foreign habits and Italian devotions, opened out before the dismayed eyes of the Old Catholics; they determined to resist to the utmost; and it was upon the question of the control of St Edmund's that the first battle in the long campaign between Errington and Manning was fought.

Cardinal Wiseman was now obviously declining towards the grave. A man of vast physique – 'your immense,'* an Irish servant used respectfully to call him – of sanguine temperament, of genial disposition, of versatile capacity, he seemed to have engrafted upon the robustness of his English nature the facile, child-like, and expansive qualities of the South. So far from being a Bishop Blougram* (as the rumour went) he was, in fact, the very antithesis of that subtle and worldly-wise ecclesiastic. He had innocently looked forward all his life to the reunion of England to the See of Peter, and eventually had come to believe that, in God's hand, he was the instrument destined to bring about this miraculous consummation. Was not the Oxford Movement, with its flood of converts, a clear sign of the Divine will? Had he not himself been the author of that momentous article on St Augustine and the Donatists, which had finally convinced Newman that the Church of England was in schism? And then had he not been able to set on foot a Crusade of Prayer throughout Catholic Europe for the conversion of England? He awaited the result with eager expectation, and in the meantime he set himself to smooth away the hostility of his countrymen by delivering courses of popular lectures on literature and archæology. He devoted much time and attention to the ceremonial details of his princely office. His knowledge of rubric and ritual and of the symbolical significations of vestments has rarely been equalled, and he took a profound delight in the ordering and the performance of elaborate processions. During one of these functions an unexpected difficulty arose: the Master of the Ceremonies suddenly gave the word for a halt, and, on being asked the reason, replied that he had been instructed that moment by special revelation to stop the procession. The Cardinal, however, was not at a loss. 'You may let the procession go on,' he smilingly replied. 'I have just obtained permission, by special revelation, to proceed with it.' His leisure hours he spent in the writing of edifying novels,* the composition of acrostics in Latin Verse, and in playing battledore and shuttlecock with his little nieces. There was, indeed, only one point in which he resembled Bishop Blougram – his love of a good table. Some of Newman's disciples were astonished and grieved to find that he sat down to four courses of fish during Lent. 'I am sorry to say,' remarked one of them afterwards, 'that there is a lobster salad side to the Cardinal.'*

It was a melancholy fate which ordained that the last years of this comfortable, easy-going, innocent old man should be distracted and embittered by the fury of opposing principles and the venom of personal animosities. But so it was. He had fallen into the hands of one who cared very little for the gentle pleasures of repose. Left to himself, Wiseman might have compromised with the Old Catholics and Dr Errington; but when Manning had once appeared upon the scene all compromise became impossible. The late Archdeacon of Chichester, who had understood so well and practised with such careful skill the precept of the golden mean so dear to the heart of the Church of England, now, as Provost of Westminster, flung himself into the fray with that unyielding intensity of fervour, that passion for the extreme and the absolute, which is the very life-blood of the Church of Rome. Even the redoubtable Dr Errington, short, thickset, determined, with his 'hawk-like expression of face,' as a contemporary described him, 'as he looked at you through his blue spectacles,' had been known to quail in the presence of his antagonist, with his tall and graceful figure, his pale ascetic features, his compressed and icy lips, his calm and penetrating gaze. As for the poor Cardinal, he was helpless indeed. Henceforward there was to be no paltering with that dangerous spirit of independence – was it not almost Gallicanism? – which possessed the Old Catholic families of England. The supremacy of the Vicar of Christ must be maintained at all hazards. Compared with such an object, what were the claims of personal affection and domestic peace? The Cardinal pleaded in vain; his lifelong friendship with Dr Errington was plucked up by the roots, and the harmony of his private life was utterly destroyed. His own household was turned against him. His favourite nephew, whom he had placed among the Oblates under Manning's special care, left the congregation and openly joined the party of Dr Errington. His secretary followed suit; but saddest of all was the case of Monsignor Searle. Monsignor Searle,* in the capacity of confidential man of affairs, had dominated over the Cardinal in private for years with the autocratic fidelity of a servant who has grown indispensable. His devotion, in fact, seemed to have taken the form of physical imitation, for he was hardly less gigantic than his master. The two were inseparable; their huge figures loomed together like neighbouring mountains; and on one occasion, meeting them in the street, a gentleman congratulated Wiseman on 'your Eminence's fine son.' Yet now even this companionship was broken up. The relentless Provost here too brought a sword. There were explosions and recriminations. Monsignor Searle, finding that his power was slipping from him, made scenes and protests, and at last was foolish enough to accuse Manning of peculation to his face; after that it was clear that his day was over; he was forced to slink snarling into the background, while the Cardinal shuddered through all his immensity and wished many times that he were already dead.

Yet he was not altogether without his consolations; Manning took care to see to that. His piercing eye had detected the secret way into the recesses of the Cardinal's heart – had discerned the core of simple faith which underlay that jovial manner and that facile talk. Others were content to laugh and chatter and transact their business; Manning was more artistic. He watched his opportunity, and then, when the moment came, touched with a deft finger the chord of the Conversion of England. There was an immediate response, and he struck the same chord again, and yet again. He became the repository of the Cardinal's most intimate aspirations. He alone sympathised and understood. 'If God gives me strength to undertake a great wrestling-match with infidelity,' Wiseman wrote, 'I shall owe it to him.'

But what he really found himself undertaking was a wrestling-match with Dr Errington. The struggle over St Edmund's College* grew more and more acute. There were high words in the Chapter, where Monsignor Searle led the assault against the Provost, and carried a resolution declaring that the Oblates of St Charles had intruded themselves illegally into the Seminary. The Cardinal quashed the proceedings of the Chapter; whereupon the Chapter appealed to Rome. Dr Errington, carried away by the fury of the controversy, then appeared as the avowed opponent of the Provost and the Cardinal. With his own hand he drew up a document justifying the appeal of the Chapter to Rome by Canon Law and the decrees of the Council of Trent. Wiseman was deeply pained. 'My own coadjutor,' he exclaimed, 'is acting as solicitor against me in a lawsuit.' There was a rush to Rome, where, for several ensuing years, the hostile English parties were to wage a furious battle in the antechambers of the Vatican. But the dispute over the Oblates now sank into insignificance beside the rage of contention which centred round a new and far more deadly question; for the position of Dr Errington himself was at stake. The Cardinal, in spite of illness, indolence, and the ties of friendship, had been brought at last to an extraordinary step: he was petitioning the Pope for nothing less than the deprivation and removal of the Archbishop of Trebizond.

The precise details of what followed are doubtful. It is only possible to discern with clearness, amid a vast cloud of official documents and unofficial correspondences in English, Italian, and Latin, of Papal decrees and voluminous *scritture*,* of confidential reports of episcopal whispers and the secret agitations of Cardinals, the form of Manning, restless and indomitable, scouring like a stormy petrel the angry ocean of debate. Wiseman, dilatory, unbusinesslike, and infirm, was ready enough to leave the conduct of affairs in his hands. Nor was it long before Manning saw where the key of the whole position lay. As in the old days, at Chichester, he had secured the goodwill of Bishop Shuttleworth by cultivating the friendship of Archdeacon Hare, so now, on this vaster scale of operations, his sagacity led him swiftly and unerringly up the little winding staircase in the Vatican and through the humble door which opened into the cabinet of Monsignor Talbot,* the private secretary of the Pope. Monsignor Talbot was a priest who embodied in a singular manner, if not the highest, at least the most persistent traditions of the Roman Curia.* He was a master of various arts which the practice of ages has brought to perfection under the friendly shadow of the triple tiara. He could mingle together astuteness and holiness without any difficulty; he could make innuendoes as naturally as an ordinary man makes statements of fact; he could apply flattery with so unsparing a hand that even Princes of the Church found it sufficient; and, on occasion, he could ring the changes of torture on a human soul with a tact which called forth universal approbation. With such accomplishments, it could hardly be expected that Monsignor Talbot should be remarkable either for a delicate sense of conscientiousness or for an extreme refinement of feeling, but then it was not for those qualities that Manning was in search when he went up the winding stair. He was looking for the man who had the ear of Pio Nono; and, on the other side of the low-arched door, he found him. Then he put forth all his efforts; his success was complete; and an alliance began which was destined to have the profoundest effect upon Manning's career, and was only dissolved when, many years later, Monsignor Talbot was unfortunately obliged to exchange his apartment in the Vatican for a private lunatic asylum at Passy.

It was determined that the coalition should be ratified by the ruin of Dr Errington. When the moment of crisis was seen to be approaching, Wiseman was summoned to Rome, where he began to draw up an immense *scrittura* containing his statement of the case. For months past the redoubtable energies of the Archbishop of Trebizond had been absorbed in a similar task. Folio was being piled upon folio, when a sudden blow threatened to put an end to the whole proceeding in a summary manner. The Cardinal was seized by violent illness, and appeared to be upon his deathbed. Manning thought for a moment that his labours had been in vain and that all was lost. But the Cardinal recovered; Monsignor Talbot used his influence as he alone knew how; and a papal decree was issued by which Dr Errington was 'liberated' from the Coadjutorship of Westminster, together with the right of succession to the See.

It was a supreme act of authority – a 'colpo di stato di Dominiddio,'* as the Pope himself said – and the blow to the Old Catholics was correspondingly severe. They found themselves deprived at one fell swoop both of the influence of their most energetic supporter and of the certainty of coming into power at Wiseman's death. And in the meantime Manning was redoubling his energies at Bayswater. Though his Oblates had been checked over St Edmund's, there was still no lack of work for them to do. There were missions to be carried on, schools to be managed, funds to be collected. Several new churches were built; a community of most edifying nuns of the Third Order of St Francis was established; and £30,000, raised from Manning's private resources and from those of his friends, was spent in three years. 'I hate that man,' one of the Old Catholics exclaimed; 'he is such a forward piece.' The words were reported to Manning, who shrugged his shoulders. 'Poor man,' he said, 'what is he made of? Does he suppose, in his foolishness, that after working day and night for twenty years in heresy and schism, on becoming a Catholic I should sit in an easy-chair and fold my hands all the rest of my life?' But his secret thoughts were of a different caste. 'I am conscious of a desire,' he wrote in his Diary, 'to be in such a position (1) as I had in times past, (2) as my present circumstances imply, (3) as my friends think me fit for, (4) as I feel my own faculties tend to.

'But, God being my helper, I will not seek it by the lifting of a finger or the speaking of a word.'

So Manning wrote, and thought, and prayed; but what are words, and thoughts, and even prayers, to the mysterious and relentless powers of circumstance and character? Cardinal Wiseman was slowly dying; the tiller of the Church was slipping from his feeble hand; and Manning was beside him, the one man with the energy, the ability, the courage, and the conviction to steer the ship upon her course. More than that; there was the sinister figure of a Dr Errington crouching close at hand, ready to seize the helm and make straight – who could doubt it? – for the rocks. In such a situation the voice of self-abnegation must needs grow still and small indeed. Yet it spoke on, for it was one of the paradoxes in Manning's soul that

that voice was never silent. Whatever else he was, he was not unscrupulous. Rather, his scruples deepened with his desires; and he could satisfy his most exorbitant ambitions in a profundity of self-abasement. And so now he vowed to Heaven that he would *seek* nothing – no, not by the lifting of a finger or the speaking of a word. But, if something came to him—? He had vowed not to seek; he had not vowed not to take. Might it not be his plain duty to take? Might it not be the will of God?

Something, of course, did come to him, though it seemed for a moment that it would elude his grasp. Wiseman died, and there ensued in Rome a crisis of extraordinary intensity. 'Since the creation of the hierarchy,' Monsignor Talbot wrote, 'it is the greatest moment for the Church that I have yet seen.' It was the duty of the Chapter of Westminster to nominate three candidates for succession to the Archbishopric; they made one last effort, and had the temerity to place upon the list, besides the names of two Old Catholic bishops, that of Dr Errington. It was a fatal blunder. Pius IX was furious; the Chapter had committed an 'insulta al Papa,' he exclaimed, striking his breast three times in his rage. 'It was the Chapter that did it,' said Manning afterwards; but even after the Chapter's indiscretion, the fatal decision hung in the balance for weeks. 'The great point of anxiety with me,' wrote Monsignor Talbot to Manning, 'is whether a Congregation will be held, or whether the Holy Father will perform a Pontifical act. He himself is doubting. I therefore say mass and pray every morning that he may have the courage to choose for himself, instead of submitting the matter to a Congregation. Although the Cardinals are determined to reject Dr Errington, nevertheless I am afraid that they should select one of the others. You know very well that Congregations are guided by the documents that are placed before them; it is for this reason that I should prefer the Pope's acting himself.'

But the Holy Father himself was doubting. In his indecision, he ordered a month of prayers and masses. The suspense grew and grew. Everything seemed against Manning. The whole English episcopate was opposed to him; he had quarrelled with the Chapter; he was a convert of but few years' standing; even the congregated Cardinals did not venture to suggest the appointment of such a man. But suddenly the Holy Father's doubts came to an end. He heard a voice – a mysterious inward voice – whispering something in his ear.

'*Mettetelo lì! Mettetelo lì!*'* the voice repeated, over and over again. *Mettetelo lì!*. It was an inspiration; and Pius IX, brushing aside the recommendations of the Chapter and the deliberations of the Cardinals, made Manning, by a Pontifical act, Archbishop of Westminster.*

Monsignor Talbot's felicity was complete; and he took occasion, in conveying his congratulations to his friend, to make some illuminating reflections upon the great event. '*My* policy throughout,' he wrote, 'was never to propose you *directly* to the Pope, but to make others do so; so that both you and I can always say that it was not I who induced the Holy Father to name you, which would lessen the weight of your appointment. This I say, because many have said that your being named was all my doing. I do not say that the Pope did not know that I thought you the only man eligible; as I took care to tell him over and over again what was against all the other candidates; and in consequence he was almost driven into naming you. After he had named you, the Holy Father said to me, 'What a diplomatist you are, to make what you wished come to pass!'

'Nevertheless,' concluded Monsignor Talbot, 'I believe your appointment was specially directed by the Holy Ghost.'

Manning himself was apparently of the same opinion. 'My dear Child,' he wrote to a lady penitent, 'I have in these last three weeks felt as if our Lord had called me by name. Everything else has passed out of my mind. The firm belief that I have long had that the Holy Father is the most supernatural person I have ever seen has given me this feeling more deeply still. I feel as if I had been brought, contrary to all human wills, by the Divine Will, into an immediate relation to our Divine Lord.'

'If indeed,' he wrote to Lady Herbert, 'it were the will of our Divine Lord to lay upon me this heavy burden, He could have done it in no way more strengthening and consoling to me. To receive it from the hands of His Vicar, and from Pius IX, and after long invocation of the Holy Ghost, and not only without human influences, but in spite of manifold and powerful human opposition, gives me the last strength for such a cross.'

VI

MANNING's appointment filled his opponents with alarm. Wrath and vengeance seemed to be hanging over them; what might not be expected from the formidable enemy against whom they had struggled for so long, and who now stood among them armed with archiepiscopal powers and invested with the special confidence of Rome? Great was their amazement, great was their relief, when they found that their dreaded master breathed nothing but kindness, gentleness, and conciliation. The old scores, they found, were not to be paid off, but to be wiped out. The new archbishop poured forth upon every side all the tact, all the courtesy, all the dignified graces of a Christian magnanimity. It was impossible to withstand such treatment. Bishops who had spent years in thwarting him became his devoted adherents; even the Chapter of Westminster forgot its hatred. Monsignor Talbot was extremely surprised. 'Your greatest enemies have entirely come round,' he wrote. 'I received the other day a panegyric of you from Searle. This change of feeling I cannot attribute to anything but the Holy Ghost.' Monsignor Talbot was very fond of the Holy Ghost; but, so far at any rate as Searle was concerned, there was another explanation. Manning, instead of dismissing Searle from his position of 'œconomus'* in the episcopal household, had kept him on – at an increased salary; and the poor man, who had not scrupled in the days of his pride to call Manning a thief, was now duly grateful.

As to Dr Errington, he gave an example of humility and submission by at once withdrawing into a complete obscurity. For years the Archbishop of Trebizond, the ejected heir to the See of Westminster, laboured as a parish priest in the Isle of Man. He nursed no resentment in his heart, and, after a long and edifying life of peace and silence, he died in 1886, a professor of theology at Clifton.

It might be supposed that Manning could now feel that his triumph was complete. His position was secure; his power was absolute; his prestige was daily growing. Yet there was something that irked him still. As he cast his eyes over the Roman Catholic community in England, he was aware of one figure which, by virtue of a peculiar eminence, seemed to challenge the supremacy of his own. That figure was Newman's.

Since his conversion, Newman's life had been a long series of misfortunes and disappointments. When he had left the Church of England, he was its most distinguished, its most revered member, whose words, however strange, were listened to with profound attention, and whose opinions, however dubious, were followed in all their fluctuations with an eager and indeed a trembling respect. He entered the Church of Rome, and found himself forthwith an unimportant man. He was received at the Papal Court with a politeness which only faintly concealed a total lack of interest and understanding. His delicate mind, with its refinements, its hesitations, its complexities – his soft, spectacled, Oxford manner, with its half-effeminate diffidence – such things were ill calculated to impress a throng of busy Cardinals and Bishops, whose days were spent amid the practical details of ecclesiastical organisation, the long-drawn involutions of papal diplomacy, and the delicious bickerings of personal intrigue. And when, at last, he did succeed in making some impression upon these surroundings, it was no better; it was worse. An uneasy suspicion gradually arose; it began to dawn upon the Roman authorities that Dr Newman was a man of ideas. Was it possible that Dr Newman did not understand that ideas in Rome were, to say the least of it, out of place? Apparently he did not; nor was that all; not content with having ideas, he positively seemed anxious to spread them. When that was known, the politeness in high places was seen to be wearing decidedly thin. His Holiness, who on Newman's arrival had graciously expressed the wish to see him 'again and again,' now, apparently, was constantly engaged. At first Newman supposed that the growing coolness was the result of misapprehension; his Italian was faulty, Latin was not spoken at Rome, his writings had only appeared in garbled translations. And even Englishmen had sometimes found his arguments difficult to follow. He therefore determined to take the utmost care to make his views quite clear; his opinions upon religious probability, his distinction between demonstrative and circumstantial evidence, his theory of the development of doctrine and the aspects of ideas – these and many other matters, upon which he had written so much, he would now explain in the simplest language. He would show that there was nothing dangerous in what he held, that there was a passage in De Lugo which supported him, that Perrone, by maintaining that the Immaculate Conception could be defined, had implicitly admitted one of his main positions, and that his language about Faith had been confused, quite erroneously, with the fideism of M. Bautain. Cardinal Barnabò,* Cardinal Reisach, Cardinal Antonelli, looked at him with their shrewd eyes and hard faces, while he poured into their ears – which, as he had already noticed with distress, were large and not too clean – his careful disquisitions; but it was all in vain; they had clearly never read De Lugo or Perrone, and as for M. Bautain, they had never heard of him. Newman in despair fell back upon St Thomas Aquinas; but, to his horror, he observed that St Thomas himself did not mean very much to the Cardinals. With a sinking heart, he realised at last the painful truth: it was not the nature of his views, it was his having views at all, that was objectionable. He had hoped to devote the rest of his life to the teaching of Theology; but what sort of Theology could he teach which would be acceptable to such superiors? He left Rome, and settled down in Birmingham as the head of a small community of Oratorians.* He did not complain; it was God's will; it was better so. He would watch and pray.

But God's will was not quite so simple as that. Was it right, after all, that a man with Newman's intellectual gifts, his devoted ardour, his personal celebrity, should sink away out of sight and use in the dim recesses of the Oratory at Birmingham? If the call were to come to him to take his talent out of the napkin, how could he refuse? And the call did come. A Catholic University was being started in Ireland, and Dr Cullen, the Archbishop of Armagh,* begged Newman to become the Rector. At first he hesitated, but when he learnt that it was the Holy Father's wish that he should take up the work, he could doubt no longer; the offer was sent from Heaven. The difficulties before him were very great; not only had a new University to be called up out of the void, but the position was complicated by the presence of a rival institution – the undenominational Queen's Colleges, founded by Peel a few years earlier with the object of giving Irish Catholics facilities for University education on the same terms as their fellow-countrymen.* Yet Newman had the highest hopes. He dreamt of something greater than a merely Irish University – of a noble and flourishing centre of learning for the Catholics of Ireland and England alike. And why should not his dream come true? 'In the midst of our difficulties,' he said, 'I have one ground of hope, just one stay, but, as I think, a sufficient one, which serves me in the stead of all other argument whatever. It is the decision of the Holy See; St Peter has spoken.'

The years that followed showed to what extent it was safe to depend upon St Peter. Unforeseen obstacles cropped up on every side. Newman's energies were untiring, but so was the inertia of the Irish authorities. On his appointment, he wrote to Dr Cullen asking that arrangements might be made for his reception in Dublin. Dr Cullen did not reply. Newman wrote again, but still there was no answer. Weeks passed, months passed, years passed, and not a word, not a sign, came from Dr Cullen. At last, after dangling for more than two years in the uncertainties and perplexities of so strange a situation, Newman was summoned to Dublin. There he found nothing but disorder and discouragement. The laity took no interest in the scheme, the clergy actively disliked it;* Newman's authority was disregarded. He appealed to Cardinal Wiseman, and then at last a ray of hope dawned. The cardinal suggested that a bishopric should be conferred upon him, to give him a status suitable to his position; Dr Cullen acquiesced, and Pius IX was all compliance. 'Manderemo a Newman la crocetta,'* he said to Wiseman, smilingly drawing his hands down each side of his neck to his breast, 'lo faremo vescovo di Porfirio, o qualche luogo.'* The news spread among Newman's friends, and congratulations began to come in. But the official intimation seemed to be unaccountably delayed; no *crocetta* came from Rome, and Cardinal Wiseman never again referred to the matter. Newman was left to gather that the secret representations of Dr Cullen had brought about a change of counsel in high quarters. His pride did not allow him to inquire further; but one of his lady penitents, Miss Giberne, was less discreet. 'Holy Father,' she suddenly said to the Pope in an audience one day, 'why don't you make Father Newman a bishop?' Upon which the Holy Father looked much confused and took a great deal of snuff.*

For the next five years Newman, unaided and ignored, struggled desperately, like a man in a bog, with the overmastering difficulties of his task. His mind, whose native haunt was among the far aerial boundaries of fancy and philosophy, was now clamped down under the fetters of petty detail and fed upon the mean diet of compromise and routine. He had to force himself to scrape together money, to write articles for the students' Gazette, to make plans for medical laboratories, to be ingratiating with the City Council; he was obliged to spend months travelling through the remote regions of Ireland in the company of extraordinary ecclesiastics and barbarous squireens. He was a thoroughbred harnessed to a four-wheeled cab; and he knew it. Eventually he realised something else: he saw that the whole project of a Catholic University* had been evolved as a political and ecclesiastical weapon against the Queen's Colleges of Peel, and that was all. As an instrument of education, it was simply laughed at; and he himself had been called in because his name would be a valuable asset in a party game. When he understood that, he resigned his rectorship and returned to the Oratory.

But his tribulations were not yet over. It seemed to be God's will that he should take part in a whole succession of schemes, which, no less than the project of the Irish University, were to end in disillusionment and failure. He was persuaded by Cardinal Wiseman to undertake the editorship of a new English version of the Scriptures, which was to be a monument of Catholic scholarship and an everlasting glory to Mother Church. He made elaborate preparations; he collected subscriptions, engaged contributors, and composed a long and learned *prolegomena* to the work. It was all useless; Cardinal Wiseman began to think of other things; and the scheme faded imperceptibly into thin air. Then a new task was suggested to him. The *Rambler*, a Catholic periodical, had fallen on evil days; would Dr Newman come to the rescue, and accept the editorship? This time he hesitated rather longer than usual; he had burnt his fingers so often; he must be specially careful now. 'I did all I could to ascertain God's will,' he said, and he came to the conclusion that it was his duty to undertake the work. He did so, and after two numbers had appeared Dr Ullathorne, the Bishop of Birmingham, called upon him, and gently hinted that he had better leave the paper alone. Its tone was not liked at Rome; it had contained an article criticising St Pius V, and, most serious of all, the orthodoxy of one of Newman's own essays had appeared to be doubtful. He resigned, and in the anguish of his heart determined never to write again. One of his friends asked him why he was publishing nothing. 'Hannibal's elephants,' he replied, 'never could learn the goose-step.'*

Newman was now an old man – he was sixty-three years of age. What had he to look forward to? A few last years of insignificance and silence. What had he to look back upon? A long chronicle of wasted efforts, disappointed hopes, neglected possibilities, unappreciated powers. And now all his labours had ended by his being accused at Rome of lack of orthodoxy. He could no longer restrain his indignation, and in a letter to one of his lady penitents he gave vent to the bitterness of his soul. When his *Rambler* article had been complained of, he said, there had been some talk of calling him to Rome. 'Call me to Rome,' he burst out – 'what does that mean? It means to sever an old man from his home, to subject him to inter-course with persons whose languages are strange to him – to food and to fashions which are almost starvation on the one hand, and involve restless days and nights on the other – it means to oblige him to dance attendance on Propaganda week after week and month after month – it means his death. (It was the punishment on Dr Baines,* 1840–41, to keep him at the door of Propaganda for a year.)

'This is the prospect which I cannot but feel probable, did I say anything which one Bishop in England chose to speak against and report. Others have been killed before me. Lucas* went of his own accord indeed – but when he got there, oh! how much did he, as loyal a son of the Church and the Holy See as ever was, what did he suffer because Dr Cullen was against him? He wandered (as Dr Cullen *said* in a letter he published in a sort of triumph), he wandered from Church to Church without a friend, and hardly got an audience from the Pope. And I too should go from St Philip to Our Lady, and to St Peter and St Paul, and to St Laurence and to St Cecilia, and, if it happened to me as to Lucas, should come back to die.'

Yet, in spite of all, in spite of these exasperations of the flesh, these agitations of the spirit, what was there to regret? Had he not a mysterious consolation which outweighed every grief? Surely, surely, he had.

'Unveil, O Lord, and on us shine,
In glory and in grace,'

he exclaims in a poem written at this time, called 'The Two Worlds':

'This gaudy world grows pale before
The beauty of Thy face.

'Till Thou art seen it seems to be
A sort of fairy ground,
Where suns unsetting light the sky,
And flowers and fruit abound.

'But when Thy keener, purer beam
    Is poured upon our sight,
It loses all its power to charm,
    And what was day is night. . . .

'And thus, when we renounce for Thee
    Its restless aims and fears,
The tender memories of the past,
    The hopes of coming years,

'Poor is our sacrifice, whose eyes
    Are lighted from above;
We offer what we cannot keep,
    What we have ceased to love.'

Such were Newman's thoughts when an unexpected event occurred which produced a profound effect upon his life. Charles Kingsley attacked his good faith and the good faith of Catholics in general in a magazine article; Newman protested, and Kingsley rejoined in an irate pamphlet. Newman's reply was the *Apologia pro Vita Sua*, which he wrote in seven weeks, sometimes working twenty-two hours at a stretch,* 'constantly in tears, and constantly crying out with distress.' The success of the book, with its transparent candour, its controversial brilliance, the sweep and passion of its rhetoric, the depth of its personal feeling, was immediate and overwhelming; it was recognised at once as a classic, not only by Catholics, but by the whole English world. From every side expressions of admiration, gratitude, and devotion poured in. It was impossible for one so sensitive as Newman to the opinions of other people to resist the happy influence of such an unlooked-for, such an enormous triumph. The cloud of his dejection began to lift; *et l'espoir malgré lui s'est glissé dans son cœur.**

It was only natural that at such a moment his thoughts should return to Oxford. For some years past proposals had been on foot for establishing there a Hall, under Newman's leadership, for Catholic undergraduates. The scheme had been looked upon with disfavour in Rome, and it had been abandoned; but now a new opportunity presented itself; some land in a suitable position came into the market; Newman, with his reviving spirits, felt that he could not let this chance go by, and bought the land. It was his intention to build there not a Hall, but a Church, and to set on foot a 'House of the Oratory.' What possible objection could there be to such a scheme? He approached the Bishop of Birmingham, who gave his approval; in Rome itself there was no hostile sign. The laity were enthusiastic and subscriptions began to flow in. Was it possible that all was well at last? Was it conceivable that the strange and weary pilgrimage of so many years should end at length, in quietude if not in happiness, where it had begun?

It so happened that it was at this very time that Manning was appointed to the See of Westminster. The destinies of the two men, which had run parallel to one another in so strange a fashion and for so many years, were now for a moment suddenly to converge. Newly clothed with all the attributes of ecclesiastical supremacy, Manning found himself face to face with Newman, upon whose brows were glittering the fresh laurels of spiritual victory – the crown of an apostolical life. It was the meeting of the eagle and the dove. What followed showed, more clearly perhaps than any other incident in his career, the stuff that Manning was made of. Power had come to him at last; and he seized it with all the avidity of a born autocrat, whose appetite for supreme dominion had been whetted by long years of enforced abstinence and the hated simulations of submission. He was the ruler of Roman Catholic England, and he would rule. The nature of Newman's influence it was impossible for him to understand, but he saw that it existed; for twenty years he had been unable to escape the unwelcome iterations of that singular, that alien, that rival renown; and now it stood in his path, alone and inexplicable, like a defiant ghost. 'It is remarkably interesting,' he observed coldly, when somebody asked him what he thought of the *Apologia;* 'it is like listening to the voice of one from the dead.' And such voices, with their sepulchral echoes, are apt to be more dangerous than living ones; they attract too much attention; they must be silenced at all costs. It was the meeting of the eagle and the dove; there was a hovering, a swoop, and then the quick beak and the relentless talons did their work.

Even before his accession to the Archbishopric, Manning had scented a peculiar peril in Newman's Oxford scheme, and so soon as he came into power he privately determined that the author of the *Apologia* should never be allowed to return to his old University. Nor was there any lack of excellent reasons for such a decision. Oxford was by this time a nest of liberalism; it was no fit place for Catholic youths, and they would inevitably be attracted there by the presence of Father Newman. And then, had not Father Newman's orthodoxy been impugned? Had he not been heard to express opinions of most doubtful propriety upon the question of the Temporal Power? Was it not known that he might almost be said to have an independent mind? An influence? Yes, he had an influence, no doubt; but what a fatal kind of influence to which to subject the rising generation of Catholic Englishmen!

Such were the reflections which Manning was careful to pour into the receptive ear of Monsignor Talbot. That useful priest, at his post of vantage in the Vatican, was more than ever the devoted servant of the new Archbishop. A league, offensive and defensive, had been established between the two friends. 'I daresay I shall have many opportunities to serve you in Rome,' wrote Monsignor Talbot modestly, 'and I do not think any support will be useless to you, especially on account of the peculiar character of the Pope, and the spirit which pervades Propaganda; therefore I wish you to understand that a compact exists between us; if you help me, I shall help you.' And a little later he added, 'I am glad you accept the league. As I have already done for years, I shall support you, and I have a hundred ways of doing so. A word dropped at the proper occasion works wonders.' Perhaps it was hardly necessary to remind his correspondent of that.

So far as Newman was concerned it so fell out that Monsignor Talbot* needed no prompting. During the sensation caused by the appearance of the *Apologia*, it had occurred to him that it would be an excellent plan to secure Newman as a preacher during Lent for the fashionable congregation which attended his church in the Piazza del Popolo; and he had accordingly written to invite him to Rome. His letter was unfortunately not a tactful one. He assured Newman that he would find in the Piazza del Popolo 'an audience of Protestants more educated than could ever be the case in England,' and 'I think myself,' he had added by way of extra inducement, 'that you will derive great benefit from visiting Rome, and showing yourself to the Ecclesiastical Authorities.' Newman smiled grimly at this; he declared to a friend that the letter was 'insolent'; and he could not resist the temptation of using his sharp pen.

'Dear Monsignor Talbot,' he wrote in reply, 'I have received your letter, inviting me to preach in your Church at Rome to an audience of Protestants more educated than could ever be the case in England.

'However, Birmingham people have souls; and I have neither taste nor talent for the sort of work which you cut out for me. And I beg to decline your offer.

'I am, yours truly,
'JOHN H. NEWMAN.'

Such words were not the words of wisdom. It is easy to imagine the feelings of Monsignor Talbot. 'Newman's work none here can understand,' he burst out to his friend. 'Poor man, by living almost ever since he has been a Catholic surrounded by a set of inferior men who idolise him, I do not think he has ever acquired the Catholic instincts.' As for his views on the Temporal Power – well, people said that he had actually sent a subscription to Garibaldi. Yes, the man was incomprehensible, heretical, dangerous; he was 'uncatholic and unchristian.' Monsignor Talbot even trembled for the position of Manning in England. 'I am afraid that the old school of Catholics will rally round Newman in opposition to you and Rome. Stand firm, do not yield a bit in the line you have taken. As I have promised, I shall stand by you. You will have battles to fight, because every Englishman is naturally anti-Roman. To be Roman is to an Englishman an effort. Dr Newman is more English than the English. His spirit must be crushed.'

His spirit must be crushed! Certainly there could be no doubt of that. 'What you write about Dr Newman,' Manning replied, 'is true. Whether he knows it or not, he has become the centre of those who hold low views about the Holy See, are anti-Roman, cold and silent, to say no more, about the Temporal Power, national, English, critical of Catholic devotions, and always on the lower side. . . . You will take care,' he concluded, 'that things are correctly known and understood where you are.'

The confederates matured their plans. While Newman was making his arrangements for the Oxford Oratory, Cardinal Reisach visited London. 'Cardinal Reisach* has just left,' wrote Manning to Monsignor Talbot: 'he has seen and *understands* all that is going on in England.' But Newman had no suspicions. It was true that persistent rumours of his unorthodoxy and his anti-Roman leanings had begun to float about, and these rumours had been traced to Rome. But what were rumours? Then, too, Newman found out that Cardinal Reisach had been to Oxford without his knowledge, and had inspected the land for the Oratory. That seemed odd; but all doubts were set at rest by the arrival from Propaganda of an official ratification of his scheme. There would be nothing but plain sailing now. Newman was almost happy; radiant visions came into his mind of a wonderful future in Oxford, the gradual growth of Catholic principles, the decay of liberalism, the inauguration of a second Oxford Movement, the conversion – who knows? – of Mark Pattison,* the triumph of the Church. . . . 'Earlier failures do not matter now,' he exclaimed to a friend. 'I see that I have been reserved by God for this.'

Just then a long blue envelope was brought into the room. Newman opened it. 'All is over,' he said, 'I am not allowed to go.' The envelope contained a letter from the Bishop announcing that, together with the formal permission for an Oratory at Oxford, Propaganda had issued a secret instruction to the effect that Newman himself was by no means to reside there. If he showed signs of doing so, he was blandly and suavely ('blande suaviterque' were the words of the Latin instrument) to be prevented. And now the secret instruction had come into operation: *blande suaviterque* Dr Newman's spirit had been crushed.

His friends made some gallant efforts to retrieve the situation; but it was in vain. Father St John hurried to Rome; and the indignant laity of England, headed by Lord Edward Howard, the guardian of the young Duke of Norfolk, seized the opportunity of a particularly virulent anonymous attack upon Newman to send him an address, in which they expressed their feeling that 'every blow that touches you inflicts a wound upon the Catholic Church in this country.' The only result was an outburst of redoubled fury upon the part of Monsignor Talbot. The address, he declared, was an insult to the Holy See. 'What is the province of the laity?' he interjected. 'To hunt, to shoot, to entertain. These matters they understand, but to meddle with ecclesiastical matters they have no right at all.' Once more he warned Manning to be careful. 'Dr Newman is the most dangerous man in England,* and you will see that he will make use of the laity against your Grace. You must not be afraid of him. It will require much prudence, but you must be firm. The Holy Father still places his confidence in you; but if you yield and do not fight the battle of the Holy See against the detestable spirit growing up in England, he will begin to regret Cardinal Wiseman, who knew how to keep the laity in order.' Manning had no thought of 'yielding'; but he pointed out to his agitated friend that an open conflict between himself and Newman would be 'as great a scandal to the Church in England, and as great a victory to the Anglicans, as could be.' He would act quietly, and there would be no more difficulty. The Bishops were united, and the Church was sound.

On this, Monsignor Talbot hurried round to Father St John's lodgings in Rome to express his regret at the misunderstanding that had arisen, to wonder how it could possibly have occurred, and to hope that Dr Newman might consent to be made a Protonotary Apostolic. That was all the satisfaction that Father St John was to obtain from his visit to Rome. A few weeks later the scheme of the Oxford Oratory was finally quashed.

When all was over, Manning thought that the time had come for a reconciliation. He made advances through a common friend; what had he done, he asked, to offend Dr Newman? Letters passed, and, naturally enough, they only widened the breach. Newman was not the man to be polite. 'I can only repeat,' he wrote at last, 'what I said when you last heard from me. I do not know whether I am on my head or my heels when I have active relations with you. In spite of my friendly feelings, this is the judgment of my intellect.' 'Meanwhile,' he concluded, 'I propose to say seven masses for your intention amid the difficulties and anxieties of your ecclesiastical duties.' And Manning could only return the compliment.

At about this time the Curate of Littlemore had a singular experience. As he was passing by the Church he noticed an old man, very poorly dressed in an old grey coat with the collar turned up, leaning over the lych gate, in floods of tears. He was apparently in great trouble, and his hat was pulled down over his eyes, as if he wished to hide his features. For a moment, however, he turned towards the Curate, who was suddenly struck by something familiar in the face. Could it be—? A photograph hung over the Curate's mantelpiece of the man who had made Littlemore famous by his sojourn there more than twenty years ago; he had never seen the original; but now, was it possible—? He looked again, and he could doubt no longer. It was Dr Newman. He sprang forward, with proffers of assistance. Could he be of any use? 'Oh no, no!' was the reply. 'Oh no, no!' But the Curate felt that he could not run away, and leave so eminent a character in such distress. 'Was it not Dr Newman he had the honour of addressing?' he asked, with all the respect and sympathy at his command. 'Was there nothing that could be done?' But the old man hardly seemed to understand what was being said to him. 'Oh no, no!' he repeated, with the tears streaming down his face, 'Oh no, no!'*

VII

MEANWHILE a remarkable problem was absorbing the attention of the Catholic Church. Once more, for a moment, the eyes of all Christendom were fixed upon Rome. The temporal Power of the Pope had now almost vanished; but, as his worldly dominions steadily diminished, the spiritual pretensions of the Holy Father no less steadily increased. For seven centuries the immaculate conception of the Virgin had been highly problematical; Pio Nono spoke, and the doctrine became an article of faith. A few years later, the Court of Rome took another step: a *Syllabus Errorum** was issued, in which all the favourite beliefs of the modern world – the rights of democracies, the claims of science, the sanctity of free speech, the principles of toleration – were categorically denounced, and their supporters abandoned to the Divine wrath. Yet it was observed that the modern world proceeded as before. Something more drastic appeared to be necessary – some bold and striking measure which should concentrate the forces of the faithful, and confound their enemies. The tremendous doctrine of Papal Infallibility,* beloved of all good Catholics, seemed to offer just the opening that was required. Let that doctrine be proclaimed, with the assent of the whole Church, an article of faith, and, in the face of such an affirmation, let the modern world do its worst! Accordingly a General Council – the first to be held since the Council of Trent more than 300 years before – was summoned to the Vatican, for the purpose, so it was announced, of providing 'an adequate remedy to the disorders, intellectual and moral, of Christendom.' The programme might seem a large one, even for a General Council; but every one knew what it meant.

Every one, however, was not quite of one mind. There were those to whom even the mysteries of Infallibility caused some searchings of heart. It was true, no doubt, that Our Lord, by saying to Peter, 'Thou art Cephas, which is by interpretation a stone,' thereby endowed that Apostle with the supreme and full primacy and principality over the Universal Catholic Church; it was equally certain that Peter afterwards became the Bishop of Rome; nor could it be doubted that the Roman Pontiff was his successor. Thus it followed directly that the Roman Pontiff was the head, heart, mind, and tongue of the Catholic Church; and moreover it was plain that when Our Lord prayed for Peter that his faith should not fail, that prayer implied the doctrine of Papal Infallibility. All these things were obvious, and yet – and yet——Might not the formal declaration of such truths in the year of grace 1870 be, to say the least of it, inopportune? Might it not come as an offence, as a scandal even, to those unacquainted with the niceties of Catholic dogma? Such were the uneasy reflections of grave and learned ecclesiastics and theologians in England, France, and Germany. Newman was more than usually upset; Monseigneur Dupanloup was disgusted; and Dr Döllinger* prepared himself for resistance. It was clear that there would be a disaffected minority at the Council.

Catholic apologists have often argued that the Pope's claim to infallibility implies no more than the necessary claim of every ruler, of every government, to the right of supreme command. In England, for instance, the Estates of the Realm exercise an absolute authority in secular matters; no one questions this authority, no one suggests that it is absurd or exorbitant; in other words, by general consent, the Estates of the Realm are, within their sphere, infallible. Why, therefore, should the Pope, within *his* sphere – the sphere of the Catholic Church – be denied a similar infallibility? If there is nothing monstrous in an Act of Parliament laying down what all men shall *do*, why should there be anything monstrous in a Papal Encyclical laying down what all men shall *believe?* The argument is simple; in fact, it is too simple; for it takes for granted the very question which is in dispute. Is there indeed no radical and essential distinction between supremacy and infallibility? between the right of a Borough Council to regulate the traffic and the right of the Vicar of Christ to decide upon the qualifications for Everlasting Bliss? There is one distinction, at any rate, which is palpable: the decisions of a supreme authority can be altered; those of an infallible authority cannot. A Borough Council may change its traffic regulations at the next meeting; but the Vicar of Christ, when, in certain circumstances and with certain precautions, he has once spoken, has expressed, for all the ages, a part of the immutable, absolute, and eternal Truth. It is this that makes the papal pretensions so extraordinary and so enormous. It is also this that gives them their charm. Catholic apologists, when they try to tone down those pretensions and to explain them away, forget that it is in their very exorbitance that their fascination lies. If the Pope were indeed nothing more than a magnified Borough Councillor, we should hardly have heard so much of him. It is not because he satisfies the reason, but because he astounds it, that men abase themselves before the Vicar of Christ.

And certainly the doctrine of Papal Infallibility presents to the reason a sufficiency of stumbling-blocks. In the fourteenth century, for instance, the following case arose. John XXII asserted in his bull 'Cum inter nonnullos'* that the doctrine of the poverty of Christ was heretical. Now, according to the light of reason, one of two things must follow from this – either John XXII was himself a heretic or he was no Pope. For his predecessor, Nicholas III, had asserted in his bull 'Exiit qui seminat' that the doctrine of the poverty of Christ was the true doctrine, the denial of which was heresy. Thus if John XXII was right Nicholas III* was a heretic, and in that case Nicholas's nominations of Cardinals were void, and the conclave which elected John was illegal; so that John was no Pope, *his* nominations of Cardinals were void, and the whole Papal succession vitiated. On the other hand, if John was wrong – well, he was a heretic; and the same inconvenient results followed. And, in either case, what becomes of Papal Infallibility?

But such crude and fundamental questions as these were not likely to trouble the Council. The discordant minority took another line. Infallibility they admitted readily enough – the infallibility, that is to say, of the Church; what they shrank from was the pronouncement that this infallibility was concentrated in the Bishop of Rome. They would not actually deny that, as a matter of fact, it was so concentrated; but to *declare* that it was, to make the belief that it was an article of faith – what could be more – it was their favourite expression – more inopportune? In truth, the Gallican* spirit still lingered among them. At heart, they hated the autocracy of Rome – the domination of the centralised Italian organisation over the whole vast body of the Church. They secretly hankered, even at this late hour, after some form of constitutional government, and they knew that the last faint vestige of such a dream would vanish utterly with the declaration of the infallibility of the Pope. It did not occur to them, apparently, that a constitutional Catholicism might be a contradiction in terms, and that the Catholic Church without the absolute dominion of the Pope might resemble the play of *Hamlet* without the Prince of Denmark.

Pius IX himself was troubled by no doubts. 'Before I was Pope,' he observed, 'I *believed* in Papal Infallibility, now I *feel* it.' As for Manning, his certainty was no less complete than his master's. Apart from the Holy Ghost, his appointment to the See of Westminster had been due to Pio Nono's shrewd appreciation of the fact that he was the one man in England upon whose fidelity the Roman Government could absolutely rely. The voice which kept repeating 'Mettetelo lì, mettetelo lì' in his Holiness's ear, whether or not it was inspired by God, was certainly inspired by political sagacity. For now Manning was to show that he was not unworthy of the trust which had been reposed in him. He flew to Rome in a whirlwind of Papal enthusiasm. On the way, in Paris, he stopped for a moment to interview those two great props of French respectability, M. Guizot and M. Thiers.* Both were careful not to commit themselves, but both were exceedingly polite. 'I am awaiting your Council,' said M. Guizot, 'with great anxiety. It is the last great moral power and may restore the peace of Europe.' M. Thiers delivered a brief harangue in favour of the principles of the Revolution, which, he declared, were the very marrow of all Frenchmen; yet, he added, he had always supported the Temporal Power of the Pope. 'Mais, M. Thiers,' said Manning, 'vous êtes effectivement croyant.' 'En Dieu,'* replied M. Thiers.

The Rome which Manning reached towards the close of 1869 was still the Rome which, for so many centuries, had been the proud and visible apex, the palpitating heart, the sacred sanctuary, of the most extraordinary mingling of spiritual and earthly powers that the world has ever known. The Pope now, it is true, ruled over little more than the City itself – the Patrimony of St Peter – and he ruled there less by the Grace of God than by the goodwill of Napoleon III;* yet he was still a sovereign Prince; and Rome was still the capital of the Papal State; she was not yet the capital of Italy. The last hour of this strange dominion had almost struck. As if she knew that her doom was upon her the Eternal City arrayed herself to meet it in all her glory. The whole world seemed to be gathered together within her walls. Her streets were filled with crowned heads and Princes of the Church, great ladies and great theologians, artists and friars, diplomats and newspaper reporters. Seven hundred bishops were there, from all the corners of Christendom, and in all the varieties of ecclesiastical magnificence – in falling lace and sweeping purple and flowing violet veils. Zouaves* stood in the colonnade of St Peter's, and Papal troops were on the Quirinal.* Cardinals passed, hatted and robed, in their enormous carriage of state, like mysterious painted idols. Then there was a sudden hush: the crowd grew thicker and expectation filled the air. Yes! it was he! He was coming! The Holy Father! But first there appeared, mounted on a white mule and clothed in a magenta mantle, a grave dignitary bearing aloft a silver cross. The golden coach followed, drawn by six horses gorgeously caparisoned, and within, the smiling white-haired Pio Nono, scattering his benedictions, while the multitude fell upon its knees as one man. Such were the daily spectacles of coloured pomp and of antique solemnity, which – so long as the sun was shining, at any rate – dazzled the onlooker into a happy forgetfulness of the reverse side of the Papal dispensation – the nauseating filth of the highways, the cattle stabled in the palaces of the great, and the fever flitting through the ghastly tenements of the poor.

In St Peter's, the North Transept had been screened off; rows of wooden seats had been erected, covered with Brussels carpet; and upon these seats sat, each crowned with a white mitre, the seven hundred Bishops in Council. Here all day long rolled forth, in sonorous Latin, the interminable periods of episcopal oratory; but it was not here that the issue of the Council was determined. The assembled Fathers might talk till the marbles of St Peter's themselves grew weary of the reverberations; the fate of the Church was decided in a very different manner – by little knots of influential persons meeting quietly of a morning in the back room of some inconspicuous lodging-house, by a sunset rendezvous in the Borghese Gardens between a Cardinal and a Diplomatist, by a whispered conference in an alcove at a Princess's evening party, with the gay world chattering all about. And, of course, on such momentous occasions as these, Manning was in his element. None knew those difficult ropes better than he; none used them with a more serviceable and yet discreet alacrity. In every juncture he had the right word, or the right silence; his influence ramified in all directions, from the Pope's audience chamber to the English Cabinet. 'Il

Diavolo del Concilio'* his enemies called him; and he gloried in the name.

The real crux of the position was less ecclesiastical than diplomatic. The Papal Court, with its huge majority of Italian Bishops, could make sure enough, when it came to the point, of carrying its wishes through the Council; what was far more dubious was the attitude of the foreign Governments – especially those of France and England. The French Government dreaded a schism among its Catholic subjects; it disliked the prospect of an extension of the influence of the Pope over the mass of the population of France; and, since the very existence of the last remnant of the Pope's Temporal Power depended upon the French army, it was able to apply considerable pressure upon the Vatican. The interests of England were less directly involved, but it happened that at this moment Mr Gladstone was Prime Minister,* and Mr Gladstone entertained strong views upon the Infallibility of the Pope. His opinions upon the subject were in part the outcome of his friendship with Lord Acton,* a historian to whom learning and judgment had not been granted in equal proportions, and who, after years of incredible and indeed well-nigh mythical research, had come to the conclusion that the Pope could err. In this Mr Gladstone entirely concurred, though he did not share the rest of his friend's theological opinions; for Lord Acton, while straining at the gnat of Infallibility, had swallowed the camel of the Roman Catholic Faith. 'Que diable allait-il faire dans cette galère?'* one cannot help asking, as one watched that laborious and scrupulous scholar, that lifelong enthusiast for liberty, that almost hysterical reviler of priesthood and persecution, trailing his learning so discrepantly along the dusty Roman way. But there are some who know how to wear their Rome with a difference; and Lord Acton was one of these.

He was now engaged in fluttering like a moth round the Council, and in writing long letters to Mr Gladstone, impressing upon him the gravity of the situation, and urging him to bring his influence to bear. If the Dogma were carried, he declared, no man who accepted it could remain a loyal subject, and Catholics would everywhere become 'irredeemable enemies of civil and religious liberty.' In these circumstances, was it not plainly incumbent upon the English Government, involved as it was with the powerful Roman Catholic forces in Ireland, to intervene? Mr Gladstone allowed himself to become convinced, and Lord Acton began to hope that his efforts would be successful. But he had forgotten one element in the situation; he had reckoned without the Archbishop of Westminster. The sharp nose of Manning sniffed out the whole intrigue. Though he despised Lord Acton almost as much as he disliked him – 'such men,' he said, 'are all vanity: they have the inflation of German professors, and the ruthless talk of undergraduates' – yet he realised clearly enough the danger of his correspondence with the Prime Minister, and immediately took steps to counteract it. There was a semi-official agent of the English Government in Rome, Mr Odo Russell,* and round him Manning set to work to spin his spider's web of delicate and clinging diplomacy. Preliminary politenesses were followed by long walks upon the Pincio, and the gradual interchange of more and more important and confidential communications. Soon poor Mr Russell was little better than a fly buzzing in gossamer. And Manning was careful to see that he buzzed on the right note. In his dispatches to the Foreign Secretary, Lord Clarendon, Mr Russell explained in detail the true nature of the Council, that it was merely a meeting of a few Roman Catholic prelates to discuss some internal matters of Church discipline, that it had no political significance whatever, that the question of Infallibility, about which there had been so much random talk, was a purely theological question, and that, whatever decision might be come to on the subject, the position of Roman Catholics throughout the world would remain unchanged. Whether the effect of these affirmations upon Lord Clarendon was as great as Manning supposed, is somewhat doubtful; but it is at any rate certain that Mr Gladstone failed to carry the Cabinet with him; and when at last a proposal was definitely made that the English Government should invite the Powers of Europe to intervene at the Vatican, it was rejected. Manning always believed that this was the direct result of Mr Russell's dispatches, which had acted as an antidote to the poison of Lord Acton's letters, and thus carried the day. If that was so – the discretion of biographers has not yet entirely lifted the veil from these proceedings – Manning had assuredly performed no small service for his cause. Yet his modesty would not allow him to assume for himself a credit which, after all, was due elsewhere; and when he told the story of those days, he would add, with more than wonted seriousness, 'It was by the Divine Will that the designs of His enemies were frustrated.'

Meanwhile, in the North Transept of St Peter's a certain amount of preliminary business had been carried through. Various miscellaneous points in Christian doctrine had been satisfactorily determined. Among others, the following Canons were laid down by the Fathers. 'If any one do not accept for sacred and canonical the whole and every part of the Books of Holy Scripture, or deny that they are divinely inspired, let him be anathema.' 'If any one say that miracles cannot be, and therefore the accounts of them, even those in Holy Scriptures, must be assigned a place among fables and myths, or that the divine origin of the Christian religion cannot rightly be proved from them, let him be anathema.' 'If any one say that the doctrines of the Church can ever receive a sense in accordance with the progress of science, other than that sense which the Church has understood and still understands, let him be anathema.' 'If any one say that it is not possible, by the natural light of human reason, to acquire a certain knowledge of the One and True God, let him be anathema.' In other words, it became an article of Faith that Faith was not necessary for a true knowledge of God. Having disposed of these minor matters, the Fathers found themselves at last approaching the great question of Infallibility. Two main issues, it soon appeared, were before them: the Pope's Infallibility was admitted, ostensibly at least, by all; what remained to be determined was, (1) whether the definition of the Pope's Infallibility was opportune, and (2) what the definition of the Pope's Infallibility was. (1) It soon became clear that the sense of the Council was overwhelmingly in favour of a definition. The Inopportunists* were a small minority; they were outvoted, and they were obliged to give way. It only remained, therefore, to come to a decision upon the second question – what the definition should actually be. (2) It now became the object of the Inopportunists to limit the scope of the definition as much as possible, while the Infallibilists were no less eager to extend it. Now every one – or nearly every one – was ready to limit the Papal Infallibility to pronouncements *ex cathedrâ** – that is to say, to those made by the Pope in his capacity of Universal Doctor; but this only served to raise the ulterior, the portentous, and indeed the really crucial question – to *which* of the Papal pronouncements *ex cathedrâ* did Infallibility adhere? The discussions which followed were, naturally enough, numerous, complicated, and embittered, and in all of them Manning played a conspicuous part. For two months the

Fathers deliberated; through fifty sessions they sought the guidance of the Holy Ghost. The wooden seats, covered though they were with Brussels carpet, grew harder and harder; and still the mitred Councillors sat on. The Pope himself began to grow impatient; for one thing, he declared, he was being ruined by the mere expense of lodging and keeping the multitude of his adherents. 'Questi infallibilisti mi faranno fallire,'* said his Holiness. At length it appeared that the Inopportunists were dragging out the proceedings in the hope of obtaining an indefinite postponement. Then the authorities began to act; a bishop was shouted down, and the closure was brought into operation. At this point the French Government, after long hesitation, finally decided to intervene, and Cardinal Antonelli* was informed that if the Definition was proceeded with the French troops would be withdrawn from Rome. But the astute Cardinal judged that he could safely ignore the threat. He saw that Napoleon III was tottering to his fall and would never risk an open rupture with the Vatican. Accordingly it was determined to bring the proceedings to a close by a final vote. Already the Inopportunists, seeing that the game was up, had shaken the dust of Rome from their feet. On July 18th, 1870, the Council met for the last time. As the first of the Fathers stepped forward to declare his vote, a storm of thunder and lightning suddenly burst over St Peter's. All through the morning the voting continued, and every vote was accompanied by a flash and a roar from heaven. Both sides, with equal justice, claimed the portent as a manifestation of the Divine Opinion. When the votes were examined, it was found that 533 were in favour of the proposed definition and two against it. Next day war was declared between France and Germany, and a few weeks later the French troops were withdrawn from Rome. Almost in the same moment the successor of St Peter had lost his Temporal Power and gained Infallibility.

What the Council had done was merely to assent to a definition of the dogma of the Infallibility of the Roman Pontiff which Pius IX had issued, proprio motu,* a few days before. The definition itself was perhaps somewhat less extreme than might have been expected. The Pope, it declared, is possessed, when he speaks *ex cathedrâ*, of 'that infallibility with which the Redeemer willed that His Church should be endowed for defining doctrine regarding faith or morals.' Thus it became a dogma of faith that a Papal definition regarding faith or morals is infallible; but beyond that both the Holy Father and the

Council maintained a judicious reserve. Over what *other* matters besides faith and morals the Papal infallibility might or might not extend still remained in doubt. And there were further questions, no less serious, to which no decisive answer was then, or ever has been since, provided. How was it to be determined, for instance, which particular Papal decisions did in fact come within the scope of the definition? Who was to decide what was or was not a matter of faith or morals? Or precisely *when* the Roman Pontiff was speaking *ex cathedrâ*? Was the famous *Syllabus Errorum*, for example, issued *ex cathedrâ* or not? Grave theologians have never been able to make up their minds. Yet to admit doubts in such matters as these is surely dangerous. 'In duty to our supreme pastoral office,' proclaimed the Sovereign Pontiff, 'by the bowels of Christ we earnestly entreat all Christ's faithful people, and we also command them by the authority of God and our Saviour, that they study and labour to expel and eliminate errors and display the light of the purest faith.' Well might the faithful study and labour to such ends! For, while the offence remained ambiguous, there was no ambiguity about the penalty. One hair's-breadth from the unknown path of truth, one shadow of impurity in the mysterious light of faith – and there shall be anathema! anathema! anathema! When the framers of such edicts called upon the bowels of Christ to justify them, might they not have done well to have paused a little, and to have called to mind the counsel of another sovereign ruler, though a heretic – Oliver Cromwell? 'Bethink ye, bethink ye, in the bowels of Christ, that ye may be mistaken!'*

One of the secondary results of the Council was the excommunication of Dr Döllinger* and a few more of the most uncompromising of the Inopportunists. Among these, however, Lord Acton was not included. Nobody ever discovered why. Was it because he was too important for the Holy See to care to interfere with him? Or was it because he was not important enough?

Another ulterior consequence was the appearance of a pamphlet by Mr Gladstone, entitled 'Vaticanism,'* in which the awful implications involved in the declaration of Infallibility were laid before the British Public. How was it possible, Mr Gladstone asked, with all the fulminating accompaniments of his most agitated rhetoric, to depend henceforward upon the civil allegiance of Roman Catholics? To this question the words of Cardinal Antonelli to the Austrian

Ambassador might have seemed a sufficient reply. 'There is a great difference,' said his Eminence, 'between theory and practice. No one will ever prevent the Church from proclaiming the great principles upon which its Divine fabric is based; but, as regards the *application* of those sacred laws, the Church, imitating the example of its Divine Founder, is inclined to take into consideration the natural weaknesses of mankind.' And, in any case, it was hard to see how the system of Faith, which had enabled Pope Gregory XIII to effect, by the hands of English Catholics, a whole series of attempts to murder Queen Elizabeth, can have been rendered a much more dangerous engine of disloyalty by the Definition of 1870. But such considerations failed to reassure Mr Gladstone; the British Public was of a like mind; and 145,000 copies of the pamphlet were sold within two months. Various replies appeared, and Manning was not behindhand. His share in the controversy led to a curious personal encounter.

His conversion had come as a great shock to Mr Gladstone. Manning had breathed no word of its approach to his old and intimate friend, and when the news reached him, it seemed almost an act of personal injury. 'I felt,' Mr Gladstone said, 'as if Manning had murdered my mother by mistake.' For twelve years the two men did not meet, after which they occasionally saw each other and renewed their correspondence. This was the condition of affairs when Mr Gladstone published his pamphlet. As soon as it appeared Manning wrote a letter to the *New York Herald*, contradicting its conclusions, and declaring that its publication was 'the first event that has overcast a friendship of forty-five years.' Mr Gladstone replied to this letter in a second pamphlet. At the close of his theological arguments, he added the following passage: 'I feel it necessary, in concluding this answer, to state that Archbishop Manning has fallen into most serious inaccuracy in his letter of November 10th, where he describes my Expostulation as the first event which has overcast a friendship of forty-five years. I allude to the subject with regret; and without entering into details.' Manning replied in a private letter.

'My dear Gladstone,' he wrote, 'you say that I am in error in stating that your former pamphlet is the first act which has overcast our friendship.

'If you refer to my act in 1851 in submitting to the Catholic

Church, by which we were separated for some twelve years, I can understand it.

'If you refer to any other act either on your part or mine I am not conscious of it, and would desire to know what it may be.

'My act in 1851 may have overcast your friendship for me. It did not overcast my friendship for you, as I think the last years have shown.

'You will not, I hope, think me over-sensitive in asking for this explanation. Believe me, yours affectionately,

'✠H. E. M.'

'My dear Archbishop Manning,' Mr Gladstone answered, 'it did, I confess, seem to me an astonishing error to state in public that a friendship had not been overcast for forty-five years until now, which your letter declares has been suspended as to all action for twelve. . . .

'I wonder, too, at your forgetting that during the forty-five years I had been charged by you with doing the work of Antichrist in regard to the Temporal Power of the Pope. . . .

'Our differences, my dear Archbishop, are indeed profound. We refer them, I suppose, in humble silence to a Higher Power. . . . You assured me once of your prayers at all and at the most solemn time. I received that assurance with gratitude and still cherish it. As and when they move upwards, there is a meeting-point for those whom a chasm separates below. I remain always, affectionately yours,

'W. E. GLADSTONE.'

Speaking of this correspondence in after years, Cardinal Manning said: 'From the way in which Mr Gladstone alluded to the overcasting of our friendship, people might have thought that I had picked his pocket.'

VIII

IN 1875 Manning's labours received their final reward: he was made a Cardinal. His long and strange career, with its high hopes, its bitter disappointments, its struggles, its renunciations, had come at last to fruition in a Princedom of the Church. 'Ask in faith and in perfect confidence,' he himself once wrote, 'and God will give us what we ask. You may say, "But do you mean that He will give us the very thing?" That, God has not said. God has said that He will give you whatsoever you ask; but the form in which it will come, and the time in which He will give it, He keeps in His own power. Sometimes our prayers are answered in the very things which we put from us; sometimes it may be a chastisement, or a loss, or a visitation against which our hearts rise, and we seem to see that God has not only forgotten us, but has begun to deal with us in severity. Those very things are the answers to our prayers. He knows what we desire, and He gives us the things which we ask; but in the form which His own Divine Wisdom sees to be best.'

There was one to whom Manning's elevation would no doubt have given a peculiar satisfaction – his old friend Monsignor Talbot. But this was not to be. That industrious worker in the cause of Rome had been removed some years previously to a sequestered Home at Passy, whose padded walls were impervious to the rumours of the outer world. Pius IX had been much afflicted by this unfortunate event; he had not been able to resign himself to the loss of his secretary, and he had given orders that Monsignor Talbot's apartment in the Vatican should be preserved precisely as he had left it, in case of his return. But Monsignor Talbot never returned. Manning's feelings upon the subject appear to have been less tender than the Pope's. In all his letters, in all his papers, in all his biographical memoranda, not a word of allusion is to be found to the misfortune, nor to the death, of the most loyal of his adherents. Monsignor Talbot's name disappears suddenly and for ever – like a stone cast into the waters.

Manning was now an old man, and his outward form had assumed that appearance of austere asceticism which is, perhaps, the one thing immediately suggested by his name to the ordinary Englishman. The spare and stately form,* the head, massive, emaciated, terrible, with the great nose, the glittering eyes, and the mouth drawn back and compressed into the grim rigidities of age, self-mortification, and authority – such is the vision that still lingers in the public mind – the vision which, actual and palpable like some embodied memory of the Middle Ages, used to pass and repass, less than a generation since, through the streets of London. For the activities of this extraordinary figure were great and varied. He ruled his diocese with the despotic zeal of a born administrator. He threw himself into social work of every kind;* he organised charities, he lectured on temperance. He delivered innumerable sermons; he produced an unending series of devotional books. And he brooked no brother near the throne: Newman languished in Birmingham; and even the Jesuits trembled and obeyed.

Nor was it only among his own community that his energy and his experience found scope. He gradually came to play an important part in public affairs, upon questions of labour, poverty, and education. He sat on Royal Commissions, and corresponded with Cabinet Ministers. At last no philanthropic meeting at the Guildhall was considered complete without the presence of Cardinal Manning. A special degree of precedence was accorded to him. Though the rank of a Cardinal-Archbishop is officially unknown in England, his name appeared in public documents – as a token, it must be supposed, of personal consideration – above the names of peers and bishops, and immediately below that of the Prince of Wales.

In his private life he was secluded. The ambiguities of his social position and his desire to maintain intact the peculiar eminence of his office combined to hold him aloof from the ordinary gatherings of society, though on the rare occasions of his appearance among fashionable and exalted persons he carried all before him. His favourite haunt was the Athenæum Club, where he sat scanning the newspapers, or conversing with the old friends of former days. He was a member, too, of that distinguished body, the Metaphysical Society, which met once a month during the palmy years of the seventies to discuss, in strict privacy, the fundamental problems of the destiny of man. After a comfortable dinner at the Grosvenor Hotel, the Society, which included Professor Huxley and Professor Tyndall, Mr John Morley and Sir James Stephen, the Duke of Argyll, Lord Tennyson, and Dean Church, would gather round to hear and discuss a paper read by one of the members upon such questions as 'What is death?' 'Is God unknowable?' or 'The nature of the Moral Principle.' Sometimes, however, the speculations of the Society ranged in other directions. 'I think the paper that interested me most of all that were ever read at our meetings,' says Sir Mountstuart Elphinstone Grant-Duff, 'was one on "Wherein consists the special beauty of imperfection and decay?" in which were propounded the questions "Are not ruins recognised and felt to be more beautiful than perfect structures? Why are they so? Ought they to be so?" ' Unfortunately, however, the answers given to these questions by the Metaphysical Society have not been recorded for the instruction of mankind.

Manning read several papers, and Professor Huxley and Mr John Morley listened with attention while he expressed his views upon 'The Soul before and after Death,' or explained why it is 'That legitimate Authority is an Evidence of Truth.' Yet, somehow or other, his Eminence never felt quite at ease in these assemblies; he was more at home with audiences of a different kind; and we must look in other directions for the free and full manifestation of his speculative gifts. In a series of lectures, for instance, delivered in 1861 – it was the first year of the unification of Italy – upon 'The Present Crisis of the Holy See, tested by Prophecy,' we catch some glimpses of the kind of problems which were truly congenial to his mind. 'In the following pages,' he said, 'I have endeavoured, but for so great a subject most insufficiently, to show that what is passing in our times is the prelude of the antichristian period of the final dethronement of Christendom, and of the restoration of society without God in the world.' 'My intention is,' he continued, 'to examine the present relation of the Church to the civil powers of the world, by the light of a prophecy recorded by St Paul.' This prophecy (2 Thess. ii. 3 to 11) is concerned with the coming of Antichrist, and the greater part of the lectures is devoted to a minute examination of this subject. There is no passage in Scripture, Manning pointed out, relating to the coming of Christ more explicit and express than those foretelling Antichrist; it therefore behoved the faithful to consider the matter more fully than they are wont to do. In the first place, Antichrist is a person. 'To deny the personality of Antichrist is to deny the plain testimony of Holy Scripture.' And we must remember that 'it is a law of Holy Scripture that when persons are prophesied of, persons appear.' Again, there was every reason to believe that Antichrist, when he did appear, would turn out to be a Jew. 'Such was the opinion of St Irenæus, St Jerome, and of the author of the work *De Consummatione Mundi*, ascribed to St Hippolytus, and of a writer of a Commentary on the Epistle to the Thessalonians, ascribed to St Ambrose, of many others, who add, that he will be of the tribe of Dan: as, for instance, St Gregory the Great, Theodoret, Aretas of Cæsarea, and many more. Such also is the opinion of Bellarmine, who calls it certain. Lessius affirms that the Fathers, with unanimous consent, teach as undoubted that Antichrist will be a Jew. Ribera repeats the same opinion, and adds that Aretas, St Bede, Haymo, St Anselm, and Rupert affirm that for this reason the tribe of Dan is not numbered among those who are sealed in the Apocalypse. . . . Now I think no one can consider the dispersion and providential preservation of the Jews among all the nations of the world and the indestructible vitality of their race without believing that they are reserved for some future action of His Judgement and Grace. And this is foretold again and again in the New Testament.'

'Our Lord,' continued Manning, widening the sweep of his speculations, 'has said of these latter times: "There shall arise false Christs and false prophets, insomuch as to deceive even the elect"; that is, they shall not be deceived; but those who have lost faith in the Incarnation, such as humanitarians, rationalists, and pantheists, may well be deceived by any person of great political power and success, who should restore the Jews to their own land, and people Jerusalem once more with the sons of the Patriarchs. And there is nothing in the political aspect of the world which renders such a combination impossible; indeed, the state of Syria, and the tide of European diplomacy, which is continually moving eastward, render such an event within a reasonable probability.' Then Manning threw out a bold suggestion. 'A successful medium,' he said, 'might well pass himself off by his preternatural endowments as the promised Messias.'

Manning went on to discuss the course of events which would lead to the final catastrophe. But this subject, he confessed, 'deals with agencies so transcendent and mysterious, that all I shall venture to do will be to sketch in outline what the broad and luminous prophecies, especially of the Book of Daniel and the Apocalypse, set forth; without attempting to enter into minute details, which can only be interpreted by the event.' While applauding his modesty, we need follow Manning no further in his commentary upon those broad and luminous works; except to observe that 'the apostasy of the City of Rome from the Vicar of Christ and its destruction by Antichrist' was, in his opinion, certain. Nor was he without authority for this belief. For it was held by 'Malvenda, who writes expressly on the subject,' and who, besides, 'states as the opinion of Ribera, Gaspar Melus, Viegas, Suarez, Bellarmine, and Bosius that Rome shall apostatise from the faith.'*

IX

THE death of Pius IX* brought to Manning a last flattering testimony of the confidence with which he was regarded at the Court of Rome. In one of the private consultations preceding the Conclave, a Cardinal suggested that Manning should succeed to the Papacy. He replied that he was unfitted for the position, because it was essential for the interests of the Holy See that the next Pope should be an Italian. The suggestion was pressed, but Manning held firm. Thus it happened that the Triple Tiara seemed to come, for a moment, within the grasp of the late Archdeacon of Chichester; and the cautious hand refrained.

Leo XIII was elected, and there was a great change in the policy of the Vatican. Liberalism became the order of the day. And now at last the opportunity seemed ripe for an act which, in the opinion of the majority of English Catholics, had long been due – the bestowal of some mark of recognition from the Holy See upon the labours and the sanctity of Father Newman. It was felt that a Cardinal's hat was the one fitting reward for such a life, and accordingly the Duke of Norfolk, representing the Catholic laity of England, visited Manning, and suggested that he should forward the proposal to the Vatican. Manning agreed, and then there followed a curious series of incidents – the last encounter in the jarring lives of those two men. A letter was drawn up by Manning for the eye of the Pope, embodying the Duke of Norfolk's proposal; but there was an unaccountable delay in the transmission of this letter; months passed, and it had not reached the Holy Father. The whole matter would, perhaps, have dropped out of sight and been forgotten, in a way which had become customary when honours for Newman were concerned, had not the Duke of Norfolk himself, when he was next in Rome, ventured to recommend to Leo XIII that Dr Newman should be made a Cardinal. His Holiness welcomed the proposal; but, he said, he could do nothing until he knew the views of Cardinal Manning. Thereupon the Duke of Norfolk wrote to Manning, explaining what had occurred; shortly afterwards Manning's letter of recommendation, after a delay of six months, reached the Pope, and the offer of a Cardinalate was immediately dispatched to Newman.

But the affair was not yet over. The offer had been made; would it be accepted? There was one difficulty in the way. Newman was now an infirm old man of seventy-eight; and it is a rule that all Cardinals who are not also diocesan Bishops or Archbishops reside, as a matter of course, at Rome. The change would have been impossible for one of his years – for one, too, whose whole life was now bound up with the Oratory at Birmingham. But, of course, there was nothing to prevent His Holiness from making an exception in Newman's case, and allowing him to end his days in England. Yet how was Newman himself to suggest this? The offer of the Hat had come to him as an almost miraculous token of renewed confidence, of ultimate reconciliation. The old, long, bitter estrangement was ended at last. 'The cloud is lifted from me for ever!' he exclaimed when the news reached him. It would be melancholy indeed if the cup were now to be once more dashed from his lips and he was obliged to refuse the signal honour. In his perplexity he went to the Bishop of Birmingham, and explained the whole situation. The Bishop assured him that all would be well; that he himself would communicate with the authorities, and put the facts of the case before them. Accordingly, while Newman wrote formally refusing the Hat, on the ground of his unwillingness to leave the Oratory, the Bishop wrote two letters to Manning, one official and one private, in which the following passages occurred:

'Dr Newman has far too humble and delicate a mind to dream of thinking or saying anything which would look like hinting at any kind of terms with the Sovereign Pontiff. . . . I think, however, that I ought to express my own sense of what Dr Newman's dispositions are, and that it will be expected of me. . . . I am thoroughly confident that nothing stands in the way of his most grateful acceptance, except what he tells me greatly distresses him, namely, the having to leave the Oratory at a critical period of its existence and the impossibility of his beginning a new life at his advanced age.'

And in his private letter the Bishop said: 'Dr Newman is very much aged, and softened with age and the trials he has had, especially the loss of his two brethren, St John and Caswall; he can never refer to these losses without weeping and becoming speechless for the time. He is very much affected by the Pope's kindness, would, I know, like to receive the great honour offered him, but feels the whole difficulty at his age of changing his life, or having to leave the Oratory, which I am sure he could not do. If the Holy Father thinks

well to confer on him the dignity, leaving him where he is, I know
how immensely he would be gratified, and you will know how generally the conferring on him the Cardinalate will be applauded.'

These two letters, together with Newman's refusal, reached Manning as he was on the point of starting for Rome. After he had left
England, the following statement appeared in the *Times*:

'Pope Leo XIII has intimated his desire to raise Dr Newman to
the rank of Cardinal, but with expressions of deep respect for the
Holy See, Dr Newman has excused himself from accepting the
Purple.'

When Newman's eyes fell upon the announcement, he realised at
once that a secret and powerful force was working against him. He
trembled, as he had so often trembled before; and certainly the danger was not imaginary. In the ordinary course of things, how could
such a paragraph have been inserted without his authority? And
consequently, did it not convey to the world, not only an absolute
refusal which he had never intended, but a wish on his part to
emphasise publicly his rejection of the proffered honour? Did it not
imply that he had lightly declined a proposal for which in reality he
was deeply thankful? And when the fatal paragraph was read in
Rome, might it not actually lead to the offer of the Cardinalate being
finally withheld?

In great agitation, Newman appealed to the Duke of Norfolk. 'As
to the statement,' he wrote, 'of my refusing a Cardinal's Hat, which
is in the papers, you must not believe it, for this reason:

'Of course it implies that an offer has been made me, and I have
sent an answer to it. Now I have ever understood that it is a point of
propriety and honour to consider such communications sacred. This
statement therefore cannot come from me. Nor could it come from
Rome, for it was made public before my answer got to Rome.

'It could only come, then, from some one who not only read my
letter, but, instead of leaving to the Pope to interpret it, took upon
himself to put an interpretation upon it, and published that interpretation to the world.

'A private letter, addressed to Roman Authorities, is interpreted
on its way and published in the English papers. How is it possible
that any one can have done this?'

The crushing indictment pointed straight at Manning.* And it was
true. Manning had done the impossible deed. Knowing what he did,

with the Bishop of Birmingham's two letters in his pocket, he had put it about that Newman had refused the Hat. But a change had come over the spirit of the Holy See. Things were not as they had once been: Monsignor Talbot was at Passy, and Pio Nono was – where? The Duke of Norfolk intervened once again; Manning was profuse in his apologies for having misunderstood Newman's intentions, and hurried to the Pope to rectify the error. Without hesitation, the Sovereign Pontiff relaxed the rule of Roman residence, and Newman became a Cardinal.

He lived to enjoy his glory for more than ten years. Since he rarely left the Oratory, and since Manning never visited Birmingham, the two Cardinals met only once or twice. After one of these occasions, on returning to the Oratory, Cardinal Newman said, 'What do you think Cardinal Manning did to me? He kissed me!'

On Newman's death, Manning delivered a funeral oration, which opened thus:

'We have lost our greatest witness for the Faith, and we are all poorer and lower by the loss.

'When these tidings came to me, my first thought was this, in what way can I, once more, show my love and veneration for my brother and friend of more than sixty years?'

In private, however, the surviving Cardinal's tone was apt to be more . . . direct. 'Poor Newman!' he once exclaimed in a moment of genial expansion. 'Poor Newman! He was a great hater!'

X

IN that gaunt and gloomy building – more like a barracks than an Episcopal palace – Archbishop's House, Westminster, Manning's existence stretched itself out into an extreme old age. As his years increased, his activities, if that were possible, increased too. Meetings, missions, lectures, sermons, articles, interviews, letters – such things came upon him in redoubled multitudes, and were dispatched with an unrelenting zeal. But this was not all; with age, he seemed to acquire what was almost a new fervour, an unaccustomed, unexpected, freeing of the spirit, filling him with preoccupations which he had hardly felt before. 'They say I am ambitious,' he noted in his Diary, 'but do I rest in my ambition?' No, assuredly he did not rest; but he worked now with no *arrière pensée* for the greater glory of God. A kind of frenzy fell upon him. Poverty, drunkenness, vice, all the horrors and terrors of our civilisation, seized upon his mind, and urged him forward to new fields of action and new fields of thought. The temper of his soul assumed almost a revolutionary cast. 'I am a Mosaic Radical,' he exclaimed; and, indeed, in the exaltation of his energies, the incoherence of his conceptions, the democratic urgency of his desires, combined with his awe-inspiring aspect and his venerable age, it was easy enough to trace the mingled qualities of the patriarch, the prophet, and the demagogue. As, in his soiled and shabby garments, the old man harangued the crowds of Bermondsey or Peckham upon the virtues of Temperance, assuring them, with all the passion of conviction, as a final argument, that the majority of the Apostles were total abstainers, this Prince of the Church might have passed as a leader of the Salvation Army. His popularity was immense, reaching its height during the great Dock Strikes of 1889, when, after the victory of the men was assured, Manning was able, by his persuasive eloquence and the weight of his character, to prevent its being carried to excess. After other conciliators – among whom was the Bishop of London – had given up the task in disgust, the octogenarian Cardinal worked on with indefatigable resolution. At last, late at night, in the schools in Kirby Street, Bermondsey, he rose to address the strikers. An enthusiastic eye-witness has described the scene. 'Unaccustomed tears glistened in the eyes of his rough and work-stained hearers as the Cardinal raised his hand, and solemnly urged them not to prolong one moment more than they could help the perilous uncertainty and the sufferings of their wives and children. Just above his uplifted hand was a figure of the Madonna and Child; and some among the men tell how a sudden light seemed to swim round it as the speaker pleaded for the women and children. When he sat down all in the room knew that he had won the day, and that, so far as the Strike Committee was concerned, the matter was at an end.'

In those days, there were strange visitors at Archbishop's House. Careful priests and conscientious secretaries wondered what the world was coming to when they saw labour leaders like Mr John Burns and Mr Ben Tillett, and land-reformers like Mr Henry George,* being ushered into the presence of his Eminence. Even the notorious Mr Stead appeared, and his scandalous paper with its unspeakable revelations lay upon the Cardinal's table. This proved too much for one of the faithful tonsured dependents of the place, and he ventured to expostulate with his master. But he never did so again.

When the guests were gone, and the great room was empty, the old man would draw himself nearer to the enormous fire, and review once more, for the thousandth time, the long adventure of his life. He would bring out his diaries and his memoranda, he would rearrange his notes, he would turn over again the yellow leaves of faded correspondences; seizing his pen, he would pour out his comments and reflections, and fill, with an extraordinary solicitude, page after page with elucidations, explanations, justifications, of the vanished incidents of a remote past. He would snip with scissors the pages of ancient journals, and with delicate ecclesiastical fingers drop unknown mysteries into the flames.

Sometimes he would turn to the four red folio scrapbooks with their collection of newspaper cuttings concerning himself over a period of thirty years. Then the pale cheeks would flush and the close-drawn lips grow more menacing even than before. 'Stupid, mulish malice,' he would note. 'Pure lying – conscious, deliberate and designed.' 'Suggestive lying. Personal animosity is at the bottom of this.'

And then he would suddenly begin to doubt. After all, where was he? What had he accomplished? Had any of it been worth while? Had he not been out of the world all his life! Out of the world! 'Croker's "Life and Letters," and Hayward's "Letters," '* he notes, 'are so full of politics, literature, action, events, collision of mind with mind, and that with such a multitude of men in every state of life, that when I look back, it seems as if I had been simply useless.' And again, 'The complete isolation and exclusion from the official life of England in which I have lived, makes me feel as if I had done nothing.' He struggled to console himself with the reflexion that all this was only 'the natural order.' 'If the natural order is moved by the supernatural order, then I may not have done nothing. Fifty years of witness for God and His Truth, I hope, has not been in vain.' But the same thoughts recurred. 'In reading Macaulay's life I had a haunting feeling that his had been a life of public utility and mine a *vita umbratilis*, a life in the shade.' Ah! it was God's will. 'Mine has been a life of fifty years out of the world as Gladstone's has been in it. The work of his life in this world is manifest. I hope mine may be in the next. I suppose our Lord called me out of the world because He saw that I should lose my soul in it.' Clearly, that was the explanation.

And yet he remained sufficiently in the world to discharge with absolute efficiency the complex government of his diocese almost up to the last moment of his existence. Though his bodily strength gradually ebbed, the vigour of his mind was undismayed. At last, supported by cushions, he continued, by means of a dictated correspondence, to exert his accustomed rule. Only occasionally would he lay aside his work, to plunge into the yet more necessary duties of devotion. Never again would he preach; never again would he put into practice those three salutary rules of his in choosing a subject for a sermon: '(1) asking God to guide the choice; (2) applying the matter to myself; (3) making the sign of the cross on my head and heart and lips in honour of the Sacred Mouth'; but he could still pray; he could turn especially to the Holy Ghost. 'A very simple but devout person,' he wrote in one of his latest memoranda, 'asked me why in my first volume of sermons I said so little about the Holy Ghost. I was not aware of it; but I found it to be true. I at once resolved that I would make a reparation every day of my life to the Holy Ghost. This I have never failed to do to this day. To this I owe the light and faith which brought me into the true fold. I bought all the books I could about the Holy Ghost. I worked out the truths about His personality, His presence, and His office. This made me understand the last paragraph in the Apostles' Creed and made me a Catholic Christian.'

So, though Death came slowly, struggling step by step with that bold and tenacious spirit, when he did come at last the Cardinal was ready. Robed in his archiepiscopal vestments, his rochet, his girdle, and his mozzetta, with the scarlet biretta* on his head, and the pectoral cross upon his breast, he made his solemn Profession of Faith in the Holy Roman Church. A crowd of lesser dignitaries, each in the garments of his office, attended the ceremonial. The Bishop of Salford held up the Pontificale and the Bishop of Amycla bore the wax taper. The provost of Westminster, on his knees, read aloud the Profession of Faith, surrounded by the Canons of the Diocese. Towards those who gathered about him the dying man was still able to show some signs of recognition, and even, perhaps, of affection; yet it seemed that his chief preoccupation, up to the very end, was with his obedience to the rules prescribed by the Divine Authority. 'I am glad to have been able to do everything in due order,' were among his last words. 'Si fort qu'on soit,' says one of the profoundest of the observers of the human heart, 'on peut éprouver le besoin de s'incliner devant quelqu'un ou quelque chose. S'incliner devant Dieu, c'est toujours le moins humiliant.'*

Manning died on January 14th, 1892, in the eighty-fifth year of his age. A few days later Mr Gladstone took occasion, in a letter to a friend, to refer to his relations with the late Cardinal. Manning's conversion was, he said, 'altogether the severest blow that ever befell me. In a late letter the Cardinal termed it a quarrel, but in my reply I told him it was not a quarrel, but a death; and that was the truth. Since then there have been vicissitudes. But I am quite certain that to the last his personal feelings never changed; and I believe also that he kept a promise made in 1851, to remember me before God at the most solemn moments; a promise which I greatly valued. The whole subject is to me at once of extreme interest and of considerable restraint.' 'His reluctance to die,' concluded Mr Gladstone, 'may be explained by an intense anxiety to complete unfulfilled service.'

The funeral was the occasion of a popular demonstration such as has rarely been witnessed in the streets of London. The route of the procession was lined by vast crowds of working people, whose imaginations, in some instinctive manner, had been touched. Many who had hardly seen him declared that in Cardinal Manning they had lost their best friend. Was it the magnetic vigour of the dead man's spirit that moved them? Or was it his valiant disregard of common custom and those conventional reserves and poor punctilios which are wont to hem about the great? Or was it something untameable in his glances and in his gestures? Or was it, perhaps, the mysterious glamour lingering about him of the antique organisation of Rome? For whatever cause, the mind of the people had been impressed; and yet, after all, the impression was more acute than lasting. The Cardinal's memory is a dim thing to-day. And he who descends into the crypt of that Cathedral which Manning never lived to see,* will observe, in the quiet niche with the sepulchral monument, that the dust lies thick on the strange, the incongruous, the almost impossible object which, with its elaborations of dependent tassels, hangs down from the dim vault like some forlorn and forgotten trophy – the Hat.*

BIBLIOGRAPHY

E. S. Purcell. *Life of Cardinal Manning.*

A. W. Hutton. *Cardinal Manning.*

J. E. C. Bodley. *Cardinal Manning and Other Essays.*

F. W. Cornish. *The English Church in the Nineteenth Century.*

Dean Church. *The Oxford Movement.*

Sir J. T. Coleridge. *Memoir of the Rev. John Keble.*

Hurrell Froude. *Remains.*

Cardinal Newman. *Letters and Correspondence in the English Church. Apologia pro Vita Sua.*

Wilfrid Ward. *Life of Cardinal Newman. W. G. Ward and the Oxford Movement. W. G. Ward and the Catholic Revival. Life of Cardinal Wiseman.*

H. P. Liddon. *Life of E. B. Pusey.*

Tracts for the Times, by Members of the University of Oxford.

Lord Morley. *Life of Gladstone.*

Lives of the Saints, edited by J. H. Newman.

Herbert Paul. *Life of J. A. Froude.*

Mark Pattison. *Autobiography.*

T. Mozley. *Letters from Rome on the Occasion of the Œcumenical Council.*

Lord Acton. *Letters.*

H. L. Smith and V. Nash. *The Story of the Dockers' Strike.*

FLORENCE
NIGHTINGALE

FLORENCE NIGHTINGALE

I

EVERY one knows* the popular conception of Florence Nightingale. The saintly, self-sacrificing woman, the delicate maiden of high degree who threw aside the pleasures of a life of ease to succour the afflicted, the Lady with the Lamp,* gliding through the horrors of the hospital at Scutari, and consecrating with the radiance of her goodness the dying soldier's couch – the vision is familiar to all. But the truth was different. The Miss Nightingale of fact was not as facile fancy painted her. She worked in another fashion, and towards another end; she moved under the stress of an impetus which finds no place in the popular imagination. A Demon possessed her. Now demons, whatever else they may be, are full of interest. And so it happens that in the real Miss Nightingale there was more that was interesting than in the legendary one; there was also less that was agreeable.

Her family was extremely well-to-do, and connected by marriage with a spreading circle of other well-to-do families. There was a large country house in Derbyshire; there was another in the New Forest; there were Mayfair rooms for the London season and all its finest parties; there were tours on the Continent with even more than the usual number of Italian operas and of glimpses at the celebrities of Paris. Brought up among such advantages, it was only natural to suppose that Florence would show a proper appreciation of them by doing her duty in that state of life unto which it had pleased God to call her – in other words, by marrying, after a fitting number of dances and dinner-parties, an eligible gentleman, and living happily ever afterwards. Her sister, her cousins, all the young ladies of her acquaintance, were either getting ready to do this or had already done it. It was inconceivable that Florence should dream of anything else; yet dream she did. Ah! To do her duty in that state of life unto which it had pleased God to call her! Assuredly she would not be behindhand in doing her duty; but unto what state of life *had* it pleased God to call her? That was the question. God's calls are many, and they are strange. Unto what state of life had it pleased Him to call Charlotte Corday, or Elizabeth of Hungary?* What was that secret voice in her ear, if it was not a call?* Why had she felt, from her earliest years, those mysterious promptings towards . . . she hardly knew what, but certainly towards something very different from anything around her? Why, as a child in the nursery, when her sister had shown a healthy pleasure in tearing her dolls to pieces, had *she* shown an almost morbid one in sewing them up again? Why was she driven now to minister to the poor in their cottages, to watch by sick-beds, to put her dog's wounded paw into elaborate splints as if it was a human being? Why was her head filled with queer imaginations of the country house at Embley* turned, by some enchantment, into a hospital, with herself as matron moving about among the beds? Why was even her vision of heaven itself filled with suffering patients to whom she was being useful? So she dreamed and wondered; and, taking out her diary, she poured into it the agitations of her soul. And then the bell rang, and it was time to go and dress for dinner.

As the years passed, a restlessness began to grow upon her. She was unhappy, and at last she knew it. Mrs Nightingale, too, began to notice that there was something wrong. It was very odd; what could be the matter with dear Flo? Mr Nightingale suggested that a hus-band might be advisable; but the curious thing was that she seemed to take no interest in husbands. And with her attractions, and her accomplishments, too! There was nothing in the world to prevent her making a really brilliant match. But no! She would think of nothing but how to satisfy that singular craving of hers to be *doing* something. As if there was not plenty to do in any case, in the ordinary way, at home. There was the china to look after, and there was her father to be read to after dinner. Mrs Nightingale could not understand it; and then one day her perplexity was changed to con-sternation and alarm. Florence announced an extreme desire to go to Salisbury Hospital for several months as a nurse; and she confessed to some visionary plan of eventually setting up in a house of her own in a neighbouring village, and there founding 'something like a Prot-estant Sisterhood,* without vows, for women of educated feelings.' The whole scheme was summarily brushed aside as preposterous; and Mrs Nightingale, after the first shock of terror, was able to settle down again more or less comfortably to her embroidery. But Florence, who was now twenty-five and felt that the dream of her life had been shattered, came near to desperation.

And, indeed, the difficulties in her path were great. For not only was it an almost unimaginable thing in those days for a woman of means to make her own way in the world and to live in independence, but the particular profession for which Florence was clearly marked out both by her instincts and her capacities was at that time a peculiarly disreputable one. A 'nurse' meant then a coarse old woman, always ignorant, usually dirty, often brutal, a Mrs Gamp,* in bunched-up sordid garments, tippling at the brandy bottle or indulging in worse irregularities. The nurses in the hospitals were especially notorious for immoral conduct; sobriety was almost unknown among them; and they could hardly be trusted to carry out the simplest medical duties. Certainly, things have changed since those days; and that they *have* changed is due, far more than to any other human being, to Miss Nightingale herself. It is not to be wondered at that her parents should have shuddered at the notion of their daughter devoting her life to such an occupation. 'It was as if,' she herself said afterwards, 'I had wanted to be a kitchen-maid.'* Yet the want, absurd, impracticable as it was, not only remained fixed immovably in her heart, but grew in intensity day by day. Her wretchedness deepened into a morbid melancholy. Everything about her was vile, and she herself, it was clear, to have deserved such misery, was even viler than her surroundings. Yes, she had sinned – 'standing before God's judgment seat.' 'No one,' she declared, 'has so grieved the Holy Spirit'; of that she was quite certain. It was in vain that she prayed to be delivered from vanity and hypocrisy, and she could not bear to smile or to be gay, 'because she hated God to hear her laugh, as if she had not repented of her sin.'

A weaker spirit would have been overwhelmed by the load of such distresses – would have yielded or snapped. But this extraordinary young woman held firm, and fought her way to victory. With an amazing persistency, during the eight years that followed her rebuff over Salisbury Hospital, she struggled and worked and planned. While superficially she was carrying on the life of a brilliant girl in high society, while internally she was a prey to the tortures of regret and of remorse, she yet possessed the energy to collect the knowledge and to undergo the experience which alone could enable her to do what she had determined she would do in the end. In secret she devoured the reports of medical commissions, the pamphlets of sanitary authorities, the histories of hospitals and homes. She spent the

intervals of the London season in ragged schools and workhouses.*
When she went abroad with her family, she used her spare time so
well that there was hardly a great hospital in Europe with which she
was not acquainted, hardly a great city whose slums she had not
passed through. She managed to spend some days in a convent
school in Rome, and some weeks as a '*Sœur de Charité*' in Paris.
Then, while her mother and sister were taking the waters at
Carlsbad, she succeeded in slipping off to a nursing institution at
Kaiserswerth, where she remained for more than three months. This
was the critical event of her life.* The experience which she gained as
a nurse at Kaiserswerth formed the foundation of all her future
action and finally fixed her in her career.

But one other trial awaited her. The allurements of the world she
had brushed aside with disdain and loathing; she had resisted the
subtler temptation which, in her weariness, had sometimes come
upon her, of devoting her baffled energies to art or literature; the last
ordeal appeared in the shape of a desirable young man.* Hitherto, her
lovers had been nothing to her but an added burden and a mockery;
but now——For a moment, she wavered. A new feeling swept over
her – a feeling which she had never known before, which she was
never to know again. The most powerful and the profoundest of all
the instincts of humanity laid claim upon her. But it rose before her,
that instinct, arrayed – how could it be otherwise? – in the inevitable
habiliments of a Victorian marriage; and she had the strength to
stamp it underfoot. 'I have an intellectual nature which requires
satisfaction,' she noted, 'and that would find it in him. I have a
passional nature which requires satisfaction, and that would find it in
him. I have a moral, an active nature which requires satisfaction, and
that would not find it in his life. Sometimes I think that I will satisfy
my passional nature at all events. . . .' But no, she knew in her heart
that it could not be. 'To be nailed to a continuation and exaggeration
of my present life . . . to put it out of my power ever to be able to
seize the chance of forming for myself a true and rich life' – that
would be a suicide. She made her choice, and refused what was at
least a certain happiness for a visionary good which might never
come to her at all. And so she returned to her old life of waiting and
bitterness. 'The thoughts and feelings that I have now,' she wrote, 'I
can remember since I was six years old. A profession, a trade, a
necessary occupation, something to fill and employ all my faculties, I

have always felt essential to me, I have always longed for. The first thought I can remember, and the last, was nursing work; and in the absence of this, education work, but more the education of the bad than of the young. . . . Everything has been tried, foreign travel, kind friends, everything. My God! What is to become of me?' A desirable young man? Dust and ashes! What was there desirable in such a thing as that? 'In my thirty-first year,' she noted in her diary, 'I see nothing desirable but death.'*

Three more years passed, and then at last the pressure of time told; her family seemed to realise that she was old enough and strong enough to have her way; and she became the superintendent of a charitable nursing home in Harley Street. She had gained her independence, though it was in a meagre sphere enough; and her mother was still not quite resigned: surely Florence might at least spend the summer in the country. At times, indeed, among her intimates, Mrs Nightingale almost wept. 'We are ducks,' she said with tears in her eyes, 'who have hatched a wild swan.' But the poor lady was wrong; it was not a swan that they had hatched; it was an eagle.*

II

MISS NIGHTINGALE had been a year in her nursing-home in Harley Street, when Fate knocked at the door. The Crimean War broke out;* the battle of the Alma was fought; and the terrible condition of our military hospitals at Scutari began to be known in England. It sometimes happens that the plans of Providence are a little difficult to follow, but on this occasion all was plain; there was a perfect co-ordination of events. For years Miss Nightingale had been getting ready; at last she was prepared – experienced, free, mature, yet still young – she was thirty-four – desirous to serve, accustomed to command: at that precise moment the desperate need of a great nation came, and she was there to satisfy it. If the war had fallen a few years earlier, she would have lacked the knowledge, perhaps even the power, for such a work; a few years later and she would, no doubt, have been fixed in the routine of some absorbing task, and moreover, she would have been growing old. Nor was it only the coincidence of Time that was remarkable. It so fell out that Sidney

Herbert* was at the War Office and in the Cabinet; and Sidney Herbert was an intimate friend of Miss Nightingale's, convinced, from personal experience in charitable work, of her supreme capacity. After such premises, it seems hardly more than a matter of course that her letter, in which she offered her services for the East, and Sidney Herbert's letter, in which he asked for them, should actually have crossed in the post. Thus it all happened, without a hitch. The appointment was made, and even Mrs Nightingale, overawed by the magnitude of the venture, could only approve. A pair of faithful friends offered themselves as personal attendants; thirty-eight nurses were collected; and within a week of the crossing of the letters* Miss Nightingale, amid a great burst of popular enthusiasm, left for Constantinople.*

Among the numerous letters which she received on her departure was one from Dr Manning, who at that time was working in comparative obscurity as a Catholic priest in Bayswater. 'God will keep you,' he wrote, 'and my prayer for you will be that your one object of Worship, Pattern of Imitation, and source of consolation and strength may be the Sacred Heart of our Divine Lord.'*

To what extent Dr Manning's prayer was answered must remain a matter of doubt; but this much is certain, that, if ever a prayer was needed, it was needed then for Florence Nightingale. For dark as had been the picture of the state of affairs at Scutari, revealed to the English public in the dispatches of the *Times* correspondent and in a multitude of private letters, yet the reality turned out to be darker still. What had occurred was, in brief, the complete breakdown of our medical arrangements at the seat of war. The origins of this awful failure were complex and manifold; they stretched back through long years of peace and carelessness in England; they could be traced through endless ramifications of administrative incapacity – from the inherent faults of confused systems to the petty bunglings of minor officials, from the inevitable ignorance of Cabinet Ministers to the fatal exactitudes of narrow routine. In the inquiries which followed it was clearly shown that the evil was in reality that worst of all evils – one which has been caused by nothing in particular and for which no one in particular is to blame. The whole organisation of the war machine was incompetent and out of date. The old Duke* had sat for a generation at the Horse Guards repressing innovations with an iron hand. There was an extraordinary overlapping of authorities, an almost incredible shifting of responsibilities to and fro. As for such a notion as the creation and the maintenance of a really adequate medical service for the army – in that atmosphere of aged chaos, how could it have entered anybody's head? Before the war, the easy-going officials at Westminster were naturally persuaded that all was well – or at least as well as could be expected; when some one, for instance, actually had the temerity to suggest the formation of a corps of Army nurses, he was at once laughed out of court. When the war had begun, the gallant British officers in control of affairs had other things to think about than the petty details of medical organisation. Who had bothered with such trifles in the Peninsula?* And surely, on that occasion, we had done pretty well. Thus the most obvious precautions were neglected, the most necessary preparations put off from day to day. The principal medical officer of the Army, Dr Hall,* was summoned from India at a moment's notice, and was unable to visit England before taking up his duties at the front. And it was not until after the battle of the Alma, when we had been at war for many months, that we acquired hospital accommodation at Scutari for more than a thousand men. Errors, follies, and vices on the part of individuals there doubtless were; but, in the general reckoning, they were of small account – insignificant symptoms of the deep disease of the body politic – the enormous calamity of administrative collapse.

Miss Nightingale arrived at Scutari – a suburb of Constantinople, on the Asiatic side of the Bosphorus – on November 4th, 1854; it was ten days after the battle of Balaclava, and the day before the battle of Inkerman. The organisation of the hospitals, which had already given way under the stress of the battle of the Alma, was now to be subjected to the further pressure which these two desperate and bloody engagements implied. Great detachments of wounded were already beginning to pour in. The men, after receiving such summary treatment as could be given them at the smaller hospitals in the Crimea itself, were forthwith shipped in batches of two hundred across the Black Sea to Scutari. This voyage was in normal times one of four days and a half; but the times were no longer normal, and now the transit often lasted for a fortnight or three weeks. It received, not without reason, the name of the 'middle passage.'* Between, and sometimes on the decks, the wounded, the sick, and the dying were crowded – men who had just undergone the amputation of limbs, men in the clutches of fever or of frostbite, men in the last stages of dysentry and cholera – without beds, sometimes without blankets, often hardly clothed. The one or two surgeons on board did what they could; but medical stores were lacking, and the only form of nursing available was that provided by a handful of invalid soldiers, who were usually themselves prostrate by the end of the voyage. There was no other food beside the ordinary salt rations of ship diet; and even the water was sometimes so stored that it was out of reach of the weak. For many months, the average of deaths during these voyages was seventy-four in the 1,000; the corpses were shot out into the waters; and who shall say that they were the most unfortunate? At Scutari, the landing-stage, constructed with all the perverseness of Oriental ingenuity, could only be approached with great difficulty, and, in rough weather, not at all. When it was reached, what remained of the men in the ships had first to be disembarked, and then conveyed up a steep slope of a quarter of a mile to the nearest of the hospitals. The most serious cases might be put upon stretchers – for there were far too few for all; the rest were carried or dragged up the hill by such convalescent soldiers as could be got together, who were not too obviously infirm for the work. At last the journey was accomplished; slowly, one by one, living or dying, the wounded were carried up into the hospital. And in the hospital what did they find?

*Lasciate ogni speranza, voi ch'entrate:** the delusive doors bore no such inscription; and yet behind them Hell yawned. Want, neglect, confusion, misery – in every shape and in every degree of intensity – filled the endless corridors and the vast apartments of the gigantic barrack-house, which, without forethought or preparation, had been hurriedly set aside as the chief shelter for the victims of the war. The very building itself was radically defective. Huge sewers underlay it, and cesspools loaded with filth wafted their poison into the upper rooms. The floors were in so rotten a condition that many of them could not be scrubbed; the walls were thick with dirt; incredible multitudes of vermin swarmed everywhere. And, enormous as the building was, it was yet too small. It contained four miles of beds, crushed together so close that there was but just room to pass between them. Under such conditions, the most elaborate system of ventilation might well have been at fault; but here there was no ventilation. The stench was indescribable. 'I have been well acquainted,' said Miss Nightingale, 'with the dwellings of the worst parts of most of the great cities in Europe, but have never been in any atmosphere which I could compare with that of the Barrack Hospital at night.' The structural defects were equalled by the deficiencies in the commonest objects of hospital use. There were not enough bedsteads; the sheets were of canvas, and so coarse that the wounded men recoiled from them, begging to be left in their blankets; there was no bedroom furniture of any kind, and empty beer bottles were used for candlesticks.* There were no basins, no towels, no soap, no brooms, no mops, no trays, no plates; there were neither slippers nor scissors, neither shoe-brushes nor blacking; there were no knives or forks or spoons. The supply of fuel was constantly deficient. The cooking arrangements were preposterously inadequate, and the laundry was a farce. As for purely medical materials, the tale was no better. Stretchers, splints, bandages – all were lacking; and so were the most ordinary drugs.

To replace such wants, to struggle against such difficulties, there was a handful of men overburdened by the strain of ceaseless work, bound down by the traditions of official routine, and enfeebled either by old age or inexperience or sheer incompetence. They had proved utterly unequal to their task. The principal doctor was lost in the imbecilities of a senile optimism. The wretched official whose business it was to provide for the wants of the hospital was tied fast hand and foot by red tape. A few of the younger doctors struggled valiantly, but what could they do? Unprepared, disorganised, with such help only as they could find among the miserable band of convalescent soldiers* drafted off to tend their sick comrades, they were faced with disease, mutilation, and death in all their most appalling forms, crowded multitudinously about them in an ever-increasing mass. They were like men in a shipwreck, fighting, not for safety, but for the next moment's bare existence – to gain, by yet another frenzied effort, some brief respite from the waters of destruction.

In these surroundings, those who had been long inured to scenes of human suffering – surgeons with a world-wide knowledge of agonies, soldiers familiar with fields of carnage, missionaries with remembrances of famine and of plague – yet found a depth of horror which they had never known before. There were moments, there were places, in the Barrack Hospital at Scutari, where the strongest hand was struck with trembling, and the boldest eye would turn away its gaze.

Miss Nightingale came, and she, at any rate, in that inferno, did not abandon hope. For one thing, she brought material succour. Before she left London she had consulted Dr Andrew Smith, the head of the Army Medical Board, as to whether it would be useful to take out stores of any kind to Scutari; and Dr Andrew Smith had told her that 'nothing was needed.'* Even Sidney Herbert had given her similar assurances; possibly, owing to an oversight, there might have been some delay in the delivery of the medical stores, which, he said, had been sent out from England 'in profusion,' but 'four days would have remedied this.' She preferred to trust her own instincts, and at Marseilles purchased a large quantity of miscellaneous provisions, which were of the utmost use at Scutari. She came, too, amply provided with money – in all, during her stay in the East, about £7000 reached her from private sources; and, in addition, she was able to avail herself of another valuable means of help. At the same time as herself, Mr Macdonald, of the *Times*, had arrived at Scutari, charged with the duty of administering the large sums of money collected through the agency of that newspaper in aid of the sick and wounded; and Mr Macdonald had the sense to see that the best use he could make of the *Times* Fund was to put it at the disposal of Miss Nightingale. 'I cannot conceive,' wrote an eye-witness, 'as I now calmly look back on the first three weeks after the arrival of the wounded from Inkerman, how it could have been possible to have avoided a state of things too disastrous to contemplate, had not Miss Nightingale been there, with the means placed at her disposal by Mr Macdonald.' But the official view was different. What! Was the public service to admit, by accepting outside charity, that it was unable to discharge its own duties without the assistance of private and irregular benevolence? Never! And accordingly when Lord Stratford de Redcliffe, our ambassador at Constantinople, was asked by Mr Macdonald to indicate how the *Times* Fund could best be employed, he answered that there was indeed one object to which it might very well be devoted – the building of an English Protestant Church at Pera.*

Mr Macdonald did not waste further time with Lord Stratford, and immediately joined forces with Miss Nightingale. But, with such a frame of mind in the highest quarters, it is easy to imagine the kind of disgust and alarm with which the sudden intrusion of a band of amateurs and females must have filled the minds of the ordinary officer and the ordinary military surgeon. They could not understand it; what had women to do with war? Honest Colonels relieved their spleen by the cracking of heavy jokes about 'the Bird'; while poor Dr Hall, a rough terrier of a man, who had worried his way to the top of his profession, was struck speechless with astonishment, and at last observed that Miss Nightingale's appointment was extremely droll.

Her position was, indeed, an official one, but it was hardly the easier for that. In the hospitals it was her duty to provide the services of herself and her nurses when they were asked for by the doctors, and not until then. At first some of the surgeons would have nothing to say to her, and, though she was welcomed by others, the majority were hostile and suspicious. But gradually she gained ground. Her good will could not be denied, and her capacity could not be disregarded. With consummate tact, with all the gentleness of supreme strength, she managed at last to impose her personality upon the susceptible, overwrought, discouraged, and helpless group of men in authority who surrounded her. She stood firm; she was a rock in the angry ocean; with her alone was safety, comfort, life. And so it was that hope dawned at Scutari. The reign of chaos and old night began to dwindle; order came upon the scene, and common sense, and forethought, and decision, radiating out from the little room off the great gallery in the Barrack Hospital where, day and night, the Lady Superintendent was at her task. Progress might be slow, but it was sure. The first sign of a great change came with the appearance of some of those necessary objects with which the hospitals had been unprovided for months. The sick men began to enjoy the use of towels and soap, knives and forks, combs and tooth-brushes. Dr Hall might snort when he heard of it, asking, with a growl, what a soldier wanted with a tooth-brush; but the good work went on. Eventually the whole business of purveying to the hospitals was, in effect, carried out by Miss Nightingale. She alone, it seemed, whatever the contingency, knew where to lay her hands on what was wanted; she alone could dispense her stores with readiness; above all she alone possessed the art of circumventing the pernicious influences of official etiquette. This was her greatest enemy, and sometimes even she was baffled by it. On one occasion 27,000 shirts, sent out at her

instance by the Home Government, arrived, were landed, and were
only waiting to be unpacked. But the official 'Purveyor' intervened;
'he could not unpack them,' he said, 'without a Board.' Miss Nightingale pleaded in vain; the sick and wounded lay half-naked shiver-
ing for want of clothing; and three weeks elapsed before the Board
released the shirts. A little later, however, on a similar occasion, Miss
Nightingale felt that she could assert her own authority. She ordered
a Government consignment to be forcibly opened, while the miserable 'Purveyor' stood by, wringing his hands in departmental agony.

Vast quantities of valuable stores sent from England lay, she
found, engulfed in the bottomless abyss of the Turkish Customs
House. Other ship-loads, buried beneath munitions of war destined
for Balaclava, passed Scutari without a sign, and thus hospital
materials were sometimes carried to and fro three times over the
Black Sea, before they reached their destination. The whole system
was clearly at fault, and Miss Nightingale suggested to the home
authorities that a Government Store House should be instituted at
Scutari for the reception and distribution of the consignments. Six
months after her arrival this was done.

In the meantime she had reorganised the kitchens and the laun-
dries in the hospitals. The ill-cooked hunks of meat, vilely served at
irregular intervals, which had hitherto been the only diet for the sick
men were replaced by punctual meals, well-prepared and appetising,
while strengthening extra foods – soups and wines and jellies ('preposterous luxuries,' snarled Dr Hall) – were distributed to those who
needed them. One thing, however, she could not effect. The separation of the bones from the meat was no part of official cookery: the
rule was that the food must be divided into equal portions, and if
some of the portions were all bone – well, every man must take his
chance. The rule, perhaps, was not a very good one; but there it was.
'It would require a new Regulation of the Service,' she was told, 'to
bone the meat.'* As for the washing arrangements, they were revolutionised. Up to the time of Miss Nightingale's arrival the number
of shirts the authorities had succeeded in washing was seven. The
hospital bedding, she found, was 'washed' in cold water. She took a
Turkish house, had boilers installed, and employed soldiers' wives to
do the laundry work. The expenses were defrayed from her own
funds and that of the *Times*; and henceforward the sick and wounded
had the comfort of clean linen.

Then she turned her attention to their clothing. Owing to military exigencies the greater number of the men had abandoned their kit; their knapsacks were lost for ever; they possessed nothing but what was on their persons, and that was usually only fit for speedy destruction. The 'Purveyor,' of course, pointed out that, according to the regulations, all soldiers should bring with them into hospital an adequate supply of clothing, and he declared that it was no business of his to make good their deficiencies. Apparently, it was the business of Miss Nightingale. She procured socks, boots, and shirts in enormous quantities; she had trousers made, she rigged up dressing-gowns. 'The fact is,' she told Sidney Herbert, 'I am now clothing the British Army.'*

All at once, word came from the Crimea that a great new contingent of sick and wounded might shortly be expected. Where were they to go? Every available inch in the wards was occupied; the affair was serious and pressing, and the authorities stood aghast. There were some dilapidated rooms in the Barrack Hospital, unfit for human habitation, but Miss Nightingale believed that if measures were promptly taken they might be made capable of accommodating several hundred beds. One of the doctors agreed with her; the rest of the officials were irresolute: it would be a very expensive job, they said; it would involve building; and who could take the responsibility?* The proper course was that a representation should be made to the Director-General of the Army Medical Department in London; then the Director-General would apply to the Horse Guards, the Horse Guards would move the Ordnance, the Ordnance would lay the matter before the Treasury, and, if the Treasury gave its consent, the work might be correctly carried through, several months after the necessity for it had disappeared. Miss Nightingale, however, had made up her mind, and she persuaded Lord Stratford – or thought she had persuaded him – to give his sanction to the required expenditure. One hundred and twenty-five workmen were immediately engaged, and the work was begun. The workmen struck; whereupon Lord Stratford washed his hands of the whole business. Miss Nightingale engaged 200 other workmen on her own authority, and paid the bill out of her own resources. The wards were ready by the required date; five hundred sick men were received in them; and all the utensils, including knives, forks, spoons, cans and towels, were supplied by Miss Nightingale.

This remarkable woman was in truth performing the function of an administrative chief. How had this come about? Was she not in reality merely a nurse? Was it not her duty simply to tend the sick? And indeed, was it not as a ministering angel, a gentle 'lady with a lamp' that she actually impressed the minds of her contemporaries? No doubt that was so; and yet it is no less certain that, as she herself said, the specific business of nursing was 'the least important of the functions into which she had been forced.' It was clear that in the state of disorganisation into which the hospitals at Scutari had fallen, the most pressing, the really vital, need was for something more than nursing; it was for the necessary elements of civilised life – the commonest material objects, the most ordinary cleanliness, the rudimentary habits of order and authority. 'Oh, dear Miss Nightingale,' said one of her party as they were approaching Constantinople, 'when we land, let there be no delays, let us get straight to nursing the poor fellows!' 'The strongest will be wanted at the wash-tub,'* was Miss Nightingale's answer. And it was upon the wash-tub, and all that the wash-tub stood for, that she expended her greatest energies. Yet to say that is perhaps to say too much. For to those who watched her at work among the sick, moving day and night from bed to bed, with that unflinching courage, with that indefatigable vigilance, it seemed as if the concentrated force of an undivided and unparalleled devotion could hardly suffice for that portion of her task alone. Wherever, in those vast wards, suffering was at its worst and the need for help was greatest, there, as if by magic, was Miss Nightingale. Her superhuman equanimity would, at the moment of some ghastly operation, nerve the victim to endure and almost to hope. Her sympathy would assuage the pangs of dying and bring back to those still living something of the forgotten charm of life. Over and over again her untiring efforts rescued those whom the surgeons had abandoned as beyond the possibility of cure. Her mere presence brought with it a strange influence. A passionate idolatry spread among the men: they kissed her shadow as it passed. They did more. 'Before she came,' said a soldier, 'there was cussin' and swearin', but after that it was as 'oly as a church.'* The most cherished privilege of the fighting man was abandoned for the sake of Miss Nightingale. In those 'lowest sinks of human misery,' as she herself put it, she never heard the use of one expression 'which could distress a gentlewoman.'

She was heroic; and these were the humble tributes paid by those of grosser mould to that high quality. Certainly, she was heroic. Yet her heroism was not of that simple sort so dear to the readers of novels and the compilers of hagiologies – the romantic sentimental heroism with which mankind loves to invest its chosen darlings: it was made of sterner stuff. To the wounded soldier on his couch of agony she might well appear in the guise of a gracious angel of mercy; but the military surgeons, and the orderlies, and her own nurses, and the 'Purveyor,' and Dr Hall, and even Lord Stratford himself could tell a different story. It was not by gentle sweetness and womanly self-abnegation that she had brought order out of chaos in the Scutari hospitals, that, from her own resources, she had clothed the British Army, that she had spread her dominion over the serried and reluctant powers of the official world; it was by strict method, by stern discipline, by rigid attention to detail, by ceaseless labour, by the fixed determination of an indomitable will. Beneath her cool and calm demeanour lurked fierce and passionate fires. As she passed through the wards in her plain dress, so quiet, so unassuming, she struck the casual observer simply as the pattern of a perfect lady; but the keener eye perceived something more than that – the serenity of high deliberation in the scope of the capacious brow, the sign of power in the dominating curve of the thin nose, and the traces of a harsh and dangerous temper – something peevish, something mocking, and yet something precise – in the small and delicate mouth. There was humour in the face; but the curious watcher might wonder whether it was humour of a very pleasant kind; might ask himself, even as he heard the laughter and marked the jokes with which she cheered the spirits of her patients, what sort of sardonic merriment this same lady might not give vent to, in the privacy of her chamber. As for her voice, it was true of it, even more than of her countenance, that it 'had that in it one must fain call master.'* Those clear tones were in no need of emphasis: 'I never heard her raise her voice,' said one of her companions. Only, when she had spoken, it seemed as if nothing could follow but obedience. Once, when she had given some direction, a doctor ventured to remark that the thing could not be done. 'But it must be done,' said Miss Nightingale. A chance bystander, who heard the words, never forgot through all his life the irresistible authority of them. And they were spoken quietly – very quietly indeed.

Late at night, when the long miles of beds lay wrapped in darkness, Miss Nightingale would sit at work in her little room, over her correspondence. It was one of the most formidable of all her duties. There were hundreds of letters to be written to the friends and relations of soldiers; there was the enormous mass of official documents to be dealt with; there were her own private letters to be answered; and, most important of all, there was the composition of her long and confidential reports to Sidney Herbert. These were by no means official communications. Her soul, pent up all day in the restraint and reserve of a vast responsibility, now at last poured itself out in these letters with all its natural vehemence, like a swollen torrent through an open sluice. Here, at least, she did not mince matters. Here she painted in her darkest colours the hideous scenes which surrounded her; here she tore away remorselessly the last veils still shrouding the abominable truth. Then she would fill pages with recommendations and suggestions, with criticisms of the minutest details of organisation, with elaborate calculations of contingencies, with exhaustive analyses and statistical statements piled up in breathless eagerness one on the top of the other. And then her pen, in the virulence of its volubility, would rush on to the discussion of individuals, to the denunciation of an incompetent surgeon or the ridicule of a self-sufficient nurse. Her sarcasm searched the ranks of the officials with the deadly and unsparing precision of a machine-gun.* Her nicknames were terrible. She respected no one: Lord Stratford, Lord Raglan, Lady Stratford, Dr Andrew Smith, Dr Hall, the Commissary-General, the Purveyor – she fulminated against them all. The intolerable futility of mankind obsessed her like a nightmare, and she gnashed her teeth against it. 'I do well to be angry,' was the burden of her cry. How many just men were there at Scutari? How many who cared at all for the sick, or had done anything for their relief? Were there ten? Were there five? Was there even one? She could not be sure.

At one time, during several weeks, her vituperations descended upon the head of Sidney Herbert himself.* He had misinterpreted her wishes, he had traversed her positive instructions, and it was not until he had admitted his error and apologised in abject terms that he was allowed again into favour. While this misunderstanding was at its height an aristocratic young gentleman* arrived at Scutari with a recommendation from the Minister. He had come out from England filled with a romantic desire to render homage to the angelic heroine of his dreams. He had, he said, cast aside his life of ease and luxury; he would devote his days and nights to the service of that gentle lady; he would perform the most menial offices, he would 'fag' for her, he would be her footman – and feel requited by a single smile. A single smile, indeed, he had, but it was of an unexpected kind. Miss Nightingale at first refused to see him, and then, when she consented, believing that he was an emissary sent by Sidney Herbert to put her in the wrong over their dispute, she took notes of her conversation with him, and insisted on his signing them at the end of it. The young gentleman returned to England by the next ship.

This quarrel with Sidney Herbert was, however, an exceptional incident. Alike by him, and by Lord Panmure, his successor at the War Office, she was firmly supported; and the fact that during the whole of her stay at Scutari she had the Home Government at her back, was her trump card in her dealings with the hospital authorities. Nor was it only the Government that was behind her; public opinion in England early recognised the high importance of her mission, and its enthusiastic appreciation of her work soon reached an extraordinary height. The Queen herself was deeply moved. She made repeated inquiries as to the welfare of Miss Nightingale; she asked to see her accounts of the wounded, and made her the intermediary between the throne and the troops. 'Let Mrs Herbert know,' she wrote to the War Minister, 'that I wish Miss Nightingale and the ladies would tell these poor noble, wounded, and sick men that *no one* takes a warmer interest or feels *more* for their sufferings or admires their courage and heroism *more* than their Queen. Day and night she thinks of her beloved troops. So does the Prince. Beg Mrs Herbert to communicate these my words to those ladies, as I know that *our* sympathy is much valued by these noble fellows.'* The letter was read aloud in the wards by the Chaplain. 'It is a very feeling letter,' said the men.

And so the months passed, and that fell winter which had begun with Inkerman and had dragged itself out through the long agony of the investment of Sebastopol, at last was over. In May, 1855, after six months of labour, Miss Nightingale could look with something like satisfaction at the condition of the Scutari hospitals. Had they done nothing more than survive the terrible strain which had been put upon them, it would have been a matter for congratulation; but they had done much more than that; they had marvellously improved. The confusion and the pressure in the wards had come to an end; order reigned in them, and cleanliness; the supplies were bountiful and prompt; important sanitary works had been carried out. One simple comparison of figures was enough to reveal the extraordinary change: the rate of mortality among the cases treated had fallen from 42 per cent to twenty-two per thousand. But still the indefatigable lady was not satisfied. The main problem had been solved – the physical needs of the men had been provided for; their mental and spiritual needs remained. She set up and furnished reading-rooms and recreation-rooms. She started classes and lectures. Officers were amazed to see her treating their men as if they were human beings, and assured her that she would only end by 'spoiling the brutes.' But that was not Miss Nightingale's opinion, and she was justified. The private soldier began to drink less, and even – though that seemed impossible – to save his pay. Miss Nightingale became a banker for the Army, receiving and sending home large sums of money every month. At last, reluctantly, the Government followed suit, and established machinery of its own for the remission of money. Lord Panmure, however, remained sceptical; 'it will do no good,' he pronounced; 'the British soldier is not a remitting animal.'* But, in fact, during the next six months, £71,000 was sent home.

Amid all these activities, Miss Nightingale took up the further task of inspecting the hospitals in the Crimea itself.* The labour was extreme, and the conditions of life were almost intolerable. She spent whole days in the saddle, or was driven over those bleak and rocky heights in a baggage cart. Sometimes she stood for hours in the heavily falling snow, and would only reach her hut at dead of night after walking for miles through perilous ravines. Her powers of resistance seemed incredible, but at last they were exhausted. She was attacked by fever, and for a moment came very near to death. Yet she worked on; if she could not move, she could at least write; and write she did until her mind had left her; and after it had left her, in what seemed the delirious trance of death itself, she still wrote. When, after many weeks, she was strong enough to travel, she was implored to return to England, but she utterly refused. She would not go back, she said, before the last of the soldiers had left Scutari.

This happy moment had almost arrived, when suddenly the

smouldering hostilities of the medical authorities burst out into a flame. Dr Hall's labours had been rewarded by a K.C.B. – letters which, as Miss Nightingale told Sidney Herbert, she could only suppose to mean 'Knight of the Crimean Burial-grounds' – and the honour had turned his head. He was Sir John, and he would be thwarted no longer. Disputes had lately arisen between Miss Nightingale and some of the nurses in the Crimean hospitals. The situation had been embittered by rumours of religious dissensions, for, while the Crimean nurses were Roman Catholics, many of those at Scutari were suspected of a regrettable propensity towards the tenets of Dr Pusey. Miss Nightingale was by no means disturbed by these sectarian differences, but any suggestion that her supreme authority over all the nurses with the Army was in doubt was enough to rouse her to fury; and it appeared that Mrs Bridgeman, the Reverend Mother in the Crimea, had ventured to call that authority in question. Sir John Hall thought that his opportunity had come, and strongly supported Mrs Bridgeman – or, as Miss Nightingale preferred to call her, the 'Reverend Brickbat.'* There was a violent struggle; Miss Nightingale's rage was terrible. Dr Hall, she declared, was doing his best to 'root her out of the Crimea.' She would bear it no longer; the War Office was playing her false; there was only one thing to be done – Sidney Herbert must move for the production of papers in the House of Commons, so that the public might be able to judge between her and her enemies. Sidney Herbert with great difficulty calmed her down. Orders were immediately dispatched putting her supremacy beyond doubt, and the Reverend Brickbat withdrew from the scene. Sir John, however, was more tenacious. A few weeks later, Miss Nightingale and her nurses visited the Crimea for the last time, and the brilliant idea occurred to him that he could crush her by a very simple expedient – he would starve her into submission; and he actually ordered that no rations of any kind should be supplied to her. He had already tried this plan with great effect upon an unfortunate medical man whose presence in the Crimea he had considered an intrusion; but he was now to learn that such tricks were thrown away upon Miss Nightingale. With extraordinary foresight, she had brought with her a great supply of food; she succeeded in obtaining more at her own expense and by her own exertions; and thus for ten days, in that inhospitable country, she was able to feed herself and twenty-four nurses. Eventually the military authorities intervened in her favour, and Sir John had to confess that he was beaten.

It was not until July, 1856 – four months after the Declaration of Peace – that Miss Nightingale left Scutari for England. Her reputation was now enormous, and the enthusiasm of the public was unbounded. The royal approbation was expressed by the gift of a brooch, accompanied by a private letter. 'You are, I know, well aware,' wrote Her Majesty, 'of the high sense I entertain of the Christian devotion which you have displayed during this great and bloody war, and I need hardly repeat to you how warm my admiration is for your services, which are fully equal to those of my dear and brave soldiers, whose sufferings you have had the *privilege* of alleviating in so merciful a manner. I am, however, anxious of marking my feelings in a manner which I trust will be agreeable to you, and therefore send you with this letter a brooch, the form and emblems of which commemorate your great and blessed work, and which I hope you will wear as a mark of the high approbation of your Sovereign!

'It will be a very great satisfaction to me,' Her Majesty added, 'to make the acquaintance of one who has set so bright an example to our sex.'

The brooch, which was designed by the Prince Consort, bore a St George's cross in red enamel, and the Royal cipher surmounted by diamonds. The whole was encircled by the inscription 'Blessed are the Merciful.'*

III

THE name of Florence Nightingale lives in the memory of the world by virtue of the lurid and heroic adventure of the Crimea. Had she died – as she nearly did – upon her return to England, her reputation would hardly have been different; her legend would have come down to us almost as we know it to-day – that gentle vision of female virtue which first took shape before the adoring eyes of the sick soldiers at Scutari. Yet, as a matter of fact, she lived for more than half a century after the Crimean War; and during the greater part of that long period all the energy and all the devotion of her extraordinary nature were working at their highest pitch. What she accomplished in those years of unknown labour could, indeed, hardly have been more glorious than her Crimean triumphs; but it was certainly more important. The true history was far stranger even than the myth. In Miss Nightingale's own eyes the adventure of the Crimea was a mere incident – scarcely more than a useful stepping-stone in her career. It was the fulcrum with which she hoped to move the world; but it was only the fulcrum. For more than a generation she was to sit in secret, working her lever: and her real life began at the very moment when, in the popular imagination, it had ended.

She arrived in England in a shattered state of health. The hardships and the ceaseless effort of the last two years had undermined her nervous system; her heart was pronounced to be affected; she suffered constantly from fainting-fits and terrible attacks of utter physical prostration. The doctors declared that one thing alone would save her – a complete and prolonged rest. But that was also the one thing with which she would have nothing to do. She had never been in the habit of resting; why should she begin now? Now, when her opportunity had come at last; now, when the iron was hot, and it was time to strike? No; she had work to do; and, come what might, she would do it. The doctors protested in vain; in vain her family lamented and entreated, in vain her friends pointed out to her the madness of such a course. Madness? Mad – possessed – perhaps she was. A demoniac frenzy had seized upon her. As she lay upon her sofa, gasping, she devoured blue-books, dictated letters, and, in the intervals of her palpitations, cracked her febrile jokes. For months at a stretch she never left her bed. For years she was in daily expectation of death. But she would not rest. At this rate, the doctors assured her, even if she did not die, she would become an invalid for life. She could not help that; there was the work to be done; and, as for rest, very likely she might rest . . . when she had done it.

Wherever she went, in London or in the country, in the hills of Derbyshire, or among the rhododendrons at Embley, she was haunted by a ghost. It was the spectre of Scutari – the hideous vision of the organisation of a military hospital. She would lay that phantom, or she would perish. The whole system of the Army Medical Department, the education of the Medical Officer, the regulations of hospital procedure . . . *rest?* How could she rest while these things were as they were, while, if the like necessity were to arise again, the like results would follow? And, even in peace and at home, what was the sanitary condition of the Army? The mortality in the barracks was, she found, nearly double the mortality in civil life. 'You might as well take 1100 men every year out upon Salisbury Plain and shoot them,' she said. After inspecting the hospitals at Chatham, she smiled grimly. 'Yes, this is one more symptom of the system which, in the Crimea, put to death 16,000 men.' Scutari had given her knowledge; and it had given her power too: her enormous reputation was at her back – an incalculable force. Other work, other duties, might lie before her; but the most urgent, the most obvious, of all was to look to the health of the Army.

One of her very first steps was to take advantage of the invitation which Queen Victoria had sent her to the Crimea, together with the commemorative brooch. Within a few weeks of her return she visited Balmoral,* and had several interviews with both the Queen and the Prince Consort. 'She put before us,' wrote the Prince in his diary, 'all the defects of our present military hospital system, and the reforms that are needed.' She related 'the whole story' of her experiences in the East; and, in addition, she managed to have some long and confidential talks with His Royal Highness on metaphysics and religion. The impression which she created was excellent. 'Sie gefällt uns sehr,' noted the Prince, 'ist sehr bescheiden.'* Her Majesty's comment was different – 'Such a *head!* I wish we had her at the War Office.'*

But Miss Nightingale was not at the War Office, and for a very simple reason; she was a woman. Lord Panmure, however, *was* (though indeed the reason for that was not quite so simple); and it was upon Lord Panmure that the issue of Miss Nightingale's efforts for reform must primarily depend. That burly Scottish nobleman had not, in spite of his most earnest endeavours, had a very easy time of it as Secretary of State for War. He had come into office in the middle of the Sebastopol Campaign, and had felt himself very well fitted for the position, since he had acquired in former days an inside knowledge of the Army – as a Captain of Hussars. It was this inside knowledge which had enabled him to inform Miss Nightingale with such authority that 'the British soldier is not a remitting animal.' And perhaps it was this same consciousness of a command of his subject which had impelled him to write a dispatch to Lord Raglan, blandly informing the Commander-in-Chief in the Field just how he was neglecting his duties, and pointing out to him that if he would only try he really might do a little better next time. Lord Raglan's reply, calculated as it was to make its recipient sink into the earth, did not quite have that effect upon Lord Panmure, who, whatever might have been his faults, had never been accused of being super-sensitive. However, he allowed the matter to drop; and a little later Lord Raglan died – worn out, some people said, by work and anxiety. He was succeeded by an excellent red-nosed old gentleman, General Simpson,* whom nobody has ever heard of, and who took Sebastopol. But Lord Panmure's relations with him were hardly more satisfac-tory than his relations with Lord Raglan; for, while Lord Raglan had been too independent, poor General Simpson erred in the opposite direction, perpetually asked advice, suffered from lumbago, doubted, his nose growing daily redder and redder, whether he was fit for his post, and, by alternate mails, sent in and withdrew his resignation. Then, too, both the General and the Minister suffered acutely from that distressingly useful new invention, the electric telegraph. On one occasion General Simpson felt obliged actually to expostulate. 'I think, my Lord,' he wrote, 'that some telegraphic messages reach us that cannot be sent under due authority, and are perhaps unknown to you, although under the protection of your Lordship's name. For instance, I was called up last night, a dragoon having come express with a telegraphic message in these words, "Lord Panmure to Gen-eral Simpson – Captain Jarvis has been bitten by a centipede. How is he now?" ' General Simpson might have put up with this, though to be sure it did seem 'rather too trifling an affair to call for a dragoon to ride a couple of miles in the dark that he may knock up the Com-mander of the Army out of the very small allowance of sleep permit-ted him'; but what was really more than he could bear was to find 'upon sending in the morning another mounted dragoon to inquire after Captain Jarvis, four miles off, that he never has been bitten at all, but has had a boil, from which he is fast recovering.' But Lord Panmure had troubles of his own. His favourite nephew, Captain Dowbiggin, was at the front, and to one of his telegrams to the Commander-in-Chief the Minister had taken occasion to append the following carefully qualified sentence – 'I recommend Dowbiggin to your notice, should you have a vacancy, and if he is fit.' Unfortunately, in those early days, it was left to the discretion of the telegraphist to compress the messages which passed through his hands; so that the result was that Lord Panmure's delicate appeal

reached its destination in the laconic form of 'Look after Dowb.'
The Headquarters Staff were at first extremely puzzled; they were at
last extremely amused. The story spread; and 'Look after Dowb'
remained for many years the familiar formula for describing official
hints in favour of deserving nephews.

And now that all this was over, now that Sebastopol had been,
somehow or another, taken, now that peace was, somehow or
another, made, now that the troubles of office might surely be
expected to be at an end at last – here was Miss Nightingale breaking
in upon the scene, with her talk about the state of the hospitals and
the necessity for sanitary reform. It was most irksome; and Lord
Panmure almost began to wish that he was engaged upon some more
congenial occupation – discussing, perhaps, the constitution of the
Free Church of Scotland – a question in which he was profoundly
interested. But no; duty was paramount; and he set himself, with a
sigh of resignation, to the task of doing as little of it as he possibly
could.

'The Bison' his friends called him;* and the name fitted both his
physical demeanour and his habit of mind. That large low head
seemed to have been created for butting rather than for anything
else. There he stood, four-square and menacing, in the doorway of
reform; and it remained to be seen whether the bulky mass, upon
whose solid hide even the barbed arrows of Lord Raglan's scorn had
made no mark, would prove amenable to the pressure of Miss Nightingale. Nor was he alone in the doorway. There loomed behind him
the whole phalanx of professional conservatism, the stubborn supporters of the out-of-date, the worshippers and the victims of War
Office routine. Among these it was only natural that Dr Andrew
Smith, the head of the Army Medical Department, should have
been pre-eminent – Dr Andrew Smith, who had assured Miss
Nightingale before she left England that 'nothing was wanted at
Scutari.' Such were her opponents; but she too was not without
allies. She had gained the ear of Royalty – which was something; at
any moment that she pleased she could gain the ear of the public –
which was a great deal. She had a host of admirers and friends;
and – to say nothing of her personal qualities – her knowledge, her
tenacity, her tact – she possessed, too, one advantage which then, far
more even than now, carried an immense weight – she belonged to
the highest circle of society. She moved naturally among Peers and

Cabinet Ministers – she was one of their own set; and in those days their set was a very narrow one. What kind of attention would such persons have paid to some middle-class woman with whom they were not acquainted, who possessed great experience of Army nursing and had decided views upon hospital reform? They would have politely ignored her; but it was impossible to ignore Flo Nightingale. When she spoke, they were obliged to listen; and, when they had once begun to do that – what might not follow? She knew her power, and she used it. She supported her weightiest minutes with familiar witty little notes. The Bison began to look grave. It might be difficult – it might be damned difficult – to put down one's head against the white hand of a lady.

Of Miss Nightingale's friends, the most important was Sidney Herbert. He was a man upon whom the good fairies seemed to have showered, as he lay in his cradle, all their most enviable goods. Well born, handsome, rich, the master of Wilton – one of those great country-houses, clothed with the glamour of a historic past, which are the peculiar glory of England – he possessed, besides all these advantages, so charming, so lively, so gentle a disposition that no one who had once come near him could ever be his enemy. He was, in fact, a man of whom it was difficult not to say that he was a perfect English gentleman. For his virtues were equal even to his good fortune. He was religious – deeply religious: 'I am more and more convinced every day,' he wrote, when he had been for some years a Cabinet Minister, 'that in politics, as in everything else, nothing can be right which is not in accordance with the spirit of the Gospel.' No one was more unselfish; he was charitable and benevolent to a remarkable degree; and he devoted the whole of his life with an unwavering conscientiousness to the public service. With such a character, with such opportunities, what high hopes must have danced before him, what radiant visions of accomplished duties, of ever-increasing usefulness, of beneficent power, of the consciousness of disinterested success! Some of those hopes and visions were, indeed, realised; but, in the end, the career of Sidney Herbert seemed to show that, with all their generosity, there was some gift or other – what was it? – some essential gift – which the good fairies had withheld, and that even the qualities of a perfect English gentleman may be no safeguard against anguish, humiliation, and defeat.

That career would certainly have been very different if he had never known Miss Nightingale. The alliance between them which had begun with her appointment to Scutari, which had grown closer and closer while the war lasted, developed, after her return, into one of the most extraordinary of friendships. It was the friendship of a man and a woman intimately bound together by their devotion to a public cause; mutual affection, of course, played a part in it, but it was an incidental part; the whole soul of the relationship was a community of work. Perhaps out of England such an intimacy could hardly have existed – an intimacy so utterly untinctured not only by passion itself but by the suspicion of it. For years Sidney Herbert saw Miss Nightingale almost daily, for long hours together, corresponding with her incessantly when they were apart; and the tongue of scandal was silent; and one of the most devoted of her admirers was his wife. But what made the connection still more remarkable was the way in which the parts that were played in it were divided between the two. The man who acts, decides, and achieves; the woman who encourages, applauds, and – from a distance – inspires: the combination is common enough; but Miss Nightingale was neither an Aspasia nor an Egeria.* In her case it is almost true to say that the roles were reversed; the qualities of pliancy and sympathy fell to the man, those of command and initiative to the woman. There was one thing only which Miss Nightingale lacked in her equipment for public life; she had not – she never could have – the public power and authority which belong to the successful politician. That power and authority Sidney Herbert possessed; that fact was obvious, and the conclusions no less so: it was through the man that the woman must work her will. She took hold of him, taught him, shaped him, absorbed him, dominated him through and through. He did not resist – he did not wish to resist; his natural inclination lay along the same path as hers; only that terrific personality swept him forward at her own fierce pace and with her own relentless stride. Swept him – where to? Ah! Why had he ever known Miss Nightingale? If Lord Panmure was a bison, Sidney Herbert, no doubt, was a stag – a comely, gallant creature springing through the forest; but the forest is a dangerous place. One has the image of those wide eyes fascinated suddenly by something feline, something strong; there is a pause; and then the tigress has her claws in the quivering haunches; and then——!

Besides Sidney Herbert, she had other friends who, in a more restricted sphere, were hardly less essential to her. If, in her condition of bodily collapse, she were to accomplish what she was determined that she should accomplish, the attentions and the services of others would be absolutely indispensable. Helpers and servers she must have; and accordingly there was soon formed about her a little group of devoted disciples upon whose affections and energies she could implicitly rely. Devoted, indeed, these disciples were, in no ordinary sense of the term; for certainly she was no light taskmistress, and he who set out to be of use to Miss Nightingale was apt to find, before he had gone very far, that he was in truth being made use of in good earnest – to the very limit of his endurance and his capacity. Perhaps, even beyond those limits; why not? Was she asking of others more than she was giving herself? Let them look at her lying there pale and breathless on the couch; could it be said that she spared herself? Why, then, should she spare others? And it was not for her own sake that she made these claims. For her own sake, indeed! No! They all knew it! it was for the sake of the work. And so the little band, bound body and soul in that strange servitude, laboured on ungrudgingly. Among the most faithful was her 'Aunt Mai,' her father's sister,* who from the earliest days had stood beside her, who had helped her to escape from the thraldom of family life, who had been with her at Scutari, and who now acted almost the part of a mother to her, watching over her with infinite care in all the movements and uncertainties which her state of health involved. Another constant attendant was her brother-in-law, Sir Harry Verney,* whom she found particularly valuable in parliamentary affairs. Arthur Clough, the poet, also a connection by marriage, she used in other ways. Ever since he had lost his faith at the time of the Oxford Movement, Clough had passed his life in a condition of considerable uneasiness, which was increased rather than diminished by the practice of poetry. Unable to decide upon the purpose of an existence whose savour had fled together with his belief in the Resurrection, his spirits lowered still further by ill-health, and his income not all that it should be, he had determined to seek the solution of his difficulties in the United States of America. But, even there, the solution was not forthcoming; and when, a little later, he was offered a post in a government department at home, he accepted it, came to live in London, and immediately fell under the influence of Miss

Nightingale. Though the purpose of existence might be still uncertain and its nature still unsavoury, here, at any rate, under the eye of this inspired woman, was something real, something earnest: his only doubt was – could he be of any use? Certainly he could. There were a great number of miscellaneous little jobs which there was nobody handy to do. For instance, when Miss Nightingale was travelling, there were the railway-tickets to be taken; and there were proof-sheets to be corrected; and then there were parcels to be done up in brown paper,* and carried to the post. Certainly he could be useful. And so, upon such occupations as these, Arthur Clough was set to work. 'This that I see, is not all,' he comforted himself by reflecting, 'and this that I do is but little; nevertheless it is good, though there is better than it.'

As time went on, her 'Cabinet,' as she called it, grew larger. Officials with whom her work brought her into touch and who sympathised with her objects, were pressed into her service; and old friends of the Crimean days gathered round her when they returned to England. Among these the most indefatigable was Dr Sutherland, a sanitary expert,* who for more than thirty years acted as her confidential private secretary, and surrendered to her purposes literally the whole of his life. Thus sustained and assisted, thus slaved for and adored, she prepared to beard the Bison.

Two facts soon emerged, and all that followed turned upon them. It became clear, in the first place, that that imposing mass was not immovable, and, in the second, that its movement, when it did move, would be exceeding slow. The Bison was no match for the Lady. It was in vain that he put down his head and planted his feet in the earth; he could not withstand her; the white hand forced him back. But the process was an extraordinarily gradual one. Dr Andrew Smith and all his War Office phalanx stood behind, blocking the way; the poor Bison groaned inwardly, and cast a wistful eye towards the happy pastures of the Free Church of Scotland; then slowly, with infinite reluctance, step by step, he retreated, disputing every inch of the ground.

The first great measure, which, supported as it was by the Queen, the Cabinet, and the united opinion of the country, it was impossible to resist, was the appointment of a Royal Commission to report upon the health of the Army. The question of the composition of the Commission then immediately arose; and it was over this matter that the first hand-to-hand encounter between Lord Panmure and Miss Nightingale took place. They met, and Miss Nightingale was victorious; Sidney Herbert was appointed Chairman; and, in the end, the only member of the Commission opposed to her views was Dr Andrew Smith. During the interview, Miss Nightingale made an important discovery: she found that 'the Bison was bullyable' – the hide was the hide of a Mexican buffalo, but the spirit was the spirit of an Alderney calf. And there was one thing above all others which the huge creature dreaded – an appeal to public opinion. The faintest hint of such a terrible eventuality made his heart dissolve within him; he would agree to anything – he would cut short his grouse-shooting – he would make a speech in the House of Lords – he would even overrule Dr Andrew Smith – rather than that. Miss Nightingale held the fearful threat in reserve – she would speak out what she knew; she would publish the truth to the whole world, and let the whole world judge between them. With supreme skill, she kept this sword of Damocles poised above the Bison's head, and more than once she was actually on the point of really dropping it. For his recalcitrancy grew and grew. The personnel of the Commission once determined upon, there was a struggle, which lasted for six months, over the nature of its powers. Was it to be an efficient body, armed with the right of full inquiry and wide examination, or was it to be a polite official contrivance for exonerating Dr Andrew Smith?* The War Office phalanx closed its ranks, and fought tooth and nail; but it was defeated: the Bison was bullyable. 'Three months from this day,' Miss Nightingale had written at last, 'I publish my experience of the Crimean Campaign, and my suggestions for improvement, unless there has been a fair and tangible pledge by that time for reform.' Who could face that?

And, if the need came, she meant to be as good as her word. For she had now determined, whatever might be the fate of the Commission, to draw up her own report upon the questions at issue. The labour involved was enormous; her health was almost desperate; but she did not flinch, and after six months of incredible industry she had put together and written with her own hand her 'Notes affecting the Health, Efficiency, and Hospital Administration of the British Army.'* This extraordinary composition, filling more than eight hundred closely printed pages, laying down vast principles of far-reaching reform, discussing the minutest details of a multitude

of controversial subjects, containing an enormous mass of information of the most varied kinds – military, statistical, sanitary, archi-
tectural – was never given to the public, for the need never came; but
it formed the basis of the Report of the Royal Commission; and it
remains to this day the leading authority on the medical administration of armies.

Before it had been completed the struggle over the powers of the
Commission had been brought to a victorious close. Lord Panmure
had given way once more; he had immediately hurried to the Queen
to obtain her consent; and only then, when Her Majesty's initials
had been irrevocably affixed to the fatal document, did he dare to tell
Dr Andrew Smith what he had done.* The Commission met, and
another immense load fell upon Miss Nightingale's shoulders. To-
day she would, of course, have been one of the Commission herself;
but at that time the idea of a woman appearing in such a capacity was
unheard of; and no one even suggested the possibility of Miss Nightingale's doing so. The result was that she was obliged to remain
behind the scenes throughout, to coach Sidney Herbert in private at
every important juncture, and to convey to him and to her other
friends upon the Commission the vast funds of her expert knowledge – so essential in the examination of witnesses – by means of
innumerable consultations, letters, and memoranda. It was even
doubtful whether the proprieties would admit of her giving evidence; and at last, as a compromise, her modesty only allowed her to
do so in the form of written answers to written questions. At length
the grand affair was finished. The Commission's Report, embodying
almost word for word the suggestions of Miss Nightingale, was
drawn up by Sidney Herbert. Only one question remained to be
answered – would anything, after all, be done? Or would the Royal
Commission, like so many other Royal Commissions before and
since, turn out to have achieved nothing but the concoction of a very
fat blue-book on a very high shelf?

And so the last and the deadliest struggle with the Bison began.
Six months had been spent in coercing him into granting the Commission effective powers; six more months were occupied by the
work of the Commission; and now yet another six were to pass in
extorting from him the means whereby the recommendations of the
Commission might be actually carried out. But, in the end, the thing
was done. Miss Nightingale seemed, indeed, during these months, to

be upon the very brink of death. Accompanied by the faithful Aunt Mai, she moved from place to place – to Hampstead, to Highgate, to Derbyshire, to Malvern – in what appeared to be a last desperate effort to find health somewhere; but she carried that with her which made health impossible. Her desire for work could now scarcely be distinguished from mania. At one moment she was writing a 'last letter' to Sidney Herbert; at the next she was offering to go out to India to nurse the sufferers in the Mutiny. When Dr Sutherland wrote, imploring her to take a holiday, she raved. Rest! – 'I am lying without my head, without my claws, and you all peck at me. It is *de rigueur, d'obligation*, like the saying something to one's hat, when one goes into church, to say to me all that has been said to me 110 times a day during the last three months. It is the *obbligato* on the violin, and the twelve violins all practise it together, like the clocks striking twelve o'clock at night all over London, till I say like Xavier de Maistre, *Assez, je le sais, je ne le sais que trop*.* I am not a penitent; but you are like the R.C. confessor, who says what is *de rigueur*. . . .' Her wits began to turn, and there was no holding her. She worked like a slave in a mine. She began to believe, as she had begun to believe at Scutari, that none of her fellow-workers had their hearts in the business; if they had, why did they not work as she did? She could only see slackness and stupidity around her. Dr Sutherland, of course, was grotesquely muddle-headed; and Arthur Clough incurably lazy. Even Sidney Herbert . . . oh yes, he had simplicity and candour and quickness of perception, no doubt; but he was an eclectic; and what could one hope for from a man who went away to fish in Ireland just when the Bison most needed bullying? As for the Bison himself he had fled to Scotland, where he remained buried for many months. The fate of the vital recommendation in the Commission's Report – the appointment of four Sub-Commissions charged with the duty of determining upon the details of the proposed reforms and of putting them into execution – still hung in the balance. The Bison consented to everything; and then, on a flying visit to London, withdrew his consent and hastily returned to Scotland. Then for many weeks all business was suspended; he had gout – gout in the hands, so that he could not write. 'His gout was always handy,'* remarked Miss Nightingale. But eventually it was clear even to the Bison that the game was up, and the inevitable surrender came.

There was, however, one point in which he triumphed over Miss

Nightingale. The building of Netley Hospital* had been begun, under his orders, before her return to England. Soon after her arrival she examined the plans, and found that they reproduced all the worst faults of an out-of-date and mischievous system of hospital construction. She therefore urged that the matter should be reconsidered, and in the meantime the building stopped. But the Bison was obdurate; it would be very expensive, and in any case it was too late. Unable to make any impression on him, and convinced of the extreme importance of the question, she determined to appeal to a higher authority. Lord Palmerston was Prime Minister; she had known him from her childhood; he was a near neighbour of her father's in the New Forest. She went down to the New Forest, armed with the plans of the proposed hospital and all the relevant information, stayed the night at Lord Palmerston's house, and convinced him of the necessity of rebuilding Netley. 'It seems to me,' Lord Palmerston wrote to Lord Panmure, 'that at Netley all consideration of what would best tend to the comfort and recovery of the patients has been sacrificed to the vanity of the architect, whose sole object has been to make a building which should cut a dash when looked at from the Southampton river. . . . Pray, therefore, stop all further progress in the work until the matter can be duly considered.'* But the Bison was not to be moved by one peremptory letter, even if it was from the Prime Minister. He put forth all his powers of procrastination, Lord Palmerston lost interest in the subject, and so the chief military hospital in England was triumphantly completed on insanitary principles, with unventilated rooms, and with all the patients' windows facing north-east.

But now the time had come when the Bison was to trouble and to be troubled no more. A vote in the House of Commons brought about the fall of Lord Palmerston's Government, and Lord Panmure found himself at liberty to devote the rest of his life to the Free Church of Scotland. After a brief interval, Sidney Herbert became Secretary of State for War. Great was the jubilation in the Nightingale Cabinet: the day of achievement had dawned at last. The next two and a half years (1859–61) saw the introduction of the whole system of reforms for which Miss Nightingale had been struggling so fiercely – reforms which make Sidney Herbert's tenure of power at the War Office an important epoch in the history of the British Army. The four Sub-Commissions, firmly established under the immediate control of the Minister, and urged forward by the relentless perseverance of Miss Nightingale, set to work with a will. The barracks and the hospitals were remodelled; they were properly ventilated and warmed and lighted for the first time; they were given a water supply which actually supplied water, and kitchens where, strange to say, it was possible to cook. Then the great question of the Purveyor – that portentous functionary whose powers and whose lack of powers had weighed like a nightmare upon Scutari – was taken in hand, and new regulations were laid down, accurately defining his responsibilities and his duties. One Sub-Commission reorganised the medical statistics of the Army. Another established – in spite of the last convulsive efforts of the Department – an Army Medical School.* Finally the Army Medical Department itself was completely reorganised; an administrative code was drawn up; and the great and novel principle was established that it was as much a part of the duty of the authorities to look after the soldier's health as to look after his sickness. Besides this, it was at last officially admitted that he had a moral and intellectual side. Coffee-rooms and reading-rooms, gymnasiums and workshops were instituted. A new era did in truth appear to have begun. Already by 1861 the mortality in the Army had decreased by one half since the days of the Crimea.* It was no wonder that even vaster possibilities began now to open out before Miss Nightingale. One thing was still needed to complete and to assure her triumphs. The Army Medical Department was indeed reorganised; but the great central machine was still untouched. The War Office itself –!* – If she could remould *that* nearer to her heart's desire – there indeed would be a victory! And until that final act was accomplished, how could she be certain that all the rest of her achievements might not, by some capricious turn of Fortune's wheel – a change of Ministry, perhaps, replacing Sidney Herbert by some puppet of the permanent official gang – be swept to limbo in a moment?

Meanwhile, still ravenous for more and yet more work, her activities had branched out into new directions. The Army in India claimed her attention. A Sanitary Commission, appointed at her suggestion, and working under her auspices, did for our troops there what the four Sub-Commissions were doing for those at home. At the same time, these very years which saw her laying the foundations of the whole modern system of medical work in the Army, saw her also beginning to bring her knowledge, her influence, and her activity into the service of the country at large. Her *Notes on Hospitals* (1859) revolutionised the theory of hospital construction and hospital management. She was immediately recognised as the leading expert upon all the questions involved; her advice flowed unceasingly and in all directions, so that there is no great hospital to-day which does not bear upon it the impress of her mind. Nor was this all. With the opening of the Nightingale Training School for Nurses at St Thomas's Hospital* (1860), she became the founder of modern nursing.

But a terrible crisis was now fast approaching. Sidney Herbert had consented to undertake the root and branch reform of the War Office. He had sallied forth into that tropical jungle of festooned obstructiveness, of intertwisted irresponsibilities, of crouching prejudices, of abuses grown stiff and rigid with antiquity, which for so many years to come was destined to lure reforming Ministers to their doom. 'The War Office,' said Miss Nightingale, 'is a very slow office, an enormously expensive office, and one in which the Minister's intentions can be entirely negatived by all his sub-departments, and those of each of the sub-departments by every other.' It was true; and, of course, at the first rumour of a change, the old phalanx of reaction was bristling with its accustomed spears. At its head stood no longer Dr Andrew Smith, who, some time since, had followed the Bison into outer darkness,* but a yet more formidable figure, the Permanent Under-Secretary himself, Sir Benjamin Hawes* – Ben Hawes the Nightingale Cabinet irreverently dubbed him – a man remarkable even among civil servants for adroitness in baffling inconvenient inquiries, resource in raising false issues, and, in short, a consummate command of all the arts of officially sticking in the mud. 'Our scheme will probably result in Ben Hawes's resignation,' Miss Nightingale said; 'and that is another of its advantages.' Ben Hawes himself, however, did not quite see it in that light. He set himself to resist the wishes of the Minister by every means in his power. The struggle was long and desperate; and, as it proceeded, it gradually became evident to Miss Nightingale that something was the matter with Sidney Herbert. What was it? His health, never very strong, was, he said, in danger of collapsing under the strain of his work. But, after all, what is illness, when there is a War Office to be reorganised? Then he began to talk of retiring altogether from public life. The doctors were consulted, and declared that, above all things, what was necessary was rest. Rest! She grew seriously alarmed. Was it possible that, at the last moment, the crowning wreath of victory was to be snatched from her grasp? She was not to be put aside by doctors; they were talking nonsense; the necessary thing was not rest but the reform of the War Office; and, besides, she knew very well from her own case what one could do even when one was on the point of death. She expostulated vehemently, passionately; the goal was so near, so very near; he could not turn back now! At any rate, he could not resist Miss Nightingale. A compromise was arranged. Very reluctantly, he exchanged the turmoil of the House of Commons for the dignity of the House of Lords, and he remained at the War Office. She was delighted. 'One fight more, the best and the last,' she said.

For several more months the fight did indeed go on. But the strain upon him was greater even than she perhaps could realise. Besides the intestine war in his office, he had to face a constant battle in the Cabinet with Mr Gladstone – a more redoubtable antagonist even than Ben Hawes – over the estimates. His health grew worse and worse. He was attacked by fainting-fits; and there were some days when he could only just keep himself going by gulps of brandy.* Miss Nightingale spurred him forward with her encouragements and her admonitions, her zeal and her example. But at last his spirit began to sink as well as his body. He could no longer hope; he could no longer desire; it was useless, all useless; it was utterly impossible. He had failed. The dreadful moment came when the truth was forced upon him: he would never be able to reform the War Office. But a yet more dreadful moment lay behind; he must go to Miss Nightingale and tell her that he was a failure, a beaten man.

'Blessed are the merciful!' What strange ironic prescience had led Prince Albert, in the simplicity of his heart, to choose that motto for the Crimean brooch? The words hold a double lesson; and, alas! when she brought herself to realise at length what was indeed the fact and what there was no helping, it was not in mercy that she turned upon her old friend. 'Beaten!' she exclaimed. 'Can't you see that you've simply thrown away the game? And with all the winning cards in your hands!* And so noble a game! Sidney Herbert beaten!* And beaten by Ben Hawes! It is a worse disgrace . . .' her full rage burst out at last, '. . . a worse disgrace than the hospitals at Scutari.'

He dragged himself away from her, dragged himself to Spa,* hoping vainly for a return to health, and then, despairing, back again to England, to Wilton, to the majestic house standing there resplendent in the summer sunshine, among the great cedars which had lent their shade to Sir Philip Sidney, and all those familiar, darling haunts of beauty which he loved, each one of them, 'as if they were persons'; and at Wilton he died. After having received the Eucharist, he had become perfectly calm; then, almost unconscious, his lips were seen to be moving. Those about him bent down. 'Poor Florence! Poor Florence!' they just caught. '. . . Our joint work . . . unfinished . . . tried to do . . .' and they could hear no more.*

When the onward rush of a powerful spirit sweeps a weaker one to its destruction, the commonplaces of the moral judgment are better left unmade. If Miss Nightingale had been less ruthless, Sidney Herbert would not have perished;* but then, she would not have been Miss Nightingale. The force that created was the force that destroyed. It was her Demon that was responsible. When the fatal news reached her, she was overcome by agony. In the revulsion of her feelings, she made a worship of the dead man's memory; and the facile instrument which had broken in her hand she spoke of for ever after as her 'Master.' Then, almost at the same moment, another blow fell on her. Arthur Clough, worn out by labours very different from those of Sidney Herbert, died too: never more would he tie up her parcels.* And yet a third disaster followed. The faithful Aunt Mai did not, to be sure, die; no, she did something almost worse: she left Miss Nightingale.* She was growing old, and she felt that she had closer and more imperative duties with her own family. Her niece could hardly forgive her. She poured out, in one of her enormous letters,* a passionate diatribe upon the faithlessness, the lack of sympathy, the stupidity, the ineptitude of women. Her doctrines had taken no hold among them; she had never known one who had *appris à apprendre;** she could not even get a woman secretary; 'they don't know the names of the Cabinet Ministers – they don't know which of the Churches has Bishops and which not.' As for the spirit of self-sacrifice, well – Sidney Herbert and Arthur Clough were men, and they indeed had shown their devotion; but women—! She would mount three widow's caps 'for a sign.' The first two would be for Clough and for her Master; but the third – 'the biggest widow's cap of all' – would be for Aunt Mai. She did well to be angry; she was deserted in her hour of need; and, after all, could she be sure that even the male sex was so impeccable? There was Dr Sutherland, bungling as usual. Perhaps even he intended to go off, one of these days, too? She gave him a look, and he shivered in his shoes. No! – she grinned sardonically; she would always have Dr Sutherland. And then she reflected that there was one thing more that she would always have – her work.

IV

SIDNEY HERBERT's death finally put an end to Miss Nightingale's dream of a reformed War Office. For a moment, indeed, in the first agony of her disappointment, she had wildly clutched at a straw; she had written to Mr Gladstone to beg him to take up the burden of Sidney Herbert's work. And Mr Gladstone had replied with a sympathetic account of the funeral.*

Succeeding Secretaries of State managed between them to undo a good deal of what had been accomplished, but they could not undo it all; and for ten years more (1862–72) Miss Nightingale remained a potent influence at the War Office. After that, her direct connection with the Army came to an end, and her energies began to turn more and more completely towards more general objects. Her work upon hospital reform assumed enormous proportions; she was able to improve the conditions in infirmaries and workhouses; and one of her most remarkable papers forestalls the recommendations of the Poor Law Commission of 1909.* Her training school for nurses, with all that it involved in initiative, control, responsibility, and combat, would have been enough in itself to have absorbed the whole efforts of at least two lives of ordinary vigour. And at the same time her work in connection with India, which had begun with the Sanitary Commission on the Indian Army, spread and ramified in a multitude of directions. Her tentacles reached the India Office and succeeded in establishing a hold even upon those slippery high places. For many years it was *de rigueur* for the newly appointed Viceroy, before he left England, to pay a visit to Miss Nightingale.

After much hesitation, she had settled down in a small house in South Street,* where she remained for the rest of her life. That life was a very long one; the dying woman reached her ninety-first year.

Her ill health gradually diminished; the crises of extreme danger became less frequent, and at last altogether ceased; she remained an invalid, but an invalid of a curious character – an invalid who was too weak to walk downstairs and who worked far harder than most Cabinet Ministers. Her illness, whatever it may have been, was certainly not inconvenient. It involved seclusion; and an extraordinary, an unparalleled seclusion was, it might almost have been said, the mainspring of Miss Nightingale's life. Lying on her sofa in the little upper room in South Street, she combined the intense vitality of a dominating woman of the world with the mysterious and romantic quality of a myth. She was a legend in her lifetime, and she knew it. She tasted the joys of power, like those Eastern Emperors whose autocratic rule was based upon invisibility, with the mingled satisfactions of obscurity and fame. And she found the machinery of illness hardly less effective as a barrier against the eyes of men than the ceremonial of a palace. Great statesmen and renowned generals were obliged to beg for audiences; admiring princesses from foreign countries found that they must see her at her own time, or not at all; and the ordinary mortal had no hope of ever getting beyond the downstairs sitting-room and Dr Sutherland. For that indefatigable disciple did, indeed, never desert her. He might be impatient, he might be restless, but he remained. His 'incurable looseness of thought,' for so she termed it, continued at her service to the end. Once, it is true, he had actually ventured to take a holiday; but he was recalled, and he did not repeat the experiment. He was wanted downstairs. There he sat, transacting business, answering correspondence, interviewing callers, and exchanging innumerable notes with the unseen power above. Sometimes word came down that Miss Nightingale was just well enough to see one of her visitors. The fortunate man was led up, was ushered, trembling, into the shaded chamber, and, of course, could never afterwards forget the interview. Very rarely, indeed, once or twice a year, perhaps, but nobody could be quite certain, in deadly secrecy, Miss Nightingale went out for a drive in the Park,* Unrecognised, the living legend flitted for a moment before the common gaze. And the precaution was necessary; for there were times when, at some public function, the rumour of her presence was spread abroad; and ladies, mistaken by the crowd for Miss Nightingale, were followed, pressed upon, and vehemently supplicated – 'Let me touch your shawl'; 'Let me stroke your arm'; such was the strange adoration in the hearts of the people. That vast reserve of force lay there behind her; she could use it, if she would. But she preferred never to use it. On occasions, she might hint or threaten; she might balance the sword of Damocles over the head of the Bison; she might, by a word, by a glance, remind some refractory Minister, some unpersuadable Viceroy, sitting in audience with her in the little upper room, that she was something more than a mere sick woman, that she had only, so to speak, to go to the window and wave her handkerchief, for . . . dreadful things to follow. But that was enough; they understood; the myth was there – obvious, portentous, impalpable; and so it remained to the last.

With statesmen and governors at her beck and call, with her hands on a hundred strings, with mighty provinces at her feet, with foreign governments agog for her counsel, building hospitals, training nurses – she still felt that she had not enough to do. She sighed for more worlds to conquer – more, and yet more. She looked about her – what was there left? Of course! Philosophy! After the world of action, the world of thought. Having set right the health of the British Army, she would now do the same good service for the religious convictions of mankind. She had long noticed – with regret – the growing tendency towards free-thinking among artisans. With regret, but not altogether with surprise: the current teaching of Christianity was sadly to seek; nay, Christianity itself was not without its defects. She would rectify these errors. She would correct the mistakes of the Churches; she would point out just where Christianity was wrong; and she would explain to the artisans what the facts of the case really were. Before her departure for the Crimea, she had begun this work; and now, in the intervals of her other labours, she completed it. Her 'Suggestions for Thought to the Searchers after Truth among the Artisans of England' (1860), unravels, in the course of three portly volumes, the difficulties – hitherto, curiously enough, unsolved – connected with such matters as Belief in God, the Plan of Creation, the Origin of Evil, the Future Life. Necessity and Free Will, Law, and the Nature of Morality. The Origin of Evil, in particular, held no perplexities for Miss Nightingale. 'We cannot conceive,' she remarks, 'that Omnipotent Righteousness would find satisfaction in *solitary existence*.' This being so, the only question remaining to be asked is, 'What beings should we then conceive that God would create?' Now, He cannot create perfect beings, 'since, essentially, perfection is one'; if He did so, He would only be adding to Himself. Thus the conclusion is obvious: He *must* create *im*perfect ones. Omnipotent Righteousness, faced by the intolerable *impasse* of a solitary existence, finds itself bound, by the very nature of the case, to create the hospitals at Scutari. Whether this argument would have satisfied the artisans, was never discovered, for only a very few copies of the book were printed for private circulation. One copy was sent to Mr Mill, who acknowledged it in an extremely polite letter. He felt himself obliged, however, to confess that he had not been altogether convinced by Miss Nightingale's proof of the existence of God. Miss Nightingale was surprised and mortified; she had thought better of Mr Mill; for surely her proof of the existence of God could hardly be improved upon. 'A law,' she had pointed out, 'implies a lawgiver.' Now the Universe is full of laws – the law of gravitation, the law of the excluded middle, and many others; hence it follows that the Universe has a lawgiver – and what would Mr Mill be satisfied with, if he was not satisfied with that?

Perhaps Mr Mill might have asked why the argument had not been pushed to its logical conclusion. Clearly, if we are to trust the analogy of human institutions, we must remember that laws are, as a matter of fact, not dispensed by lawgivers, but passed by Act of Parliament. Miss Nightingale, however, with all her experience of public life, never stopped to consider the question whether God might not be a Limited Monarchy.

Yet her conception of God was certainly not orthodox. She felt towards Him as she might have felt towards a glorified sanitary engineer; and in some of her speculations she seems hardly to distinguish between the Deity and the Drains. As one turns over these singular pages, one has the impression that Miss Nightingale has got the Almighty too into her clutches, and that, if He is not careful, she will kill Him with overwork.

Then, suddenly, in the very midst of the ramifying generalities of her metaphysical disquisitions there is an unexpected turn, and the reader is plunged all at once into something particular, something personal, something impregnated with intense experience – a virulent invective upon the position of women in the upper ranks of society. Forgetful alike of her high argument and of the artisans, the bitter creature rails through a hundred pages of close print at the falsities of family life, the ineptitudes of marriage, the emptinesses of convention, in the spirit of an Ibsen or a Samuel Butler. Her fierce pen, shaking with intimate anger, depicts in biting sentences the fearful fate of an unmarried girl in a wealthy household. It is a *cri du cœur;* and then, as suddenly, she returns once more to instruct the artisans upon the nature of Omnipotent Righteousness.

Her mind was, indeed, better qualified to dissect the concrete and distasteful fruits of actual life than to construct a coherent system of abstract philosophy. In spite of her respect for Law, she was never at home with a generalisation. Thus, though the great achievement of her life lay in the immense impetus which she gave to the scientific treatment of sickness, a true comprehension of the scientific method itself was alien to her spirit. Like most great men of action – perhaps like all – she was simply an empiricist. She believed in what she saw, and she acted accordingly; beyond that she would not go. She had found in Scutari that fresh air and light played an effective part in the prevention of the maladies with which she had to deal; and that was enough for her; she would not inquire further; what were the general principles underlying that fact – or even whether there were any – she refused to consider. Years after the discoveries of Pasteur and Lister, she laughed at what she called the 'germ-fetish.'* There was no such thing as 'infection'; she had never seen it, therefore it did not exist. But she *had* seen the good effects of fresh air; therefore there could be no doubt about them; and therefore it was essential that the bedrooms of patients should be well ventilated. Such was her doctrine; and in those days of hermetically sealed windows it was a very valuable one. But it was a purely empirical doctrine, and thus it led to some unfortunate results. When, for instance, her influence in India was at its height, she issued orders that all hospital windows should be invariably kept open.* The authorities, who knew what an open window in the hot weather meant, protested, but in vain; Miss Nightingale was incredulous. She knew nothing of the hot weather, but she did know the value of fresh air – from personal experience; the authorities were talking nonsense; and the windows must be kept open all the year round. There was a great outcry from all the doctors in India, but she was firm; and for a moment it seemed possible that her terrible commands would have to be put into execution. Lord Lawrence, however, was Viceroy,* and he was able to intimate to Miss Nightingale, with sufficient authority, that he himself had decided upon the question, and that his decision must stand, even against her own. Upon that, she gave way, but reluctantly and quite unconvinced; she was only puzzled by the unexpected weakness of Lord Lawrence. No doubt, if she had lived to-day, and if her experience had lain, not among cholera cases at Scutari, but among yellow-fever cases in Panama,* she would have declared fresh air a fetish, and would have maintained to her dying day that the only really effective way of dealing with disease was by the destruction of mosquitoes.

Yet her mind, so positive, so realistic, so ultra-practical, had its singular revulsions, its mysterious moods of mysticism and of doubt. At times, lying sleepless in the early hours, she fell into long, strange, agonised meditations, and then, seizing a pencil, she would commit to paper the confessions of her soul. The morbid longings of her pre-Crimean days came over her once more; she filled page after page with self-examination, self-criticism, self-surrender. 'O Father,' she wrote, 'I submit, I resign myself, I accept with all my heart this stretching out of Thy hand to save me. . . . O how vain it is, the vanity of vanities, to live in men's thoughts instead of God's!' She was lonely, she was miserable. 'Thou knowest that through all these horrible twenty years, I have been supported by the belief that I was working with Thee who wert bringing every one, even our poor nurses, to perfection' – and yet, after all, what was the result? Had not even she been an unprofitable servant? One night, waking suddenly, she saw, in the dim light of the night-lamp, tenebrous shapes upon the wall. The past rushed back upon her. 'Am I she who once stood on that Crimean height?' she wildly asked – ' "The Lady with a lamp shall stand. . . ." The lamp shows me only my utter shipwreck.'*

She sought consolation in the writings of the Mystics and in a correspondence with Mr Jowett.* For many years the Master of Balliol acted as her spiritual adviser. He discussed with her in a series of enormous letters the problems of religion and philosophy; he criticised her writings on those subjects with the tactful sympathy of a cleric who was also a man of the world; and he even ventured to attempt at times to instil into her rebellious nature some of his own peculiar suavity. 'I sometimes think,' he told her, 'that you ought seriously to consider how your work may be carried on, not with less energy, but in a calmer spirit. I am not blaming the past. . . . But I want the peace of God to settle on the future.' He recommended her to spend her time no longer in 'conflicts with Government offices,' and to take up some literary work. He urged her to 'work out her notion of Divine Perfection,' in a series of essays for *Frazer's Magazine*.* She did so; and the result was submitted to Mr Froude, who pronounced the second essay to be 'even more pregnant than the first. I cannot tell,' he said, 'how sanitary, with disordered intellects, the effects of such papers will be.' Mr Carlyle, indeed, used different language, and some remarks of his about a lost lamb bleating on the mountains having been unfortunately repeated to Miss Nightingale, all Mr Jowett's suavity was required to keep the peace. In a letter of fourteen sheets, he turned her attention from this painful topic towards a discussion of Quietism. 'I don't see why,' said the Master of Balliol, 'active life might not become a sort of passive life too.' And then, he added, 'I sometimes fancy there are possibilities of human character much greater than have been realised.' She found such sentiments helpful, underlining them in blue pencil; and, in return, she assisted her friend with a long series of elaborate comments upon the Dialogues of Plato,* most of which he embodied in the second edition of his translation. Gradually her interest became more personal; she told him never to work again after midnight, and he obeyed her. Then she helped him to draw up a special form of daily service for the College Chapel, with selections from the Psalms under the heads of 'God the Lord, God the Judge, God the Father, and God the Friend' – though, indeed, this project was never realised; for the Bishop of Oxford disallowed the alterations, exercising his legal powers, on the advice of Sir Travers Twiss.*

Their relations became intimate. 'The spirit of the Twenty-third Psalm and the spirit of the Nineteenth Psalm should be united in our lives,' Mr Jowett said. Eventually, she asked him to do her a singular favour. Would he, knowing what he did of her religious views, come to London and administer to her the Holy Sacrament?* He did not hesitate, and afterwards declared that he would always regard the occasion as a solemn event in his life. He was devoted to her; though the precise nature of his feelings towards her never quite transpired. Her feelings towards him were more mixed. At first, he was 'that great and good man' – 'that true saint, Mr Jowett'; but, as time went on, some gall was mingled with the balm; the acrimony of her nature asserted itself. She felt that she gave more sympathy than she received; she was exhausted, she was annoyed, by his conversation. Her tongue, one day, could not refrain from shooting out at him. 'He comes to me, and he talks to me,' she said, 'as if I were some one else.'

V

AT one time she had almost decided to end her life in retirement, as a patient at St Thomas's Hospital.* But partly owing to the persuasions of Mr Jowett, she changed her mind; for forty-five years she remained in South Street; and in South Street she died. As old age approached, though her influence with the official world gradually diminished, her activities seemed to remain as intense and widespread as before. When hospitals were to be built, when schemes of sanitary reform were in agitation, when wars broke out, she was still the adviser of all Europe. Still, with a characteristic self-assurance, she watched from her Mayfair bedroom over the welfare of India. Still, with an indefatigable enthusiasm, she pushed forward the work, which, perhaps, was nearer to her heart, more completely her own, than all the rest – the training of nurses. In her moments of deepest depression, when her greatest achievements seemed to lose their lustre, she thought of her nurses, and was comforted. The ways of God, she found, were strange indeed. 'How inefficient I was in the Crimea,' she noted. 'Yet He has raised up from it trained nursing.'

At other times she was better satisfied. Looking back, she was amazed by the enormous change which, since her early days, had come over the whole treatment of illness, the whole conception of public and domestic health – a change in which, she knew, she had played her part. One of her Indian admirers, the Aga Khan, came to visit her. She expatiated on the marvellous advances she had lived to see in the management of hospitals, in drainage, in ventilation, in sanitary work of every kind. There was a pause; and then, 'Do you think you are improving?'* asked the Aga Khan. She was a little taken aback, and said, 'What do you mean by "improving"?' He replied, 'Believing more in God.' She saw that he had a view of God which was different from hers. 'A most interesting man,' she noted after the interview; 'but you could never teach him sanitation.'

When old age actually came, something curious happened. Destiny, having waited very patiently, played a queer trick on Miss Nightingale. The benevolence and public spirit of that long life had only been equalled by its acerbity. Her virtue had dwelt in hardness, and she had poured forth her unstinted usefulness with a bitter smile upon her lips. And now the sarcastic years brought the proud woman her punishment. She was not to die as she had lived. The sting was to be taken out of her: she was to be made soft; she was to be reduced to compliance and complacency. The change came gradually, but at last it was unmistakable. The terrible commander who had driven Sidney Herbert to his death, to whom Mr Jowett had applied the words of Homer, ἄμοτον μεμανῖα – raging insatiably – now accepted small compliments with gratitude, and indulged in sentimental friendships with young girls. The author of *Notes on Nursing** – that classical compendium of the besetting sins of the sisterhood, drawn up with the detailed acrimony, the vindictive relish, of a Swift – now spent long hours in composing sympathetic Addresses to Probationers, whom she petted and wept over in turn. And, at the same time, there appeared a corresponding alteration in her physical mould. The thin, angular woman, with her haughty eye and her acrid mouth, had vanished; and in her place was the rounded, bulky form of a fat old lady,* smiling all day long. Then something else became visible. The brain which had been steeled at Scutari was indeed, literally, growing soft. Senility – an ever more and more amiable senility – descended. Towards the end, consciousness itself grew lost in a roseate haze, and melted into nothingness. It was just then, three years before her death, when she was eighty-seven years old (1907), that those in authority bethought them that the opportune moment had come for bestowing a public honour on Florence Nightingale. She was offered the Order of Merit. That Order, whose roll contains, among other distinguished names, those of Sir Lawrence Alma Tadema and Sir Edward Elgar,* is remarkable chiefly for the fact that, as its title indicates, it is bestowed because its recipient deserves it, and for no other reason. Miss Nightingale's representatives accepted the honour, and her name, after a lapse of many years, once more appeared in the Press. Congratulations from all sides came pouring in. There was a universal burst of enthusiasm – a final revivification of the ancient myth. Among her other admirers, the German Emperor took this opportunity of expressing his feelings towards her. 'His Majesty,' wrote the German Ambassador, 'having just brought to a close a most enjoyable stay in the beautiful neighbourhood of your old home near Romsey, has commanded me to present you with some flowers as a token of his esteem.' Then, by Royal command, the Order of Merit was brought to South Street, and there was a little ceremony of presentation. Sir Douglas Dawson, after a short speech, stepped forward, and handed the insignia of the Order to Miss Nightingale. Propped up by pillows, she dimly recognised that some compliment was being paid her. 'Too kind – too kind,' she murmured; and she was not ironical.*

BIBLIOGRAPHY

Sir E. Cook. *Life of Florence Nightingale.*
A. W. Kinglake. *The Invasion of the Crimea.*
Lord Sidney Godolphin Osborne. *Scutari and its Hospitals.*
S. M. Mitra. *Life of Sir John Hall.*
Lord Stanmore. *Sidney Herbert.*
Sir G. Douglas. *The Panmure Papers.*
Sir H. Maxwell. *Life and Letters of the Fourth Earl of Clarendon.*
E. Abbott and L. Campbell. *Life and Letters of Benjamin Jowett.*
A. H. Clough. *Poems and Memoir.*

DR ARNOLD

DR ARNOLD

In 1827 the headmastership of Rugby School fell vacant, and it became necessary for the twelve trustees, noblemen and gentlemen of Warwickshire,* to appoint a successor to the post. Reform was in the air – political, social, religious; there was even a feeling abroad that our great public schools were not quite all that they should be, and that some change or other – no one precisely knew what – but *some* change in the system of their management, was highly desirable. Thus it was natural that when the twelve noblemen and gentlemen, who had determined to be guided entirely by the merits of the candidates, found among the testimonials pouring in upon them a letter from Dr Hawkins, the Provost of Oriel, predicting that if they elected Mr Thomas Arnold he would 'change the face of education all through the public schools of England,'* they hesitated no longer: obviously, Mr Thomas Arnold was their man. He was elected therefore; received, as was fitting, priest's orders; became, as was no less fitting, a Doctor of Divinity; and in August, 1828, took up the duties of his office.

All that was known of the previous life of Dr Arnold seemed to justify the prediction of the Provost of Oriel, and the choice of the Trustees. The son of a respectable Collector of Customs, he had been educated at Winchester and at Oxford, where his industry and piety had given him a conspicuous place among his fellow-students. It is true that, as a schoolboy, a certain pompousness in the style of his letters home suggested to the more clear-sighted among his relatives the possibility that young Thomas might grow up into a prig; but, after all, what else could be expected from a child who, at the age of three, had been presented by his father, as a reward for proficiency in his studies, with the twenty-four volumes of Smollett's *History of England*?* His career at Oxford had been a distinguished one, winding up with an Oriel fellowship. It was at about this time that the smooth and satisfactory progress of his life was for a moment interrupted: he began to be troubled by religious doubts. These doubts, as we learn from one of his contemporaries, who afterwards became Mr Justice Coleridge, 'were not low nor rationalistic in their tendency, according to the bad sense of that term; there was no indisposition in him to believe merely because the article transcended his reason; he doubted the proof and the interpretation of the textual authority.'* In his perturbation, Arnold consulted Keble, who was at that time one of his closest friends, and a Fellow of the same College. 'The subject of these distressing thoughts,' Keble wrote to Coleridge,* 'is that most awful one, on which all *very* inquisitive reasoning minds are, I believe, most liable to such temptations – I mean, the doctrine of the blessed Trinity. Do not start, my dear Coleridge; I do not believe that Arnold has any serious scruples of the *understanding* about it, but it is a defect of his mind that he cannot get rid of a certain feeling of objections.' What was to be done? Keble's advice was peremptory. Arnold was 'bid to pause in his inquiries, to pray earnestly for help and light from above, and turn himself more strongly than ever to the practical duties of a holy life.' He did so, and the result was all that could be wished. He soon found himself blessed with perfect peace of mind, and a settled conviction.

One other difficulty, and one only, we hear of, at this period of his life. His dislike of early rising amounted, we are told, 'almost to a constitutional infirmity.'* This weakness too he overcame, yet not quite so successfully as his doubts upon the doctrine of the Trinity. For in afterlife the Doctor would often declare 'that early rising continued to be a daily effort to him, and that in this instance he never found the truth of the usual rule, that all things are made easy by custom.'

He married young,* and settled down in the country as a private tutor for youths preparing for the Universities. There he remained for ten years – happy, busy, and sufficiently prosperous. Occupied chiefly with his pupils, he nevertheless devoted much of his energy to wider interests. He delivered a series of sermons in the parish church; and he began to write a History of Rome,* in the hope, as he said, that its tone might be such 'that the strictest of what is called the Evangelical party would not object to putting it into the hands of their children.' His views on the religious and political condition of the country began to crystallise. He was alarmed by the 'want of Christian principle in the literature of the day,' looking forward anxiously to 'the approach of a greater struggle between good and evil than the world has yet seen'; and, after a serious conversation with Dr Whately,* began to conceive the necessity of considerable alterations in the Church Establishment. All who knew him during these years were profoundly impressed by the earnestness of his religious convictions and feelings, which, as one observer said, 'were ever bursting forth.' It was impossible to disregard his 'deep consciousness of the invisible world' and 'the peculiar feeling of love and adoration which he entertained towards our Lord Jesus Christ.' 'His manner of awful reverence when speaking of God or of the Scriptures' was particularly striking. 'No one could know him even a little,' said another friend, 'and not be struck by his absolute wrestling with evil, so that like St Paul he seemed to be battling with the wicked one, and yet with a feeling of God's help on his side.'*

Such was the man who, at the age of thirty-three, became headmaster of Rugby. His outward appearance was the index of his inward character; everything about him denoted energy, earnestness, and the best intentions. His legs, perhaps, were shorter than they should have been;* but the sturdy athletic frame, especially when it was swathed (as it usually was) in the flowing robes of a Doctor of Divinity,* was full of an imposing vigour; and his head, set decisively upon the collar, stock, and bands of ecclesiastical tradition, clearly belonged to a person of eminence. The thick, dark clusters of his hair, his bushy eyebrows and curling whiskers, his straight nose and bulky chin, his firm and upward-curving lower lip – all these revealed a temperament of ardour and determination. His eyes were bright and large; they were also obviously honest. And yet – why was it? Was it in the lines of the mouth or the frown on the forehead? – it was hard to say, but it was unmistakable – there was a slightly puzzled look* upon the face of Dr Arnold.

And certainly, if he was to fulfil the prophecy of the Provost of Oriel, the task before him was sufficiently perplexing. The public schools of those days were still virgin forests, untouched by the hand of reform. Keate was still reigning at Eton;* and we possess, in the records of his pupils, a picture of the public-school education of the early nineteenth century, in its most characteristic state. It was a system of anarchy tempered by despotism. Hundreds of boys, herded together in miscellaneous boarding-houses, or in that grim 'Long Chamber' at whose name in after years aged statesmen and warriors would turn pale, lived, badgered and overawed by the furious incursions of an irascible little old man carrying a bundle of birch-twigs, a life in which licensed barbarism was mingled with the daily and hourly study of the niceties of Ovidian verse. It was a life of freedom and terror, of prosody and rebellion, of interminable floggings and appalling practical jokes. Keate ruled, unaided – for the under-masters were few and of no account – by sheer force of character. But there were times when even that indomitable will was overwhelmed by the flood of lawlessness. Every Sunday afternoon he attempted to read sermons to the whole school assembled; and every Sunday afternoon the whole school assembled shouted him down. The scenes in Chapel were far from edifying: while some antique Fellow doddered in the pulpit, rats would be let loose to scurry among the legs of the exploding boys. But next morning the hand of discipline would reassert itself; and the savage ritual of the whipping-block would remind a batch of whimpering children that, though sins against man and God might be forgiven them, a false quantity could only be expiated in tears and blood.

From two sides, this system of education was beginning to be assailed by the awakening public opinion of the upper middle classes. On the one hand, there was a desire for a more liberal curriculum; on the other, there was a demand for a higher moral tone. The growing utilitarianism of the age viewed with impatience a course of instruction which excluded every branch of knowledge except classical philology; while its growing respectability was shocked by such a spectacle of disorder and brutality as was afforded by the Eton of Keate. 'The public schools,' said the Rev. Mr Bowdler, 'are the very seats and nurseries of vice.'*

Dr Arnold agreed. He was convinced of the necessity for reform. But it was only natural that to one of his temperament and education it should have been the moral rather than the intellectual side of the question which impressed itself upon his mind. Doubtless it was important to teach boys something more than the bleak rigidities of the ancient tongues; but how much more important to instil into them the elements of character and the principles of conduct! His great object, throughout his career at Rugby, was, as he repeatedly said, to 'make the school a place of really Christian education.'* To introduce 'a religious principle into education,' was his 'most earnest wish,' he wrote to a friend when he first became headmaster; 'but to do this would be to succeed beyond all my hopes; it would be a happiness so great, that, I think, the world would yield me nothing comparable to it.' And he was constantly impressing these sentiments upon his pupils. 'What I have often said before,' he told them, 'I repeat now: what we must look for here is, first, religious and moral principle; secondly, gentlemanly conduct; thirdly, intellectual ability.'*

There can be no doubt that Dr Arnold's point of view was shared by the great mass of English parents. They cared very little for classical scholarship; no doubt they would be pleased to find that their sons were being instructed in history or in French; but their real hopes, their real wishes, were of a very different kind. 'Shall I tell him to mind his work, and say he's sent to school to make himself a good scholar?' meditated old Squire Brown when he was sending off Tom for the first time to Rugby. 'Well, but he isn't sent to school for that – at any rate, not for that mainly. I don't care a straw for Greek particles, or the digamma; no more does his mother. What is he sent to school for? . . . If he'll only turn out a brave, helpful, truth-telling Englishman, and a Christian, that's all I want.'*

That was all; and it was that that Dr Arnold set himself to accomplish. But how was he to achieve his end? Was he to improve the character of his pupils by gradually spreading round them an atmosphere of cultivation and intelligence? By bringing them into close and friendly contact with civilised men, and even, perhaps, with civilised women? By introducing into the life of his school all that he could of the humane, enlightened, and progressive elements in the life of the community? On the whole, he thought not. Such considerations left him cold, and he preferred to be guided by the general laws of Providence. It only remained to discover what those general laws were. He consulted the Old Testament, and could doubt no longer. He would apply to his scholars, as he himself explained to them in one of his sermons, 'the principle which seemed to him to have been adopted in the training of the childhood of the human race itself.' He would treat the boys at Rugby as Jehovah had treated the Chosen People: he would found a theocracy; and there should be Judges in Israel.

For this purpose, the system, prevalent in most of the public schools of the day, by which the elder boys were deputed to keep order in the class-rooms, lay ready to Dr Arnold's hand. He found the 'Præpostor' a mere disciplinary convenience, and he converted him into an organ of government. Every boy in the Sixth Form became *ipso facto* a Præpostor, with powers extending over every department of school life; and the Sixth Form as a body was erected into an authority responsible to the headmaster, and to the headmaster alone, for the internal management of the school.

This was the means by which Dr Arnold hoped to turn Rugby into 'a place of really Christian education.' The boys were to work out their own salvation, like the human race. He himself, involved in awful grandeur, ruled remotely, through his chosen instruments, from an inaccessible heaven. Remotely – and yet with an omnipresent force. As the Israelite of old knew that his almighty Lawgiver might at any moment thunder to him from the whirlwind, or appear before his very eyes, the visible embodiment of power or wrath, so the Rugby schoolboy walked in a holy dread of some sudden manifestation of the sweeping gown, the majestic tone, the piercing glance, of Dr Arnold. Among the lower forms of the school his appearances were rare and transitory, and upon these young children 'the chief impression,' we are told, 'was of extreme fear.' The older boys saw more of him, but they did not see much. Outside the Sixth Form, no part of the school came into close intercourse with him;* and it would often happen that a boy would leave Rugby without having had any personal communication with him at all. Yet the effect which he produced upon the great mass of his pupils was remarkable. The prestige of his presence and the elevation of his sentiments were things which it was impossible to forget. In class, every line of his countenance, every shade of his manner imprinted themselves indelibly on the minds of the boys who sat under him. One of these, writing long afterwards, has described, in phrases still impregnated with awestruck reverence, the familiar details of the scene: 'the glance with which he looked round in the few moments of silence before the lesson began, and which seemed to speak his sense of his own position' – 'the attitude in which he stood, turning over the pages of Facciolati's Lexicon, or Pole's synopsis,* with his eye fixed upon the boy who was pausing to give an answer' – 'the pleased look and the cheerful "thank you," which followed upon a successful translation' – 'the fall of his countenance with its deepening severity, the stern elevation of the eyebrows, the sudden "sit down" which followed upon the reverse' – 'the startling earnestness with which he would check in a moment the slightest approach to levity.'

To be rebuked, however mildly, by Dr Arnold was a notable experience. One boy could never forget how he drew a distinction between 'mere amusement' and 'such as encroached on the next day's duties,' nor the tone of voice with which the Doctor added 'and then it immediately becomes what St Paul calls *revelling*.' Another remembered to his dying day his reproof of some boys who had behaved badly during prayers. 'Nowhere,' said Dr Arnold, 'nowhere is Satan's work more evidently manifest than in turning holy things to ridicule.' On such occasions, as another of his pupils described it, it was impossible to avoid 'a consciousness almost amounting to solemnity' that, 'when his eye was upon you, he looked into your inmost heart.'

With the boys in the Sixth Form, and with them alone, the severe formality of his demeanour was to some degree relaxed. It was his wish, in his relations with the Præpostors, to allow the Master to be occasionally merged in the Friend. From time to time, he chatted with them in a familiar manner; once a term he asked them to dinner; and during the summer holidays he invited them, in rotation, to stay with him in Westmorland.

It was obvious that the primitive methods of discipline which had reached their apogee under the dominion of Keate were altogether incompatible with Dr Arnold's view of the functions of a headmaster and the proper governance of a public school. Clearly, it was not for such as he to demean himself by bellowing and cuffing, by losing his temper once an hour, and by wreaking his vengeance with indiscriminate flagellations. Order must be kept in other ways. The worst boys were publicly expelled; many were silently removed; and, when Dr Arnold considered that a flogging was necessary, he administered it with gravity. For he had no theoretical objection to corporal punishment.* On the contrary, he supported it, as was his wont, by an appeal to general principles. 'There is,' he said, 'an essential inferiority in a boy as compared with a man'; and hence 'where there is no equality the exercise of superiority implied in personal chastisement' inevitably followed. He was particularly disgusted by the view that 'personal correction,' as he phrased it, was an insult or a degradation to the boy upon whom it was inflicted; and to accustom young boys to think so appeared to him to be 'positively mischievous.' 'At an age,' he wrote, 'when it is almost impossible to find a true, manly sense of the degradation of guilt or faults, where is the wisdom of encouraging a fantastic sense of the degradation of personal correction? What can be more false, or more adverse to the simplicity, sobriety, and humbleness of mind which are the best ornaments of youth, and offer the best promise of a noble manhood?' One had not to look far, he added, for 'the fruits of such a system.' In Paris, during the Revolution of 1830, an officer observed a boy of twelve insulting the soldiers, and 'though the action was then raging, merely struck him with the flat part of his sword, as the fit chastisement for boyish impertinence. But the boy had been taught to consider his person sacred, and that a blow was a deadly insult; he therefore followed the officer, and having watched his opportunity, took deliberate aim at him with a pistol and murdered him.' Such were the alarming results of insufficient whipping.

Dr Arnold did not apply this doctrine to the Præpostors; but the boys in the lower parts of the school felt its benefits with a double force. The Sixth Form was not only excused from chastisement; it was given the right to chastise. The younger children, scourged both by Dr Arnold and by the elder children, were given every opportunity of acquiring the simplicity, sobriety, and humbleness of mind, which are the best ornaments of youth.

In the actual sphere of teaching, Dr Arnold's reforms were tentative and few. He introduced modern history, modern languages, and mathematics into the school curriculum; but the results were not encouraging. He devoted to the teaching of history one hour a week; yet, though he took care to inculcate in these lessons a wholesome hatred of moral evil, and to point out from time to time the indications of the providential government of the world, his pupils never seemed to make much progress in the subject. Could it have been that the time allotted to it was insufficient? Dr Arnold had some suspicions that this might be the case. With modern languages there was the same difficulty. Here his hopes were certainly not excessive. 'I assume it,' he wrote, 'as the foundation of all my view of the case, that boys at a public school never will learn to speak or pronounce French well, under any circumstances.'* It would be enough if they could 'learn it grammatically as a dead language.' But even this they very seldom managed to do. 'I know too well,' he was obliged to confess, 'that most of the boys would pass a very poor examination even in French grammar. But so it is with their mathematics; and so it will be with any branch of knowledge that is taught but seldom, and is felt to be quite subordinate to the boys' main study.'

The boys' main study remained the dead languages of Greece and

Rome. That the classics should form the basis of all teaching was an axiom with Dr Arnold. 'The study of language,' he said, 'seems to me as if it was given for the very purpose of forming the human mind in youth; and the Greek and Latin languages seem the very instruments by which this is to be effected.'* Certainly, there was something providential about it – from the point of view of the teacher as well as of the taught. If Greek and Latin had not been 'given' in that convenient manner, Dr Arnold, who had spent his life in acquiring those languages, might have discovered that he had acquired them in vain. As it was, he could set the noses of his pupils to the grindstone of syntax and prosody with a clear conscience. Latin verses and Greek prepositions divided between them the labours of the week. As time went on, he became, he declared, 'increasingly convinced that it is not knowledge, but the means of gaining knowledge which I have to teach.' The reading of the school was devoted almost entirely to selected passages from the prose writers of antiquity. 'Boys,' he remarked, 'do not like poetry.' Perhaps his own poetical taste was a little dubious; at any rate, it is certain that he considered the Greek Tragedians greatly overrated,* and that he ranked Propertius as 'an indifferent poet.' As for Aristophanes, owing to his strong moral disapprobation, he could not bring himself to read him until he was forty, when, it is true, he was much struck by the 'Clouds.' But Juvenal the Doctor could never bring himself to read at all.

Physical science was not taught at Rugby. Since, in Dr Arnold's opinion, it was 'too great a subject to be studied ἐν παρέργῳ,'* obviously only two alternatives were possible: it must either take the chief place in the school curriculum, or it must be left out altogether. Before such a choice, Dr Arnold did not hesitate for a moment. 'Rather than have physical science the principal thing in my son's mind,' he exclaimed in a letter to a friend, 'I would gladly have him think that the sun went round the earth, and that the stars were so many spangles set in the bright blue firmament.* Surely the one thing needful for a Christian and an Englishman to study is Christian and moral and political philosophy.'

A Christian and an Englishman! After all, it was not in the class-room, nor in the boarding-house, that the essential elements of instruction could be imparted which should qualify the youthful neophyte to deserve those names. The final, the fundamental lesson could only be taught in the school chapel;* in the school chapel the centre of Dr Arnold's system of education was inevitably fixed. There, too, the Doctor himself appeared in the plenitude of his dignity and his enthusiasm. There, with the morning sun shining on the freshly scrubbed faces of his three hundred pupils, or, in the dusk of evening, through a glimmer of candles, his stately form, rapt in devotion or vibrant with exhortation, would dominate the scene.* Every phase of the Church service seemed to receive its supreme expression in his voice, his attitude, his look. During the Te Deum, his whole countenance would light up; and he read the Psalms with such conviction that boys would often declare, after hearing him, that they understood them now for the first time. It was his opinion that the creeds in public worship ought to be used as triumphant hymns of thanksgiving, and, in accordance with this view, although unfortunately he possessed no natural gift for music, he regularly joined in the chanting of the Nicene Creed* with a visible animation and a peculiar fervour, which it was impossible to forget. The Communion service he regarded as a direct and special counterpoise to that false communion and false companionship, which, as he often observed, was a great source of mischief in the school; and he bent himself down with glistening eyes, and trembling voice, and looks of paternal solicitude, in the administration of the elements. Nor was it only the different sections of the liturgy, but the very divisions of the ecclesiastical year that reflected themselves in his demeanour; the most careless observer, we are told, 'could not fail to be struck by the triumphant exultation of his whole manner on Easter Sunday'; though it needed a more familiar eye to discern the subtleties in his bearing which were produced by the approach of Advent, and the solemn thoughts which it awakened of the advance of human life, the progress of the human race, and the condition of the Church of England.

At the end of the evening service the culminating moment of the week had come: the Doctor delivered his sermon. It was not until then, as all who had known him agreed, it was not until one had heard and seen him in the pulpit, that one could fully realise what it was to be face to face with Dr Arnold. The whole character of the man – so we are assured – stood at last revealed. His congregation sat in fixed attention (with the exception of the younger boys, whose thoughts occasionally wandered), while he propounded the general principles both of his own conduct and that of the Almighty, or indicated the bearing of the incidents of Jewish history in the sixth century B.C. upon the conduct of English schoolboys in 1830. Then, more than ever, his deep consciousness of the invisible world became evident; then, more than ever, he seemed to be battling with the wicked one. For his sermons ran on the eternal themes of the darkness of evil, the craft of the tempter, the punishment of obliquity, and he justified the persistence with which he dwelt upon these painful subjects by an appeal to a general principle: 'The spirit of Elijah,' he said, 'must ever precede the spirit of Christ.'* The impression produced upon the boys was remarkable. It was noticed that even the most careless would sometimes, during the course of the week, refer almost involuntarily to the sermon of the past Sunday, as a condemnation of what they were doing. Others were heard to wonder how it was that the Doctor's preaching, to which they had attended at the time so assiduously, seemed, after all, to have such a small effect upon what they did. An old gentleman, recalling those vanished hours, tried to recapture in words his state of mind as he sat in the darkened chapel, while Dr Arnold's sermons, with their high-toned exhortations, their grave and sombre messages of incalculable import, clothed, like Dr Arnold's body in its gown and bands, in the traditional stiffness of a formal phraseology, reverberated through his adolescent ears. 'I used,' he said, 'to listen to those sermons from first to last with a kind of awe.'*

His success was not limited to his pupils and immediate auditors. The sermons were collected into five large volumes; they were the first of their kind; and they were received with admiration by a wide circle of pious readers. Queen Victoria herself possessed a copy, in which several passages were marked in pencil, by the Royal hand.*

Dr Arnold's energies were by no means exhausted by his duties at Rugby. He became known, not merely as a headmaster, but as a public man. He held decided opinions upon a large number of topics; and he enunciated them – based as they were almost invariably upon general principles – in pamphlets, in prefaces, and in magazine articles, with an impressive self-confidence. He was, as he constantly declared, a Liberal. In his opinion, by the very constitution of human nature, the principles of progress and reform had been those of wisdom and justice in every age of the world – except one: that which had preceded the fall of man from Paradise.* Had he lived then, Dr Arnold would have been a Conservative. As it was, his Liberalism was tempered by an 'abhorrence of the spirit of 1789, of the American War, of the French Economistes, and of the English Whigs of the latter part of the seventeenth century';* and he always entertained a profound respect for the hereditary peerage. It might almost be said, in fact, that he was an orthodox Liberal. He believed in toleration, too, within limits; that is to say, in the toleration of those with whom he agreed. 'I would give James Mill as much opportunity for advocating his opinion,' he said, 'as is consistent with a voyage to Botany Bay.'* He had become convinced of the duty of sympathising with the lower orders ever since he had made a serious study of the Epistle of St James; but he perceived clearly that the lower orders fell into two classes, and that it was necessary to distinguish between them. There were the 'good poor' – and there were the others. 'I am glad that you have made acquaintance with some of the good poor,' he wrote to a Cambridge undergraduate; 'I quite agree with you that it is most instructive to visit them.' Dr Arnold himself occasionally visited them, in Rugby;* and the con-descension with which he shook hands with old men and women of the working classes was long remembered in the neighbourhood. As for the others, he regarded them with horror and alarm. 'The dis-orders in our social state,' he wrote to the Chevalier Bunsen in 1834, 'appear to me to continue unabated. You have heard, I doubt not, of the Trades Unions; a fearful engine of mischief, ready to riot or to assassinate; and I see no counteracting power.'*

On the whole, his view of the condition of England was a gloomy one. He recommended a correspondent to read 'Isaiah iii, v, xxii; Jeremiah v, xxii, xxx; Amos iv; and Habakkuk ii,' adding, 'you will be struck, I think, with the close resemblance of our own state with that of the Jews before the second destruction of Jerusalem.'* When he was told that the gift of tongues had descended on the Irvingites at Glasgow,* he was not surprised. 'I should take it,' he said, 'merely as a sign of the coming of the day of the Lord.' And he was convinced that the day of the Lord *was* coming – 'the termination of one of the great αἰῶνες of the human race.' Of that he had no doubt whatever; wherever he looked he saw 'calamities, wars, tumults, pestilences, earthquakes, etc., all marking the time of one of God's peculiar seasons of visitation.' His only uncertainty was whether this termination of an αἰών would turn out to be the absolutely final one; but that he believed 'no created being knows or can know.' In any case he had 'not the slightest expectation of what is commonly meant by the Millennium.' And his only consolation was that he preferred the present Ministry, inefficient as it was, to the Tories.

He had planned a great work on Church and State, in which he intended to lay bare the causes and to point out the remedies of the evils which afflicted society. Its theme was to be, not the alliance or union, but the absolute identity of the Church and the State; and he felt sure that if only this fundamental truth were fully realised by the public, a general reformation would follow. Unfortunately, however, as time went on, the public seemed to realise it less and less. In spite of his protests, not only were Jews admitted to Parliament, but a Jew was actually appointed a governor of Christ's Hospital; and Scripture was not made an obligatory subject at the London University.*

There was one point in his theory which was not quite plain to Dr Arnold. If Church and State were absolutely identical, it became important to decide precisely which classes of persons were to be excluded, owing to their beliefs, from the community. Jews, for instance, were decidedly outside the pale; while Dissenters – so Dr Arnold argued – were as decidedly within it. But what was the position of the Unitarians? Were they, or were they not, Members of the Church of Christ? This was one of those puzzling questions which deepened the frown upon the Doctor's forehead and intensified the pursing of his lips. He thought long and earnestly upon the subject; he wrote elaborate letters on it to various correspondents; but his conclusions remained indefinite. 'My great objection to Unitarianism,' he wrote, 'in its present form in England, is that it makes Christ virtually dead.'* Yet he expressed 'a fervent hope that if we could get rid of the Athanasian Creed many good Unitarians would join their fellow Christians in bowing the knee to Him who is Lord both of the dead and the living.' Amid these perplexities, it was disquieting to learn that 'Unitarianism is becoming very prevalent in Boston.'* He inquired anxiously as to its 'complexion' there; but received no very illuminating answer. The whole matter continued to be wrapped in a painful obscurity: there were, he believed, Unitarians and Unitarians; and he could say no more.

In the meantime, pending the completion of his great work, he occupied himself with putting forward various suggestions of a

practical kind. He advocated the restoration of the Order of Deacons,* which, he observed, had long been 'quoad the reality, dead';
for he believed that 'some plan of this sort might be the small end of
the wedge, by which Antichrist might hereafter be burst asunder like
the Dragon of Bel's temple.' But the Order of Deacons was never
restored, and Dr Arnold turned his attention elsewhere, urging in a
weighty pamphlet the desirability of authorising military officers, in
congregations where it was impossible to procure the presence of
clergy, to administer the Eucharist, as well as Baptism. It was with
the object of laying such views as these before the public – 'to tell
them plainly,' as he said, 'the evils that exist, and lead them, if I can,
to their causes and remedies,'* – that he started, in 1831, a weekly
newspaper, *The Englishman's Register*. The paper was not a success,
in spite of the fact that it set out to improve its readers morally and
that it preserved, in every article, an avowedly Christian tone. After a
few weeks, and after he had spent upon it more than £200, it came to
an end.

Altogether, the prospect was decidedly discouraging. After all his
efforts, the absolute identity of Church and State remained as
unrecognised as ever. 'So deeply,' he was at last obliged to confess, 'is
the distinction between the Church and the State seated in our laws,
our language, and our very notions, that nothing less than a miraculous interposition of God's Providence seems capable of eradicating
it.' Dr Arnold waited in vain.

But he did not wait in idleness. He attacked the same question
from another side: he explored the writings of the Christian Fathers,
and began to compose a commentary on the New Testament. In his
view, the Scriptures were as fit a subject as any other book for free
inquiry and the exercise of the individual judgment, and it was in
this spirit that he set about the interpretation of them. He was not
afraid of facing apparent difficulties, of admitting inconsistencies, or
even errors, in the sacred text. Thus he observed that 'in Chronicles
xi. 20, and xiii. 2, there is a decided difference in the parentage of
Abijah's mother'; – 'which,' he added, 'is curious on any supposition.' And at one time he had serious doubts as to the authorship of
the Epistle to the Hebrews. But he was able, on various problematical
points, to suggest interesting solutions. At first, for instance, he
could not but be startled by the cessation of miracles in the early
Church; but on consideration he came to the conclusion that this

phenomenon might be 'truly accounted for by the supposition that none but the Apostles ever conferred miraculous powers, and that therefore they ceased of course after one generation.' Nor did he fail to base his exegesis, whenever possible, upon an appeal to general principles. One of his admirers* points out how Dr Arnold 'vindicated God's command to Abraham to sacrifice his son, and to the Jews to exterminate the nations of Canaan, by explaining the principles on which these commands were given, and their reference to the moral state of those to whom they were addressed; thereby educing light out of darkness, unravelling the thread of God's religious education of the human race, and holding up God's marvellous counsels to the devout wonder and meditation of the thoughtful believer.'

There was one of his friends, however, who did not share this admiration for the Doctor's methods of Scriptural interpretation. W. G. Ward, while still a young man at Oxford, had come under his influence, and had been for some time one of his most enthusiastic disciples. But the star of Newman was rising at the University; Ward soon felt the attraction of that magnetic power; and his belief in his old teacher began to waver. It was, in particular, Dr Arnold's treatment of the Scriptures which filled Ward's argumentative mind, at first with distrust, and at last with positive antagonism. To subject the Bible to free inquiry, to exercise upon it the criticism of the individual judgment – where might not such methods lead? Who could say that they would not end in Socinianism? – nay, in Atheism itself?* If the text of Scripture was to be submitted to the searchings of human reason, how could the question of its inspiration escape the same tribunal? And the proofs of revelation, and even of the existence of God? What human faculty was capable of deciding upon such enormous questions? And would not the logical result be a condition of universal doubt? 'On a very moderate computation,' Ward argued, 'five times the amount of a man's natural life might qualify a person endowed with extraordinary genius to have some faint notion (though even this we doubt) on which side truth lies.' It was not that he had the slightest doubt of Dr Arnold's orthodoxy – Dr Arnold, whose piety was universally recognised – Dr Arnold, who had held up to scorn and execration Strauss's 'Leben Jesu' without reading it.* What Ward complained of was the Doctor's lack of logic, not his lack of faith. Could he not see that if he really carried out his own principles to a logical conclusion he would eventually find himself, precisely, in the arms of Strauss? The young man, whose personal friendship remained unshaken, determined upon an interview, and went down to Rugby primed with first principles, syllogisms, and dilemmas. Finding that the headmaster was busy in school, he spent the afternoon reading novels on the sofa in the drawing-room. When at last, late in the evening, the Doctor returned, tired out with his day's work, Ward fell upon him with all his vigour. The contest was long and furious; it was also entirely inconclusive. When it was over, Ward, with none of his brilliant arguments disposed of, and none of his probing questions satisfactorily answered, returned to the University, to plunge headlong into the vortex of the Oxford Movement; and Dr Arnold, worried, perplexed, and exhausted, went to bed, where he remained for the next thirty-six hours.*

The Commentary on the New Testament was never finished, and the great work on Church and State itself remained a fragment. Dr Arnold's active mind was diverted from political and theological speculations to the study of philology and to historical composition. His Roman History, which he regarded as 'the chief monument of his historical fame,' was based partly upon the researches of Niebuhr, and partly upon an aversion to Gibbon. 'My highest ambition,' he wrote, 'is to make my history the very reverse of Gibbon – in this respect, that whereas the whole spirit of his work, from its low morality, is hostile to religion, without speaking directly against it, so my greatest desire would be, in my History, by its high morals and its general tone, to be of use to the cause without actually bringing it forward.' These efforts were rewarded, in 1841, by the Professorship of Modern History at Oxford. Meanwhile, he was engaged in the study of the Sanscrit and Slavonic languages, bringing out an elaborate edition of Thucydides, and carrying on a voluminous correspondence upon a multitude of topics with a large circle of men of learning. At his death, his published works, composed during such intervals as he could spare from the management of a great public school, filled, besides a large number of pamphlets and articles, no less than seventeen volumes. It was no wonder that Carlyle, after a visit to Rugby, should have characterised Dr Arnold as a man of 'unhasting, unresting diligence.'

Mrs Arnold, too, no doubt agreed with Carlyle. During the first eight years of their married life, she bore him six children; and four more were to follow. In this large and growing domestic circle his hours of relaxation were spent. There those who had only known him in his professional capacity were surprised to find him displaying the tenderness and jocosity of a parent. The dignified and stern headmaster was actually seen to dandle infants and to caracole upon the hearthrug on all fours. Yet, we are told, 'the sense of his authority as a father was never lost in his playfulness as a companion.' On more serious occasions, the voice of the spiritual teacher sometimes made itself heard. An intimate friend described how 'on a comparison having been made in his family circle, which seemed to place St Paul above St John,' the tears rushed to the Doctor's eyes and how, repeating one of the verses from St John, he begged that the comparison might never again be made. The longer holidays were spent in Westmorland, where, rambling with his offspring among the mountains, gathering wild flowers, and pointing out the beauties of Nature, Dr Arnold enjoyed, as he himself would often say, 'an almost awful happiness.' Music he did not appreciate, though he occasionally desired his eldest boy, Matthew, to sing him the Confirmation Hymn of Dr Hinds, to which he had become endeared, owing to its use in Rugby Chapel. But his lack of ear was, he considered, amply recompensed by his love of flowers: 'they are my music,' he declared.* Yet, in such a matter, he was careful to refrain from an excess of feeling, such as, in his opinion, marked the famous lines of Wordsworth:

'To me the meanest flower that blows can give
Thoughts that do often lie too deep for tears.'

He found the sentiment morbid. 'Life,' he said, 'is not long enough to take such intense interest in objects in themselves so little.'* As for the animal world, his feelings towards it were of a very different cast. 'The whole subject,' he said, 'of the brute creation is to me one of such painful mystery, that I dare not approach it.' The Unitarians themselves were a less distressing thought.

Once or twice he found time to visit the Continent, and the letters and journals recording in minute detail his reflections and impressions in France or Italy show us that Dr Arnold preserved, in spite of the distractions of foreign scenes and foreign manners, his accustomed habits of mind. Taking very little interest in works of art, he was occasionally moved by the beauty of natural objects; but his principal preoccupation remained with the moral aspects of things. From this point of view, he found much to reprehend in the conduct of his own countrymen. 'I fear,' he wrote, 'that our countrymen who live abroad are not in the best possible moral state, however much they may do in science or literature.' And this was unfortunate, because 'a thorough English gentleman – Christian, manly, and enlightened – is more, I believe, than Guizot or Sismondi could comprehend; it is a finer specimen of human nature than any other country, I believe, could furnish.' Nevertheless, our travellers would imitate foreign customs without discrimination, 'as in the absurd habit of not eating fish with a knife, borrowed from the French, who do it because they have no knives fit for use.' Places, no less than people, aroused similar reflections. By Pompeii, Dr Arnold was not particularly impressed. 'There is only,' he observed, 'the same sort of interest with which one would see the ruins of Sodom and Gomorrah, but indeed there is less. One is not authorised to ascribe so solemn a character to the destruction of Pompeii.' The lake of Como moved him more profoundly. As he gazed upon the overwhelming beauty around him, he thought of 'moral evil,' and was appalled by the contrast. 'May the sense of moral evil,' he prayed, 'be as strong in me as my delight in external beauty, for in a deep sense of moral evil, more perhaps than in anything else, abides a saving knowledge of God!'

His prayer was answered: Dr Arnold was never in any danger of losing his sense of moral evil. If the landscapes of Italy only served to remind him of it, how could he forget it among the boys at Rugby School? The daily sight of so many young creatures in the hands of the Evil One filled him with agitated grief. 'When the spring and activity of youth,' he wrote, 'is altogether unsanctified by anything pure and elevated in its desires, it becomes a spectacle that is as dizzying and almost more morally distressing than the shouts and gambols of a set of lunatics.' One thing struck him as particularly strange: 'It is very startling,' he said, 'to see so much of sin combined with so little of sorrow.' The naughtiest boys positively seemed to enjoy themselves most. There were moments when he almost lost faith in his whole system of education, when he began to doubt whether some far more radical reforms than any he had attempted might not be necessary, before the multitude of children under his charge – shouting, and gambolling, and yet plunged all the while deep in moral evil – could ever be transformed into a set of Christian gentlemen. But then he remembered his general principles, the conduct of Jehovah with the Chosen People, and the childhood of the human race. No, it was for him to make himself, as one of his pupils afterwards described him, in the words of Bacon, 'kin to God in spirit'; he would rule the school majestically from on high. He would deliver a series of sermons analysing 'the six vices' by which 'great schools were corrupted, and changed from the likeness of God's temple to that of a den of thieves.' He would exhort, he would denounce, he would sweep through the corridors, he would turn the pages of Facciolati's Lexicon more imposingly than ever; and the rest he would leave to the Præpostors in the Sixth Form.

Upon the boys in the Sixth Form, indeed, a strange burden would seem to have fallen. Dr Arnold himself was very well aware of this. 'I cannot deny,' he told them in a sermon, 'that you have an anxious duty – a duty which some might suppose was too heavy for your years'; and every term he pointed out to them, in a short address, the responsibilities of their position, and impressed upon them 'the enormous influence' they possessed 'for good or for evil.' Nevertheless most youths of seventeen, in spite of the warnings of their elders, have a singular trick of carrying moral burdens lightly. The Doctor might preach and look grave; but young Brooke was ready enough to preside at a fight behind the Chapel, though he was in the Sixth, and knew that fighting was against the rules. At their best, it may be supposed that the Præpostors administered a kind of barbaric justice; but they were not always at their best, and the pages of *Tom Brown's Schooldays* show us what was no doubt the normal condition of affairs under Dr Arnold, when the boys in the Sixth Form were weak or brutal, and the blackguard Flashman, in the intervals of swigging brandy-punch with his boon companions, amused himself by roasting fags before the fire.

But there was an exceptional kind of boy, upon whom the high-pitched exhortations of Dr Arnold produced a very different effect. A minority of susceptible and serious youths fell completely under his sway, responded like wax to the pressure of his influence, and moulded their whole lives with passionate reverence upon the teaching of their adored master. Conspicuous among these was Arthur

Clough. Having been sent to Rugby at the age of ten, he quickly entered into every phase of school life, though, we are told, 'a weakness in his ankles* prevented him from taking a prominent part in the games of the place.' At the age of sixteen, he was in the Sixth Form, and not merely a Præpostor, but head of the School House.* Never did Dr Arnold have an apter pupil. This earnest adolescent, with the weak ankles and the solemn face, lived entirely with the highest ends in view. He thought of nothing but moral good, moral evil, moral influence, and moral responsibility. Some of his early letters have been preserved, and they reveal both the intensity with which he felt the importance of his own position, and the strange stress of spirit under which he laboured. 'I have been in one continued state of excitement for at least the last three years,' he wrote when he was not yet seventeen, 'and now comes the time of exhaustion.' But he did not allow himself to rest, and a few months later he was writing to a schoolfellow as follows: 'I verily believe my whole being is soaked through with the wishing and hoping and striving to do the school good, or rather to keep it up and hinder it from falling in this, I do think, very critical time, so that my cares and affections and conversations, thoughts, words, and deeds look to that involuntarily. I am afraid you will be inclined to think this "cant" and I am conscious that even one's truest feelings, if very frequently put out in the light, do make a bad and disagreeable appearance; but this, however, is true, and even if I am carrying it too far, I do not think it has made me really forgetful of my personal friends, such as, in particular, Gell and Burbidge and Walrond, and yourself, my dear Simpkinson.' Perhaps it was not surprising that a young man brought up in such an atmosphere should have fallen a prey, at Oxford, to the frenzies of religious controversy; that he should have been driven almost out of his wits by the ratiocinations of W. G. Ward; that he should have lost his faith; that he should have spent the rest of his existence lamenting that loss, both in prose and verse; and that he should have eventually succumbed, conscientiously doing up brown paper parcels for Florence Nightingale.

In the earlier years of his headmastership Dr Arnold had to face a good deal of opposition. His advanced religious views were disliked, and there were many parents to whom his system of school government did not commend itself. But in time this hostility melted away. Succeeding generations of favourite pupils began to spread his fame through the Universities. At Oxford especially, men were profoundly impressed by the pious aims of the boys from Rugby. It was a new thing to see undergraduates going to Chapel more often than they were obliged, and visiting the good poor. Their reverent admiration for Dr Arnold was no less remarkable. Whenever two of his old pupils met they joined in his praises; and the sight of his picture had been known to call forth, from one who had not even reached the Sixth, exclamations of rapture lasting for ten minutes and filling with astonishment the young men from other schools who happened to be present. He became a celebrity; he became at last a great man. Rugby prospered; its numbers rose higher than ever before; and, after thirteen years as headmaster, Dr Arnold began to feel that his work there was accomplished, and that he might look forward either to other labours or, perhaps, to a dignified retirement. But it was not to be.

His father had died suddenly at the age of fifty-three from angina pectoris; and he himself was haunted by forebodings of an early death. To be snatched away without a warning, to come in a moment from the seductions of this World to the presence of Eternity – the most ordinary actions, the most casual remarks, served to keep him in remembrance of that dreadful possibility. When one of his little boys clapped his hands at the thought of the approaching holidays, the Doctor gently checked him, and repeated the story of his own early childhood; how his own father had made him read aloud a sermon on the text 'Boast not thyself of to-morrow'; and how, within the week, his father was dead. On the title-page of his MS volume of sermons he was always careful to write the date of its commencement, leaving a blank for that of its completion. One of his children asked him the meaning of this. 'It is one of the most solemn things I do,' he replied, 'to write the beginning of that sentence, and think that I may perhaps not live to finish it.'*

It was noticed that in the spring of 1842 such thoughts seemed to be even more frequently than usual in his mind. He was only in his forty-seventh year, but he dwelt darkly on the fragility of human existence. Towards the end of May, he began to keep a diary – a private memorandum of his intimate communings with the Almighty. Here, evening after evening, in the traditional language of religious devotion, he humbled himself before God, prayed for strength and purity, and threw himself upon the mercy of the Most

High. 'Another day and another month succeed,' he wrote on May 31st. 'May God keep my mind and heart fixed on Him, and cleanse me from all sin. I would wish to keep a watch over my tongue, as to vehement speaking and censuring of others. . . . I would desire to remember my latter end to which I am approaching. . . . May God keep me in the hour of death, through Jesus Christ; and preserve me from every fear, as well as from presumption.' On June 2nd he wrote, 'Again the day is over and I am going to rest. O Lord, preserve me this night, and strengthen me to bear whatever Thou shalt see fit to lay on me, whether pain, sickness, danger, or distress.' On Sunday, June 5th, the reading of the newspaper aroused 'painful and solemn' reflections* – 'So much of sin and so much of suffering in the world, as are there displayed, and no one seems able to remedy either. And then the thought of my own private life, so full of comforts, is very startling.' He was puzzled; but he concluded with a prayer: 'May I be kept humble and zealous, and may God give me grace to labour in my generation for the good of my brethren and for His Glory!'

The end of the term was approaching, and to all appearance the Doctor was in excellent spirits. On June 11th, after a hard day's work, he spent the evening with a friend in the discussion of various topics upon which he often touched in his conversation – the comparison of the art of medicine in barbarous and civilised ages, the philological importance of provincial vocabularies, and the threatening prospect of the moral condition of the United States.* Left alone, he turned to his diary. 'The day after to-morrow,' he wrote, 'is my birthday, if I am permitted to live to see it – my forty-seventh birthday since my birth. How large a portion of my life on earth is already passed! And then – what is to follow this life? How visibly my outward work seems contracting and softening away into the gentler employments of old age. In one sense how nearly can I now say, "Vixi."* And I thank God that, as far as ambition is concerned, it is, I trust, fully mortified; I have no desire other than to step back from my present place in the world, and not to rise to a higher. Still there are works which, with God's permission, I would do before the night cometh.' Dr Arnold was thinking of his great work on Church and State.

Early next morning he awoke with a sharp pain in his chest. The pain increasing, a physician was sent for; and in the meantime Mrs Arnold read aloud to her husband the Fifty-first Psalm. Upon one of their boys coming into the room, 'My son, thank God for me,' said Dr Arnold; and as the boy did not at once catch his meaning, he added, 'Thank God, Tom, for giving me this pain; I have suffered so little pain in my life that I feel it is very good for me. Now God has given it to me, and I do so thank Him for it.' Then Mrs Arnold read from the Prayer-book the 'Visitation of the Sick,' her husband listening with deep attention, and assenting with an emphatic 'Yes' at the end of many of the sentences. When the physician arrived, he perceived at once the gravity of the case: it was an attack of angina pectoris. He began to prepare some laudanum, while Mrs Arnold went out to fetch the children. All at once, as the medical man was bending over his glasses, there was a rattle from the bed; a convulsive struggle followed; and, when the unhappy woman, with the children, and all the servants, rushed into the room, Dr Arnold had passed from his perplexities for ever.

There can be little doubt that what he had achieved justified the prediction of the Provost of Oriel that he would 'change the face of education all through the public schools of England.' It is true that, so far as the actual machinery of education was concerned, Dr Arnold not only failed to effect a change, but deliberately adhered to the old system. The monastic and literary conceptions of education, which had their roots in the Middle Ages, and had been accepted and strengthened at the revival of Learning, he adopted almost without hesitation. Under him, the public school remained, in essentials, a conventional establishment, devoted to the teaching of Greek and Latin grammar. Had he set on foot reforms in these directions, it seems probable that he might have succeeded in carrying the parents of England with him. The moment was ripe; there was a general desire for educational changes; and Dr Arnold's great reputation could hardly have been resisted. As it was, he threw the whole weight of his influence into the opposite scale, and the ancient system became more firmly established than ever.

The changes which he did effect were of a very different nature. By introducing morals and religion into his scheme of education, he altered the whole atmosphere of public-school life. Henceforward the old rough-and-tumble, which was typified by the régime of Keate at Eton, became impossible. After Dr Arnold, no public school could venture to ignore the virtues of respectability. Again, by his introduction of the prefectorial system, Dr Arnold produced far-reaching effects – effects which he himself, perhaps, would have found perplexing. In his day, when the school hours were over, the boys were free to enjoy themselves as they liked; to bathe, to fish, to ramble for long afternoons in the country, collecting eggs or gathering flowers. 'The taste of the boys at this period,' writes an old Rugbæan who had been under Arnold, 'leaned strongly towards flowers'; the words have an odd look to-day. The modern reader of *Tom Brown's Schooldays* searches in vain for any reference to compulsory games, house colours, or cricket averages. In those days, when boys played games they played them for pleasure; but in those days the prefectorial system – the system which hands over the life of a school to an oligarchy of a dozen youths of seventeen – was still in its infancy, and had not yet borne its fruit. Teachers and prophets have strange after-histories; and that of Dr Arnold has been no exception. The earnest enthusiast who strove to make his pupils Christian gentlemen and who governed his school according to the principles of the Old Testament has proved to be the founder of the worship of athletics and the worship of good form. Upon those two poles our public schools have turned for so long that we have almost come to believe that such is their essential nature, and that an English public schoolboy who wears the wrong clothes and takes no interest in football is a contradiction in terms. Yet it was not so before Dr Arnold; will it always be so after him? We shall see.

BIBLIOGRAPHY

Dean Stanley. *Life and Correspondence of Dr Arnold*.
Thomas Hughes. *Tom Brown's Schooldays*.
Sir H. Maxwell-Lyte. *History of Eton College*.
Wilfrid Ward. *W. G. Ward and the Oxford Movement*.
A. H. Clough. *Letters*.
An Old Rugbæan. *Recollections of Rugby*.
Thomas Arnold. *Passages in a Wandering Life*.

THE END OF
GENERAL GORDON

THE END OF GENERAL GORDON

DURING* the year 1883 a solitary English gentleman was to be seen, wandering, with a thick book under his arm, in the neighbourhood of Jerusalem.* His unassuming figure, short and slight, with its half-gliding, half-tripping motion, gave him a boyish aspect, which contrasted, oddly, but not unpleasantly, with the touch of grey on his hair and whiskers. There was the same contrast – enigmatic and attractive – between the sunburnt brick-red complexion – the hue of the seasoned traveller – and the large blue eyes, with their look of almost childish sincerity.* To the friendly inquirer, he would explain, in a low, soft, and very distinct voice, that he was engaged in elucidating four questions – the site of the Crucifixion, the line of division between the tribes of Benjamin and Judah, the identification of Gibeon, and the position of the Garden of Eden. He was also, he would add, most anxious to discover the spot where the Ark first touched ground, after the subsidence of the Flood: he believed, indeed, that he had solved that problem, as a reference to some passages in the book which he was carrying would show.

This singular person was General Gordon, and his book was the Holy Bible.

In such complete retirement from the world and the ways of men, it might have seemed that a life of inordinate activity had found at last a longed-for, a final peacefulness. For month after month, for an entire year, the General lingered by the banks of the Jordan. But then the enchantment was suddenly broken. Once more adventure claimed him; he plunged into the whirl of high affairs; his fate was mingled with the frenzies of Empire and the doom of peoples. And it was not in peace and rest, but in ruin and horror, that he reached his end.

The circumstances of that tragic history, so famous, so bitterly debated, so often and so controversially described, remain full of suggestion for the curious examiner of the past. There emerges from those obscure, unhappy records an interest, not merely political and historical, but human and dramatic. One catches a vision of strange characters, moved by mysterious impulses, interacting in queer complication, and hurrying at last – so it almost seems – like creatures in a puppet show to a predestined catastrophe. The characters, too, have a charm of their own: they are curiously English. What other nation on the face of the earth could have produced Mr Gladstone and Sir Evelyn Baring and Lord Hartington* and General Gordon? Alike in their emphasis and their lack of emphasis, in their eccentricity and their conventionality, in their matter-of-factness and their romance, these four figures seem to embody the mingling contradictions of the English spirit. As for the *mise-en-scène*, it is perfectly appropriate. But first let us glance at the earlier adventures of the hero of the piece.

Charles George Gordon was born in 1833. His father, of Highland and military descent, was himself a Lieutenant-General,* his mother came of a family of merchants, distinguished for their sea-voyages into remote regions of the Globe. As a boy, Charlie was remarkable for his high spirits, pluck, and love of mischief. Destined for the Artillery, he was sent to the Academy at Woolwich, where some other characteristics made their appearance. On one occasion, when the cadets had been forbidden to leave the dining-room and the senior corporal stood with outstretched arms in the doorway to prevent their exit, Charlie Gordon put his head down, and, butting the officer in the pit of the stomach, projected him down a flight of stairs and through a glass door at the bottom.* For this act of insubordination he was nearly dismissed, while the captain of his company predicted that he would never make an officer. A little later, when he was eighteen, it came to the knowledge of the authorities that bullying was rife at the Academy. The new-comers were questioned, and one of them said that Charlie Gordon had hit him over the head with a clothes-brush. He had worked well, and his record was on the whole a good one; but the authorities took a serious view of the case, and held back his commission for six months. It was owing to this delay that he went into the Royal Engineers, instead of the Royal Artillery.

He was sent to Pembroke, to work at the erection of fortifications; and at Pembroke those religious convictions, which never afterwards left him, first gained a hold upon his mind. Under the influence of his sister Augusta and of a 'very religious captain of the name of Drew,'* he began to reflect upon his sins, look up texts, and hope for salvation. Though he had never been confirmed – he never *was* confirmed – he took the sacrament every Sunday; and he eagerly perused the *Priceless Diamond*, Scott's *Commentaries*, and *The Remains of the Rev. R. McCheyne*.* 'No novels or worldly books,' he wrote to his sister, 'come up to the *Commentaries* of Scott. . . . I remember well when you used to get them in numbers, and I used to laugh at them; but, thank God, it is different with me now. I feel much happier and more contented than I used to do. I did not like Pembroke, but now I would not wish for any prettier place. I have got a horse and gig, and Drew and myself drive all about the country. I hope my dear father and mother think of eternal things. . . . Dearest Augusta, pray for me, I beg of you.'

He was twenty-one; the Crimean War broke out; and before the year was over he had managed to get himself transferred to Balaclava. During the siege of Sebastopol he behaved with conspicuous gallantry. Upon the declaration of peace, he was sent to Bessarabia to assist in determining the frontier between Russia and Turkey, in accordance with the Treaty of Paris; and upon this duty he was occupied for nearly two years. Not long after his return home, in 1860, war was declared upon China.* Captain Gordon was dispatched to the scene of operations, but the fighting was over before he arrived. Nevertheless, he was to remain for the next four years in China, where he was to lay the foundations of an extraordinary renown.

Though he was too late to take part in the capture of the Taku Forts, he was in time to witness the destruction of the Summer Palace at Pekin – the act by which Lord Elgin, in the name of European civilisation, took vengeance upon the barbarism of the East.*

The war was over; but the British Army remained in the country, until the payment of an indemnity by the Chinese Government was completed. A camp was formed at Tientsin, and Gordon was occupied in setting up huts for the troops. While he was thus engaged, he had a slight attack of small-pox. 'I am glad to say,' he told his sister, 'that this disease has brought me back to my Saviour, and I trust in future to be a better Christian than I have been hitherto.'

Curiously enough a similar circumstance had, more than twenty years earlier, brought about a singular succession of events which were now upon the point of opening the way to Gordon's first great adventure. In 1837, a village schoolmaster near Canton had been attacked by illness; and, as in the case of Gordon, illness had been followed by a religious revulsion. Hong-siu-tsuen – for such was his name – saw visions, went into ecstasies, and entered into relations with the Deity. Shortly afterwards he fell in with a Methodist missionary from America, who instructed him in the Christian religion. The new doctrine, working upon the mystical ferment already in Hong's mind, produced a remarkable result. He was, he declared, the prophet of God; he was more – he was the Son of God; he was Tien Wang, the Celestial King; he was the younger brother of Jesus. The times were propitious, and proselytes soon gathered around him. Having conceived a grudge against the Government, owing to his failure in an examination, Hong gave a political turn to his teaching, which soon developed into a propaganda of rebellion against the rule of the Manchus and the Mandarins. The authorities took fright, attempted to suppress Hong by force, and failed. The movement spread. By 1850 the rebels were overrunning the populous and flourishing delta of the Yang-tse Kiang, and had become a formidable force. In 1853 they captured Nankin, which was henceforth their capital. The Tien Wang established himself in a splendid palace, and proclaimed his new evangel. His theogony included the wife of God, or the celestial Mother, the wife of Jesus, or the celestial daughter-in-law, and a sister of Jesus, whom he married to one of his lieutenants, who thus became the celestial son-in-law; the Holy Ghost, however, was eliminated. His mission was to root out Demons and Manchus from the face of the earth, and to establish Taiping, the reign of eternal peace. In the meantime, retiring into the depths of his palace, he left the further conduct of earthly operations to his lieutenants, upon whom he bestowed the title of 'Wangs' (kings), while he himself, surrounded by thirty wives and one hundred concubines, devoted his energies to the spiritual side of his mission. The Taiping Rebellion, as it came to be called, had now reached its furthest extent. The rebels were even able to occupy, for more than a year, the semi-European city of Shanghai. But then the tide turned. The latent forces of the Empire gradually asserted themselves. The rebels lost ground, their armies were defeated, and in 1859 Nankin itself was besieged and the Celestial King trembled in his palace. The end seemed to be at hand, when there was a sudden twist of Fortune's wheel. The war of 1860, the invasion of China by European armies, their march into the interior, and their occupation of Pekin, not only saved the rebels from destruction but allowed them to recover the greater part of what they had lost. Once more they seized upon the provinces of the delta, once more they menaced Shanghai. It was clear that the Imperial army was incompetent, and the Shanghai merchants determined to provide for their own safety as best they could. They accordingly got together a body of troops, partly Chinese and partly European and under European officers, to which they entrusted the defence of the town. This small force, which, after a few preliminary successes, received from the Chinese Government the title of the 'Ever Victorious Army,' was able to hold the rebels at bay, but it could do no more. For two years Shanghai was in constant danger. The Taipings, steadily growing in power, were spreading destruction far and wide. The Ever Victorious Army was the only force capable of opposing them, and the Ever Victorious Army was defeated more often than not. Its first European leader had been killed; his successor quarrelled with the Chinese Governor, Li Hung Chang,* and was dismissed. At last it was determined to ask the General at the head of the British Army of Occupation for the loan of an officer to command the force. The English, who had been at first inclined to favour the Taipings, on religious grounds, were now convinced, on practical grounds, of the necessity of suppressing them. It was in these circumstances that, early in 1863, the command of the Ever Victorious Army was offered to Gordon. He accepted it, received the title of general from the Chinese authorities, and entered forthwith upon his new task. He was just thirty.

In eighteen months, he told Li Hung Chang, the business would be finished; and he was as good as his word. The difficulties before him were very great. A vast tract of country was in the possession of the rebels – an area, at the lowest estimate, of 14,000 square miles with a population of twenty millions. For centuries this low-lying plain of the Yang-tse delta, rich in silk and tea, fertilised by elaborate irrigation, and covered with great walled cities, had been one of the most flourishing districts in China. Though it was now being rapidly ruined by the depredations of the Taipings, its strategic strength was obviously enormous. Gordon, however, with the eye of a born general, perceived that he could convert the very feature of the country which, on the face of it, most favoured an army on the defence – its complicated geographical system of interlacing roads and waterways, canals, lakes and rivers – into a means of offensive warfare. The force at his disposal was small, but it was mobile. He had a passion for map-making, and had already, in his leisure hours, made a careful survey of the country round Shanghai; he was thus able to execute a series of manœuvres which proved fatal to the enemy. By swift marches and countermarches, by sudden attacks and surprises, above all by the dispatch of armed steamboats up the circuitous waterways into positions from which they could fall upon the enemy in reverse, he was able gradually to force back the rebels, to cut them off piecemeal in the field, and to seize upon their cities. But, brilliant as these operations were, Gordon's military genius showed itself no less unmistakably in other directions. The Ever Victorious Army, recruited from the riff-raff of Shanghai, was an ill-disciplined, ill-organised body of about three thousand men, constantly on the verge of mutiny, supporting itself on plunder, and, at the slightest provocation, melting into thin air. Gordon, by sheer force of character, established over this incoherent mass of ruffians an extraordinary ascendancy. He drilled them with rigid severity; he put them into a uniform, armed them systematically, substituted pay for loot, and was even able, at last, to introduce regulations of a sanitary kind. There were some terrible scenes, in which the General, alone, faced the whole furious army, and quelled it: scenes of rage, desperation, towering courage, and summary execution. Eventually he attained to an almost magical prestige. Walking at the head of his troops, with nothing but a light cane in his hand, he seemed to pass through every danger with the scatheless equanimity of a demigod. The Taipings themselves were awed into a strange reverence. More than once their leaders, in a frenzy of fear and admiration, ordered the sharp-shooters not to take aim at the advancing figure of the faintly smiling Englishman.

It is significant that Gordon found it easier to win battles and to crush mutineers than to keep on good terms with the Chinese authorities. He had to act in co-operation with a large native force; and it was only natural that the general at the head of it should grow more and more jealous and angry as the Englishman's successes revealed more and more clearly his own incompetence. At first, indeed, Gordon could rely upon the support of the Governor. Li Hung Chang's experience of Europeans had been hitherto limited to low-class adventurers, and Gordon came as a revelation. 'It is a direct blessing from Heaven,' he noted in his diary, 'the coming of this British Gordon. . . . He is superior in manner and bearing to any of

the foreigners whom I have come into contact with, and does not
show outwardly that conceit which makes most of them repugnant
in my sight.' A few months later, after he had accompanied Gordon
on a victorious expedition, the Mandarin's enthusiasm burst forth.
'What a sight for tired eyes,' he wrote, 'what an elixir for a heavy
heart – to see this splendid Englishman fight! . . . If there is anything
that I admire nearly as much as the superb scholarship of Tseng
Kuo-fan it is the military qualities of this fine officer. He is a glorious
fellow!' In his emotion, Li Hung Chang addressed Gordon as his
brother, declaring that he 'considered him worthy to fill the place of
the brother who is departed. Could I have said more in all the words
of the world?' Then something happened which impressed and mystified the sensitive Chinaman. 'The Englishman's face was first filled
with a deep pleasure, and then he seemed to be thinking of something depressing and sad; for the smile went from his mouth and
there were tears in his eyes when he thanked me for what I had said.
Can it be that he has, or has had, some great trouble in his life, and
that he fights recklessly to forget it, or that Death has no terrors for
him?' But, as time went on, Li Hung Chang's attitude began to
change. 'General Gordon,' he notes in July, 'must control his tongue,
even if he lets his mind run loose.' The Englishman had accused him
of intriguing with the Chinese general, and of withholding money
due to the Ever Victorious Army. 'Why does he not accord me the
honours that are due to me, as head of the military and civil authority in these parts?' By September the Governor's earlier transports
have been replaced by a more judicial frame of mind. 'With his many
faults, his pride, his temper, and his never-ending demand for
money, Gordon is a noble man, and in spite of all I have said to him
or about him, I will ever think most highly of him. . . . He is an
honest man, but difficult to get on with.'

Disagreements of this kind might perhaps have been tided over
till the end of the campaign; but an unfortunate incident suddenly
led to a more serious quarrel. Gordon's advance had been fiercely
contested, but it had been constant; he had captured several important towns; and in October he laid siege to the city of Soo-chow, once
one of the most famous and splendid in China. In December, its fall
being obviously imminent, the Taiping leaders agreed to surrender
it, on condition that their lives were spared. Gordon was a party to
the agreement, and laid special stress upon his presence with the

Imperial forces as a pledge of its fulfilment. No sooner, however, was the city surrendered than the rebel 'Wangs' were assassinated. In his fury, it is said that Gordon searched everywhere for Li Hung Chang with a loaded pistol in his hand.* He was convinced of the complicity of the Governor, who, on his side, denied that he was responsible for what had happened. 'I asked him why I should plot, and go round a mountain, when a mere order, written with five strokes of the quill, would have accomplished the same thing. He did not answer, but he insulted me, and said he would report my treachery, as he called it, to Shanghai and England. Let him do so; he cannot bring the crazy Wangs back.' The agitated Mandarin hoped to placate Gordon by a large gratuity and an Imperial medal; but the plan was not successful. 'General Gordon,' he writes, 'called upon me in his angriest mood. He repeated his former speeches about the Wangs. I did not attempt to argue with him. . . . He refused the 10,000 taels, which I had ready for him, and, with an oath, said that he did not want the Throne's medal. This is showing the greatest disrespect.'

Gordon resigned his command; and it was only with the utmost reluctance that he agreed at last to resume it. An arduous and terrible series of operations followed; but they were successful, and by June, 1864, the Ever Victorious Army, having accomplished its task, was disbanded. The Imperial forces now closed round Nankin: the last hopes of the Tien Wang had vanished. In the recesses of his seraglio, the Celestial King, judging that the time had come for the conclusion of his mission, swallowed gold leaf* until he ascended to Heaven. In July, Nankin was taken, the remaining chiefs were executed, and the rebellion was at an end. The Chinese Government gave Gordon the highest rank in its military hierarchy, and invested him with the yellow jacket and the peacock's feather. He rejected an enormous offer of money; but he could not refuse a great gold medal, specially struck in his honour by order of the Emperor. At the end of the year he returned to England, where the conqueror of the Taipings was made a Companion of the Bath.

That the English authorities should have seen fit to recognise Gordon's services by the reward usually reserved for industrious clerks was typical of their attitude towards him until the very end of his career. Perhaps if he had been ready to make the most of the wave of popularity which greeted him on his return – if he had advertised his fame and, amid high circles, played the part of Chinese Gordon in a becoming manner – the results would have been different. But he was by nature *farouche;* his soul revolted against dinner-parties and stiff shirts; and the presence of ladies – especially of fashionable ladies – filled him with uneasiness. He had, besides, a deeper dread of the world's contaminations. And so, when he was appointed to Gravesend to supervise the erection of a system of forts at the mouth of the Thames, he remained there quietly for six years, and at last was almost forgotten. The forts, which were extremely expensive and quite useless, occupied his working hours; his leisure he devoted to acts of charity and to religious contemplation. The neighbourhood was a poverty-stricken one, and the kind Colonel, with his tripping step and simple manner, was soon a familiar figure in it, chatting with the seamen, taking provisions to starving families, or visiting some bedridden old woman to light her fire. He was particularly fond of boys.* Ragged street arabs and rough sailor-lads crowded about him. They were made free of his house and garden; they visited him in the evenings for lessons and advice; he helped them, found them employment, corresponded with them when they went out into the world. They were, he said, his Wangs. It was only by a singular austerity of living that he was able to afford such a variety of charitable expenses. The easy luxuries of his class and station were unknown to him: his clothes verged upon the shabby; and his frugal meals were eaten at a table with a drawer, into which the loaf and plate were quickly swept at the approach of his poor visitors. Special occasions demanded special sacrifices. When, during the Lancashire famine,* a public subscription was opened, finding that he had no ready money, he remembered his Chinese medal, and, after effacing the inscription, dispatched it as an anonymous gift.

Except for his boys and his paupers, he lived alone. In his solitude, he ruminated upon the mysteries of the universe; and those religious tendencies, which had already shown themselves, now became a fixed and dominating factor in his life. His reading was confined almost entirely to the Bible; but the Bible he read and re-read with an untiring, an unending, assiduity. There, he was convinced, all truth was to be found; and he was equally convinced that he could find it. The doubts of philosophers, the investigations of commentators, the smiles of men of the world, the dogmas of Churches – such things meant nothing to the Colonel. Two facts alone were evident: there was the Bible, and there was himself; and all that remained to be done was for him to discover what were the Bible's instructions, and to act accordingly. In order to make this discovery it was only necessary for him to read the Bible over and over again; and therefore, for the rest of his life, he did so.

The faith that he evolved was mystical and fatalistic; it was also highly unconventional. His creed, based upon the narrow foundations of Jewish Scripture, eked out occasionally by some English evangelical manual, was yet wide enough to ignore every doctrinal difference, and even, at moments, to transcend the bounds of Christianity itself. The just man was he who submitted to the Will of God, and the Will of God, inscrutable and absolute, could be served aright only by those who turned away from earthly desires and temporal temptations, to rest themselves whole-heartedly upon the indwelling Spirit. Human beings were the transitory embodiments of souls who had existed through an infinite past and would continue to exist through an infinite future. The world was vanity; the flesh was dust and ashes. 'A man,' Gordon wrote to his sister, 'who knows not the secret, who has not the indwelling of God revealed to him, is like this –

He takes the promises and curses as addressed to him as one man, and will not hear of there being any birth before his natural birth, in any existence except with the body he is in. The man to whom the secret (the indwelling of God) is revealed is like this –

He applies the promises to one and the curses to the other, if disobedient, which he must be, except the soul is enabled by God to rule. He then sees he is not of this world; for when he speaks of himself he quite disregards the body his soul lives in, which is earthly.'

Such conceptions are familiar enough in the history of religious thought: they are those of the hermit and the fakir; and it might have been expected that, when once they had taken hold upon his mind, Gordon would have been content to lay aside the activities of his profession, and would have relapsed at last into the complete retirement of holy meditation. But there were other elements in his nature, which urged him towards a very different course. He was no simple quietist. He was an English gentleman, an officer, a man of energy and action, a lover of danger and the audacities that defeat danger, a passionate creature, flowing over with the self-assertiveness of independent judgment and the arbitrary temper of command. Whatever he might find in his pocket-Bible, it was not for such as he to dream out his days in devout obscurity. But, conveniently enough, he found nothing in his pocket-Bible indicating that he should. What he did find was that the Will of God was inscrutable and absolute; that it was man's duty to follow where God's hand led; and, if God's hand led towards violent excitements and extraordinary vicissitudes, that it was not only futile, it was impious, to turn another way. Fatalism is always apt to be a double-edged philosophy; for while, on the one hand, it reveals the minutest occurrences as the immutable result of a rigid chain of infinitely predestined causes, on the other, it invests the wildest incoherences of conduct or of circumstance with the sanctity of eternal law. And Gordon's fatalism was no exception. The same doctrine that led him to dally with omens, to search for prophetic texts, and to append, in brackets, the apotropaic initials D.V.* after every statement in his letters implying futurity, led him also to envisage his moods and his desires, his passing reckless whims and his deep unconscious instincts, as the mysterious manifestations of the indwelling God. That there was danger lurking in such a creed* he was very well aware. The grosser temptations of the world – money and the vulgar attributes of power – had, indeed, no charms for him; but there were subtler and more insinuating allurements which it was not so easy to resist. More than one observer declared that ambition was, in reality, the essential motive in his life – ambition, neither for wealth nor titles, but for fame and influence, for the swaying of multitudes, and for that kind of enlarged and intensified existence 'where breath breathes most – even in the mouths of men.' Was it so? In the depths of Gordon's soul there were intertwining contradictions – intricate recesses where egoism and renunciation melted into one another, where the flesh lost itself in the spirit, and the spirit in the flesh. What *was* the

Will of God? The question, which first became insistent during his retirement at Gravesend, never afterwards left him: it might almost be said that he spent the remainder of his life in searching for the answer to it. In all his Odysseys, in all his strange and agitated adventures, a day never passed on which he neglected the voice of eternal wisdom as it spoke through the words of Paul or Solomon, of Jonah or Habakkuk. He opened his Bible, he read, and then he noted down his reflections upon scraps of paper, which, periodically pinned together, he dispatched to one or other of his religious friends, and particularly his sister Augusta. The published extracts from these voluminous outpourings lay bare the inner history of Gordon's spirit, and reveal the pious visionary of Gravesend in the restless hero of three continents.

His seclusion came to an end in a distinctly providential manner. In accordance with a stipulation in the Treaty of Paris,* an international commission had been appointed to improve the navigation of the Danube; and Gordon, who had acted on a similar body fifteen years earlier, was sent out to represent Great Britain. At Constantinople, he chanced to meet the Egyptian minister, Nubar Pasha. The Governorship of the Equatorial Provinces of the Sudan was about to fall vacant; and Nubar offered the post to Gordon, who accepted it. 'For some wise design,' he wrote to his sister, 'God turns events one way or another, whether man likes it or not, as a man driving a horse turns it to right or left without consideration as to whether the horse likes that way or not. To be happy, a man must be like a well-broken, willing horse, ready for anything. Events will go as God likes.'

And then followed six years of extraordinary, desperate, unceasing, and ungrateful labour. The unexplored and pestilential region of Equatoria, stretching southwards to the Great Lakes and the sources of the Nile, had been annexed to Egypt by the Khedive Ismail,* who, while he squandered his millions on Parisian ballet-dancers, dreamt strange dreams of glory and empire. Those dim tracts of swamp and forest in Central Africa were – so he declared – to be 'opened up,' they were to receive the blessings of civilisation, they were to become a source of eternal honour to himself and Egypt. The slave-trade, which flourished there, was to be put down; the savage inhabitants were to become acquainted with freedom, justice, and prosperity. Incidentally, a government monopoly in ivory was to be established, and the place was to be made a paying concern. Ismail, hopelessly in debt to a horde of European creditors, looked to Europe to support him in his schemes. Europe, and, in particular, England, with her passion for extraneous philanthropy, was not averse. Sir Samuel Baker* became the first Governor of Equatoria, and now Gordon was to carry on the good work. In such circumstances it was only natural that Gordon should consider himself a special instrument in God's hand. To put his disinterestedness beyond doubt, he reduced his salary, which had been fixed at £10,000, to £2000. He took over his new duties early in 1874, and it was not long before he had a first hint of disillusionment. On his way up the Nile, he was received in state at Khartoum by the Egyptian Governor-General of the Sudan, his immediate official superior. The function ended in a prolonged banquet, followed by a mixed ballet of soldiers and completely naked young women, who danced in a circle, beat time with their feet, and accompanied their gestures with a curious sound of clucking. At last the Austrian Consul, overcome by the exhilaration of the scene, flung himself in a frenzy among the dancers; the Governor-General, shouting with delight, seemed about to follow suit, when Gordon abruptly left the room, and the party broke up in confusion.

When, fifteen hundred miles to the southward, Gordon reached the seat of his government, and the desolation of the Tropics closed over him, the agonising nature of his task stood fully revealed. For the next three years he struggled with enormous difficulties – with the confused and horrible country, the appalling climate, the maddening insects and the loathsome diseases, the indifference of subordinates and superiors, the savagery of the slave-traders, the hatred of the inhabitants. One by one the small company of his European staff succumbed. With a few hundred Egyptian soldiers, he had to suppress insurrections, make roads, establish fortified posts, and enforce the government monopoly of ivory. All this he accomplished; he even succeeded in sending enough money to Cairo to pay for the expenses of the expedition. But a deep gloom had fallen upon his spirit. When, after a series of incredible obstacles had been overcome, a steamer was launched upon the unexplored Albert Nyanza, he turned his back upon the lake, leaving the glory of its navigation to his Italian lieutenant, Gessi.* 'I wish,' he wrote, 'to give a practical proof of what I think regarding the inordinate praise which is given to an explorer.' Among his distresses and self-mortifications, he loathed the thought of all such honours, and remembered the attentions of English society with a snarl. 'When, D.V., I get home, I do not dine out. My reminiscences of these lands will not be more pleasant to me than the China ones. What I shall have done will be what I have done. Men think giving dinners is conferring a favour on you. . . . Why not give dinners to those who need them?' No! His heart was set upon a very different object. 'To each is allotted a distinct work, to each a destined goal; to some the seat at the right hand or left of the Saviour. (It was not His to give; it was already given – Matthew xx. 23. Again, Judas went to "*his own place*" – Acts i. 25.) It is difficult to the flesh to accept "Ye are dead, ye have naught to do with the world." How difficult for anyone to be circumcised from the world, to be as indifferent to its pleasures, its sorrows, and its comforts as a corpse is! That is to know the resurrection.'

But the Holy Bible was not his only solace. For now, under the parching African sun, we catch glimpses, for the first time, of Gordon's hand stretching out towards stimulants of a more material quality.* For months together, we are told, he would drink nothing but pure water; and then . . . water that was not so pure. In his fits of melancholy, he would shut himself up in his tent for days at a time, with a hatchet and a flag placed at the door to indicate that he was not to be disturbed for any reason whatever; until at last the cloud would lift, the signals would be removed, and the Governor would reappear, brisk and cheerful. During one of these retirements, there was a grave danger of a native attack upon the camp. Colonel Long, the Chief of Staff,* ventured, after some hesitation, to ignore the flag and hatchet, and to enter the forbidden tent. He found Gordon seated at a table, upon which were an open Bible and an open bottle of brandy. Long explained the circumstances, but could obtain no answer beyond the abrupt words – 'You are commander of the camp' – and was obliged to retire, nonplussed, to deal with the situation as best he could. On the following morning, Gordon, cleanly shaven, and in the full-dress uniform of the Royal Engineers, entered Long's hut with his usual tripping step, exclaiming – 'Old fellow, now don't be angry with me. I was very low last night. Let's have a good breakfast – a little b. and s. Do you feel up to it?'* And, with these veering moods and dangerous restoratives, there came an intensification of the queer and violent elements in the temper of the man. His eccentricities grew upon him. He found it more and more uncomfortable to follow the ordinary course. Official routine was an agony to him. His caustic and satirical humour expressed itself in a style that astounded government departments. While he jibed at his superiors, his subordinates learnt to dread the explosions of his wrath. There were moments when his passion became utterly ungovernable; and the gentle soldier of God, who had spent the day in quoting texts for the edification of his sister, would slap the face of his Arab aide-de-camp in a sudden access of fury, or set upon his Alsatian servant and kick him till he screamed.*

At the end of three years, Gordon resigned his post in Equatoria, and prepared to return home. But again Providence intervened: the Khedive offered him, as an inducement to remain in the Egyptian service, a position of still higher consequence – the Governor-Generalship of the whole Sudan; and Gordon once more took up his task. Another three years were passed in grappling with vast revolting provinces, with the ineradicable iniquities of the slave-trade, with all the complications of weakness and corruption incident to an oriental administration extending over almost boundless tracts of savage territory which had never been effectively subdued. His headquarters were fixed in the palace at Khartoum; but there were various interludes in his government. Once, when the Khedive's finances had become peculiarly embroiled, he summoned Gordon to Cairo, to preside over a commission which should set matters to rights. Gordon accepted the post, but soon found that his situation was untenable. He was between the devil and the deep sea – between the unscrupulous cunning of the Egyptian Pashas and the immeasurable immensity of the Khedive's debts to his European creditors. The Pashas were anxious to use him as a respectable mask for their own nefarious dealings; and the representatives of the European creditors, who looked upon him as an irresponsible intruder, were anxious simply to get rid of him as soon as they could. One of these representatives was Sir Evelyn Baring, whom Gordon now met for the first time. An immediate antagonism flashed out between the two men. But their hostility had no time to mature; for Gordon, baffled on all sides, and deserted even by the Khedive, precipitately returned to his Governor-Generalship. Whatever else Providence might have decreed, it had certainly not decided that he should be a financier.

His tastes and his talents were indeed of a very different kind. In his absence, a rebellion had broken out in Darfur – one of the vast outlying provinces of his government – where a native chieftain, Zobeir, had erected, on a basis of slave-traffic, a dangerous military power. Zobeir himself had been lured to Cairo, where he was detained in a state of semi-captivity; but his son, Suleiman, ruled in his stead, and was now defying the Governor-General. Gordon determined upon a hazardous stroke. He mounted a camel, and rode, alone, in the blazing heat, across eighty-five miles of desert, to Suleiman's camp. His sudden apparition dumbfounded the rebels; his imperious bearing overawed them; he signified to them that in two days they must disarm and disperse; and the whole host obeyed. Gordon returned to Khartoum in triumph. But he had not heard the last of Suleiman. Flying southwards from Darfur to the neighbouring province of Bahr-el-Ghazal, the young man was soon once more at the head of a formidable force. A prolonged campaign, of extreme difficulty and danger, followed. Eventually, Gordon, summoned again to Cairo, was obliged to leave to Gessi the task of finally crushing the revolt. After a brilliant campaign, Gessi forced Suleiman to surrender, and then shot him as a rebel. The deed was to exercise a curious influence upon Gordon's fate.

Though Suleiman had been killed and his power broken, the slave-trade still flourished in the Sudan. Gordon's efforts to suppress it resembled the palliatives of an empiric treating the superficial symptoms of some profound constitutional disease. The root of the malady lay in the slave-markets of Cairo and Constantinople: the supply followed the demand. Gordon, after years of labour, might here and there stop up a spring or divert a tributary, but, somehow or other, the waters would reach the river-bed. In the end, he himself came to recognise this. 'When you have got the ink that has soaked into blotting-paper out of it,' he said, 'then slavery will cease in these lands.' And yet he struggled desperately on; it was not for him to murmur. 'I feel my own weakness, and look to Him who is Almighty, and I leave the issue without inordinate care to Him.'

Relief came at last. The Khedive Ismail was deposed; and Gordon felt at liberty to send in his resignation. Before he left Egypt, however, he was to experience yet one more remarkable adventure. At his own request, he set out on a diplomatic mission to the Negus of Abyssinia.* The mission was a complete failure. The Negus was intractable, and, when his bribes were refused, furious. Gordon was ignominiously dismissed; every insult was heaped on him; he was arrested, and obliged to traverse the Abyssinian Mountains in the depth of winter under the escort of a savage troop of horse. When, after great hardships and dangers, he reached Cairo, he found the whole official world up in arms against him. The Pashas had determined at last that they had no further use for this honest and peculiar Englishman. It was arranged that one of his confidential dispatches should be published in the newspapers; naturally, it contained indiscretions; there was a universal outcry – the man was insubordinate, and mad. He departed under a storm of obloquy. It seemed impossible that he should ever return to Egypt.

On his way home, he stopped in Paris, saw the English Ambassador, Lord Lyons,* and speedily came into conflict with him over Egyptian affairs. There ensued a heated correspondence, which was finally closed by a letter from Gordon, ending as follows: 'I have some comfort in thinking that in ten or fifteen years' time it will matter little to either of us. A black box, six feet six by three feet wide, will then contain all that is left of Ambassador, or Cabinet Minister, or of your humble and obedient servant.'

He arrived in England early in 1880 ill and exhausted; and it might have been supposed that after the terrible activities of his African exile he would have been ready to rest. But the very opposite was the case: the next three years were the most *mouvementés* of his life. He hurried from post to post, from enterprise to enterprise, from continent to continent, with a vertiginous rapidity. He accepted the Private Secretaryship to Lord Ripon, the new Viceroy of India,* and, three days after his arrival at Bombay, he resigned. He had suddenly realised that he was not cut out for a Private Secretary, when, on an address being sent in from some deputation, he was asked to say that the Viceroy had read it with interest. 'You know perfectly,' he said to Lord William Beresford,* 'that Lord Ripon has never read it, and I can't say that sort of thing, so I will resign, and you take in my resignation.' He confessed to Lord William that the world was not big enough for him, that there was 'no king or country big enough'; and then he added, hitting him on the shoulder, 'Yes, that is flesh, that is what I hate, and what makes me wish to die.'

Two days later, he was off for Pekin. 'Every one will say I am mad,' were his last words to Lord William Beresford; 'but you say I am not.' The position in China was critical; war with Russia appeared to be imminent; and Gordon had been appealed to, in order to use his influence on the side of peace. He was welcomed by many old friends of former days, among them Li Hung Chang, whose diplomatic views coincided with his own. Li's diplomatic language, however, was less unconventional. In an interview with the Ministers, Gordon's expressions were such that the interpreter shook with terror, upset a cup of tea, and finally refused to translate the dreadful words; upon which Gordon snatched up a dictionary, and, with his finger on the word 'idiocy,' showed it to the startled Mandarins. A few weeks later, Li Hung Chang was in power, and peace was assured. Gordon had spent two and a half days in Pekin, and was whirling through China, when a telegram arrived from the home authorities, who viewed his movements with uneasiness, ordering him to return at once to England. 'It did not produce a twitter in me,' he wrote to his sister; 'I died long ago, and it will not make any difference to me; I am prepared to follow the unrolling of the scroll.' The world, perhaps, was not big enough for him; and yet how clearly he recognised that he was 'a poor insect!' 'My heart tells me that, and I am glad of it.'*

On his return to England, he telegraphed to the Government of the Cape of Good Hope, which had become involved in a war with the Basutos, offering his services; but his telegram received no reply. Just then, Sir Howard Elphinstone* was appointed to the command of the Royal Engineers in Mauritius. It was a thankless and insignificant post; and, rather than accept it, Elphinstone was prepared to retire from the Army – unless some other officer could be induced, in return for £800, to act as his substitute. Gordon, who was an old friend, agreed to undertake the work – upon one condition: that he should receive nothing from Elphinstone; and accordingly he spent the next year in that remote and unhealthy island, looking after the barrack repairs and testing the drains. While he was thus engaged, the Cape Government, whose difficulties had been increasing, changed its mind, and early in 1882, begged for Gordon's help. Once more he was involved in great affairs: a new field of action opened before him; and then, in a moment, there was another shift of the kaleidoscope, and again he was thrown upon the world. Within a few weeks, after a violent quarrel with the Cape authorities, his mission had come to an end. What should he do next? To what remote corner or what enormous stage, to what self-sacrificing drudgeries or what resounding exploits, would the hand of God lead him now? He waited, in an odd hesitation. He opened the Bible, but neither the prophecies of Hosea nor the epistles to Timothy gave him any advice. The King of the Belgians asked if he would be willing to go to the Congo. He was perfectly willing; he would go whenever the King of the Belgians sent for him; his services, however, were not required yet. It was at this juncture that he betook himself to Palestine. His studies there were embodied in a correspondence with the Rev. Mr Barnes, filling over two thousand pages of manuscript – a correspondence which was only put an end to when, at last, the summons from the King of the Belgians came. He hurried back to England; but it was not to the Congo that he was being led by the hand of God.

Gordon's last great adventure, like his first, was occasioned by a religious revolt. At the very moment when, apparently for ever, he was shaking the dust of Egypt from his feet, Mahommed Ahmed was starting upon his extraordinary career in the Sudan. The time was propitious for revolutions. The effete Egyptian Empire was hovering upon the verge of collapse. The enormous territories of the Sudan were seething with discontent. Gordon's administration had, by its very vigour, only helped to precipitate the inevitable disaster. His attacks upon the slave-trade, his establishment of a government monopoly in ivory, his hostility to the Egyptian officials, had been so many shocks, shaking to its foundations the whole rickety machine. The result of all his efforts had been, on the one hand, to fill the most powerful classes in the community – the dealers in slaves and ivory – with a hatred of the government, and on the other to awaken among the mass of the inhabitants a new perception of the dishonesty and incompetence of their Egyptian masters. When, after Gordon's removal, the rule of the Pashas once more asserted itself over the Sudan, a general combustion became inevitable: the first spark would set off the blaze. Just then it happened that Mahommed Ahmed, the son of an insignificant priest in Dongola, having quarrelled with the Sheikh from whom he was receiving religious instruction, set up as an independent preacher, with his headquarters at Abba Island, on the Nile, a hundred and fifty miles above Khartoum. Like Hong-siu-tsuen, he began as a religious reformer, and ended as a rebel king. It was his mission, he declared, to purge the true Faith of its worldliness and corruptions, to lead the followers of the prophet into the paths of chastity, simplicity, and holiness; with the puritanical zeal of a Calvin, he denounced junketings and merrymakings, songs and dances, lewd living and all the delights of the flesh. He fell into trances, he saw visions, he saw the prophet and Jesus, and the Angel Izrail* accompanying him and watching over him for ever. He prophesied, and performed miracles, and his fame spread through the land.

There is an ancient tradition in the Mohammedan world telling of a mysterious being, the last in succession of the twelve holy Imams, who, untouched by death and withdrawn into the recesses of a mountain, was destined, at the appointed hour, to come forth again among men. His title was the Mahdi, the guide; some believed that he would be the forerunner of the Messiah; others that he would be Christ himself. Already various Mahdis had made their appearance; several had been highly successful, and two, in medieval times, had founded dynasties in Egypt. But who could tell whether all these were not impostors? Might not the twelfth Imam be still waiting, in mystical concealment, ready to emerge, at any moment, at the bidding of God? There were signs by which the true Mahdi might be recognised – unmistakable signs, if one could but read them aright. He must be of the family of the prophet; he must possess miraculous powers of no common kind; and his person must be overflowing with a peculiar sanctity. The pious dwellers beside those distant waters, where holy men by dint of a constant repetition of one of the ninety-nine names of God, secured the protection of guardian angels, and where groups of devotees, shaking their heads with a violence which would unseat the reason of less athletic worshippers, attained to an extraordinary beatitude, heard with awe of the young preacher whose saintliness was almost more than mortal and whose miracles brought amazement to the mind. Was he not also of the family of the prophet? He himself had said so; and who would disbelieve the holy man? When he appeared in person, every doubt was swept away. There was a strange splendour in his presence, an overpowering passion in the torrent of his speech. Great was the wickedness of the people, and great was their punishment! Surely their miseries were a visible sign of the wrath of the Lord. They had sinned, and the cruel tax-gatherers had come among them, and the corrupt governors, and all the oppressions of the Egyptians. Yet these things, too, should have an end. The Lord would raise up his chosen deliverer: the hearts of the people would be purified, and their enemies would be laid low. The accursed Egyptian would be driven from the land. Let the faithful take heart and make ready. How soon might not the long-predestined hour strike, when the twelfth Imam, the guide, the Mahdi, would reveal himself to the world? In that hour, the right-eous would triumph and the guilty be laid low for ever. Such was the teaching of Mahommed Ahmed. A band of enthusiastic disciples gathered round him, eagerly waiting for the revelation which would crown their hopes. At last, the moment came. One evening, at Abba Island, taking aside the foremost of his followers, the Master whispered the portentous news. He was the Mahdi.

The Egyptian Governor-General at Khartoum, hearing that a religious movement was on foot, grew disquieted, and dispatched an emissary to Abba Island to summon the impostor to his presence. The emissary was courteously received. Mahommed Ahmed, he said, must come at once to Khartoum. 'Must!' exclaimed the Mahdi, starting to his feet, with a strange look in his eyes. The look was so strange that the emissary thought it advisable to cut short the inter-view and to return to Khartoum empty-handed. Thereupon the Governor-General sent two hundred soldiers to seize the audacious rebel by force. With his handful of friends, the Mahdi fell upon the soldiers and cut them to pieces. The news spread like wild-fire through the country: the Mahdi had arisen, the Egyptians were des-troyed. But it was clear to the little band of enthusiasts at Abba Island that their position on the river was no longer tenable. The Mahdi, deciding upon a second Hegira,* retreated south-westward, into the depths of Kordofan.

The retreat was a triumphal progress. The country, groaning under alien misgovernment and vibrating with religious excitement, suddenly found in this rebellious prophet a rallying-point, a hero, a deliverer. And now another element was added to the forces of insur-rection. The Baggara tribes of Kordofan, cattle-owners and slave-traders, the most warlike and vigorous of the inhabitants of the Sudan, threw in their lot with the Mahdi. Their powerful Emirs, still smarting from the blows of Gordon, saw that the opportunity for revenge had come. A holy war was proclaimed against the Egyptian misbelievers. The followers of the Mahdi, dressed, in token of a new austerity of living, in the 'jibbeh,' or white smock of coarse cloth, patched with variously shaped and coloured patches, were rapidly organised into a formidable army. Several attacks from Khartoum were repulsed; and at last the Mahdi felt strong enough to advance against the enemy. While his lieutenants led detachments into the vast provinces lying to the west and the south – Darfur and Bahr-el-Ghazal – he himself marched upon El Obeid, the capital of Kordofan. It was in vain that reinforcements were hurried from Khartoum to the assistance of the garrison: there was some severe fighting; the town was completely cut off; and, after a six months' siege, it surrendered. A great quantity of guns and ammunition and £100,000 in specie fell into the hands of the Mahdi. He was master of Kordofan: he was at the head of a great army; he was rich; he was worshipped. A dazzling future opened before him. No possibility seemed too remote, no fortune too magnificent. A vision of universal empire hovered before his eyes. Allah, whose servant he was, who had led him thus far, would lead him onward still, to the glorious end.

For some months he remained at El Obeid, consolidating his dominion. In a series of circular letters, he described his colloquies with the Almighty and laid down the rule of living which his followers were to pursue. The faithful, under pain of severe punishment, were to return to the ascetic simplicity of ancient times. A criminal code was drawn up, meting out executions, mutilations, and floggings with a barbaric zeal. The blasphemer was to be instantly hanged, the adulterer was to be scourged with whips of rhinoceros hide, the thief was to have his right hand and his left foot hacked off in the market-place. No more were marriages to be celebrated with pomp and feasting, no more was the youthful warrior to swagger with flowing hair: henceforth the believer must banquet on dates and milk, and his head must be kept shaved. Minor transgressions were punished by confiscation of property, or by imprisonment and chains. But the rhinoceros whip was the favourite instrument of chastisement. Men were flogged for drinking a glass of wine, they were flogged for smoking; if they swore, they received eighty lashes for every expletive; and after eighty lashes it was a common thing to die. Before long, flogging grew to be so everyday an incident that the young men made a game of it, as a test of their endurance of pain. With this Spartan ferocity there was mingled the glamour and the mystery of the East. The Mahdi himself, his four Khalifas, and the principal Emirs, masters of sudden riches, surrounded themselves with slaves and women, with trains of horses and asses, with bodyguards and glittering arms. There were rumours of debaucheries in high places; of the Mahdi, forgetful of his own ordinances, revelling in the recesses of his harem, and quaffing date syrup mixed with ginger out of the silver cups looted from the church of the Christians. But that imposing figure had only to show itself for the tongue of scandal to be stilled. The tall, broad-shouldered, majestic man, with the dark face and black beard and great eyes – who could doubt that he was the embodiment of a superhuman power? Fascination dwelt in every movement, every glance. The eyes, painted with antimony, flashed extraordinary fires; the exquisite smile revealed, beneath the vigorous lips, white upper teeth with a V-shaped space between them – the certain sign of fortune. His turban was folded with faultless art, his jibbeh, speck-less, was perfumed with sandal-wood, musk, and attar of roses. He was at once all courtesy and all command. Thousands followed him, thousands prostrated themselves before him; thousands, when he lifted up his voice in solemn worship, knew that the heavens were opened and that they had come near to God. Then all at once the onbeia – the elephant's-tusk trumpet – would give out its enormous sound. The nahas – the brazen war-drums – would summon, with their weird rolling, the whole host to arms. The green flag and the red flag and the black flag would rise over the multitude. The great army would move forward, coloured, glistening, dark, violent, proud, beautiful. The drunkenness, the madness, of religion would blaze on every face; and the Mahdi, immovable on his charger, would let the scene grow under his eyes in silence.

El Obeid fell in January, 1883. Meanwhile events of the deepest importance had occurred in Egypt. The rise of Arábi had synchron-ised with that of the Mahdi. Both movements were nationalist; both were directed against alien rulers who had shown themselves unfit to rule. While the Sudanese were shaking off the yoke of Egypt, the Egyptians themselves grew impatient of their own masters – the Turkish and Circassian Pashas who filled with their incompetence all the high offices of state. The army, led by Ahmed Arábi, a Colonel of fellah origin, mutinied, the Khedive gave way, and it seemed as if a new order were about to be established. A new order was indeed upon the point of appearing: but it was of a kind undreamt of in Arábi's philosophy. At the critical moment, the English Government intervened. An English fleet bombarded Alexandria, an English

army landed under Lord Wolseley* and defeated Arábi and his supporters at Tel-el-kebir. The rule of the Pashas was nominally
restored; but henceforth, in effect, the English were masters of
Egypt.

Nevertheless, the English themselves were slow to recognise this
fact. Their Government had intervened unwillingly; the occupation
of the country was a merely temporary measure; their army was to be
withdrawn so soon as a tolerable administration had been set up. But
a tolerable administration, presided over by the Pashas, seemed long
in coming, and the English army remained. In the meantime
the Mahdi had entered El Obeid, and his dominion was rapidly
spreading over the greater part of the Sudan.

Then a terrible catastrophe took place. The Pashas, happy once
more in Cairo, pulling the old strings and growing fat over the old
flesh-pots, decided to give the world an unmistakable proof of their
renewed vigour. They would tolerate the insurrection in the Sudan
no longer; they would destroy the Mahdi, reduce his followers to
submission, and re-establish their own beneficent rule over the
whole country. To this end they collected together an army of ten
thousand men, and placed it under the command of Colonel Hicks, a
retired English officer,* He was ordered to advance and suppress the
rebellion. In these proceedings the English Government refused to
take any part. Unable, or unwilling, to realise that, so long as there
was an English army in Egypt, they could not avoid the responsibilities of supreme power, they declared that the domestic policy of
the Egyptian administration was no concern of theirs. It was a fatal
error – an error which they themselves, before many weeks were
over, were to be forced by the hard logic of events to admit. The
Pashas, left to their own devices, mismanaged the Hicks expedition
to their hearts' content. The miserable troops, swept together from
the relics of Arábi's disbanded army, were dispatched to Khartoum
in chains. After a month's drilling they were pronounced to be fit to
attack the fanatics of the Sudan. Colonel Hicks was a brave man;
urged on by the authorities in Cairo, he shut his eyes to the danger
ahead of him, and marched out from Khartoum in the direction of
El Obeid at the beginning of September, 1883. Abandoning his
communications, he was soon deep in the desolate wastes of Kordofan. As he advanced, his difficulties increased; the guides were
treacherous, the troops grew exhausted, the supply of water gave

out. He pressed on, and at last, on November 5th, not far from El Obeid, the harassed, fainting, almost desperate army plunged into a vast forest of gum-trees and mimosa scrub. There was a sudden, an appalling yell; the Mahdi, with forty thousand of his finest men, sprang from their ambush. The Egyptians were surrounded, and immediately overpowered. It was not a defeat, but an annihilation. Hicks and his European staff were slaughtered; the whole army was slaughtered; three hundred wounded wretches crept away into the forest alive.

The consequences of this event were felt in every part of the Sudan. To the westward, in Darfur, the Governor, Slatin Pasha, after a prolonged and valiant resistance, was forced to surrender, and the whole province fell into the hands of the rebels. Southwards, in the Bahr-el-Ghazal, Lupton Bey was shut up in a remote stronghold, while the country was overrun. The Mahdi's triumphs were beginning to penetrate even into the tropical regions of Equatoria; the tribes were rising, and Emin Pasha was preparing to retreat towards the Great Lakes. On the east, Osman Digna pushed the insurrection right up to the shores of the Red Sea, and laid siege to Suakin. Before the year was over, with the exception of a few isolated and surrounded garrisons, the Mahdi was absolute lord of a territory equal to the combined area of Spain, France, and Germany; and his victorious armies were rapidly closing round Khartoum.

When the news of the Hicks disaster reached Cairo, the Pashas calmly announced that they would collect another army of ten thousand men, and again attack the Mahdi; but the English Government understood at last the gravity of the case. They saw that a crisis was upon them, and that they could no longer escape the implications of their position in Egypt. What were they to do? Were they to allow the Egyptians to become more and more deeply involved in a ruinous, perhaps ultimately a fatal, war with the Mahdi? And, if not, what steps were they to take? A small minority of the party then in power in England – the Liberal Party – were anxious to withdraw from Egypt altogether and at once. On the other hand, another and a more influential minority, with representatives in the Cabinet, were in favour of a more active intervention in Egyptian affairs – of the deliberate use of the power of England to give to Egypt internal stability and external security; they were ready, if necessary, to take the field against the Mahdi with English troops. But the great bulk of the party, and the Cabinet, with Mr Gladstone at their head,* preferred a middle course. Realising the impracticability of an immediate withdrawal, they were nevertheless determined to remain in Egypt not a moment longer than was necessary, and, in the meantime, to interfere as little as possible in Egyptian affairs. From a campaign in the Sudan conducted by an English army they were altogether averse. If, therefore, the English army was not to be used, and the Egyptian army was not fit to be used, against the Mahdi, it followed that any attempt to reconquer the Sudan must be abandoned; the remaining Egyptian troops must be withdrawn, and in future military operations must be limited to those of a strictly defensive kind. Such was the decision of the English Government. Their determination was strengthened by two considerations: in the first place, they saw that the Mahdi's rebellion was largely a nationalist movement, directed against an alien power, and, in the second place, the policy of withdrawal from the Sudan was the policy of their own representative in Egypt, Sir Evelyn Baring, who had lately been appointed Consul-General at Cairo. There was only one serious obstacle in the way – the attitude of the Pashas at the head of the Egyptian Government. The infatuated old men were convinced that they would have better luck next time, that another army and another Hicks would certainly destroy the Mahdi, and that, even if the Mahdi were again victorious, yet another army and yet another Hicks would no doubt be forthcoming, and that *they* would do the trick, or, failing that . . . but they refused to consider eventualities any further. In the face of such opposition, the English Government, unwilling as they were to interfere, saw that there was no choice open to them but to exercise pressure. They therefore instructed Sir Evelyn Baring, in the event of the Egyptian Government refusing to withdraw from the Sudan, to insist upon the Khedive's appointing other Ministers who would be willing to do so.

Meanwhile, not only the Government, but the public in England were beginning to realise the alarming nature of the Egyptian situation. It was some time before the details of the Hicks expedition were fully known, but when they were, and when the appalling character of the disaster was understood, a thrill of horror ran through the country. The newspapers became full of articles on the Sudan, of personal descriptions of the Mahdi, of agitated letters from colonels and clergymen demanding vengeance, and of serious discussions of future policy in Egypt. Then, at the beginning of the new year, alarming messages began to arrive from Khartoum. Colonel Coetlogon, who was in command of the Egyptian troops, reported a menacing concentration of the enemy. Day by day, hour by hour, affairs grew worse. The Egyptians were obviously outnumbered: they could not maintain themselves in the field; Khartoum was in danger; at any moment its investment might be complete. And, with Khartoum once cut off from communication with Egypt, what might not happen? Colonel Coetlogon began to calculate how long the city would hold out. Perhaps it could not resist the Mahdi for a month, perhaps for more than a month; but he began to talk of the necessity of a speedy retreat. It was clear that a climax was approaching, and that measures must be taken to forestall it at once. Accordingly, Sir Evelyn Baring, on receipt of final orders from England, presented an ultimatum to the Egyptian Government: the Ministry must either sanction the evacuation of the Sudan, or it must resign. The Ministry was obstinate, and, on January 7th, 1884, it resigned, to be replaced by a more pliable body of Pashas. On the same day, General Gordon arrived at Southampton.

He was over fifty, and he was still, by the world's measurements, an unimportant man. In spite of his achievements, in spite of a certain celebrity – for 'Chinese Gordon' was still occasionally spoken of – he was unrecognised and almost unemployed. He had spent a life-time in the dubious services of foreign governments, punctuated by futile drudgeries at home; and now, after a long idleness, he had been sent for – to do what? – to look after the Congo for the King of the Belgians. At his age, even if he survived the work and the climate, he could hardly look forward to any subsequent appointment; he would return from the Congo, old and worn out, to a red-brick villa and extinction. Such were General Gordon's prospects on January 7th, 1884.* By January 18th, his name was on every tongue, he was the favourite of the nation, he had been declared to be the one man living capable of coping with the perils of the hour, he had been chosen, with unanimous approval, to perform a great task, and he had left England on a mission which was to bring him not only a boundless popularity but an immortal fame. The circumstances which led to a change so sudden and so remarkable are less easily explained than might have been wished. An ambiguity hangs over them – an ambiguity which the discretion of eminent persons has certainly not diminished. But some of the facts are clear enough.

The decision to withdraw from the Sudan had no sooner been taken than it had become evident that the operation would be a difficult and hazardous one, and that it would be necessary to send to Khartoum an emissary armed with special powers and possessed of special ability, to carry it out. Towards the end of November, somebody at the War Office – it is not clear who* – had suggested that this emissary should be General Gordon: Lord Granville, the Foreign Secretary, had thereupon telegraphed to Sir Evelyn Baring asking whether, in his opinion, the presence of General Gordon would be useful in Egypt; Sir Evelyn Baring had replied that the Egyptian Government were averse to this proposal, and the matter had dropped. There was no further reference to Gordon in the official dispatches until after his return to England. Nor, before that date, was any allusion made to him, as a possible unraveller of the Sudan difficulty, in the Press. In all the discussions which followed the news of the Hicks disaster, his name is only to be found in occasional and incidental references to his work in the Sudan. The *Pall Mall Gazette*, which, more than any other newspaper, interested itself in Egyptian affairs,* alluded to Gordon once or twice as a geographical expert; but, in an enumeration of the leading authorities on the Sudan, left him out of account altogether. Yet it was from the *Pall Mall Gazette* that the impulsion which projected him into a blaze of publicity finally came. Mr Stead, its enterprising editor, went down to Southampton the day after Gordon's arrival there, and obtained an interview. Now when he was in the mood – after a little b. and s., especially – no one was more capable than Gordon, with his facile speech and his free-and-easy manners, of furnishing good copy for a journalist; and Mr Stead made the most of his opportunity. The interview, copious and pointed, was published next day in the most prominent part of the paper, together with a leading article, demanding that the General should be immediately dispatched to Khartoum with the widest powers. The rest of the Press, both in London and in the provinces, at once took up the cry. General Gordon was a capable and energetic officer, he was a noble and God-fearing man, he was a national asset, he was a statesman in the highest sense of the word: the occasion was pressing and perilous; General Gordon had been for years Governor-General of the Sudan; General Gordon alone had the knowledge, the courage, the virtue, which would save the situation; General Gordon must go to Khartoum. So, for a week, the papers sang in chorus. But already those in high places had taken a step. Mr Stead's interview appeared on the afternoon of January 9th, and on the morning of January 10th Lord Granville* telegraphed to Sir Evelyn Baring, proposing, for a second time, that Gordon's services should be utilised in Egypt. But Sir Evelyn Baring, for the second time, rejected the proposal.

While these messages were flashing to and fro, Gordon himself was paying a visit to the Rev. Mr Barnes at the Vicarage of Heavitree, near Exeter. The conversation ran chiefly on Biblical and spiritual matters – on the light thrown by the Old Testament upon the geography of Palestine, and on the relations between man and his Maker; but there were moments when topics of a more worldly interest arose. It happened that Sir Samuel Baker, Gordon's predecessor in Equatoria, lived in the neighbourhood. A meeting was arranged, and the two ex-Governors, with Mr Barnes in attendance, went for a drive together. In the carriage, Sir Samuel Baker, taking up the tale of the *Pall Mall Gazette*, dilated upon the necessity of his friend's returning to the Sudan as Governor-General. Gordon was silent; but Mr Barnes noticed that his blue eyes flashed, while an eager expression passed over his face. Late that night, after the Vicar had retired to bed, he was surprised by the door suddenly opening, and by the appearance of his guest swiftly tripping into the room. 'You saw me to-day?' the low voice abruptly questioned. 'You mean in the carriage?' replied the startled Mr Barnes. 'Yes,' came the reply; 'you saw *me* – that was *myself* – the self I want to get rid of.' There was a sliding movement, the door swung to, and the Vicar found himself alone again.*

It was clear that a disturbing influence had found its way into Gordon's mind. His thoughts, wandering through Africa, flitted to the Sudan; they did not linger at the Congo. During the same visit, he took the opportunity of calling upon Dr Temple, the Bishop of Exeter, and asking him, merely as a hypothetical question, whether, in his opinion, Sudanese converts to Christianity might be permitted to keep three wives. His Lordship answered that this would be uncanonical.

A few days later, it appeared that the conversation in the carriage at Heavitree had borne fruit. Gordon wrote a letter to Sir Samuel

Baker, further elaborating the opinions on the Sudan which he had already expressed in his interview with Mr Stead; the letter was clearly intended for publication, and published it was, in the *Times* of January 14th. On the same day, Gordon's name began once more to buzz along the wires in secret questions and answers to and from the highest quarters.

'Might it not be advisable,' telegraphed Lord Granville to Mr Gladstone, 'to put a little pressure on Baring, to induce him to accept the assistance of General Gordon?' Mr Gladstone replied, also by a telegram, in the affirmative; and on the 15th Lord Wolseley telegraphed to Gordon begging him to come to London immediately. Lord Wolseley, who was one of Gordon's oldest friends, was at that time Adjutant-General of the Forces; there was a long interview; and, though the details of the conversation have never transpired, it is known that, in the course of it, Lord Wolseley asked Gordon if he would be willing to go to the Sudan, to which Gordon replied that there was only one objection – his prior engagement to the King of the Belgians. Before nightfall, Lord Granville, by private telegram, had 'put a little pressure on Baring.' 'He had,' he said, 'heard indirectly that Gordon was ready to go at once to the Sudan on the following rather vague terms. His mission to be to report to Her Majesty's Government on the military situation, and to return without any further engagement. He would be under you for instructions and will send letters through you under flying seal. . . . He might be of use,' Lord Granville added, 'in informing you and us of the situation. It would be popular at home, but there may be countervailing objections. Tell me,' such was Lord Granville's concluding injunction, 'your real opinion.' It was the third time of asking, and Sir Evelyn Baring resisted no longer. 'Gordon,' he telegraphed on the 16th, 'would be the best man if he will pledge himself to carry out the policy of withdrawing from the Sudan as quickly as is possible consistently with saving life. He must also understand that he must take his instructions from the British representative in Egypt. . . . I would rather have him than any one else, provided there is a perfectly clear understanding with him as to what his position is to be and what line of policy he is to carry out. Otherwise, not. . . . Whoever goes should be distinctly warned that he will undertake a service of great difficulty and danger.' In the meantime, Gordon, with the Sudan upon his lips, with the Sudan in his imagination, had hurried to Brussels, to obtain from the King of the Belgians a reluctant consent to the postponement of his Congo mission. On the 17th he was recalled to London by a telegram from Lord Wolseley. On the 18th the final decision was made. 'At noon,' Gordon told the Rev. Mr Barnes, 'Wolseley came to me and took me to the Ministers. He went in and talked to the Ministers, and came back and said: "Her Majesty's Government want you to undertake this. Government are determined to evacuate the Sudan, for they will not guarantee future government. Will you go and do it?" I said: "Yes." He said: "Go in." I went in and saw them. They said: "Did Wolseley tell you your orders?" I said: "Yes." I said: "You will not guarantee future government of the Sudan, and you wish me to go up and evacuate now." They said: "Yes," and it was over.'

Such was the sequence of events which ended in General Gordon's last appointment. The precise motives of those responsible for these transactions are less easy to discern.* It is difficult to understand what the reasons could have been which induced the Government, not only to override the hesitations of Sir Evelyn Baring, but to overlook the grave and obvious dangers involved in sending such a man as Gordon to the Sudan. The whole history of his life, the whole bent of his character, seemed to disqualify him for the task for which he had been chosen. He was before all things a fighter, an enthusiast, a bold adventurer;* and he was now to be entrusted with the conduct of an inglorious retreat. He was alien to the subtleties of civilised statesmanship, he was unamenable to official control, he was incapable of the skilful management of delicate situations; and he was now to be placed in a position of great complexity, requiring at once a cool judgment, a clear perception of fact, and a fixed determination to carry out a line of policy laid down from above. He had, it is true, been Governor-General of the Sudan; but he was now to return to the scene of his greatness as the emissary of a defeated and humbled power; he was to be a fugitive where he had once been a ruler; the very success of his mission was to consist in establishing the triumph of those forces which he had spent years in trampling underfoot. All this should have been clear to those in authority, after a very little reflection. It was clear enough to Sir Evelyn Baring, though, with characteristic reticence, he had abstained from giving expression to his thoughts. But, even if a general acquaintance with Gordon's life and character were not sufficient to lead to these conclusions, he himself had taken care to put their validity beyond reasonable doubt. Both in his interview with Mr Stead and in his letter to Sir Samuel Baker, he had indicated unmistakably his own attitude towards the Sudan situation. The policy which he advocated, the state of feeling in which he showed himself to be, were diametrically opposed to the declared intentions of the Government. He was by no means in favour of withdrawing from the Sudan: he was in favour, as might have been supposed, of vigorous military action. It might be necessary to abandon, for the time being, the more remote garrisons in Darfur and Equatoria; but Khartoum must be held at all costs. To allow the Mahdi to enter Khartoum would not merely mean the return of the whole of the Sudan to barbarism, it would be a menace to the safety of Egypt herself. To attempt to protect Egypt against the Mahdi by fortifying her southern frontier was preposterous. 'You might as well fortify against a fever.' Arabia, Syria, the whole Mohammedan world, would be shaken by the Mahdi's advance. 'In self-defence,' Gordon declared to Mr Stead, 'the policy of evacuation cannot possibly be justified.' The true policy was obvious. A strong man – Sir Samuel Baker, perhaps – must be sent to Khartoum, with a large contingent of Indian and Turkish troops and with two millions of money. He would very soon overpower the Mahdi, whose forces would 'fall to pieces of themselves.' For in Gordon's opinion it was 'an entire mistake to regard the Mahdi as in any sense a religious leader'; he would collapse as soon as he was face to face with an English general. Then the distant regions of Darfur and Equatoria could once more be occupied; their original Sultans could be reinstated; the whole country would be placed under civilised rule; and the slave-trade would be finally abolished. These were the views which Gordon publicly expressed on January 9th and on January 14th; and it certainly seems strange that on January 10th and on January 14th, Lord Granville should have proposed, without a word of consultation with Gordon himself, to send him on a mission which involved, not the reconquest, but the abandonment of the Sudan. Gordon, indeed, when he was actually approached by Lord Wolseley, had apparently agreed to become the agent of a policy which was exactly the reverse of his own. No doubt, too, it is possible for a subordinate to suppress his private convictions and to carry out loyally, in spite of them, the orders of his superiors. But how rare are the qualities of self-control and wisdom which such a subordinate must possess! And how little reason there was to think that General Gordon possessed them!

In fact, the conduct of the Government wears so singular an appearance that it has seemed necessary to account for it by some ulterior explanation. It has often been asserted that the true cause of Gordon's appointment was the clamour in the Press. It is said – among others, by Sir Evelyn Baring himself, who has given something like an official sanction to this view of the case – that the Government could not resist the pressure of the newspapers and the feeling in the country which it indicated; that Ministers, carried off their feet by a wave of 'Gordon cultus,' were obliged to give way to the inevitable. But this suggestion is hardly supported by an examination of the facts. Already, early in December, and many weeks before Gordon's name had begun to figure in the newspapers, Lord Granville had made his first effort to induce Sir Evelyn Baring to accept Gordon's services. The first newspaper demand for a Gordon mission appeared in the *Pall Mall Gazette* on the afternoon of January 9th; and the very next morning Lord Granville was making his second telegraphic attack upon Sir Evelyn Baring. The feeling in the Press did not become general until the 11th, and on the 14th Lord Granville, in his telegram to Mr Gladstone, for the third time proposed the appointment of Gordon. Clearly, on the part of Lord Granville at any rate, there was no extreme desire to resist the wishes of the Press. Nor was the Government as a whole by any means incapable of ignoring public opinion: a few months were to show that, plainly enough. It is difficult to avoid the conclusion that if Ministers had been opposed to the appointment of Gordon, he would never have been appointed. As it was, the newspapers were in fact forestalled, rather than followed, by the Government.

How, then, are we to explain the Government's action? Are we to suppose that its members, like the members of the public at large, were themselves carried away by a sudden enthusiasm, a sudden conviction that they had found their saviour, that General Gordon was the man – they did not quite know why, but that was of no consequence – the one man to get them out of the whole Sudan difficulty – they did not quite know how, but that was of no consequence either – if only he were sent to Khartoum? Doubtless even Cabinet Ministers are liable to such impulses; doubtless it is possible that the Cabinet of that day allowed itself to drift, out of mere lack of consideration, and judgment, and foresight, along the rapid stream of popular feeling towards the inevitable cataract. That may be so; yet there are indications that a more definite influence was at work. There was a section of the Government which had never become quite reconciled to the policy of withdrawing from the Sudan. To this section – we may call it the imperialist section – which was led, inside the Cabinet, by Lord Hartington, and outside by Lord Wolseley, the policy which really commended itself was the very policy which had been outlined by General Gordon in his interview with Mr Stead and his letter to Sir Samuel Baker. They saw that it might be necessary to abandon some of the outlying parts of the Sudan to the Mahdi; but the prospect of leaving the whole province in his hands was highly distasteful to them; above all, they dreaded the loss of Khartoum. Now, supposing that General Gordon, in response to a popular agitation in the Press, were sent to Khartoum, what would follow? Was it not at least possible that, once there, with his views and his character, he would, for some reason or other, refrain from carrying out a policy of pacific retreat? Was it not possible that in that case he might so involve the English Government that it would find itself obliged, almost imperceptibly perhaps, to substitute for its policy of withdrawal a policy of advance? Was it not possible that General Gordon might get into difficulties, that he might be surrounded and cut off from Egypt? If that were to happen, how could the English Government avoid the necessity of sending an expedition to rescue him? And, if an English expedition went to the Sudan, was it conceivable that it would leave the Mahdi as it found him? In short, would not the dispatch of General Gordon to Khartoum involve, almost inevitably, the conquest of the Sudan by British troops, followed by a British occupation? And, behind all these questions, a still larger question loomed. The position of the English in Egypt itself was still ambiguous; the future was obscure; how long, in reality, would an English army remain in Egypt? Was not one thing, at least, obvious – that if the English were to conquer and occupy the Sudan, their evacuation of Egypt would become impossible?

With our present information, it would be rash to affirm that all, or any, of these considerations were present to the minds of the imperialist section of the Government. Yet it is difficult to believe that a man such as Lord Wolseley, for instance, with his knowledge

of affairs and his knowledge of Gordon, could have altogether overlooked them. Lord Hartington, indeed, may well have failed to realise at once the implications of General Gordon's appointment – for
it took Lord Hartington some time to realise the implications of
anything; but Lord Hartington was very far from being a fool: and
we may well suppose that he instinctively, perhaps subconsciously,
apprehended the elements of a situation which he never formulated to himself. However that may be, certain circumstances are
significant. It is significant that the go-between who acted as the
Government's agent in its negotiations with Gordon was an imperialist – Lord Wolseley. It is significant that the 'Ministers' whom
Gordon finally interviewed, and who actually determined his
appointment, were by no means the whole of the Cabinet, but a small
section of it, presided over by Lord Hartington. It is significant, too,
that Gordon's mission was represented both to Sir Evelyn Baring,
who was opposed to his appointment, and to Mr Gladstone, who was
opposed to an active policy in the Sudan, as a mission merely 'to
report'; while, no sooner was the mission actually decided upon,
than it began to assume a very different complexion. In his final
interview with the 'Ministers,' Gordon, we know (though he said
nothing about it to the Rev. Mr Barnes), threw out the suggestion
that it might be as well to make him the Governor-General of the
Sudan. The suggestion, for the moment, was not taken up; but it is
obvious that a man does not propose to become a Governor-General
in order to make a report.

We are in the region of speculations; one other presents itself. Was
the movement in the Press during that second week of January a
genuine movement, expressing a spontaneous wave of popular feeling? Or was it a cause of that feeling, rather than an effect? The
engineering of a newspaper agitation may not have been an impossibility – even so long ago as 1884. One would like to know more than
one is ever likely to know of the relations of the imperialist section of
the Government with Mr Stead.

But it is time to return to the solidity of fact. Within a few hours
of his interview with the Ministers, Gordon had left England for
ever. At eight o'clock in the evening, there was a little gathering of
elderly gentlemen at Victoria Station. Gordon, accompanied by Colonel Stewart, who was to act as his second-in-command, tripped on
to the platform. Lord Granville bought the necessary tickets; the

Duke of Cambridge opened the railway-carriage door. The General jumped into the train; and then Lord Wolseley appeared, carrying a leather bag, in which was two hundred pounds in gold, collected from friends at the last moment, for the contingencies of the journey. The bag was handed through the window. The train started. As it did so, Gordon leant out, and addressed a last whispered question to Lord Wolseley. Yes, it had been done, Lord Wolseley had seen to it himself; next morning, every member of the Cabinet would receive a copy of Dr Samuel Clarke's *Scripture Promises*. That was all. The train rolled out of the station.*

Before the travellers reached Cairo, steps had been taken which finally put an end to the theory – if it had ever been seriously held – that the purpose of the mission was simply the making of a report. On the very day of Gordon's departure, Lord Granville telegraphed to Sir Evelyn Baring as follows: 'Gordon suggests that it may be announced in Egypt that he is on his way to Khartoum to arrange for the future settlement of the Sudan for the best advantage of the people.' Nothing was said of reporting. A few days later, Gordon himself telegraphed to Lord Granville suggesting that he should be made Governor-General of the Sudan, in order to 'accomplish the evacuation,' and to 'restore to the various Sultans of the Sudan their independence.' Lord Granville at once authorised Sir Evelyn Baring to issue, if he thought fit, a proclamation to this effect in the name of the Khedive. Thus the mission 'to report' had already swollen into a Governor-Generalship, with the object, not merely of effecting the evacuation of the Sudan, but also of setting up 'various Sultans' to take the place of the Egyptian Government.

In Cairo, in spite of the hostilities of the past, Gordon was received with every politeness. He was at once proclaimed Governor-General of the Sudan, with the widest powers. He was on the point of starting off again on his journey southwards, when a singular and important incident occurred. Zobeir, the rebel chieftain of Darfur, against whose forces Gordon had struggled for years, and whose son, Suleiman, had been captured and executed by Gessi, Gordon's lieutenant, was still detained at Cairo. It so fell out that he went to pay a visit to one of the Ministers at the same time as the new Governor-General. The two men met face to face, and, as he looked into the savage countenance of his old enemy, an extraordinary shock of inspiration ran through Gordon's brain. He was seized, as he explained in a State paper, which he drew up immediately after the meeting, with a 'mystic feeling' that he could trust Zobeir. It was true that Zobeir was 'the greatest slave-hunter who ever existed'; it was true that he had a personal hatred of Gordon, owing to the execution of Suleiman – 'and one cannot wonder at it, if one is a father'; it was true that, only a few days previously, on his way to Egypt, Gordon himself had been so convinced of the dangerous character of Zobeir that he had recommended by telegram his removal to Cyprus. But such considerations were utterly obliterated by that one moment of electric impact, of personal vision; henceforward there was a rooted conviction in Gordon's mind that Zobeir was to be trusted, that Zobeir must join him at Khartoum, that Zobeir's presence would paralyse the Mahdi, that Zobeir must succeed him in the government of the country after the evacuation. Did not Sir Evelyn Baring, too, have the mystic feeling? Sir Evelyn Baring confessed that he had not. He distrusted mystic feelings. Zobeir, no doubt, might possibly be useful; but before deciding upon so important a matter it was necessary to reflect and to consult.

In the meantime, failing Zobeir, something might perhaps be done with the Emir Abdul Shakur, the heir of the Darfur Sultans. The Emir, who had been living in domestic retirement in Cairo, was with some difficulty discovered, given £2000, an embroidered uniform, together with the largest decoration that could be found, and informed that he was to start at once with General Gordon for the Sudan, where it would be his duty to occupy the province of Darfur, after driving out the forces of the Mahdi. The poor man begged for a little delay; but no delay could be granted. He hurried to the railway station in his frock-coat and fez, and rather the worse for liquor. Several extra carriages for his twenty-three wives and a large quantity of luggage had then to be hitched on to the Governor-General's train; and at the last moment some commotion was caused by the unaccountable disappearance of his embroidered uniform. It was found, but his troubles were not over. On the steamer, General Gordon was very rude to him,* and he drowned his chagrin in hot rum and water. At Assuan he disembarked, declaring that he would go no farther. Eventually, however, he got as far as Dongola, whence, after a stay of a few months, he returned with his family to Cairo.

In spite of this little contretemps, Gordon was in the highest spirits. At last his capacities had been recognised by his countrymen;

at last he had been entrusted with a task great enough to satisfy even his desires. He was already famous; he would soon be glorious. Looking out once more over the familiar desert, he felt the searchings of his conscience stilled by the manifest certainty that it was for this that Providence had been reserving him through all these years of labour and of sorrow – for this! What was the Mahdi to stand up against him! A thousand schemes, a thousand possibilities sprang to life in his pullulating brain. A new intoxication carried him away. 'Il faut être toujours ivre. Tout est là: c'est l'unique question.'* Little though he knew it, Gordon was a disciple of Baudelaire. 'Pour ne pas sentir l'horrible fardeau du Temps qui brise vos épaules et vous penche vers la terre, il faut vous enivrer sans trêve.'* Yes; but how feeble were those gross resources of the miserable Abdul-Shakur! Rum? Brandy? Oh, he knew all about them; they were nothing. He tossed off a glass.* They were nothing at all. The true drunkenness lay elsewhere. He seized a paper and pencil, and dashed down a telegram to Sir Evelyn Baring. Another thought struck him, and another telegram followed. And another, and yet another. He had made up his mind; he would visit the Mahdi in person, and alone. He might do that; or he might retire to the Equator. He would decidedly retire to the Equator, and hand over the Bahr-el-Ghazal province to the King of the Belgians. A whole flock of telegrams flew to Cairo from every stopping-place. Sir Evelyn Baring was patient and discreet; he could be trusted with such confidences; but unfortunately Gordon's strange exhilaration found other outlets. At Berber, in the course of a speech to the assembled chiefs, he revealed the intention of the Egyptian Government to withdraw from the Sudan. The news was everywhere in a moment, and the results were disastrous. The tribesmen, whom fear and interest had still kept loyal, perceived that they need look no more for help or punishment from Egypt, and began to turn their eyes towards the rising sun.

Nevertheless, for the moment, the prospect wore a favourable appearance. The Governor-General was welcomed at every stage of his journey, and on February 18th he made a triumphal entry into Khartoum. The feeble garrison, the panic-stricken inhabitants, hailed him as a deliverer. Surely they need fear no more, now that the great English Pasha had come among them. His first acts seemed to show that a new and happy era had begun. Taxes were remitted, the bonds of the usurers were destroyed, the victims of Egyptian injustice were set free from the prisons; the immemorial instruments of torture – the stocks and the whips and the branding-irons – were broken to pieces in the public square. A bolder measure had been already taken. A proclamation had been issued sanctioning slavery in the Sudan. Gordon, arguing that he was powerless to do away with the odious institution, which, as soon as the withdrawal was carried out, would inevitably become universal, had decided to reap what benefit he could from the public abandonment of an unpopular policy. At Khartoum the announcement was received with enthusiasm, but it caused considerable perturbation in England. The Christian hero, who had spent so many years of his life in suppressing slavery, was now suddenly found to be using his high powers to set it up again. The Anti-Slavery Society made a menacing movement, but the Government showed a bold front, and the popular belief in Gordon's infallibility carried the day.

He himself was still radiant. Nor, amid the jubilation and the devotion which surrounded him, did he forget higher things. In all this turmoil, he told his sister, he was 'supported.' He gave injunctions that his Egyptian troops should have regular morning and evening prayers; 'they worship one God,' he said, 'Jehovah.' And he ordered an Arabic text, 'God rules the hearts of all men,' to be put up over the chair of state in his audience chamber. As the days went by, he began to feel at home again in the huge palace which he knew so well. The glare and the heat of that southern atmosphere, the movement of the crowded city, the dark-faced populace, the soldiers and the suppliants, the reawakened consciousness of power, the glamour and the mystery of the whole strange scene – these things seized upon him, engulfed him, and worked a new transformation on his intoxicated heart. England, with its complications and its policies, became an empty vision to him; Sir Evelyn Baring, with his cautions and sagacities, hardly more than a tiresome name. He was Gordon Pasha, he was the Governor-General, he was the ruler of the Sudan. He was among his people – his own people, and it was to them only that he was responsible – to them, and to God. Was he to let them fall without a blow into the clutches of a sanguinary impostor? Never! He was there to prevent that. The distant governments might mutter something about 'evacuation'; his thoughts were elsewhere. He poured them into his telegrams, and Sir Evelyn Baring sat aghast. The man who had left London a month before, with instructions to 'report upon the best means of effecting the evacuation of the Sudan,' was now openly talking of 'smashing up the Mahdi' with the aid of British and Indian troops. Sir Evelyn Baring counted up on his fingers the various stages of this extraordinary development in General Gordon's opinions. But he might have saved himself the trouble, for, in fact, it was less a development than a reversion. Under the stress of the excitements and the realities of his situation at Khartoum, the policy which Gordon was now proposing to carry out had come to tally, in every particular, with the policy which he had originally advocated with such vigorous conviction in the pages of the *Pall Mall Gazette*.

Nor was the adoption of that policy by the English Government by any means out of the question. For, in the meantime, events had been taking place in the Eastern Sudan, in the neighbourhood of the Red Sea port of Suakin, which were to have a decisive effect upon the prospects of Khartoum. General Baker, the brother of Sir Samuel Baker, attempting to relieve the beleaguered garrisons of Sinkat and Tokar, had rashly attacked the forces of Osman Digna, had been defeated, and obliged to retire. Sinkat and Tokar had then fallen into the hands of the Mahdi's general. There was a great outcry in England, and a wave of warlike feeling passed over the country. Lord Wolseley at once drew up a memorandum advocating the annexation of the Sudan. In the House of Commons even Liberals began to demand vengeance and military action, whereupon the Government dispatched Sir Gerald Graham* with a considerable British force to Suakin. Sir Gerald Graham advanced, and in the battles of El Teb and Tamai inflicted two bloody defeats upon the Mahdi's forces. It almost seemed as if the Government was now committed to a policy of interference and conquest; as if the imperialist section of the Cabinet were at last to have their way. The dispatch of Sir Gerald Graham coincided with Gordon's sudden demand for British and Indian troops with which to 'smash up the Mahdi.' The business, he assured Sir Evelyn Baring, in a stream of telegrams, could very easily be done. It made him sick, he said, to see himself held in check and the people of the Sudan tyrannised over by 'a feeble lot of stinking Dervishes.' Let Zobeir at once be sent down to him, and all would be well. The original Sultans of the country had unfortunately proved disappointing. Their place should be taken by Zobeir. After the Mahdi had been smashed up, Zobeir should rule the Sudan as a subsidised vassal of England, on a similar footing to that of the Amir of Afghanistan. The plan was perhaps feasible; but it was clearly incompatible with the policy of evacuation, as it had been hitherto laid down by the English Government. Should they reverse that policy? Should they appoint Zobeir, reinforce Sir Gerald Graham, and smash up the Mahdi? They could not make up their minds. So far as Zobeir was concerned, there were two counterbalancing considerations; on the one hand, Sir Evelyn Baring now declared that he was in favour of the appointment; but, on the other hand, would English public opinion consent to a man, described by Gordon himself as 'the greatest slave-hunter who ever existed,' being given an English subsidy and the control of the Sudan? While the Cabinet was wavering, Gordon took a fatal step. The delay was intolerable, and one evening, in a rage, he revealed his desire for Zobeir – which had hitherto been kept a profound official secret – to Mr Power,* the English Consul at Khartoum, and the special correspondent of the *Times*. Perhaps he calculated that the public announcement of his wishes would oblige the Government to yield to them; if so, he was completely mistaken, for the result was the very reverse. The country, already startled by the proclamation in favour of slavery, could not swallow Zobeir. The Anti-Slavery Society set on foot a violent agitation, opinion in the House of Commons suddenly stiffened, and the Cabinet, by a substantial majority, decided that Zobeir should remain in Cairo. The imperialist wave had risen high, but it had not risen high enough; and now it was rapidly subsiding. The Government's next action was decisive. Sir Gerald Graham and his British Army were withdrawn from the Sudan.

The critical fortnight during which these events took place was the first fortnight of March. By the close of it, Gordon's position had undergone a rapid and terrible change. Not only did he find himself deprived, by the decision of the Government, both of the hope of Zobeir's assistance and of the prospect of smashing up the Mahdi with the aid of British troops; the military movements in the Eastern Sudan produced, at the very same moment, a yet more fatal consequence. The adherents of the Mahdi had been maddened, they had not been crushed, by Sir Gerald Graham's victories. When, immediately afterwards, the English withdrew to Suakin, from which they never again emerged, the inference seemed obvious; they had been defeated, and their power was at an end. The war-like tribes to the north and the north-east of Khartoum had long been wavering. They now hesitated no longer, and joined the Mahdi. From that moment – it was less than a month from Gordon's arrival at Khartoum – the situation of the town was desperate. The line of communications was cut. Though it still might be possible for occasional native messengers, or for a few individuals on an armed steamer, to win their way down the river into Egypt, the removal of a large number of persons – the loyal inhabitants or the Egyptian garrison – was henceforward an impossibility. The whole scheme of the Gordon mission had irremediably collapsed; worse still, Gordon himself, so far from having effected the evacuation of the Sudan, was surrounded by the enemy. 'The question now is,' Sir Evelyn Baring told Lord Granville, on March 24th, 'how to get General Gordon and Colonel Stewart away from Khartoum.'

The actual condition of the town, however, was not, from a military point of view, so serious as Colonel Coetlogon, in the first moments of panic after the Hicks disaster, had supposed. Gordon was of opinion that it was capable of sustaining a siege of many months. With his usual vigour, he had already begun to prepare an elaborate system of earthworks, mines, and wire entanglements. There was a five or six months' supply of food, there was a great quantity of ammunition, the garrison numbered about 8000 men. There were, besides, nine small paddle-wheel steamers, hitherto used for purposes of communication along the Nile, which, fitted with guns and protected by metal plates, were of considerable military value. 'We are all right,' Gordon told his sister on March 15th. 'We shall, D.V., go on for months.' So far, at any rate, there was no cause for despair. But the effervescent happiness of three weeks since had vanished. Gloom, doubt, disillusionment, self-questioning, had swooped down again upon their victim. 'Either I must believe He does all things in mercy and love, or else I disbelieve His existence, there is no half way in the matter. What holes do I not put myself into! And for what? So mixed are my ideas. I believe ambition put me here in this ruin.' Was not that the explanation of it all? 'Our Lord's promise is not for the fulfilment of earthly wishes; therefore, if things come to ruin here He is still faithful, and is carrying out His great work of divine wisdom.' How could he have forgotten that? But he would not transgress again. 'I owe all to God, and nothing to myself, for, humanly speaking, I have done very foolish things. However, if I am humbled, the better for me.'

News of the changed circumstances at Khartoum was not slow in reaching England, and a feeling of anxiety began to spread. Among the first to realise the gravity of the situation was Queen Victoria. 'It is alarming,' she telegraphed to Lord Hartington on March 25th. 'General Gordon is in danger; you are bound to try to save him. . . . You have incurred fearful responsibility.' With an unerring instinct, Her Majesty forestalled and expressed the popular sentiment. During April, when it had become clear that the wire between Khartoum and Cairo had been severed, when, as time passed, no word came northward, save vague rumours of disaster, when at last a curtain of impenetrable mystery closed over Khartoum, the growing uneasiness manifested itself in letters to the newspapers, in leading articles, and in a flood of subscriptions towards a relief fund. At the beginning of May, the public alarm reached a climax. It now appeared to be certain, not only that General Gordon was in imminent danger, but that no steps had yet been taken by the Government to save him. On the 5th, there was a meeting of protest and indignation at St. James's Hall; on the 9th there was a mass meeting in Hyde Park; on the 11th there was a meeting at Manchester. The Baroness Burdett-Coutts wrote an agitated letter to the *Times* begging for further subscriptions. Somebody else proposed that a special fund should be started, with which 'to bribe the tribes to secure the General's personal safety.' A country vicar made another suggestion. Why should not public prayers be offered up for General Gordon in every church in the kingdom? He himself had adopted that course last Sunday. 'Is not this,' he concluded, 'what the godly man, the true hero, himself would wish to be done?' It was all of no avail. General Gordon remained in peril; the Government remained inactive. Finally, a vote of censure was moved in the House of Commons; but that too proved useless. It was strange. The same executive which, two months before, had trimmed its sails so eagerly to the shifting gusts of popular opinion, now, in spite of a rising hurricane, held on its course. A new spirit, it was clear – a determined, an intractable spirit – had taken control of the Sudan situation. What was it? The explanation was simple, and it was ominous. Mr Gladstone had intervened.

The old statesman was now entering upon the penultimate period

of his enormous career. He who had once been the rising hope of the
stern and unbending Tories, had at length emerged, after a lifetime
of transmutations, as the champion of militant democracy. He was at
the apex of his power. His great rival was dead; he stood pre-eminent
in the eye of the nation; he enjoyed the applause, the confidence, the
admiration, the adoration, even, of multitudes. Yet – such was the
peculiar character of the man, and such the intensity of the feelings
which he called forth – at this very moment, at the height of his
popularity, he was distrusted and loathed; already an unparalleled
animosity was gathering its forces against him. For, indeed, there
was something in his nature which invited – which demanded – the
clashing reactions of passionate extremes. It was easy to worship Mr
Gladstone; to see in him the perfect model of the upright man – the
man of virtue and of religion – the man whose whole life had been
devoted to the application of high principles to affairs of State – the
man, too, whose sense of right and justice was invigorated and
ennobled by an enthusiastic heart. It was also easy to detest him as a
hypocrite, to despise him as a demagogue, and to dread him as a
crafty manipulator of men and things for the purposes of his own
ambition. It might have been supposed that one or other of these
conflicting judgments must have been palpably absurd, that nothing
short of gross prejudice or wilful blindness, on one side or the other,
could reconcile such contradictory conceptions of a single human
being. But it was not so; 'the elements' were 'so mixed' in Mr Gladstone that his bitterest enemies (and his enemies were never mild)
and his warmest friends (and his friends were never tepid) could
justify, with equal plausibility, their denunciations or their praises.
What, then, was the truth? In the physical universe there are no
chimeras. But man is more various than nature; was Mr Gladstone,
perhaps, a chimera of the spirit? Did his very essence lie in the
confusion of incompatibles? His very essence? It eludes the hand
that seems to grasp it. One is baffled, as his political opponents were
baffled fifty years ago. The soft serpent coils harden into quick
strength that has vanished, leaving only emptiness and perplexity
behind. Speech was the fibre of his being; and, when he spoke, the
ambiguity of ambiguity was revealed. The long, winding, intricate
sentences, with their vast burden of subtle and complicated qualifications, befogged the mind like clouds, and like clouds, too, dropped
thunderbolts. Could it not then at least be said of him with certainty

that his was a complex character? But here also there was a contradiction. In spite of the involutions of his intellect and the contortions
of his spirit, it is impossible not to perceive a strain of *naïveté* in Mr
Gladstone. He adhered to some of his principles – that of the value
of representative institutions, for instance – with a faith which was
singularly literal; his views upon religion were uncritical to crude-
ness; he had no sense of humour. Compared with Disraeli's, his
attitude towards life strikes one as that of an ingenuous child. His
very egoism was simple-minded: through all the labyrinth of his
passions there ran a single thread. But the centre of the labyrinth?
Ah! the thread might lead there, through those wandering mazes, at
last. Only, with the last corner turned, the last step taken, the
explorer might find that he was looking down into the gulf of a
crater. The flame shot out on every side, scorching and brilliant; but
in the midst there was a darkness.

That Mr Gladstone's motives and ambitions were not merely
those of a hunter after popularity was never shown more clearly than
in that part of his career which, more than any other, has been
emphasised by his enemies – his conduct towards General Gordon.
He had been originally opposed to Gordon's appointment, but he
had consented to it partly, perhaps, owing to the persuasion that its
purpose did not extend beyond the making of a 'report.' Gordon
once gone, events had taken their own course; the policy of the
Government began to slide, automatically, down a slope at the bottom of which lay the conquest of the Sudan and the annexation of
Egypt. Sir Gerald Graham's bloody victories awoke Mr Gladstone
to the true condition of affairs; he recognised the road he was on and
its destination; but there was still time to turn back. It was he who
had insisted upon the withdrawal of the English army from the
Eastern Sudan. The imperialists were sadly disappointed. They had
supposed that the old lion had gone to sleep, and suddenly he had
come out of his lair, and was roaring. All their hopes now centred
upon Khartoum. General Gordon was cut off; he was surrounded,
he was in danger; he must be relieved. A British force must be sent to
save him. But Mr Gladstone was not to be caught napping a second
time. When the agitation rose, when popular sentiment was deeply
stirred, when the country, the Press, the Sovereign herself, declared
that the national honour was involved with the fate of General Gordon, Mr Gladstone remained immovable. Others might picture the

triumphant rescue of a Christian hero from the clutches of heathen savages; before *his* eyes was the vision of battle, murder, and sudden death, the horrors of defeat and victory, the slaughter and the anguish of thousands, the violence of military domination, the enslavement of a people. The invasion of the Sudan, he had flashed out in the House of Commons, would be a war of conquest against a people struggling to be free. 'Yes, those people are struggling to be free, and they are rightly struggling to be free.' Mr Gladstone – it was one of his old-fashioned simplicities – believed in liberty. If, indeed, it should turn out to be the fact that General Gordon was in serious danger, then, no doubt, it would be necessary to send a relief expedition to Khartoum. But he could see no sufficient reason to believe that it was the fact. Communications, it was true, had been interrupted between Khartoum and Cairo, but no news was not necessarily bad news, and the little information that had come through from General Gordon seemed to indicate that he could hold out for months. So his agile mind worked, spinning its familiar web of possibilities and contingencies and fine distinctions. General Gordon, he was convinced, might be hemmed in, but he was not surrounded. Surely, it was the duty of the Government to take no rash step, but to consider and to inquire, and, when it acted, to act upon reasonable conviction. And then, there was another question. If it was true – and he believed it was true – that General Gordon's line of retreat was open, why did not General Gordon use it? Perhaps he might be unable to withdraw the Egyptian garrison, but it was not for the sake of the Egyptian garrison that the relief expedition was proposed; it was simply and solely to secure the personal safety of General Gordon. And General Gordon had it in his power to secure his personal safety himself; and he refused to do so; he lingered on in Khartoum, deliberately, wilfully, in defiance of the obvious wishes of his superiors. Oh! it was perfectly clear what General Gordon was doing: he was trying to force the hand of the English Government. He was hoping that if he only remained long enough at Khartoum he would oblige the English Government to send an army into the Sudan which should smash up the Mahdi. That, then, was General Gordon's calculation! Well, General Gordon would learn that he had made a mistake. Who was he that he should dare to imagine that he could impose his will upon Mr Gladstone? The old man's eyes glared. If it came to a struggle between them – well, they should see! As the weeks passed, the strange situation grew tenser. It was like some silent deadly game of bluff. And who knows what was passing in the obscure depths of that terrifying spirit? What mysterious mixture of remorse, rage, and jealousy? Who was it that was ultimately responsible for sending General Gordon to Khartoum? But then, what did that matter? Why did not the man come back? He was a Christian hero, was he? Were there no other Christian heroes in the world? A Christian hero! Let him wait till the Mahdi's ring was really round him, till the Mahdi's spear was really about to fall! That would be the test of heroism! If he slipped back then, with his tail between his legs——! The world would judge.

One of the last telegrams sent by Gordon before the wire was cut* seemed to support exactly Mr Gladstone's diagnosis of the case. He told Sir Evelyn Baring that, since the Government refused to send either an expedition or Zobeir, he would 'consider himself free to act according to circumstances.' 'Eventually,' he said, 'you will be forced to smash up the Mahdi,' and he declared that if the Government persisted in its present line of conduct, it would be branded with an 'indelible disgrace.' The message was made public, and it happened that Mr Gladstone saw it for the first time in a newspaper, during a country visit. Another of the guests, who was in the room at the moment, thus describes the scene. 'He took up the paper, his eye instantly fell on the telegram, and he read it through. As he read, his face hardened and whitened, the eyes burned as I have seen them once or twice in the House of Commons when he was angered – burned with a deep fire, as if they would have consumed the sheet on which Gordon's message was printed, or as if Gordon's words had burnt into his soul, which was looking out in wrath and flame. He said not a word. For perhaps two or three minutes he sat still, his face all the while like the face you may read of in Milton – like none other I ever saw. Then he rose, still without a word, and was seen no more that morning.'*

It is curious that Gordon himself never understood the part that Mr Gladstone was playing in his destiny. His Khartoum Journals put this beyond a doubt. Except for one or two slight and jocular references to Mr Gladstone's minor idiosyncrasies – the shape of his collars, and his passion for felling trees – Gordon leaves him unnoticed, while he lavishes his sardonic humour upon Lord

Granville. But in truth Lord Granville was a nonentity. The error
shows how dim the realities of England had grown to the watcher in
Khartoum. When he looked towards home, the figure that loomed
largest upon his vision was – it was only natural that it should have
been so – the nearest. It was upon Sir Evelyn Baring that he fixed his
gaze. For him Sir Evelyn Baring was the embodiment of England –
or rather the embodiment of the English official classes, of English
diplomacy, of the English Government with its hesitations, its
insincerities, its double-faced schemes. Sir Evelyn Baring, he almost
came to think at moments, was the prime mover, the sole contriver,
of the whole Sudan imbroglio. In this he was wrong; for Sir Evelyn
Baring, of course, was an intermediary, without final responsibility
or final power; but Gordon's profound antipathy, his instinctive distrust, were not without their justification. He could never forget that
first meeting in Cairo, six years earlier, when the fundamental hostility between the two men had leapt to the surface. 'When oil mixes
with water,' he said, 'we will mix together.' Sir Evelyn Baring
thought so too; but *he* did not say so; it was not his way. When he
spoke, he felt no temptation to express everything that was in his
mind. In all he did, he was cautious, measured, unimpeachably correct. It would be difficult to think of a man more completely the
antithesis of Gordon. His temperament, all in monochrome, touched
in with cold blues and indecisive greys, was eminently unromantic.*
He had a steely colourlessness, and a steely pliability, and a steely
strength. Endowed beyond most men with the capacity of foresight,
he was endowed as very few men have ever been with that staying-
power which makes the fruit of foresight attainable. His views were
long, and his patience was even longer. He progressed imperceptibly;
he constantly withdrew; the art of giving way he practised with the
refinement of a virtuoso. But, though the steel recoiled and recoiled,
in the end it would spring forward. His life's work had in it an
element of paradox. It was passed entirely in the East; and the East
meant very little to him; he took no interest in it. It was something to
be looked after. It was also a convenient field for the talents of Sir
Evelyn Baring. Yet it must not be supposed that he was cynical;
perhaps he was not quite great enough for that. He looked forward to
a pleasant retirement – a country place – some literary recreations.
He had been careful to keep up his classics. His ambition can be
stated in a single phrase; it was, to become an institution; and he

achieved it. No doubt, too, he deserved it. The greatest of poets, in a bitter mood, has described the characteristics of a certain class of persons, whom he did not like. 'They,' he says,

'that have power to hurt and will do none,
That do not do the things they most do show,
Who, moving others, are themselves as stone,
Unmovèd, cold, and to temptation slow,
They rightly do inherit heaven's graces,
And husband nature's riches from expense;
They are the lords and owners of their faces. . . .'

The words might have been written for Sir Evelyn Baring.

Though, as a rule, he found it easy to despise those with whom he came into contact, he could not altogether despise General Gordon. If he could have, he would have disliked him less. He had gone as far as his caution had allowed him in trying to prevent the fatal appointment; and then, when it had become clear that the Government was insistent, he had yielded with a good grace. For a moment, he had imagined that all might yet be well; that he could impose himself, by the weight of his position and the force of his sagacity, upon his self-willed subordinate; that he could hold him in a leash at the end of the telegraph wire to Khartoum. Very soon he perceived that this was a miscalculation. To his disgust, he found that the telegraph wire, far from being an instrument of official discipline, had been converted by the agile strategist at the other end of it into a means of extending his own personality into the deliberations at Cairo. Every morning Sir Evelyn Baring would find upon his table a great pile of telegrams from Khartoum – twenty or thirty at least; and as the day went on, the pile would grow. When a sufficient number had accumulated he would read them all through, with the greatest care. There upon the table, the whole soul of Gordon lay before him – in its incoherence, its eccentricity, its impulsiveness, its romance; the jokes, the slang, the appeals to the prophet Isaiah, the whirl of contradictory policies – Sir Evelyn Baring did not know which exasperated him most. He would not consider whether, or to what degree, the man was a maniac; no, he would not. A subacid smile was the only comment he allowed himself. His position, indeed, was an extremely difficult one, and all his dexterity would be needed if he was to emerge from it with credit. On one side of him was a veering and vacillating Government; on the other, a frenzied enthusiast. It was his business to interpret to the first the wishes, or rather the inspirations, of the second, and to convey to the second the decisions, or rather the indecisions, of the first. A weaker man would have floated helplessly on the ebb and flow of the Cabinet's wavering policies; a rasher man would have plunged headlong into Gordon's schemes. He did neither; with a singular courage and a singular caution he progressed along a razor-edge. He devoted all his energies to the double task of evolving a reasonable policy out of Gordon's intoxicated telegrams, and of inducing the divided Ministers at home to give their sanction to what he had evolved. He might have succeeded, if he had not had to reckon with yet another irreconcilable; Time was a vital element in the situation, and Time was against him. When the tribes round Khartoum rose, the last hope of a satisfactory solution vanished. He was the first to perceive the altered condition of affairs; long before the Government, long before Gordon himself, he understood that the only remaining question was that of the extrication of the Englishmen from Khartoum. He proposed that a small force should be dispatched at once across the desert from Suakin to Berber, the point on the Nile nearest to the Red Sea, and thence up the river to Gordon; but, after considerable hesitation, the military authorities decided that this was not a practicable plan. Upon that, he foresaw, with perfect lucidity, the inevitable development of events. Sooner or later, it would be absolutely necessary to send a relief expedition to Khartoum; and, from that premise, it followed, without a possibility of doubt, that it was the duty of the Government to do so at once. This he saw quite clearly; but he also saw that the position in the Cabinet had now altered, that Mr Gladstone had taken the reins into his own hands. And Mr Gladstone did not wish to send a relief expedition. What was Sir Evelyn Baring to do? Was he to pit his strength against Mr Gladstone's? To threaten resignation? To stake his whole future upon General Gordon's fate? For a moment he wavered; he seemed to hint that unless the Government sent a message to Khartoum promising a relief expedition before the end of the year, he would be unable to be a party to their acts. The Government refused to send any such message; and he perceived, as he tells us, that 'it was evidently useless to continue the correspondence any further.' After all, what could he do? He was still only a secondary figure; his

resignation would be accepted; he would be given a colonial governorship, and Gordon would be no nearer safety. But then, could he
sit by, and witness a horrible catastrophe, without lifting a hand? Of
all the odious dilemmas which that man had put him into, this, he
reflected, was the most odious. He slightly shrugged his shoulders.
No; he might have 'power to hurt,' but he would 'do none.' He wrote
a dispatch – a long, balanced, guarded, grey dispatch, informing the
Government that he 'ventured to think' that it was 'a question
worthy of consideration whether the naval and military authorities
should not take some preliminary steps in the way of preparing
boats, etc., so as to be able to move, should the necessity arise.' Then,
within a week, before the receipt of the Government's answer, he left
Egypt. From the end of April till the beginning of September –
during the most momentous period of the whole crisis – he was
engaged in London upon a financial conference, while his place was
taken in Cairo by a substitute. With a characteristically convenient
unobtrusiveness, Sir Evelyn Baring had vanished from the scene.

Meanwhile, far to the southward, over the wide-spreading lands
watered by the Upper Nile and its tributaries, the power and the
glory of him who had once been Mahommed Ahmed were growing
still. In the Bahr-el-Ghazal, the last embers of resistance were
stamped out with the capture of Lupton Bey, and through the whole
of that vast province – three times the size of England – every trace
of the Egyptian Government was obliterated. Still farther south the
same fate was rapidly overtaking Equatoria, where Emin Pasha,
withdrawing into the unexplored depths of Central Africa, carried
with him the last vestiges of the old order. The Mahdi himself still
lingered in his headquarters at El Obeid; but, on the rising of the
tribes round Khartoum, he had decided that the time for an offensive movement had come, and had dispatched an army of thirty
thousand men to lay siege to the city. At the same time, in a long and
elaborate proclamation, in which he asserted, with all the elegance of
oriental rhetoric, both the sanctity of his mission and the invincibil-
ity of his troops, he called upon the inhabitants to surrender. Gordon
read aloud the summons to the assembled townspeople; with one
voice they declared that they were ready to resist. This was a false
Mahdi, they said; God would defend the right; they put their trust in
the Governor-General. The most learned Sheikh in the town drew
up a theological reply, pointing out that the Mahdi did not fulfil the

requirements of the ancient prophets. At his appearance, had the Euphrates dried up and revealed a hill of gold? Had contradiction and difference ceased upon the earth? And, moreover, did not the faithful know that the true Mahdi was born in the year of the Prophet 255, from which it surely followed that he must be now 1046 years old? And was it not clear to all men that this pretender was not a tenth of that age? These arguments were certainly forcible; but the Mahdi's army was more forcible still. The besieged sallied out to the attack; they were defeated; and the rout that followed was so disgraceful that two of the commanding officers were, by Gordon's orders, executed as traitors. From that moment the regular investment of Khartoum began. The Arab generals decided to starve the town into submission. When, after a few weeks of doubt, it became certain that no British force was on its way from Suakin to smash up the Mahdi, and when, at the end of May, Berber, the last connecting link between Khartoum and the outside world, fell into the hands of the enemy, Gordon set his teeth, and sat down to wait and to hope, as best he might. With unceasing energy he devoted himself to the strengthening of his defences and the organisation of his resources – to the digging of earthworks, the manufacture of ammunition, the collection and the distribution of food. Every day there were sallies and skirmishes; every day his little armoured steamboats paddled up and down the river, scattering death and terror as they went. Whatever the emergency, he was ready with devices and expedients. When the earthworks were still uncompleted he procured hundreds of yards of cotton, which he dyed the colour of earth, and spread out in long, sloping lines, so as to deceive the Arabs, while the real works were being prepared farther back. When a lack of money began to make itself felt, he printed and circulated a paper coinage of his own. To combat the growing discontent and disaffection of the townspeople he instituted a system of orders and medals; the women were not forgotten; and his popularity redoubled. There was terror in the thought that harm might come to the Governor-General. Awe and reverence followed him; wherever he went he was surrounded by a vigilant and jealous guard, like some precious idol, some mascot of victory. How could he go away? How could he desert his people? It was impossible. It would be, as he himself exclaimed in one of his latest telegrams to Sir Evelyn Baring, 'the climax of meanness,' even to contemplate such an act. Sir Evelyn Baring thought differently. In his opinion it was General Gordon's plain duty to have come away from Khartoum. To stay involved inevitably a relief expedition – a great expense of treasure and the loss of valuable lives; to come away would merely mean that the inhabitants of Khartoum would be 'taken prisoner by the Mahdi.' So Sir Evelyn Baring put it; but the case was not quite so simple as that. When Berber fell, there had been a massacre lasting for days – an appalling orgy of loot and lust and slaughter; when Khartoum itself was captured, what followed was still more terrible. Decidedly, it was no child's play to be 'taken prisoner by the Mahdi.' And Gordon was actually there, among those people, in closest intercourse with them, responsible, beloved. Yes; no doubt. But was that, in truth, his only motive? Did he not wish in reality, by lingering in Khartoum, to force the hand of the Government? To oblige them, whether they would or no, to send an army to smash up the Mahdi? And was that fair? Was *that* his duty? He might protest, with his last breath, that he had 'tried to do his duty'; Sir Evelyn Baring, at any rate, would not agree.

But Sir Evelyn Baring was inaudible, and Gordon now cared very little for his opinions. Is it possible that, if only for a moment, in his extraordinary predicament, he may have listened to another and a very different voice – a voice of singular quality, a voice which – for so one would fain imagine – may well have wakened some familiar echoes in his heart? One day, he received a private letter from the Mahdi. The letter was accompanied by a small bundle of clothes. 'In the name of God!' wrote the Mahdi, 'herewith a suit of clothes, consisting of a coat (jibbeh), an overcoat, a turban, a cap, a girdle, and beads. This is the clothing of those who have given up this world and its vanities, and who look for the world to come, for everlasting happiness in Paradise. If you truly desire to come to God and seek to live a godly life, you must at once wear this suit, and come out to accept your everlasting good fortune.' Did the words bear no meaning to the mystic of Gravesend? But he was an English gentleman, an English officer. He flung the clothes to the ground, and trampled on them in the sight of all. Then, alone, he went up to the roof of his high palace, and turned the telescope once more, almost mechanically, towards the north.

But nothing broke the immovability of that hard horizon; and, indeed, how was it possible that help should come to him now? He seemed to be utterly abandoned.* Sir Evelyn Baring had disappeared into his financial conference. In England, Mr Gladstone had held firm, had outfaced the House of Commons, had ignored the Press. He appeared to have triumphed. Though it was clear that no preparations of any kind were being made for the relief of Gordon, the anxiety and agitation of the public, which had risen so suddenly to such a height of vehemence, had died down. The dangerous beast had been quelled by the stern eye of its master. Other questions became more interesting – the Reform Bill, the Russians, the House of Lords. Gordon, silent in Khartoum, had almost dropped out of remembrance. And yet, help did come after all. And it came from an unexpected quarter. Lord Hartington had been for some time convinced that he was responsible for Gordon's appointment; and his conscience was beginning to grow uncomfortable.

Lord Hartington's conscience was of a piece with the rest of him. It was not, like Mr Gladstone's, a salamander-conscience – an intangible, dangerous creature, that loved to live in the fire; nor was it, like Gordon's, a restless conscience; nor, like Sir Evelyn Baring's, a diplomatic conscience; it was a commonplace affair. Lord Hartington himself would have been disgusted by any mention of it. If he had been obliged, he would have alluded to it distantly; he would have muttered that it was a bore not to do the proper thing. He was usually bored – for one reason or another; but this particular form of boredom he found more intense than all the rest. He would take endless pains to avoid it. Of course, the whole thing was a nuisance – an obvious nuisance; and every one else must feel just as he did about it. And yet people seemed to have got it into their heads that he had some kind of special faculty in such matters – that there was some peculiar value in his judgment on a question of right and wrong. He could not understand why it was; but whenever there was a dispute about cards in a club, it was brought to *him* to settle. It was most odd. But it was true. In public affairs, no less than in private, Lord Hartington's decisions carried an extraordinary weight. The feeling of his idle friends in high society was shared by the great mass of the English people; here was a man they could trust. For indeed he was built upon a pattern which was very dear to his countrymen. It was not simply that he was honest: it was that his honesty was an English honesty – an honesty which naturally belonged to one who, so it seemed to them, was the living image of what an Englishman should be. In Lord Hartington they saw, embodied and glorified, the very qualities which were nearest to their hearts – impartiality, solidity, common sense – the qualities by which they themselves longed to be distinguished, and by which, in their happier moments, they believed they were. If ever they began to have misgivings, there, at any rate, was the example of Lord Hartington to encourage them and guide them – Lord Hartington who was never self-seeking, who was never excited, and who had no imagination at all. Everything they knew about him fitted into the picture, adding to their admiration and respect. His fondness for field sports gave them a feeling of security; and certainly there could be no nonsense about a man who confessed to two ambitions – to become Prime Minister and to win the Derby – and who put the second above the first. They loved him for his casualness – for his inexactness – for refusing to make life a cut-and-dried business – for ramming an official dispatch of high importance into his coat-pocket, and finding it there, still unopened, at Newmarket, several days later. They loved him for his hatred of fine sentiments; they were delighted when they heard that at some function, on a florid speaker's avowing that 'this was the proudest moment of his life,' Lord Hartington had growled in an undertone 'the proudest moment of *my* life was when my pig won the prize at Skipton fair.' Above all, they loved him for being dull. It was the greatest comfort – with Lord Hartington they could always be absolutely certain that he would never, in any circumstances, be either brilliant, or subtle, or surprising, or impassioned, or profound. As they sat, listening to his speeches, in which considerations of stolid plainness succeeded one another with complete flatness, they felt, involved and supported by the colossal tedium, that their confidence was finally assured. They looked up, and took their fill of the sturdy, obvious presence. The inheritor of a splendid dukedom might almost have passed for a farm hand. Almost, but not quite. For an air, that was difficult to explain, of preponderating authority lurked in the solid figure; and the lordly breeding of the House of Cavendish was visible in the large, long, bearded, unimpressionable face.*

One other characteristic – the necessary consequence, or, indeed, it might almost be said, the essential expression, of all the rest – completes the portrait: Lord Hartington was slow. He was slow in movement, slow in apprehension, slow in thought and the communication of thought, slow to decide, and slow to act. More than once this disposition exercised a profound effect upon his career. A private individual may, perhaps, be slow with impunity; but a statesman who is slow – whatever the force of his character and the strength of his judgment – can hardly escape unhurt from the hurrying of Time's wingèd chariot, can hardly hope to avoid some grave disaster or some irretrievable mistake. The fate of General Gordon, so intricately interwoven with such a mass of complicated circumstance – with the policies of England and of Egypt, with the fanaticism of the Mahdi, with the irreproachability of Sir Evelyn Baring, with Mr Gladstone's mysterious passions – was finally determined by the fact that Lord Hartington was slow. If he had been even a very little quicker – if he had been quicker by two days . . . but it could not be. The ponderous machinery took so long to set itself in motion; the great wheels and levers, once started, revolved with such a laborious, such a painful deliberation, that at last their work was accomplished – surely, firmly, completely, in the best English manner, and too late.

Seven stages may be discerned in the history of Lord Hartington's influence upon the fate of General Gordon. At the end of the first stage, he had become convinced that he was responsible for Gordon's appointment to Khartoum. At the end of the second, he had perceived that his conscience would not allow him to remain inactive in the face of Gordon's danger. At the end of the third, he had made an attempt to induce the Cabinet to send an expedition to Gordon's relief. At the end of the fourth, he had realised that the Cabinet had decided to postpone the relief of Gordon indefinitely. At the end of the fifth, he had come to the conclusion that he must put pressure upon Mr Gladstone. At the end of the sixth, he had attempted to put pressure upon Mr Gladstone, and had not succeeded. At the end of the seventh, he had succeeded in putting pressure upon Mr Gladstone; the relief expedition had been ordered; he could do no more. The turning-point in this long and extraordinary process occurred towards the end of April, when the Cabinet, after the receipt of Sir Evelyn's Baring's final dispatch, decided to take no immediate measures for Gordon's relief. From that moment it was clear that there was only one course open to Lord Hartington – to tell Mr Gladstone that he would resign unless a relief expedition was sent. But it took him more than three months to come to this conclusion. He always found the proceedings at Cabinet meetings particularly hard to follow. The interchange of question and answer, of proposal and counter-proposal, the crowded counsellors, Mr

Gladstone's subtleties, the abrupt and complicated resolutions – these things invariably left him confused and perplexed. After the crucial Cabinet at the end of April, he came away in a state of uncertainty as to what had occurred; he had to write to Lord Granville to find out; and by that time, of course, the Government's decision had been telegraphed to Egypt. Three weeks later, in the middle of May, he had grown so uneasy that he felt himself obliged to address a circular letter to the Cabinet, proposing that preparations for a relief expedition should be set on foot at once. And then he began to understand that nothing would ever be done until Mr Gladstone, by some means or other, had been forced to give his consent. A singular combat followed. The slippery old man perpetually eluded the cumbrous grasp of his antagonist. He delayed, he postponed, he raised interminable difficulties, he prevaricated, he was silent, he disappeared. Lord Hartington was dauntless. Gradually, inch by inch, he drove the Prime Minister into a corner. But in the meantime many weeks had passed. On July 1st, Lord Hartington was still remarking that he 'really did not feel that he knew the mind or intention of the Government in respect of the relief of General Gordon.' The month was spent in a succession of stubborn efforts to wring from Mr Gladstone some definite statement upon the question. It was useless. On July 31st, Lord Hartington did the deed. He stated that, unless an expedition was sent, he would resign. It was, he said, 'a question of personal honour and good faith, and I don't see how I can yield upon it.' His conscience had worked itself to rest at last.

When Mr Gladstone read the words, he realised that the game was over. Lord Hartington's position in the Liberal Party was second only to his own; he was the leader of the rich and powerful Whig aristocracy; his influence with the country was immense. Nor was he the man to make idle threats of resignation; he had said he would resign, and resign he would: the collapse of the Government would be the inevitable result. On August 5th, therefore, Parliament was asked to make a grant of £300,000, in order 'to enable Her Majesty's Government to undertake operations for the relief of General Gordon, should they become necessary.' The money was voted; and even then, at that last hour, Mr Gladstone made another, final, desperate twist. Trying to save himself by the proviso which he had inserted into the resolution, he declared that he was still unconvinced of the

necessity of any operations at all. 'I nearly,' he wrote to Lord Hartington, 'but not quite, adopt words received to-day from Granville.
"It is clear, I think, that Gordon has our messages, and does not
choose to answer them." ' Nearly, but not quite! The qualification
was masterly; but it was of no avail. This time, the sinuous creature
was held by too firm a grasp. On August 26th, Lord Wolseley was
appointed to command the relief expedition; and on September 9th,
he arrived in Egypt.

The relief expedition had begun; and at the same moment a new
phase opened at Khartoum. The annual rising of the Nile was now
sufficiently advanced to enable one of Gordon's small steamers to
pass over the cataracts down to Egypt in safety. He determined to
seize the opportunity of laying before the authorities in Cairo and
London, and the English public at large, an exact account of his
position. A cargo of documents, including Colonel Stewart's Diary
of the siege and a personal appeal for assistance addressed by Gordon to all the European powers, was placed on board the *Abbas;* four
other steamers were to accompany her until she was out of danger
from attacks by the Mahdi's troops; after which, she was to proceed
alone into Egypt. On the evening of September 9th, just as she was
about to start, the English and French Consuls asked for permission
to go with her – a permission which Gordon, who had long been
anxious to provide for their safety, readily granted. Then Colonel
Stewart made the same request; and Gordon consented with the
same alacrity. Colonel Stewart was the second-in-command at Khartoum; and it seems strange that he should have made a proposal
which would leave Gordon in a position of the gravest anxiety without a single European subordinate. But his motives were to be veiled
for ever in a tragic obscurity.* The *Abbas* and her convoy set out.
Henceforward the Governor-General was alone. He had now, definitely and finally, made his decision. Colonel Stewart and his companions had gone, with every prospect of returning unharmed to
civilisation. Mr Gladstone's belief was justified; so far as Gordon's
personal safety was concerned, he might still, at this late hour, have
secured it. But he had chosen; he stayed at Khartoum.

No sooner were the steamers out of sight than he sat down at his
writing-table and began that daily record of his circumstances, his
reflections, and his feelings, which reveals to us, with such an
authentic exactitude, the final period of his extraordinary destiny.

His 'Journals,' sent down the river in batches to await the coming of the relief expedition, and addressed, first to Colonel Stewart, and later to the 'Chief of Staff, Sudan Expeditionary Force,' were official documents, intended for publication, though, as Gordon himself was careful to note on the outer covers, they would 'want pruning out' before they were printed. He also wrote, on the envelope of the first section, 'No secrets as far as I am concerned.' A more singular set of state papers was never compiled. Sitting there, in the solitude of his palace, with ruin closing round him, with anxieties on every hand, with doom hanging above his head, he let his pen rush on for hour after hour in an ecstasy of communication, a tireless unburdening of the spirit, where the most trivial incidents of the passing day were mingled pell-mell with philosophical disquisitions, where jests and anger, hopes and terrors, elaborate justifications and cynical confessions, jostled one another in reckless confusion. The impulsive, demonstrative man had nobody to talk to any more, and so he talked instead to the pile of telegraph forms, which, useless now for perplexing Sir Evelyn Baring, served very well – for they were large and blank – as the repositories of his conversation. His tone was not the intimate and religious tone which he would have used with the Rev. Mr Barnes or his sister Augusta; it was such as must have been habitual with him in his intercourse with old friends or fellow-officers, whose religious views were of a more ordinary caste than his own, but with whom he was on confidential terms. He was anxious to put his case to a select and sympathetic audience – to convince such a man as Lord Wolseley that he was justified in what he had done; and he was sparing in his allusions to the hand of Providence, while those mysterious doubts and piercing introspections, which must have filled him, he almost entirely concealed. He expressed himself, of course, with eccentric *abandon* – it would have been impossible for him to do otherwise; but he was content to indicate his deepest feelings with a fleer. Yet sometimes – as one can imagine happening with him in actual conversation – his utterance took the form of a half-soliloquy, a copious outpouring addressed to himself more than to any one else, for his own satisfaction. There are passages in the Khartoum Journals which call up in a flash the light, gliding figure, and the blue eyes with the candour of childhood still shining in them; one can almost hear the low voice, the singularly distinct articulation, the persuasive – the self-persuasive –

sentences, following each other so unassumingly between the puffs of a cigarette.

As he wrote, two preoccupations principally filled his mind. His reflections revolved round the immediate past and the impending future. With an untiring persistency he examined, he excused, he explained, his share in the complicated events which had led to his present situation. He rebutted the charges of imaginary enemies; he laid bare the ineptitude and the faithlessness of the English Government. He poured out his satire upon officials and diplomatists. He drew caricatures, in the margin, of Sir Evelyn Baring, with sentences of shocked pomposity coming out of his mouth. In some passages, which the editor of the *Journals* preferred to suppress, he covered Lord Granville with his raillery, picturing the Foreign Secretary, lounging away his morning at Walmer Castle, opening the *Times* and suddenly discovering, to his horror, that Khartoum was still holding out. 'Why, HE *said distinctly* he could *only* hold out *six months*, and that was in March (counts the months). August! why, he ought to have given in! What *is* to be done? They'll be howling for an expedition. . . . It is no laughing matter; *that abominable Mahdi!* Why on earth does he not guard his roads better? *What* IS to be done?' Several times in his bitterness he repeats the suggestion that the authorities at home were secretly hoping that the fall of Khartoum would relieve them of their difficulties. 'What that Mahdi is about,' Lord Granville is made to exclaim in another deleted paragraph, 'I cannot make out. Why does he not put all his guns on the river and stop the route? Eh what? "We will have to go to Khartoum!" Why, it will cost millions, what a wretched business! What! Send Zobeir? Our conscience recoils from *that*, it is elastic, but not equal to that, it is a pact with the Devil. . . . Do you not think there is any way of getting hold of HIM, in a quiet way?' If a boy at Eton or Harrow, he declared, had acted as the Government had acted, 'I *think* he would be kicked, and I *am sure* he would deserve it.' He was the victim of hypocrites and humbugs. There was 'no sort of parallel to all this in history – except it be David with Uriah the Hittite';* but then 'there was an Eve in the case,' and he was not aware that the Government had even that excuse.

From the past, he turned to the future, and surveyed, with a disturbed and piercing vision, the possibilities before him. Supposing that the relief expedition arrived, what would be his position?

Upon one thing he was determined: whatever happened, he would not play the part of 'the rescued lamb.' He vehemently asserted that the purpose of the expedition could only be the relief of the Sudan garrisons; it was monstrous to imagine that it had been undertaken merely to ensure his personal safety. He refused to believe it. In any case, 'I declare *positively*,' he wrote, with passionate underlinings, '*and once for all, that I will not leave the Sudan until every one who wants to go down is given the chance to do so, unless* a government is established which relieves me of the charge; therefore if any emissary or letter comes up here ordering me to come down, I WILL NOT OBEY IT, BUT WILL STAY HERE, AND FALL WITH TOWN, AND RUN ALL RISKS.' This was sheer insubordination, no doubt; but he could not help that; it was not in his nature to be obedient. 'I know if *I* was chief, I would never employ *myself*, for I am incorrigible.' Decidedly, he was not afraid to be 'what club men call insubordinate, though, of all insubordinates, the club men are the worst.'

As for the government which was to replace him, there were several alternatives: an Egyptian Pasha might succeed him as Governor-General, or Zobeir might be appointed after all, or the whole country might be handed over to the Sultan. His fertile imagination evolved scheme after scheme; and his visions of his own future were equally various. He would withdraw to the Equator; he would be delighted to spend Christmas in Brussels; he would . . . at any rate he would never go back to England. That was certain. 'I dwell on the joy of never seeing Great Britain again, with its horrid, wearisome *dinner* parties and miseries. How we can put up with those things, passes my imagination! It is a perfect bondage. . . . I would sooner live like a Dervish with the Mahdi, than go out to dinner every night in London. I hope, if any English general comes to Khartoum, he will not ask me to dinner. Why men cannot be friends without bringing the wretched stomachs in, is astounding.'

But would an English general ever have the opportunity of asking him to dinner in Khartoum? There were moments when terrible misgivings assailed him. He pieced together his scraps of intelligence with feverish exactitude; he calculated times, distances, marches; 'If,' he wrote on October 24th, 'they do not come before 30th November, the game is up, and Rule Britannia.' Curious premonitions came into his mind. When he heard that the Mahdi was approaching in person, it seemed to be the fulfilment of a destiny, for he had 'always felt we were doomed to come face to face.' What would be the end of it all? 'It is, of course, on the cards,' he noted, 'that Khartoum is taken under the nose of the Expeditionary Force, which will be *just too late.*' The splendid hawks that swooped about the palace reminded him of a text in the Bible: 'The eye that mocketh at his father and despiseth to obey his mother, the ravens of the valley shall pick it out, and the young eagles shall eat it.'* 'I often wonder,' he wrote, 'whether they are destined to pick my eyes, for I fear I was not the best of sons.'

So, sitting late into the night, he filled the empty telegraph forms with the agitations of his spirit, overflowing ever more hurriedly, more furiously, with lines of emphasis, and capitals, and exclamation-marks more and more thickly interspersed, so that the signs of his living passion are still visible to the inquirer of to-day on those thin sheets of mediocre paper and in the torrent of the ink. But he was a man of elastic temperament; he could not remain for ever upon the stretch; he sought, and he found, relaxation in extraneous matters – in metaphysical digressions, or in satirical outbursts, or in the small details of his daily life. It amused him to have the Sudanese soldiers brought in and shown their 'black pug faces' in the palace looking-glasses. He watched with a cynical sympathy the impertinence of a turkey-cock that walked in his courtyard. He made friends with a mouse who, 'judging from her swelled-out appearance,' was a lady, and came and ate out of his plate. The cranes that flew over Khartoum in their thousands, and with their curious cry, put him in mind of the poems of Schiller, which few ever read, but which he admired highly, though he only knew them in Bulwer's translation. He wrote little disquisitions on Plutarch and purgatory, on the fear of death and on the sixteenth chapter of the Koran. Then the turkey-cock, strutting with 'every feather on end, and all the colours of the rainbow on his neck,' attracted him once more, and he filled several pages with his opinions upon the immortality of animals, drifting on to a discussion of man's position in the universe, and the infinite knowledge of God. It was all clear to him. And yet – 'what a contradiction is life! I hate Her Majesty's Government for their leaving the Sudan after having caused all its troubles; yet I believe our Lord rules heaven and earth, so I ought to hate Him, which I (sincerely) do not.'

One painful thought obsessed him. He believed that the two

Egyptian officers, who had been put to death after the defeat in March, had been unjustly executed. He had given way to 'outside influences'; the two Pashas had been 'judicially murdered.' Again and again he referred to the incident, with a haunting remorse. The *Times*, perhaps, would consider that he had been justified; but what did that matter? 'If the *Times* saw this in print, it would say, "Why, then, did you act as you did?" to which I fear I have no answer.' He determined to make what reparation he could, and to send the families of the unfortunate Pashas £1000 each.

On a similar, but a less serious, occasion, he put the same principle into action. He boxed the ears of a careless telegraph clerk – 'and then, as my conscience pricked me, I gave him $5. He said he did not mind if I killed him – I was his father (a chocolate-coloured youth of twenty).' His temper, indeed, was growing more and more uncertain, as he himself was well aware. He observed with horror that men trembled when they came into his presence – that their hands shook so that they could not hold a match to a cigarette.

He trusted no one. Looking into the faces of those who surrounded him, he saw only the ill-dissimulated signs of treachery and dislike. Of the 40,000 inhabitants of Khartoum he calculated that two-thirds were willing – were perhaps anxious – to become the subjects of the Mahdi. 'These people are not worth any *great* sacrifice,' he bitterly observed. The Egyptian officials were utterly incompetent; the soldiers were cowards. All his admiration was reserved for his enemies. The meanest of the Mahdi's followers was, he realised, 'a determined warrior, who could undergo thirst and privation, who no more cared for pain or death than if he were stone.' Those were the men whom, if the choice had lain with him, he would have wished to command. And yet, strangely enough, he persistently underrated the strength of the forces against him. A handful of Englishmen – a handful of Turks – would, he believed, be enough to defeat the Mahdi's hosts and destroy his dominion. He knew very little Arabic, and he depended for his information upon a few ignorant English-speaking subordinates. The Mahdi himself he viewed with ambiguous feelings. He jibed at him as a vulgar impostor; but it is easy to perceive, under his scornful jocularities, the traces of an uneasy respect.

He spent long hours upon the palace roof, gazing northwards; but the veil of mystery and silence was unbroken. In spite of the efforts of Major Kitchener, the officer in command of the Egyptian Intelligence Service, hardly any messengers ever reached Khartoum; and when they did, the information they brought was tormentingly scanty. Major Kitchener did not escape the attentions of Gordon's pen. When news came at last, it was terrible: Colonel Stewart and his companions had been killed. The *Abbas*, after having passed uninjured through the part of the river commanded by the Mahdi's troops, had struck upon a rock; Colonel Stewart had disembarked in safety; and, while he was waiting for camels to convey the detachment across the desert into Egypt, had accepted the hospitality of a local Sheikh. Hardly had the Europeans entered the Sheikh's hut when they were set upon and murdered; their native followers shared their fate. The treacherous Sheikh was an adherent of the Mahdi, and to the Mahdi all Colonel Stewart's papers, filled with information as to the condition of Khartoum, were immediately sent. When the first rumours of the disaster reached Gordon, he pictured, in a flash of intuition, the actual details of the catastrophe. 'I feel somehow convinced,' he wrote, 'they were captured by treachery. . . . Stewart was not a bit suspicious (I am made up of it). I can see in imagination the whole scene, the Sheikh inviting them to land . . . then a rush of wild Arabs, and all is over!' 'It is very sad,' he added, 'but being ordained, we must not murmur.' And yet he believed that the true responsibility lay with him: it was the punishment of his own sins. 'I look on it,' was his unexpected conclusion, 'as being a Nemesis on the death of the two Pashas.'

The workings of his conscience did indeed take on surprising shapes. Of the three ex-governors of Darfur, Bahr-el-Ghazal, and Equatoria, Emin Pasha had disappeared, Lupton Bey had died, and Slatin Pasha was held in captivity by the Mahdi. By birth an Austrian and a Catholic, Slatin, in the last desperate stages of his resistance, had adopted the expedient of announcing his conversion to Mahommedanism, in order to win the confidence of his native troops. On his capture, the fact of his conversion procured him some degree of consideration; and, though he occasionally suffered from the caprices of his masters, he had so far escaped the terrible punishment which had been meted out to some other of the Mahdi's European prisoners – that of close confinement in the common gaol. He was now kept prisoner in one of the camps in the neighbourhood of Khartoum. He managed to smuggle through a letter to Gordon, asking for assistance, in case he could make his escape. To this letter Gordon did not reply. Slatin wrote again and again; his piteous appeals, couched in no less piteous French, made no effect upon the heart of the Governor-General. 'Excellence!' he wrote, 'J'ai envoyé deux lettres, sans avoir reçu une réponse de votre excellence. . . . Excellence! j'ai me battu *27 fois* pour le gouvernement contre l'ennemi – on m'a feri deux fois, et j'ai rien fait contre l'honneur – rien de chose qui doit empêché votre excellence de m'ecrir une réponse que je sais quoi faire. . . . *Je vous prie*, Excellence, de m'honoré avec une réponse. . . . P.S. Si votre Excellence ont peutêtre entendu que j'ai fait quelque chose contre l'honneur d'un officier et cela vous empêche de m'ecrir, je vous prie de me donner l'occasion de me defendre, et jugez apres la verité.'* The unfortunate Slatin understood well enough the cause of Gordon's silence. It was in vain that he explained the motives of his conversion, in vain that he pointed out that it had been made easier for him since he had, *'perhaps unhappily*, not received a strict religious education at home.' Gordon was adamant. Slatin had 'denied his Lord', and that was enough. His communications with Khartoum were discovered and he was put in chains. When Gordon heard of it, he noted the fact grimly in his diary, without a comment.

A more ghastly fate awaited another European who had fallen into the hands of the Mahdi. Olivier Pain, a French adventurer, who had taken part in the Commune, and who was now wandering, for reasons which have never been discovered, in the wastes of the Sudan, was seized by the Arabs, made prisoner, and hurried from camp to camp. He was attacked by fever; but mercy was not among the virtues of the savage soldiers who held him in their power. Hoisted upon the back of a camel, he was being carried across the desert, when, overcome by weakness, he lost his hold, and fell to the ground. Time or trouble were not to be wasted upon an infidel. Orders were given that he should be immediately buried; the orders were carried out; and in a few moments the cavalcade had left the little hillock far behind. But some of those who were present believed that Olivier Pain had been still breathing when his body was covered with the sand.

Gordon, on hearing that a Frenchman had been captured by the Mahdi, became extremely interested. The idea occurred to him that this mysterious individual was none other than Ernest Renan,* 'who,' he wrote, 'in his last publication takes leave of the world, and is said to have gone into Africa, not to reappear again.' He had met Renan at the rooms of the Royal Geographical Society, had noticed that he looked bored – the result, no doubt, of too much admiration – and had felt an instinct that he would meet him again. The instinct now seemed to be justified. There could hardly be any doubt that it *was* Renan; who else could it be? 'If he comes to the lines,' he decided, 'and it is Renan, I shall go and see him, for whatever one may think of his unbelief in our Lord, he certainly dared to say what he thought, and he has not changed his creed to save his life.' That the mellifluous author of the *Vie de Jésus* should have determined to end his days in the depths of Africa, and have come, in accordance with an intuition, to renew his acquaintance with General Gordon in the lines of Khartoum, would indeed have been a strange occurrence; but who shall limit the strangeness of the possibilities that lie in wait for the sons of men? At that very moment, in the south-eastern corner of the Sudan, another Frenchman, of a peculiar eminence, was fulfilling a destiny more extraordinary than the wildest romance. In the town of Harrar, near the Red Sea, Arthur Rimbaud* surveyed with splenetic impatience the tragedy of Khartoum. 'C'est justement les Anglais,' he wrote, 'avec leur absurde politique, qui minent désormais le commerce de toutes ces côtes. Ils ont voulu tout remanier et ils sont arrivés à faire pire que les Egyptiens et les Turcs, ruinés par eux. Leur Gordon est un idiot, leur Wolseley un âne, et toutes leurs entreprises une suite insensée d'absurdités et de déprédations.' So wrote the amazing poet of the *Saison d'Enfer* amid those futile turmoils of petty commerce, in which, with an inexplicable deliberation, he had forgotten the enchantments of an unparalleled adolescence, forgotten the fogs of London and the streets of Brussels, forgotten Paris, forgotten the subtleties and the frenzies of inspiration, forgotten the agonised embraces of Verlaine.

When the contents of Colonel Stewart's papers had been interpreted to the Mahdi, he realised the serious condition of Khartoum, and decided that the time had come to press the siege to a final conclusion. At the end of October, he himself, at the head of a fresh army, appeared outside the town. From that moment, the investment assumed a more and more menacing character. The lack of provisions now for the first time began to make itself felt. November 30th – the date fixed by Gordon as the last possible moment of his resistance – came and went; the Expeditionary Force had made no sign. The fortunate discovery of a large store of grain, concealed by some merchants for purposes of speculation, once more postponed the catastrophe. But the attacking army grew daily more active, the skirmishes round the lines and on the river more damaging to the besieged, and the Mahdi's guns began an intermittent bombardment of the palace. By December 10th it was calculated that there was not fifteen days' food in the town; 'truly I am worn to a shadow with the food question,' Gordon wrote; 'it is one continued demand.' At the same time he received the ominous news that five of his soldiers had deserted to the Mahdi. His predicament was terrible; but he calculated, from a few dubious messages that had reached him, that the relieving force could not be very far away. Accordingly, on the 14th, he decided to send down one of his four remaining steamers, the *Bordeen*, to meet it at Metemmah, in order to deliver to the officer in command the latest information as to the condition of the town. The *Bordeen* carried down the last portion of the Journals, and Gordon's final messages to his friends. Owing to a misunderstanding, he believed that Sir Evelyn Baring was accompanying the expedition from Egypt, and some of his latest and most successful satirical fancies played round the vision of the distressed Consul-General perched for days upon the painful eminence of a camel's hump. 'There was a slight laugh when Khartoum heard Baring was bumping his way up here – a regular Nemesis.' But, when Sir Evelyn Baring actually arrived – in whatever condition – what would happen? Gordon lost himself in the multitude of his speculations. His own object, he declared, was, 'of course, to make tracks.' Then in one of his strange premonitory rhapsodies, he threw out, half in jest and half in earnest, that the best solution of all the difficulties of the future would be the appointment of Major Kitchener as Governor-General of the Sudan. The Journal ended upon a note of menace and disdain. 'Now MARK THIS, if the Expeditionary Force, and I ask for no more than two hundred men, does not come in ten days, *the town may fall;* and I have done my best for the honour of our country. Good-bye. – C. G. GORDON.'

'You send me no information, though you have lots of money. – C. G. G.'

To his sister Augusta he was more explicit. 'I decline to agree,' he told her, 'that the expedition comes for my relief; it comes for the relief of the garrisons, which I failed to accomplish. I expect Her Majesty's Government are in a precious rage with me for holding out and forcing their hand.' The admission is significant. And then came the final adieux. 'This may be the last letter you will receive from me, for we are on our last legs, owing to the delay of the expedition. However, God rules all, and, as He will rule to His glory and our welfare, His will be done. I fear, owing to circumstances, that my affairs are pecuniarily not over bright ... your affectionate brother, C. G. GORDON.

'P.S. I am quite happy, thank God, and, like Lawrence, I have *tried* to do my duty.'*

The delay of the expedition was even more serious than Gordon had supposed. Lord Wolseley had made the most elaborate preparations. He had collected together a picked army of 10,000 of the finest British troops; he had arranged a system of river transports with infinite care. For it was his intention to take no risks; he would advance in force up the Nile; he had determined that the fate of Gordon should not depend upon the dangerous hazards of a small and hasty exploit. There is no doubt – in view of the opposition which the relieving force actually met with – that his decision was a wise one; but unfortunately he had miscalculated some of the essential elements in the situation. When his preparations were at last complete, it was found that the Nile had sunk so low that the flotillas, over which so much care had been lavished, and upon which depended the whole success of the campaign, would be unable to surmount the cataracts. At the same time – it was by then the middle of November – a message arrived from Gordon indicating that Khartoum was in serious straits. It was clear that an immediate advance was necessary; the river route was out of the question; a swift dash across the desert was the only possible expedient after all. But no preparations for land transport had been made; weeks elapsed before a sufficient number of camels could be collected; and more weeks before those collected were trained for a military march. It was not until December 30th – more than a fortnight after the last entry in Gordon's Journal – that Sir Herbert Stewart, at the head of 1100 British troops, was able to leave Korti on his march towards Metemmah, 170 miles across the desert. His advance was slow, and it was tenaciously disputed by the Mahdi's forces. There was a desperate engagement on January 17th at the wells of Abu Klea; the British square was broken; for a moment victory hung in the balance; but the Arabs were repulsed. On the 19th, there was another furiously contested fight, in which Sir Herbert Stewart was killed. On the 21st, the force, now diminished by over 250 casualties, reached Metemmah. Three days elapsed in reconnoitring the country, and strengthening the position of the camp. On the 24th, Sir Charles Wilson, who had succeeded to the command, embarked on the *Bordeen*, and started up the river for Khartoum. On the following evening, the vessel struck on a rock, causing a further delay of twenty-four hours. It was not until January 28th that Sir Charles Wilson, arriving under a heavy fire within sight of Khartoum, saw that the Egyptian flag was not flying from the roof of the palace. The signs of ruin and destruction on every hand showed clearly enough that the town had fallen. The relief expedition was two days late.

The details of what passed within Khartoum during the last weeks of the siege are unknown to us. In the diary of Bordeini Bey, a Levantine merchant, we catch a few glimpses of the final stages of the catastrophe – of the starving populace, the exhausted garrison, the fluctuations of despair and hope, the dauntless energy of the Governor-General. Still he worked on, indefatigably, apportioning provisions, collecting ammunition, consulting with the townspeople, encouraging the soldiers. His hair had suddenly turned quite white. Late one evening, Bordeini Bey went to visit him in the palace, which was being bombarded by the Mahdi's cannon. The high building, brilliantly lighted up, afforded an excellent mark. As the shot came whistling round the windows, the merchant suggested that it would be advisable to stop them up with boxes full of sand. Upon this, Gordon Pasha became enraged. 'He called up the guard, and gave them orders to shoot me if I moved; he then brought a very large lantern which would hold twenty-four candles. He and I then put the candles into the sockets, placed the lantern on the table in front of the window, lit the candles, and then we sat down at the table. The Pasha then said, "When God was portioning out fear to all the people in the world, at last it came to my turn, and there was no fear left to give me. Go, tell all the people in Khartoum that Gordon fears nothing, for God has created him without fear." '

On January 5th, Omdurman, a village on the opposite bank of the Nile, which had hitherto been occupied by the besieged, was taken by the Arabs. The town was now closely surrounded, and every chance of obtaining fresh supplies was cut off. The famine became terrible; dogs, donkeys, skins, gum, palm fibre, were devoured by the desperate inhabitants. The soldiers stood on the fortifications like pieces of wood. Hundreds died of hunger daily: their corpses filled the streets; and the survivors had not the strength to bury the dead. On the 20th, the news of the battle of Abu Klea reached Khartoum. The English were coming at last. Hope rose; every morning the Governor-General assured the townspeople that one day more would see the end of their sufferings; and night after night his words were proved untrue.

On the 23rd, a rumour spread that a spy had arrived with letters, and that the English army was at hand. A merchant found a piece of newspaper lying in the road, in which it was stated that the strength of the relieving forces was 15,000 men. For a moment, hope flickered up again, only to relapse once more. The rumour, the letters, the printed paper, all had been contrivances of Gordon to inspire the garrison with the courage to hold out. On the 25th, it was obvious that the Arabs were preparing an attack, and a deputation of the principal inhabitants waited upon the Governor-General. But he refused to see them; Bordeini Bey was alone admitted to his presence. He was sitting on a divan, and, as Bordeini Bey came into the room, he snatched the fez from his head and flung it from him. 'What more can I say?' he exclaimed, in a voice such as the merchant had never heard before. 'The people will no longer believe me. I have told them over and over again that help would be here, but it has never come, and now they must see I tell them lies. I can do nothing more. Go, and collect all the people you can on the lines, and make a good stand. Now leave me to smoke these cigarettes.' Bordeini Bey knew then, he tells us, that Gordon Pasha was in despair. He left the room, having looked upon the Governor-General for the last time.

When the English force reached Metemmah, the Mahdi, who had originally intended to reduce Khartoum to surrender through starvation, decided to attempt its capture by assault. The receding Nile had left one portion of the town's circumference undefended: as the river withdrew, the rampart had crumbled; a broad expanse of mud was left between the wall and the water, and the soldiers, overcome by hunger and the lassitude of hopelessness, had trusted to the morass to protect them, and neglected to repair the breach. Early on the morning of the 26th, the Arabs crossed the river at this point. The mud, partially dried up, presented no obstacle; nor did the ruined fortification, feebly manned by some half-dying troops. Resistance was futile, and it was scarcely offered: the Mahdi's army swarmed into Khartoum. Gordon had long debated with himself what his action should be at the supreme moment. 'I shall never (D.V.),' he had told Sir Evelyn Baring, 'be taken alive.' He had had gunpowder put into the cellars of the palace, so that the whole building might, at a moment's notice, be blown into the air. But then misgivings had come upon him; was it not his duty 'to maintain the faith, and, if necessary, to suffer for it?' – to remain a tortured and humiliated witness of his Lord in the Mahdi's chains? The blowing up of the palace would have, he thought, 'more or less the taint of suicide,' would be, 'in a way, taking things out of God's hands.' He remained undecided; and meanwhile, to be ready for every contingency, he kept one of his little armoured vessels close at hand on the river, with steam up, day and night, to transport him, if so he should decide, southward, through the enemy, to the recesses of Equatoria. The sudden appearance of the Arabs, the complete collapse of the defence, saved him the necessity of making up his mind. He had been on the roof, in his dressing-gown, when the attack began; and he had only time to hurry to his bedroom, to slip on a white uniform, and to seize up a sword and a revolver, before the foremost of the assailants were in the palace. The crowd was led by four of the fiercest of the Mahdi's followers – tall and swarthy Dervishes, splendid in their many-coloured jibbehs, their great swords drawn from their scabbards of brass and velvet, their spears flourishing above their heads. Gordon met them at the top of the staircase. For a moment, there was a deathly pause, while he stood in silence, surveying his antagonists. Then it is said that Taha Shahin, the Dongolawi, cried in a loud voice, 'Mala' oun el yom yomek!' (O cursèd one, your time is come), and plunged his spear into the Englishman's body. His only reply was a gesture of contempt. Another spear transfixed him; he fell, and the swords of the three other Dervishes instantly hacked him to death. Thus, if we are to believe the official chroniclers, in the dignity of unresisting disdain, General Gordon met his end. But it is only fitting that the last moments of one whose whole life was passed in contradiction should be involved in mystery and doubt. Other witnesses told a very different story. The man whom they saw die was not a saint but a warrior. With intrepidity, with skill, with desperation, he flew at his enemies. When his pistol was exhausted, he fought on with his sword; he forced his way almost to the bottom of the staircase; and, among a heap of corpses, only succumbed at length to the sheer weight of the multitudes against him.

That morning, while Slatin Pasha was sitting in his chains in the camp at Omdurman, he saw a group of Arabs approaching, one of whom was carrying something wrapped up in a cloth. As the group passed him, they stopped for a moment, and railed at him in savage mockery. Then the cloth was lifted, and he saw before him Gordon's head. The trophy was taken to the Mahdi: at last the two fanatics had indeed met face to face. The Mahdi ordered the head to be fixed between the branches of a tree in the public highway, and all who passed threw stones at it. The hawks of the desert swept and circled about it – those very hawks which the blue eyes had so often watched.

The news of the catastrophe reached England,* and a great outcry arose. The public grief vied with the public indignation. The Queen, in a letter to Miss Gordon, immediately gave vent both to her own sentiments and those of the nation. '*How* shall I write to you,' she exclaimed, 'or how shall I attempt to express *what I feel!* To *think* of your dear, noble, heroic Brother, who served his Country and his Queen so truly, so heroically, with a self-sacrifice so edifying to the World, not having been rescued. That the promises of support were not fulfilled – which I so frequently and constantly pressed on those who asked him to go – is to me *grief inexpressible!* indeed, it has made me ill. . . . Would you express to your other sisters and your elder Brother my true sympathy, and what I do so keenly feel, the *stain* left upon England, for your dear Brother's cruel, though heroic, fate!' In reply, Miss Gordon presented the Queen with her brother's Bible, which was placed in one of the corridors at Windsor, open, on a white satin cushion, and enclosed in a crystal case. In the meanwhile, Gordon was acclaimed in every newspaper as a national martyr; State services were held in his honour at Westminster and St Paul's; £20,000 was voted to his family; and a great sum of money was raised by subscription to endow a charity in his memory. Wrath and execration fell, in particular, upon the head of Mr Gladstone. He was little better than a murderer; he was a traitor; he was a heartless villain, who had been seen at the play on the very night when Gordon's death was announced. The storm passed; but Mr Gladstone had soon to cope with a still more serious agitation. The cry was raised on every side that the national honour would be irreparably tarnished if the Mahdi were left in the peaceful possession of Khartoum, and that the Expeditionary Force should be at once employed to chastise the false prophet and to conquer the Sudan. But it was in vain that the imperialists clamoured, in vain that Lord Wolseley wrote several dispatches, proving over and over again that to leave the Mahdi unconquered must involve the ruin of Egypt, in vain that Lord Hartington at last discovered that he had come to the same conclusion. The old man stood firm. Just then, a crisis with Russia on the Afghan frontier supervened; and Mr Gladstone, pointing out that every available soldier might be wanted at any moment for a European war, withdrew Lord Wolseley and his army from Egypt. The Russian crisis disappeared. The Mahdi remained supreme lord of the Sudan.

And yet it was not with the Mahdi that the future lay. Before six months were out, in the plenitude of his power, he died, and the Khalifa Abdullahi reigned in his stead. The future lay with Major Kitchener and his Maxim-Nordenfeldt guns.* Thirteen years later the Mahdi's empire was abolished for ever in the gigantic hecatomb of Omdurman; after which it was thought proper that a religious ceremony in honour of General Gordon should be held at the palace at Khartoum. The service was conducted by four chaplains – of the Catholic, Anglican, Presbyterian, and Methodist persuasions – and concluded with a performance of 'Abide with Me' – the General's favourite hymn – by a select company of Sudanese buglers.* Every one agreed that General Gordon had been avenged at last. Who could doubt it? General Gordon himself, possibly, fluttering, in some remote Nirvana, the pages of a phantasmal Bible, might have ventured on a satirical remark. But General Gordon had always been a contradictious person – even a little off his head, perhaps, though a hero; and besides, he was no longer there to contradict. . . . At any rate, it had all ended very happily – in a glorious slaughter of twenty thousand Arabs, a vast addition to the British Empire, and a step in the Peerage for Sir Evelyn Baring.*

BIBLIOGRAPHY

General Gordon. *Reflections in Palestine. Letters. Khartoum Journals.*

A. E. Hake. *The Story of Chinese Gordon.*

H. W. Gordon. *Events in the Life of C. G. Gordon.*

D. C. Boulger. *Life of General Gordon.*

Sir W. Butler. *General Gordon.*

Rev. R. H. Barnes and C. E. Brown. *Charles George Gordon: A Sketch.*

A. Biovès. *Un Grand Aventurier.*

Li Hung Chang. *Memoirs.*[1]

Colonel Chaillé-Long. *My Life in Four Continents.*

Lord Cromer. *Modern Egypt.*

Sir R. Wingate. *Mahdiism and the Sudan.*

Sir R. Slatin. *Fire and Sword in the Sudan.*

J. Ohrwalder. *Ten Years of Captivity in the Mahdi's Camp.*

C. Neufeld. *A Prisoner of the Khaleefa.*

Wilfrid Blunt. *A Secret History of the English Occupation of Egypt. Gordon at Khartoum.*

Winston Churchill. *The River War.*

F. Power. *Letters from Khartoum.*

Lord Morley. *Life of Gladstone.*

George W. Smalley. *Mr Gladstone. Harper's Magazine,* 1898.

B. Holland. *Life of the Eighth Duke of Devonshire.*

Lord Fitzmaurice. *Life of the Second Earl Granville.*

S. Gwynn and Gertrude Tuckwell. *Life of Sir Charles Dilke.*

Arthur Rimbaud. *Lettres.*

G. F. Steevens. *With Kitchener to Khartoum.*

---

[1] The authenticity of the Diary contained in this book has been disputed, notably by Mr. J. O. P. Bland in his *Li Hung Chang.* (Constable, 1917.)

APPENDIX
BIOGRAPHICAL SKETCHES

Cardinal Manning

HENRY EDWARD MANNING (1808–92) was born on 15 July 1808 at his family's home, Copped Hall, Totteridge, Hertfordshire. He was the son of a city merchant, an MP (in the 1790s), and sometime Governor of the Bank of England. William Manning married twice and Henry was the youngest son of his father's second wife, whose family may have had Catholic connections. Manning attended Harrow School where he made a name for himself as a scholar and a sportsman. He enrolled at Balliol College Oxford in 1827 where he formed what was to be a long friendship with W. E. Gladstone, who succeeded him as President of the Union (their friendship died a 'natural death' on Manning's going over to Rome). Manning took the expected first-class degree in Classics, in 1830. It had been intended he should follow his father into banking and politics, but these plans were scotched by financial reverses. He worked for a while as a clerk at the Colonial Office and immersed himself in political economy.

His conversion to enthusiastic Christianity is credited to Miss Favell Lee Bevan (later Mrs Mortimer), his 'spiritual mother'. He returned to Oxford, with a fellowship at Merton, in 1832 and was ordained in the same year. For eighteen years he served as a country parson at Lavington-with-Graffham, in Sussex. In 1833 he married Caroline Sargent. The Sargent family had been strongly influenced by the 'Rome-ward' drift of the Anglican Church and had intermarried with the Wilberforces (Robert Wilberforce was to be Manning's closest friend over his years in the Anglican Church). Caroline died in 1837 of consumption; the marriage was childless. In 1840 Manning was appointed Archdeacon of Chichester.

He was, at this stage of his career, High Church, but staunchly Anglican. He preached against Newman and Tract 90, at the Church of St Mary the Virgin Oxford, on Guy Fawkes Day, 1843. In May 1848 he visited Rome and had an audience with Pope Pius IX. A decisive event in his religious career was the 1850 Gorham judgement on baptismal regeneration. The issue centred, essentially, on temporal versus spiritual power in the Church of England (were the Prime Minister and English monarch ultimate arbiters on points of religious doctrine?). On 6 April 1850 Manning joined the Roman Catholic Church. In 1851 he was appointed Father Superior of the newly established Oblates of St

Charles—a Catholic mission in Bayswater, London. The following eight years in this 'infant community' were the 'happiest of his life'. In 1856 Archbishop Wiseman appointed him Diocesan Inspector of Schools. Manning was consistently distrusted by the 'Old Catholics' (that is, those who had been in the faith before the agitation of the Oxford Movement). On Wiseman's death in 1865 Pius IX (against some resistance from his English opponents) appointed Manning the Roman Catholic Archbishop of Westminster. In 1869–70 Manning played a leading part in the Vatican Council, which affirmed the doctrine of Papal Infallibility. In 1875 he was appointed a Cardinal-Priest. In his later years, he was active in public affairs playing a moderating role in the 1889 London dock strike. As Archbishop he had uneasy relations with Cardinal Newman—advocate of a 'purer' Catholicism.

Florence Nightingale

FLORENCE NIGHTINGALE was born in Florence, Italy, on 12 May 1820 and named after that city. Her family was wealthy and her upbringing was privileged. Much of her childhood was spent in the family homes in Derbyshire and Hampshire. She was educated at home. In 1837 she felt a 'call' from God—instructing her to do good work. A visit (with her friends, Charles and Selina Bracebridge) to Kaiserswerth, in northern Germany, inspired her life's vocation—nursing (not then a profession for well-bred ladies). After some struggle with her family, she took an appointment at a nursing home for gentlewomen, in Harley Street. Political connections (particularly with the then Secretary for War, Sidney Herbert) led to her being sent, with a company of nurses, to the base hospitals of the Crimean War, which broke out in March 1854. She was supported by charitable subscriptions, raised principally through *The Times*. At Scutari, Nightingale wholly reformed nursing care and, making use of the publicity attaching to her as the 'Lady with the Lamp', hospital care in Britain. She returned from the Crimea in August 1856, thereafter living the life of a recluse, but working discreetly for further reforms with her 'inner cabinet' of powerful (male) friends and contacts. In 1860, with the aid of public donations, she established the Nightingale School for Nurses, at St Thomas's Hospital, London. Always a favourite of the monarch, she was awarded the Royal Red Cross by Queen Victoria, in 1883, and the Order of Merit in 1907 (the first woman to receive the latter). She died, aged 90, on 13 August 1910, and was buried near her family home, Embley Park in Hampshire.

Dr Arnold

THOMAS ARNOLD was born at Cowes on the Isle of Wight on 13 June 1795, the seventh child of the Collector of Customs on the island. His father died (as would Thomas himself) prematurely, of angina, in 1801. Young Thomas's early home education was entrusted to a family friend, Miss Delafield. In 1807 he went as a boarder to Winchester College. He was elected a scholar of Corpus Christi College Oxford in 1811 taking a first-class degree in Literae Humaniores in 1814, and was elected a fellow of Oriel College the following year. He won prizes at Oxford for his scholarship. He meanwhile broadened his outlook with visits to France (recently defeated in war) and to the English Lakes (he had a lifelong passion for Wordsworth's poetry). He was ordained deacon (the rank below priest) in late 1818: a necessary qualification if he wished to pursue a career in scholarship, education, or the Church. In 1820 he married Mary Penrose, settling down in a house at Laleham, on the Thames. Here he took pupils with his brother-in-law, John Buckland. The first of the Arnolds' nine children was born in 1821 (Matthew, the most famous to posterity, was born in 1822). In 1827 Arnold failed to be elected to a professorship at the newly established London University. Later in the same year, he was appointed headmaster of Rugby School, a post he accepted with some reluctance. He was ordained priest in 1828 and awarded a doctorate in Divinity later the same year. His first volume of *Sermons* was published in 1829. During the fourteen years of his headship at Rugby he published a stream of religious and scholarly writings in addition to quantities of material for the magazines. His magnum opus was the *History of Rome*, published in three volumes, 1838–42. His even greater work on Church and State was never completed. He was elected Regius Professor of Modern History at Oxford in 1841 (it did not require him to give up his headship). He died, aged 47, on 12 June 1842 and is buried in Rugby School Chapel.

The End of General Gordon

CHARLES GEORGE GORDON (known to friends as 'Charlie' and to posterity as 'Gordon of Khartoum') was born into a military family at Woolwich, on 28 January 1833. He entered the Royal Military Academy at Woolwich in 1848 and was commissioned into the Royal Engineers in June 1852. After an initial posting on the fortifications (his specialism) at Pembroke Docks, he was posted to the Crimea in December 1854, where he distinguished himself in action at the siege of Sebastopol. After the Treaty of Paris he was dispatched on a mission to determine post-war boundaries between Russia and Turkey. In April 1859 he was promoted to the rank of Captain. From 1860 to 1864 he was seconded to China, still turbulent from the Second Opium War. His service there earned him the first of his public nicknames: 'Chinese Gordon'. He was, at the end of this tour, grudgingly promoted to Lieutenant-Colonel (in China he had commanded an army). From 1866 to 1871 he superintended the building of forts around Gravesend, in response to war on the Continent. In February 1872 he was made a full Colonel. In January 1874 he was seconded to Egypt, where he was appointed Governor of the Equatorial Provinces. In 1877 he was appointed Governor-General of the Soudan. On his resignation, in December 1879, he travelled widely around the world as a soldier and (in the Holy Land) as a devout student of biblical archaeology. In January 1884 Gordon was sent—largely as a result of newspaper pressure—to the Soudan, again as Governor-General. It was not clear what the British government interest was, other than preserving the corrupt regime of the Pashas in Egypt (where Britain had colonial interests). Gordon found himself essentially abandoned in Khartoum, surrounded by the fanatic hordes of the Mahdi. He resisted heroically and was killed (the details are uncertain) when the city fell on 26 January 1885.

EXPLANATORY NOTES

Annotating *Eminent Victorians* is, I can testify, a useful exercise for those wishing to get to know the text. I think, however, that the four essays require a somewhat different treatment. The Manning biography will be, for modern readers, the least accessible by virtue of the intricacies of nineteenth-century religious factionalism. It is also the section for which Strachey did his heaviest reading. The notes I offer here are correspondingly factual and numerous. In the other three sections I have annotated (as I believe Strachey researched) more sparingly. I make reference to the manuscripts now in the British Library, Add. 54219–23. The following abbreviations are used:

Cook	Edward Cook, *The Life of Florence Nightingale*, 2 vols. (1914 edn.; first published 1913)
EVDE	*Eminent Victorians: The Definitive Edition*, ed. Paul Levy (2002)
Holroyd	Michael Holroyd, *Lytton Strachey: A Critical Biography*, 2 vols. (1967–8)
Purcell	E. S. Purcell, *The Life of Cardinal Manning*, 2 vols. (1895)
Stanley	A. P. Stanley, *The Life of Thomas Arnold, DD* (1892 edn.; first published 1844)
Ward	Wilfrid Ward, *The Life and Times of Cardinal Newman*, 2 vols. (1912 edn.; first published 1897)

3 *Dedication*: H. T. J. Norton—Strachey's friend from Eton days, Harry Norton. The two were undergraduates together at Cambridge. Norton was a mathematician. He gave Strachey crucially necessary financial help with which to pursue his literary career. With the sales success of *Eminent Victorians*, Strachey repaid him in full.

5 *Ranke*: Leopold von Ranke (1795–1886), founder of the modern historiography dedicated to discovering, objectively, 'how it really was'. Given the ongoing war, it was provocative to cite a German authority so prominently. Strachey was a conscientious objector.

Gibbon: Edward Gibbon (1737–94), English historian. Strachey was strongly influenced by the ironic, iconoclastic (and anti-Christian) tone of Gibbon's *Decline and Fall of the Roman Empire* (particularly Gibbon's chapters 15 and 16). Strachey is, of course, recording the fall of a more recent empire.

attack his subject . . . searchlight: serious composition on *Eminent Victorians* was begun with the outbreak of war and the book was published a few months before Armistice Day, in 1918. The reference here is to Elmer Sperry's high-intensity arc searchlights which came into service against enemy aircraft around London after 1916. The Preface was probably the last section Strachey wrote.

6 *we have never had, like the French, a great biographical tradition*: controversial. One could cite Boswell and Carlyle—and, ongoing as Strachey wrote, the *Dictionary of National Biography*.

Fontenelles and Condorcets: Bernard le Bovier de Fontenelle (1657–1757), man of letters and French Academician; he wrote *éloges* of Academy members (the French word means 'eulogy'). Marie-Jean Antoine Caritat Condorcet (1743–1794), philosopher, mathematician, and revolutionary; Strachey is here thinking of Condorcet's *Vie de Turgot* (1784) and *Vie de Voltaire* (1787)—written just before the French Revolution. Strachey, writing *Eminent Victorians*, was fresh from publishing *Landmarks in French Literature*.

Standard Biographies: Strachey is evidently thinking of Leslie Stephen's 'English Men of Letters' series.

Je n'impose rien ... j'expose: as Michael Holroyd has shown, Strachey invented this quotation.

Cook's: Sir Edward Tyas Cook (1857–1919) was still living as Strachey wrote and was one of the giants among Victorian journalist-editors. His *Life of Florence Nightingale* came out in 1913. Strachey had himself, at one point, been invited to undertake this venture.

CARDINAL MANNING

STRACHEY'S SOURCES

Strachey draws on two main sources. For Manning, he relies almost entirely on Edmund Sheridan Purcell's two-volume *The Life of Cardinal Manning* (1895). He has been much criticized for doing so. David Newsome summarizes the tainted background to Purcell's biography:

> Manning never commissioned him. Purcell, virtually bankrupt through the failure of the *Westminster Gazette*, of which he had been editor, blamed Manning—actually quite unfairly—for the collapse of the paper; sought financial assistance from the Cardinal, who allowed him to take his journal of his visit to Rome in 1847–8, from which he might write an article. Using this as his credential as the Cardinal's would-be biographer, Purcell contrived to wheedle letters and papers from many of Manning's friends and—until he was rumbled—a substantial part of the Manning archives, after the Cardinal's death. Every effort to block the publication failed. Purcell then had a free hand to do his worst. It is almost inconceivable that Strachey did not know something of this story. (*EVDE*, 110)

For the sections on Newman Strachey used the more reliable Wilfrid Ward's *The Life and Times of Cardinal Wiseman*, 2 vols. (1897).

9 *1807*: Strachey takes this wrong birth date from Purcell. As newspaper announcements and his gravestone confirm, Manning was born on 15 July 1808. As his notebook indicates, Strachey initially intended to open

this section rather more discursively: 'The life of Manning is a singular example of the power of innate characteristics ...' (Add. 54219). This was to be followed with some description of his feud with Dr Errington for the archbishopric of Westminster after Wiseman's death. Strachey clearly saw this struggle for power as the key event in Manning's life.

Francis ... Aquinas ... Innocent: the allusions are chosen for their 'eminence'—which reflects ironically on Manning. St Francis of Assisi (1182–1226) was the founder of the Franciscan Order and a saintly receiver of the stigmata. In 1979 he was recognized by Pope John Paul II as the patron saint of ecology—something which would have amused Strachey. Thomas Aquinas (1225–74) was a scholastic theologian, who founded the so-called 'Thomist' school of theology. The 'Innocent' Strachey is thinking of is Innocent III (1160–1216), the greatest Pope of the Middle Ages, credited with reforming the Catholic Church.

Cardinal Wolsey: Thomas Wolsey (1475?–1530), adviser to Henry VIII and the greatest of English politician-prelates.

Exeter Hall ... the Docks: Exeter Hall, built in the 1830s in London's Strand, was used for philanthropic mass meetings and religious assemblies (famously of an evangelical nature) until 1907. Manning actively mediated in the 1889 London dockers' strike.

10 *Keble*: John Keble (1792–1866), divine, poet, and leading spirit in the Oxford Movement. The movement is supposed to have taken off with his 1833 sermon on 'national apostasy'. The issue of baptismal regeneration was to be crucial in Manning's eventual going over to Rome. There was a general indifference to baptism in the Church of England until Pusey's tracts on the subject and the Gorham case of 1850.

Manning's biographer: E. S. Purcell.

de sexu: 'of a sexual nature'. The negro story would have been provoked by William Wilberforce's long campaign against slavery. A bill prohibiting trade in slavery was passed in 1808, although the use of slave labour was not abolished in the West Indian colonies (with which Manning's family had commercial connections) until the 1830s.

11 *the Apocalypse*: the Book of Revelation, 19–20. The allusion to 'the lake that burneth with fire and brimstone' is Rev. 20: 10. These juvenile testimonies are taken from Manning's own autobiographical writings, via Purcell.

Paley's Evidences: William Paley's (1743–1805) *Evidences of Christianity*, first published in 1794, introduced what Creationists (with whom Paley is still popular) call the 'intelligent design' argument. (If you came across a watch, lying in the road, would you assume it had just 'happened', or that someone had made it?)

Hessian top-boots: full-length boots, originally worn by troops from Hesse in Germany.

Samuel Wilberforce ... Gladstone: Samuel (1805–73) was the third son of the philosopher and philanthropist, William Wilberforce. He was at Oriel College Oxford at the same period in the late 1820s that Manning was at Balliol. Samuel Wilberforce went into the Church and was appointed Chaplain to Prince Albert in 1841. He was subsequently Bishop of Oxford and later (from 1869) of Winchester. Anthony Trollope satirizes him as 'Soapy Sam' in *The Warden* (1855). William Ewart Gladstone (1809–98) was another contemporary of Manning's at Oxford. He was elected to Parliament in 1832, as a Conservative, by the patronage of the Duke of Newcastle, who had the borough of Newark in his pocket. Gladstone went on to become the greatest Liberal politician of the century. He was a lifelong student of theology, and fanatic in his Anglicanism.

12 *a pious lady*: Miss Favell Lee Bevan (1802–78). She married Thomas Mortimer in 1841 and gained a public reputation with uplifting works for the young.

13 *getting rid of Manning*: there follows, crossed out in the MS: 'Nevertheless within a few months he had forsaken Miss Deffell and become engaged to the Rector's daughter. A few months more the Rector was dead, Manning was in his shoes, and the bells were ringing for his marriage with the young lady who among other advantages was a . . .' (Add. 54220). On second thoughts, Strachey may have felt this was too harsh.

ad veritatem et ad seipsum: to the truth and to himself. Some dates may be helpful. Manning received his degree on 2 December 1830 and was elected to a fellowship at Merton on 27 April 1832. He was ordained on 23 December 1832 and took a curacy under the Revd John Sargent, Rector of Woolavington-cum-Graffham, in Sussex. Sargent died on 10 June 1833 and Manning succeeded to the rectorship. On 7 November 1833 he married the late Rector's third daughter, Caroline. The ceremony was performed by his friend, Samuel Wilberforce. Strachey angles his account to Manning's disadvantage.

God's special mercies: because, as a married man, he would never have been able to enter the Catholic priesthood. Caroline Manning died in July 1837, evidently of consumption. There were no children.

But, when the grave was yet fresh . . . writing his sermons: this account of Manning's bereavement caused offence to early readers. Purcell is originally responsible for the imputation that Manning saw an advantage in being single. But his account of this 'hidden episode of his life' is less razor-edged than Strachey's:

> In the frequent and intimate conversations I had with the Cardinal about his Anglican days he only alluded to the subject twice, and that in an indirect fashion . . . On another occasion Cardinal Manning told me that he had received a letter from the church-wardens, announcing that the grave at Lavington was falling into decay, and asking for instructions about putting and keeping it in repair. 'My reply was: "It is best so; let it be. Time effaces all things." ' (Purcell, i. 124)

The detail about his 'destroying' *every* record of his married life is, apparently, a Stracheyan invention.

Tracts for the Times: the first of these pamphlets (defending Apostolic Succession, by J. H. Newman), around which the Oxford Movement mobilized, came out on 9 September 1833. The tracts continued to be published until Newman finally went over to Rome in 1845. Initially, they aimed to inject High Church rigour into Anglicanism. But they were given extra force by the general anxiety (especially in traditional University and Church circles) generated by the 1829 Catholic Emancipation Act. The leaders of the Oxford Movement were John Keble, Newman, and E. B. Pusey. The Movement is seen to have been triggered by Keble's sermon on 14 July 1833 on 'National Apostasy'. It climaxed, doctrinally, with Newman's Tract 90, which was condemned publicly by many Anglican bishops. Newman retired from Oxford to rural Littlemore, and was received into the Catholic Church in autumn 1845.

14 *Laud*: William Laud (1573–1645), the Archbishop of Canterbury who opposed Puritanism in all its doctrinal forms. He was executed (martyred, as his coreligionists thought) at Tower Hill, maintaining to the end his 'true' Protestantism.

Benthams and the Mills: Jeremy Bentham (1748–1832), the champion of utilitarianism. Strachey presumably indicates both James Mill (1773–1836) and his son John Stuart Mill (1806–73)—both were confessed disciples of Bentham.

Dr Whateley was so bold: Richard Whateley (1787–1863), Anglican Archbishop of Dublin (and earlier Professor of Political Economy at Oxford). Whateley was one of the leaders of the so-called 'Noetics' (i.e. philosophers addressing matters pertaining to the mind, or intellect). He advocated a broader, more generous Anglican doctrine.

15 *Dr Arnold . . . the admission of Unitarians*: Thomas Arnold (1795–1842), headmaster of Rugby and the third of Strachey's eminent Victorians. The reference here is to Arnold's *Principles of Church Reform* (1833). Unitarianism was a Nonconformist branch of Christian belief, popular among intellectuals, which rejected the Trinity and the divinity of Christ in favour of the unipersonality of God.

John Keble: Keble was for nineteen years a fellow of Oriel College Oxford, spiritual home of the Oxford Movement. In 1827 he published his immensely successful collection of poems, *The Christian Year*, verse designed for Sundays and holy days. In 1831 he was elected Professor of Poetry at Oxford. On 14 July 1833 he preached an assize sermon (i.e. before the Judges of Assize, at the Church of St Mary the Virgin) at the University, on 'National Apostasy', which is usually taken as the starting-point of the Oxford Movement.

Hurrell Froude: Richard Hurrell Froude (1803–36), a rigorous Tractarian, was elected a fellow of Oriel in 1826. He exercised a strong early influence on both Newman and Keble. Afflicted with consumption, he died abroad, prematurely, leaving the four volumes of his *Remains* to be edited by Newman as one of the founding texts of the Oxford Movement.

17 *Were Timothy and Titus bishops?*: Timothy and Titus were companions of St Paul on his second missionary journey. Both were made saints. Titus is supposed to have been the first bishop of Crete; Timothy the first bishop of Ephesus. Bishops are the highest order of minister in the Christian Church with the power of consecration. There was in the nineteenth century much controversy about the origins of the episcopate, and the bishops' link to the Apostles.

The time was out of joint ... born to set it right: Hamlet's despairing ejaculation (*Hamlet*, I. v. 211–12)

John Henry Newman: Newman (1801–90) was the most famous convert of the century. He was brought up in an Evangelical household. After graduation, he was made a fellow of Oriel in 1822 and ordained deacon (the order below priest) in 1824. From 1832 to 1833 he toured southern Europe. On his return, he became the acknowledged leader of the Oxford Movement. His Tract 90, published in 1841 (on the Thirty-nine Articles) marked his inability to continue in the Anglican Church and he went over on 9 October 1845.

the fatal morning: the episode is recorded in Wilfrid Ward's biography and originates in Newman's own autobiographical records. Little else is known about his childhood. Cambridge was more 'rational' than Oxford. It was Strachey's university and had strong connections with Bloomsbury.

Meleager ... lapis lazuli ... Fra Angelico ... palæstra ... Chartres: Meleager, first-century BC Greek epigrammatist. Fra Angelico (Giovanni da Fiesole, 1387–1455), painter of the Florentine School and a member of the Dominican Order; when offered an archbishopric, he turned it down, to devote himself to his art. Lapis lazuli is a semi-precious stone—here the allusion is to Fra Angelico's distinctive tint of blue paint. The palaestra is a gymnasium. Strachey alludes, of course, to Chartres Cathedral, and the statuettes of saints which embellish it.

Gray's footsteps: Thomas Gray (1716–71), the poet.

Lyra Apostolica: a collection of devotional poems, mostly by Newman, published in 1834.

at Oxford he was doomed: there follows, crossed out in the MS: 'The whirlpool of theological controversy sucked him ruthlessly into its depths. All his noble qualities—his high-mindedness, his sensitiveness of spirit, his passion, his subtlety of thought—fell a prey to the infection of the hour and the place. There is always a danger that high-mindedness may turn to narrow-minded, that passion may ...' (Add. 54220). Strachey evidently checked himself from becoming too much of a preacher.

18 *St Walburga*: Walburga (*c.* 710–79) was born in England and did mission-

ary work in Germany. She passed much of her adult life as the Abbess of Heidenheim. The summer festival of Walpurgisnacht is named after her.

his Apologia: his *Apologia pro Vita Sua* (1864).

au pied de la lettre: absolutely literally.

Athanasian Creed … the Thirty-nine Articles: the Athanasian Creed, or profession of faith to be made publicly at church service, differs in doctrinal points from the Nicene and Apostles' Creeds. The Athanasian is that used most widely in Western churches. The Thirty-nine Articles are a set of formulas accepted communally by the Church of England in the late sixteenth century, defining its dogmatic position. Subscription to them is required by entering clergy and, until the nineteenth century, by entrants to Oxford and Cambridge.

20 *the wand of Newman to strike the rock*: the allusion is to Moses striking the rock to bring forth water for the Israelites (Exodus 17: 2–6).

'The only good I know of Cranmer,' said Hurrell Froude: Thomas Cranmer (1486–1556), Archbishop of Canterbury, burnt at the stake by Queen Mary at Oxford for his unyielding opposition to Catholicism. Cranmer was responsible for the Book of Common Prayer (1549) and an early version of the Thirty-nine Articles. He was a 'convinced Erastian'—that is, he believed in the supremacy of State over Church. Hence Froude's homicidal comment.

Dr Pusey: Edward Bouverie Pusey (1800–82), a leading Tractarian. He was elected a fellow of Oriel College in 1823 and became formally involved with the Oxford Movement at the end of 1833 with Tract 17, on 'Fasting'. He had visited Germany in 1824–5.

and the Movement was launched upon the world: Strachey initially wrote: 'and the fat was in the fire'. He changed it in proof, presumably, because of the mention of 'fire' in the following sentence.

Dr Pusey … on Baptismal Regeneration: Strachey seems to be in error here. Tract 56 on 'Baptismal Regeneration' (September 1836) was by Newman.

21 τὰ αἰσθητὰ … τὰ νοητὰ i.e. the visible and sensible universe just referred to.

Origen: (*c.*185–254), Alexandrian biblical commentator. The reference here is to his *Hexapla*, a (six-fold) commentary.

St Barnabas: early Christian disciple, resident in Jerusalem. The reference is to the (dubious) Epistle of Barnabas, an attack on Judaism. 'Tau' is the Greek letter 'T', symbolic (pictographically) of the Crucifixion. Strachey is guying Tractarian mumbo-jumbo.

The Rev. Mr Maitland: Samuel Roffey Maitland (1799–1866), ordained into the Church of England in 1821. The reference is to his 'Letter to a Friend on Tract 89' (1841). Tract 89 is Keble's on 'Mysticism'; here mocked at length.

22 *'Credo in Newmannum'*: 'I believe in Newman'. This mild blasphemy is described in J. A. Froude's *Short Studies in Great Subjects* (1867–73).

23 *some years younger*: seven years.

Optatus: St Optatus (*fl.* 370), African bishop, only one of whose works survives: 'Against Parmenian the Donatist'. The Donatists were African schismatics of the fourth century. They saw themselves as 'rigorists' defending the holiness of the Church against laxity.

the celebrated Mr Bowdler: not the celebrated bowdlerizer of Shakespeare, Thomas Bowdler (1754–1825), but his nephew Thomas Bowdler (1782–1856).

the Ecclesiastical Commission: set up in 1835 to examine the estates and revenues of the Church of England.

24 *1 Cor. vii*: the chapter in Paul's First Epistle to the Corinthians opens: 'Now concerning the things whereof ye wrote unto me: It is good for a man not to touch a woman.'

in festo S. Car. 1838: the feast day of St Charles [the Martyr] (30 January)

The Record newspaper: the first Anglican weekly newspaper, launched in January 1828. Newman, then an Evangelical, was one of its sponsors.

the neighbouring Archdeacon, Mr Hare: Julius Charles Hare (1795–1855), a Cambridge graduate. He was strongly influenced by German theologians and was 'broad' in his Anglican beliefs. His career as a popular author was launched with *Guesses at Truth*. He was promoted to Archdeacon of Lewes in 1840 and was thus a neighbour when, also in 1840, Manning became Archdeacon of Chichester.

Gal. vi. 15: Paul's Epistle to the Galatians: 'For in Christ Jesus neither circumcision availeth any thing, nor uncircumcision, but a new creature.'

removing the high pews: the Tractarian 'war against pews' was at its height in the 1840s. Manning was opposed to them, and in favour of surplices about which there was similarly internecine quarrelling.

25 *a new bishop, Dr Shuttleworth*: Philip Nicholas Shuttleworth (1782–1842), a notable anti-Tractarian, was appointed in September 1840—two months before Manning was made Archdeacon. Pusey saw God's hand in Shuttleworth's prompt death shortly afterwards (aged a youthful 60).

26 *the publication of Tract No. 90*: 'Remarks on Certain Passages in the Thirty-Nine Articles', published 25 January 1841. It provoked a storm and led, after a four-year retreat, to Newman's going over to Rome.

the Monophysite heresy: the doctrine that Christ incarnated divine nature only, not a combination of divine and human. It was condemned as heretical in the fifth century.

the Council of Trent: 1545–63, formulated the terms of the Counter-Reformation and revived Catholic militancy in the face of advancing Protestantism in Europe.

27 *Apologia*: Newman's *Apologia pro Vita Sua* (1864). See note to p. 64 below.

28 *'of imagination all compact'*: Shakespeare, *A Midsummer Night's Dream*, v. i. 7–9: 'The lunatic, the lover, and the poet, Are of imagination all compact.'

the liquefaction of St Januarius's blood: Newman visited Italy in 1846. Januarius is the patron saint of Naples. The liquefaction of his blood (preserved in a phial in the city's cathedral) is supposed to take place eighteen times a year. The feast of San Gennaro, mentioned in the next sentence, is commemorated on 19 September.

the Octave: eight days after the feast.

Sir H. Davy: the scientist Sir Humphry Davy visited Naples in 1818, on a mission to preserve manuscripts recently discovered at Pompeii.

29 *St Patrizia*: a seventh-century saint. She was martyred near Naples for refusing marriage. In 1549 her relics were exhumed and from them two vials of liquefied blood were taken.

St Pantaleon: tortured and martyred in the fourth century; one of the patron saints of physicians. Milk is supposed to have flowed from his head. Strachey takes all these details from Ward's life of Newman.

it is always liquid: Strachey wrote, and deleted, a long section here exculpating Newman from any deceit and acknowledging (along with insuperable gullibility) his 'transparent honesty'.

Loreto: the 'Holy House' near Ancona, Italy. It is supposed to have been occupied by the Blessed Virgin Mary at the time of the Annunciation, transported there by angels.

Elias: this episode of the transport of Elias (i.e. Elijah) in a whirlwind to heaven is narrated in 2 Kings 2.

30 *'wished he could believe the Arabian Nights were true'*: a detail given in Ward. In his notebook, Strachey jotted down: 'Truth question. (a) Desire to deceive (b) Love of scientific truth. Januarius. Arabian Nights' (Add. 54219).

a virulently Protestant harangue: at this time Manning thought Tract 90 casuistical.

retirement to Littlemore: Newman went into seclusion at Littlemore, near Oxford, in 1842 where he set up a quasi-monastic establishment with a few friends.

31 *one of his proselytes, W. G. Ward*: William George Ward (1812–82), philosopher and theologian, a fellow of Balliol 1834–45, and a close adherent to Newman. Ward was the most vehement of the Tractarians.

a priori reasoning: that is, jumping to conclusions.

Opéra Bouffe: the first chapter of Wilfrid Ward's *W. G. Ward and the Oxford Movement* describes his 'passion for music and the drama and for mathematics'.

31 ... *the rooms next door were Dr Pusey's*: the preceding passage, when compared with Wilfrid Ward's (piously affectionate) life of his father (1889), indicates Strachey's 'mischievous' way with his sources:

> with his magnificent voice he [Ward] would go right through some of the best *arias* in Mozart's and Rossini's operas, in true dramatic style, before a select audience. 'Non piu andrai,' from the *Nozze di Figaro* and the *bouffe* song, 'Largo al factotum,' from the *Barbiere*, were among those most frequently chosen ... After he had joined the Newmanites he considerably curtailed the amount of dramatic and musical recreation he allowed himself. He never entered a theatre at all for eleven years, and in Lent by Dr Pusey's advice, as the ordinary corporal austerities injured his health, he made a rule to forego all music whatever. One Lent when three weeks had passed in this way he met Coffin in the High Street and said 'I have such an awful fit of depression that I feel as if I should go out of my mind; don't you think that a little music for once may be allowed?' After some discussion it was agreed that a little strictly sacred music might pass. Beginning with Cherubini's 'O Salutaris' they gradually passed to 'Possenti Numi' in the 'Flauto magico.' But this opened a book containing songs somewhat lighter, and the duet between Papageno and Papagena followed. The music waxed faster and livelier till it culminated in 'Largo al factotum', the lightest and raciest of buffo songs, in the middle of which one of the company suddenly recollected that the room in Christ Church in which he was singing was separated only by a thin wall from Dr Pusey's own rooms. (*W. G. Ward and the Oxford Movement* 40–1)

Strachey, among all else, changes 'Coffin' to the more dramatically effective 'Dr Pusey'. The faint knocking on the wall is another embellishment. In his notebook, Strachey jotted down the memorandum: 'Largo al factotum. (Symbolic of the landslide!)' (Add. 54219).

entrain: enthusiasm.

32 *Ward at last published a devastating book*: The Ideal of a Christian Church (1844). It began as a pamphlet and together with Newman's Tract 90 attracted condemnation by Oxford's Convocation, on 4 February 1845. In the vote to deprive Ward of his degrees, Gladstone, Manning, and Pusey supported him. Ward and his newly married wife were received into the Catholic Church, a few months later, in September 1845. Ward's book earned him the nickname 'Ideal Ward'.

a prolonged study of the English saints: Frederick William Faber had begun a series of translations of lives of the Continental saints some time earlier. Newman proposed to continue the series, bringing in English saints. He himself did only the lives of St Edilwald and St Gundleas and part of the life of St Bettelin. He soon retired from the editorship. The lives were published serially, 1844–5, and reprinted as *The Lives of the English Saints, Written by Various Hands at the Suggestion of John Henry Newman*. Newman later claimed that this work was produced on his 'deathbed' as an Anglican and it was designed to establish lines of continuity with the medieval Catholic Church. Of the intended 300 lives only 33 were completed. Although Newman stressed the 'mythic' element embellishing these lives they were, for decades, attacked by militant Protestants as spreaders of superstition and untruth.

33 *up to his neck in water*: the opportunity for a 'cold shower and masturbation' joke was too tempting for Strachey to resist. What the life of St Cuthbert records is:

> Yet such was the reputation of St Ebba's sanctity, and the spiritual wisdom of her discourse, that St Bede informs us that when she sent messengers to the man of God [St Cuthbert], desiring him to come to her monastery, he went and stopped several days in conversation with her, going out of the gates at nightfall and spending the hours of darkness in prayer, either up to his neck in the water, or in the chilly air.

The 'indignant commentator', as Strachey's notes indicate, was J. C. Crossthwaite in his 1846 polemic: 'Modern Hagiology: An Examination of the Lives of the Saints'. Strachey took extensive notes on 'silly miracles'.

James Anthony Froude, the younger brother of Hurrell: J. A. Froude (1818–94) is remembered as, in later life, the biographer and disciple of Carlyle. Like his brother he attended Oriel, but a decade later, in the mid-1830s. He was less amenable to the Tractarians than Hurrell. It was James who was given (by Newman) the Life of St Neot. He opened his account with a caveat; and eventually James Froude came to regard the lives as 'nonsense'. He broke with religion altogether with his satirical novel *The Nemesis of Faith* (1847)—one of that select library of Victorian fiction that has the distinction of having been publicly burned for profanity. In 1872 Froude belatedly divested himself of his deacon's orders.

to feel some qualms: it is worth quoting Herbert Paul's account, in his *Life of Froude* (1905), from which Strachey freely draws:

> Froude chose St Neot, a contemporary of Alfred, in whose life the supernatural played a comparatively small part. He told the story as legend, not quite as Newman wanted it. 'This is all,' he said at the end, 'and perhaps rather more than all that is known of the life of the blessed St Neot.' His connection with the series ceased. But his curiosity was excited. He read far and wide in the Benedictine biographies. No trace of the investigation into facts could he discover. If a tale was edifying, it was believed, and credibility had nothing to do with it. The saints were beatified conjurers, and any nonsense about them was swallowed, if it involved the miraculous element. The effect upon Froude may be left to his own words. 'St Patrick I found once lighted a fire with icicles, changed a French marauder into a wolf, and floated to Ireland on an altar stone. I thought it nonsense. I found it eventually uncertain whether Patricius was not a title, and whether any single apostle of that name had so much as existed.' (p. 34)

Froude (like Gibbon) was, clearly, a congenial spirit for Strachey (even though he misquotes him, inserting here, for example, 'known *to men*').

34 *trousers . . . grey*: Strachey gleefully seizes on the delicious detail from Purcell:

> The guest from Oscott was on the look-out for the smallest sign of his intentions from one who was apt, as Dean Stanley has said, 'like the slave of Midas to whisper his secret to the reeds.' And the sign came— slight but unmistakable. At dinner Newman was attired in grey trousers—which to Bernard Smith, who knew his punctiliousness in matters of dress, was conclusive evidence that he no longer regarded himself as a clergyman. Mr Smith returned to Oscott and reported that the end was near. (Purcell, i. 183).

Mr Sibthorpe . . . returned to the Church of his fathers: Richard Waldo Sibthorp (*sic*) (1792–1879) was received into the Catholic Church in 1841 by Wiseman, reverted to Anglicanism two years later, and again went over to Rome in 1865.

Mr Morris: John Brande Morris (1812–80), fellow at Exeter College Oxford, converted to Catholicism in 1846, entering the priesthood three years later. In 1843 he published his 'Essay towards the Conversion of Learned and Philosophical Hindus', which won a £200 prize awarded by the Bishop of Calcutta. Wiseman's approbation seems to be a Strachey embellishment.

Arthur Clough, the poet: Arthur Hugh Clough (1819–61), who appears in three of the *Eminent Victorians* portraits, was a pupil of Arnold's at Rugby, 1829–36. After graduation he was elected to a fellowship at Oriel in 1842. He lost his faith and resigned his University post in October 1848.

35 *the tight-rope has its dancers still*: in his notes, Strachey added a memorandum to himself at this point: 'Newman struggling with the dogma, organization, and policy of the R. Church [was] like a fly in a spider's web' (Add. 54220).

Samuel Wilberforce . . . made a bishop: Wilberforce was made Bishop of Oxford in 1845.

Sir James Graham: Sir James Robert George Graham (1792–1861), Home Secretary under Peel, 1841–6. If, as this chapter begins by informing us, Manning is 38, the date is 1845. The first of the letters below from which Strachey quotes (not entirely accurately) is dated 26 November 1841 (see Purcell, i. 198). The later letter, on 'filtration,' belongs to 28 December 1844.

36 *'Oh, Manning! No power on earth can keep him from a bishopric!'*: Strachey's gloss on what Purcell writes, apropos Wilberforce's getting his bishopric in 1845: 'The promotion of Wilberforce set men thinking and talking of Manning's chances of preferment' (Purcell, i. 269).

37 *the Readership of Lincoln's Inn . . . sub-almoner to the Queen*: Manning

applied for the readership in December 1843. The sub-almonership was offered him in December 1845. The 'For/Against' columns are taken (as are all quotations from Manning's papers) from Purcell, here i. 278–9.

38 *he might die at any moment*: the strain on him was, Purcell confirms, exacerbated by the Newman crisis. In June 1847 three doctors examined his chest and ordered Manning abroad—they suspected that (like his dead wife) he was consumptive. He left in July. By choosing Italy (specifically Rome), he turned this invalidism into a defining spiritual moment in his life. In the following pages, Strachey draws very closely on Purcell's selections from Manning's private papers, going no further or deeper, and deliberately fixing on the tellingly ludicrous as in 'I do not include plain biscuits'.

39 *the Church of England seems to me to be diseased*: the extracts here are from entries made by Manning (and quoted by Purcell) in May and August 1846 (see Purcell, i. 483–7). Their placement by Strachey suggests a later date.

40 *precisely what passed on that occasion never transpired*: this (following Purcell) is a passage in *Eminent Victorians* which has caused great offence; specifically the Stracheyan innuendo that some kind of deal was struck, or bribe offered. What Purcell writes is:

> More difficult, however, of interpretation is the strange silence observed in the diary in regard to two events of singular interest and importance, namely Archdeacon Manning's meeting with John Henry Newman at Rome in 1847 and his audience with the Pope ... still more unaccountable is the utter absence of any record in his Diary of this writer's private audience with Pope Pius IX. Not a line, not a word, not a syllable, beyond the mere record of the fact, and that in the baldest form: 'Audience to-day at the Vatican.' The Pope's name even is not mentioned ... To a man of Archdeacon Manning's antecedents, not to speak of his position in the 'sister Church,' a private meeting, still more a long conversation with the Pope of Rome, could not but be an occasion or an occurrence of exceptional interest. Was the wise and cautious archdeacon afraid that, if once committed to paper, an account of his conversation with the Pope might somehow or other reach suspicious ears? (Purcell, i. 415–16)

The Pope's astonished comments on the lack of sacramental hygiene in the Anglican Church was, apparently, supplied to Purcell in conversation. Manning was in Rome in winter 1847 (when he met Newman) and early summer 1848 (when he met the Pope).

from an agitated lady: Mrs Ryle's letter is dated 15 October 1850. Strachey takes some liberties with transcription, as given in Purcell.

42 *St Cyprian ... St Chrysostom*: this sonorous and saintly catalogue is taken, almost verbatim, from Purcell (i. 471).

42 *the Reverend Mr Gorham*: a key figure in Manning's spiritual travails on the road to Rome. The Gorham affair preoccupies chapters 24–6 of Purcell's *Life*. George Cornelius Gorham (1787–1857) took orders in 1811. When, in the mid-1840s, he was appointed to a new living at Brampford Speke, near Exeter, Phillpotts insisted on testing his orthodoxy. There followed an interrogation lasting four days in December 1847 and a further three days in March 1848. Gorham was found to deny the Anglican doctrine of baptismal regeneration (essentially, Gorham argued that salvation must be 'prevenient'—it did not depend on the ritual). The Bishop refused to appoint him. The case went on to the Church's 'Court of Arches' (the 'archbishops' court', with responsibility for ecclesiastical matters) in August 1849. Initially, Phillpotts was supported. But the decision was subsequently reversed by the Privy Council (the body of statesmen who advise the monarch). For clerics like Manning, a 'temporal' body had no authority to pronounce on matters spiritual. They were appalled that politicians could strike out an article of the creed. Manning discussed the issue at great length with confidants, like Robert Wilberforce, marking his letters, as Strachey notes, 'under seal' (i.e. of the confessional—never to be divulged).

    Dr Phillpotts: Henry Phillpotts (1778–1869), Bishop of Exeter. A high churchman, Phillpotts had no sympathy with the Tractarian Movement. Popularly known as the 'fighting bishop', he vehemently attacked Tract 90.

45 *Wegg-Prosser*: Francis Richard Wegg-Prosser (1824–1911) gave up a promising career in Parliament in 1852, when he converted to Roman Catholicism. He thereafter became a political power in his newly adopted Church.

    prevented the functions of the Church of England: this is from a letter of Manning's dated 3 January 1851. As I read Purcell (from whom Strachey took it), the letter was addressed to T. T. Carter, not Robert Wilberforce (Purcell, i. 614–15).

    a meagre meaning: Purcell quotes much of the excited correspondence between Gladstone and Manning over the summer of 1850. By September, Manning was convinced that the Church of England was 'in schism' (Purcell, i. 560). The letter from Gladstone quoted here dates from 1 April when the battle was, effectively, lost. Five days later Manning's decisive step would be taken.

    Soon afterwards: Purcell (i. 617) recalls this poignant episode being described to him by Manning 'five or six years ago' (as he writes) which would make it the late 1880s, early 1890s. Strachey, in transcribing it from Purcell, leaves out a telling phrase: 'I rose up—"St Paul is standing by his side"—and laying my hand . . .'

46 *"Land of Shadows"*: proverbial for 'land of the dead.'

    θεολογία: theology. 'Nice' refers to the Council of Nicaea (325).

    Cathedra Petri: the church founded on a rock, and the church of Peter.

47 *What did Pio Nono say? . . .*: this is another Stracheyan embellishment

which has caused huge offence. David Newsome pours scorn on this speculation: 'It is not in the least easy to imagine such a ludicrous situation. To quote F. A. Simpson: "A nineteenth-century Pope, at the first audience of a Protestant Archdeacon charged with a semi-official errand, promptly digging him the ribs, as it were, and proffering him a bribe: crudely told the story might tax the credulity of a cretin" ' (*EVDE* 112). See also F. A. Simpson, 'Max Beerbohm on Lytton Strachey', *Cambridge Review*, 4 Dec. 1943, p. 67.

the Rev. Mr Tierney: evidently Mark Aloysius Tierney (1795–1862), although I cannot locate the exchange which Strachey describes here. Tierney was a Roman Catholic historian. As the *DNB* records: 'For many years he was a member of the ancient chapter of England, and when the diocese of Southwark was erected by Pope Pius IX in 1852, he became the first canon penitentiary of the cathedral chapter. Throughout life he was an opponent of Cardinal Wiseman and of undue interference on the part of the Pope.' As Purcell records (i. 627), Manning was received into the Catholic communion by Father Brownhill, at Hill Street in London, on 6 April 1851. He was ordained a priest by Cardinal Wiseman on 14 June 1851. This was the period of the so-called 'Papal Aggression'—that is, the setting up of a Catholic hierarchy in England, with Wiseman at its head as (Catholic) Archbishop of Westminster. It caused huge public agitation.

48 *the Oblates of St Charles*: a Catholic mission, comprising a community of secularly inclined priests, set up in 1857. As Strachey goes on to say, the Archbishop of Milan (a city identified with the Saint) endowed the mission with some of Charles's sacred relics. Strachey has leapt forward (without informing the reader) half a dozen years. He does not mention the death of Robert Wilberforce in 1857. Nor does he stress the fact that Manning prepared himself for his new career with years of study of Catholic theology.

the accession of Manning to the Archbishopric: in 1865. Manning was Father Superior of the Oblates of St Charles from 1857 to 1865.

49 *triple crowns*: the Papal insignia.

50 *W. G. Ward . . . the ancient traditions of Douay*: Ward (see note to p. 31), who was a student at Christ Church Oxford as the Tractarian Movement got under way, went on to lecture in mathematics at the University. He fell under Newman's influence. Through the influence of Wiseman (and with a Ph.D. awarded by the Pope) he had a post at St Edmund's College, Ware (a Catholic institution) from 1851 to 1858. Douay, or Douai, in northern France was the centre for exiled English Roman Catholics in the seventeenth and eighteenth centuries.

the uneasiness of the Old Catholics was becoming intense: between 1852 and 1853 Manning was moving incessantly between London and Rome. He took up permanent residence in London in 1854. Having been in the Church only three years, he was too junior for serious preferment. In

April 1857, on the resignation of the incumbent, he was appointed Provost of the Chapter of Westminster. This moved him away from the missionary work with the Oblates of St Charles into the power structure of the Catholic Church. His appointment (as a very new Catholic) marked the beginning of friction with the old-established Catholic families in England.

50 *Dr Errington*: George Errington (1804–86). According to Purcell, the appointment of Errington as his 'coadjutor' (with right of succession to the archbishopric) in 1855 was 'the greatest mistake of Wiseman's life' (Purcell, ii. 76). On the establishment of the new Catholic hierarchy in England, Errington was nominated in September 1850 the first Bishop of Plymouth. In 1855 he was promoted to the Archbishopric of Trebizond 'in partibus infidelium' (i.e. ruling in a region fallen away from the Catholic faith). Errington was a 'man of business' (Purcell, ii. 82), unlike the unworldly Wiseman. Errington was also implacably hostile to Manning.

your immense: a comic corruption of 'Your Eminence'. Strachey took the joke from Ward, and slightly misrepresents his source:

> Wiseman loved to visit the poor. While at St Leonard's he gave deep pleasure by his visits to a coast-guard's wife who was ill of some mortal disease. Her designation of the Cardinal, as she looked at him with profound admiration as 'your Immense', which he ascribed to her sense of the applicability of the title to his portly figure delighted him. (Ward, ii, 174)

Strachey evidently confuses this pious lady with the 'Irish servant' jokes against Wiseman in *Punch* in the early 1850s.

a Bishop Blougram: as Ward observes, Bishop Blougram in Browning's poem, 'Bishop Blougram's Apology' (1855) was generally taken to be based on Wiseman who was 'ruddy and portly'.

51 *edifying novels*: Strachey is thinking of Wiseman's *Fabiola, or the Church of the Catacombs*, published in 1854 as the first title in the 'Catholic Popular Library', designed to oppose Charles Kingsley's ultra-Protestant novel, *Hypatia*.

a lobster salad side to the Cardinal: a misquotation from Ward:

> He likewise kept the table of a Roman cardinal, and surprised some Puseyite guests by four courses of fish in Lent—in lieu of the herbs and bread and water which the strictest to the party were accustomed to at Oxford. 'The Cardinal has a lobster salad side as well as a spiritual side', one of the Puseyite wits remarked. (Ward, ii. 189)

52 *Monsignor Searle*: Wiseman's private secretary. The two men had become friends at the English College, in Rome (see Ward, ii. 279). Searle, a 'rough diamond', took charge of all Wiseman's business and household affairs. The event in which Searle was mistaken for the Cardinal's son is

narrated in Purcell (ii. 283), as is the long feud between Searle and Manning (ii. 285–6). Manning was driven into a 'berserker rage' (Purcell, ii. 284) by Searle's accusation that he was motivated by financial greed for the Oblates of St Charles (what Strachey calls 'peculation').

53 *the struggle over St Edmund's College*: Searle and Errington were united in their insistence that St Edmund's College (a seminary) be wholly independent of Manning's influence. It devolved into a power struggle between old and new Catholics.

scritture: documents.

54 *Monsignor Talbot*: George Talbot, a relative of Lord John Talbot, and— with Newman—a notable Anglican convert to Catholicism. His 'collapse of mind' is alluded to (sarcastically) by Strachey in section VIII below.

Curia: the administration of the Roman Catholic Church.

55 *colpo di stato di Dominiddio*: a formal decision by the Papal office.

57 *Mettetelo lì!*: put him (it) in.

Archbishop of Westminster: Wiseman died in February 1865 and Manning was consecrated on 8 June 1865. It was expected, given his age and frail health, that he would not hold the post long.

58 *œconomus*: bursar.

60 *De Lugo . . . Perrone . . . M. Bautain . . . Barnabò*: Francisco de Lugo, Spanish Jesuit theologian (1580–1652); Giovanni Perrone, Italian Jesuit theologian (1794–1876); Louis-Eugène-Marie Bautain, French philosopher and theologian (1796–1867); Barnabò was currently Prefect of Propaganda at the Vatican and the official channel for communications on English affairs to the Vatican.

a small community of Oratorians: i.e. a pious community based on the Oratory of Saint Philip Neri. The Birmingham Oratory was founded by Newman in 1847, after his return from Rome, and on the advice of Pius IX. He would, until 1854, be rusticated in Edgbaston, away from the centres of British Catholicism.

Dr Cullen, the Archbishop of Armagh: Paul Cullen (1803–74) Archbishop of Armagh 1849–52, later (after 1866) a Cardinal.

their fellow-countrymen: Peel's government, in 1845, established three colleges for 'superior education' at Belfast, Cork, and Galway, on the principle of uniting all denominations, both as professors and as students. These 'Queen's Colleges' opened in 1849–50.

61 *the laity . . . the clergy actively disliked it*: Strachey initially wrote: 'The laity actively disliked the scheme, the clergy were bored by it.' He changed the sentence because, presumably, the fall of the prose (as revised) pleased his ear better.

'Manderemo a Newman la crocetta': let us give Newman the [bishop's] crook.

lo faremo vescovo di Porfirio, o qualche luogo: we shall make him bishop of Porfirio, or somewhere.

61 *a great deal of snuff*: Strachey took this from Ward:

> On my return from Rome in February 1856, Badeley wrote to me
> under date of March 25th: 'I was in some hope that, when the Pope got
> you at the Vatican, he would take the opportunity to make you a
> Bishop, before he sent you home. When is this to be?' Miss Giberne, to
> my great vexation, one day when she had an audience of the Pope, said
> without circumlocution what she had also said to Cardinal Antonelli:
> 'Holy Father, why don't you make Father Newman a Bishop?' She
> reported that he looked much confused and took a great deal of snuff.
> (Ward, i. 358)

62 *the whole project of a Catholic University*: this project was launched at the
Synod of Thurles in 1850. The Holy See gave approval in 1852 and
money for it was raised and Newman nominated as Rector. The University opened in November 1854.

Hannibal's elephants ... goose-step: Strachey, as elsewhere in this section
on Newman's vexations, took the detail from Ward. The friend was
James Laird Patterson. Newman, in fact, gave seven reasons for 'not
writing more books':

> (1) because in matters of controversy I am a *miles emeritus, rude dona-
> tus*. (2) because no one serves on Parliamentary Committees after he is
> sixty. (3) because Rigaud's steam engine which was hard to start was
> hard to stop. (4) because Hannibal's elephants never could learn the
> goose-step. (5) because Garibaldi's chaplains in ordinary never do
> write. (6) because books that do not sell do not pay. (7) because just
> now I am teaching little boys nonsense verses. (Ward, i. 579)

63 *Call me to Rome ... Dr Baines*: Strachey takes this from Ward, specifically a letter of 29 August 1864 in which Newman refers, bitterly, to 'the hot
water I might get into with Propaganda. Perhaps I should have to kick my
heels at its door for a whole year, like poor Dr. Baines. It would kill me'
(Ward, ii. 52).

Lucas: Frederick Lucas (1812–55), Catholic journalist and politician. He
went over to Rome in 1830, publishing, at the same time, 'Reasons for
Becoming a Roman Catholic'.

64 *Charles Kingsley ... a magazine article ... twenty-two hours at a stretch*:
see Ward:

> At Christmas 1863 there appeared in *Macmillan's Magazine* a review by
> Charles Kingsley of J. A. Froude's *History of England*. In it occurred
> the following passage: 'Truth for its own sake had never been a virtue
> with the Roman clergy. Father Newman informs us that it need not be,
> and on the whole ought not to be;—that cunning is the weapon which
> Heaven has given to the Saints wherewith to withstand the brute male
> force of the wicked world which marries and is given in marriage.
> Whether his notion be doctrinally correct or not, it is, at least, historic-

ally so.' Newman wrote to the publishers, not, he said, to ask for reparation, but 'to draw their attention as gentlemen to a grave and gratuit-
ous slander.' Kingsley at once wrote to him . . . acknowledging the
authorship of the review . . . 'I never had such a time of it,' [Newman]
adds to another of the Dominican sisters. 'When I was at Oxford I have
twice written a pamphlet in a night, and once in a day, but now I had
writing and printing upon me at once, and I have done a book of 562
pages all at a heat; but with so much suffering, such profuse crying,
such long spells of work—sometimes sixteen hours, once twenty-two
hours at once,—that it is a prodigious, awful marvel that I have got
through it and that I am not simply knocked up by it.' (Ward, ii. 53)

l'espoir . . . son cœur: and hope, in spite of himself, began to slip into his
heart.

66 *Monsignor Talbot*: the account of Talbot's deviousness, taken from Ward,
chapter 25.

67 *Cardinal Reisach*: Carl von Reisach (1800–69).

68 *Mark Pattison*: Pattison (1813–84), Rector of Lincoln College Oxford
(after 1861), was regarded as one of the greatest English scholars of his
time and his *Memoirs* (1883) were considered the greatest of British
intellectual autobiographies. He was an early candidate to be one of
Strachey's eminent Victorians.

Dr Newman is the most dangerous man in England: this episode about the
Oxford Oratory is taken, often practically verbatim, from Ward, chapter
24.

70 *'Oh, no, no!'*: Strachey subtly alters what Ward wrote:

Fortunately there are extant the written impressions of one who acci-
dentally met him there, which help to fill in the picture. I owe them to
the kindness of Canon Irvine. 'I was passing by the Church at Littlemore when I observed a man very poorly dressed leaning over the
lych gate crying. He was to all appearance in great trouble. He was
dressed in an old gray coat with the collar turned up and his hat pulled
down over his face as if he wished to hide his features. As he turned
towards me I thought it was a face I had seen before. The thought
instantly flashed through my mind it was Dr. Newman. I had never
seen him, but I remember Mr. Crawley had got a photo of Dr. Newman. I went and told Mr. Crawley I thought Dr. Newman was in the
village, but he said I must be mistaken, it could not be. I asked him to
let me see the photo, which he did. I then told him I felt sure it was
[he]. Mr. Crawley wished me to have another look at him. I went and
met him in the churchyard. He was walking with Mr. St. John. I made
bold to ask him if he was not an old friend of Mr. Crawley's, because if
he was I felt sure Mr. Crawley would be very pleased to see him; as he
was a great invalid and not able to get out himself, would he please to
go and see Mr. Crawley. He instantly burst out crying and said, "Oh no,

oh no!" Mr. St. John begged him to go, but he said, "I cannot." Mr. St. John asked him then to send his name, but said "Oh no!" At last Mr. St. John said, "You may tell Mr. Crawley Dr. Newman is here." I did so, and Mr. Crawley sent his compliments, begged him to come and see him, which he did and had a long chat with him. After that he went and saw several of the old people in the village.' (Ward, ii. 207)

As Michael Holroyd points out, Strachey skews his source here, ascribing Newman's tears not to nostalgia (which, according to Ward they were) but to frustrated careerism—'obliquely attributing to Newman an aspiring nature hardly less keen than Manning's own' (Holroyd, ii. 282).

70 *Syllabus Errorum*: a catalogue of errors.

   Papal Infallibility: this assertion of what was called 'ultramontane' authority (centring on Papal Infallibility) over the years 1867–8 is dealt with in Ward, chapter 27.

71 *Monseigneur Dupanloup . . . Dr Döllinger*: Félix-Antoine-Philibert Dupanloup (1802–1878), Bishop of Orléans; Johann Joseph Ignaz von Döllinger (1799–1890), German historian and theologian.

72 *John XXII . . . 'Cum inter nonnullos'*: Pope John XXII (1249–1334, enthroned 1316). Papal 'bulls' (ordinances) are identified by their first words. *Cum inter nonnullos* was directed against the Franciscans, and their ultra-austere interpretations of Christ's poverty and the spiritual virtues of owning nothing.

   Nicholas III: Pope Nicholas III (1216–80, enthroned 1277).

   Gallican: a term used to designate doctrines associated with France opposing the 'ultramontane' authority of Rome.

73 *M. Guizot and M. Thiers*: François Guizot (1787–1874), a French historian specialising in grand surveys of his country's civilization; Adolphe Thiers (1797–1877), a statesman and also a historian, having written a history of the French Revolution in his youth.

   'Mais, M. Thiers . . . vous êtes effectivement croyant,' 'En Dieu': But, M. Thiers, you are, effectively, a believer? 'In God.'

   Napoleon III: the historical background in this section of Strachey's account is intricate. In November 1852 Louis-Napoleon became Emperor Napoleon III of France. He led his country, successfully, in the Crimean campaign and dominated the subsequent Congress of Paris. An expansionist, he turned his attention to Italy, supporting that country's insurgent nationalist movement and its aim to overthrow Austrian occupation and the authority of the Vatican. War broke out in 1859. Napoleon's troops entered Italy. After the costly victory of the French and Sardinians at Solferino, Napoleon made a separate peace with Austria—partly under pressure from the French Catholic Church.

74 *Zouaves*: French light infantry. The name was applied to this *corps d'élite* from North African fighters, who had joined the French military in 1830.

They retained a distinctively Moroccan uniform. Louis-Napoleon established them as the nucleus of his army.

the Quirinal: one of the seven hills of Rome. In the sixteenth century a Papal palace was built there. It is now the home of the President of Italy.

75 *Il Diavolo del Concilio*: the mischief-maker at the Council.

Mr Gladstone was Prime Minister: Gladstone became Prime Minister in 1868.

Lord Acton: 'historian and moralist (1834–1904)', as the *DNB* describes him. In the 1860s Acton took an active part in the European debate on the separation of religious and political powers. Pope Pius IX's encyclical *Quanta Cura* with the appended *Syllabus Errorum* (1864) 'deliberately condemned all such efforts as those of Acton to make terms between the church and modern civilisation'.

'Que diable allait-il faire dans cette galère?': literally, 'What the devil was he going to do in that galley?' Figuratively, 'why was he getting involved in all that?' Proverbial in French. It originates as an exclamation by Géronte in Molière's *Les Fourberies de Scapin*.

76 *Mr Odo Russell*: a career diplomat (1829–84). He moved from Washington to Rome in 1858, and was resident there (serving British government interests) until 1870. After a distinguished career he was raised to the peerage in 1881.

77 *Inopportunists*: the history of the First General Council of the Vatican (1869–70) is intricate, and Strachey's account is both lucid and, apparently, accurate (taken, as it is, from chapter 20 of Ward). At this council various factions competed among themselves: the 'Gallicans' opposed the 'Ultramontanes' on the question of Papal authority. The 'Inopportunists' took a moderate line against the 'Infallibilists' (those who believed in absolute and final Papal jurisdiction).

ex cathedrâ: from on high.

78 *Questi infallibilisti mi faranno fallire*: these proponents of infallibility will be the death of me.

Antonelli: Cardinal Giacomo Antonelli (1806–76), Secretary of State to Pius IX.

proprio motu: at his own instigation.

79 *'Bethink ye ... mistaken!'*: before the battle of Dunbar, in July 1650, Cromwell implored his Scottish foes 'I beseech you, in the bowels of Christ, think it possible you may be mistaken.' The Scots ignored his request, and were slaughtered.

the excommunication of Dr Döllinger: Döllinger was excommunicated in April 1871. He continued to teach, however, at his university in Germany and maintained his post as royal councillor to King Louis II of Bavaria.

Vaticanism: Gladstone intervened in the current Catholic disputes with two pamphlets: *Vatican Decrees in their Bearing on Civil Allegiance* (1874) and its sequel, *Vaticanism* (1875). Like Manning (although with opposite views) he was preoccupied with the tensions of temporal and spiritual authority.

82 *the spare and stately form*: Strachey was insistent with his publishers that the four sections of *Eminent Victorians* be headed by an appropriately imposing portrait. The photograph of Manning, in late life, shows him as excessively 'spare and stately'.

83 *He threw himself into social work of every kind*: in his later years, Manning campaigned vigorously for abstinence and founded, in 1868, a temperance society, 'The League of the Cross'. He associated himself with hospitals and practical educational initiatives for the working classes. His most effective intervention was as a peace-maker in the London dock strike of August 1889.

85 *. . . shall apostatise from the faith*: this, as are other details in this section, is taken from Purcell and is introduced, one supposes, to suggest an incipient religious mania in Manning's later years about the 'End-times'.

86 *the death of Pius IX*: the Pope died on 7 February 1878. As Strachey notes, Manning took part in the conclave to elect a successor and himself received some votes. The election finally went to Leo XIII.

88 *the crushing indictment pointed straight at Manning*: Strachey draws here on Ward, chapter 33, 'The Cardinalate (1879)'. Ward, however, gives Manning some benefit of the doubt in the business of the *Times* leak, observing:

> Although the letter sent to Dr. Ullathorne for Cardinal Nina to see did bear this interpretation prima facie, it was addressed to one to whom Newman himself explained its true meaning, and had been shown by the Bishop only to Cardinal Manning, to whom he had carefully conveyed Newman's real wishes. Manning, however, appears to have taken Newman's own written words as decisive, and to have regarded the Bishop's impressions as unauthoritative. Newman was greatly pained by the appearance of such a statement in the papers, and at a loss to account for it. In the ordinary course of things such a paragraph could not have been inserted without Newman's express authority . . . 'A private letter, addressed to Roman Authorities, is interpreted on its way and published in the English papers. How is it possible that any one can have done this?' (Ward, ii. 444)

90 *Mr John Burns . . . Mr Ben Tillett . . . Mr Henry George*: John Burns (1858–1953) and Benjamin Tillett (1860–1943) were the trade union leaders directly involved in the 1889 dock strike (the basic demand was for 'a tanner [6*d.*] an hour'). The strike brought them into close connection with Manning, who acted as an intermediary with the employers. Henry George (1839–97) was a self-taught American economist whose treatise *Progress and Poverty* (1879) was inspirational for pioneers of the British Labour movement.

91 *Croker's 'Life and Letters' . . . Hayward's 'Letters'*: John Wilson Croker (1780–1857), politician; and Abraham Hayward (1801–1884), essayist. Strachey implies that Manning, at this stage of his life, missed the hurly-burly of English political life.

92 *rochet . . . mozzetta . . . biretta*: vestments of the cardinal. The 'rochet' is an over-tunic usually made of fine white linen. The 'mozzetta' is a short cape. The 'biretta' is the beret, or flat hat, which is placed on the new cardinal by the Pope himself.

93 *'Si fort qu'on soit . . . c'est toujours le moins humiliant'*: 'however strong one is, one can feel the need to bow down before someone or something. To bow down before God is always the least humbling.'

the cathedral which Manning never lived to see: Manning's body lay in state in his house at Westminster. He was buried at Kensal Green Cemetery. Some years later, his remains were re-interred in the crypt of the newly built Catholic Cathedral of Westminster.

the Hat: Manning received the biretta of a cardinal-priest from the Pope Pius IX, at Rome, on 31 March 1875. He did not receive 'the hat' (i.e. full cardinalate status, with the Pope's ceremonially placing the hat on his head) until 31 December 1877. Pius IX was then in his last illness, and Manning remained at Rome, and was present at his death on 7 February 1878. This final promotion, Strachey intimates, was the end to which Manning, arch-careerist that he was, had devoted all his life.

FLORENCE NIGHTINGALE

STRACHEY'S SOURCES

Strachey's piece on Nightingale is, like those on Manning and Arnold, taken principally from one source. With Nightingale, however, it was—as he protests in his Preface—a source which he admired and trusted: 'Sir Edward Cook's excellent *Life of Florence Nightingale*, without which my own study, though composed on a very different scale and from a decidedly different angle, could not have been written.' Strachey himself had been contracted, before Cook was authorized, to undertake Nightingale's biography. Cook's life, which came out in 1913, was very popular and was reprinted twice in its first years. Strachey's borrowings are referenced below to the two-volume edition of 1914. Mark Bostridge notes that 'No enormous liberties were taken with the truth in [Strachey's] "Florence Nightingale", though Strachey did embroider details in order to poke fun at individuals as well as to heighten comic effects' (*EVDE* 174). One obvious example is his caricature of the poet, Arthur Clough. Strachey had finished Manning by Christmas 1914, and had resolved to do Nightingale next. He worked on it during the first half of 1915.

97 *Every one knows*: Strachey wrote, and deleted (in proof, presumably), a more florid introduction to this section, as the manuscript (Add. 54221) indicates:

There are some who come to greatness by devious paths and accidental by-ways; who linger for long—unconscious of their destiny, in idleness or in misdirected effort, and who drift at last into glory without pre-vision and even perhaps, without desire. There are others who bear, so to speak, the mark of fate upon their brows, who, sealed from the first tribe of Heroes, rush through thick and thin straight at their life's achievement, like hounds upon their quarry; and of these was Florence Nightingale. Every one knows . . .

97 *the Lady with the Lamp*: this iconic image was invented by Mr Macdonald (his initials are elusive), the *Times'* almoner (i.e. manager of the newspaper's fund for nurses in the Crimea) in a dispatch describing Nightingale's habitual midnight patrol of the wards at Scutari:

> She is a 'ministering angel' without any exaggeration in these hos-pitals, and as her slender form glides quietly along each corridor, every poor fellow's face softens with gratitude at the sight of her. When all the medical officers have retired for the night and silence and darkness have settled down upon those miles of prostrate sick, she may be observed alone, with a little lamp in her hand, making her solitary rounds. (Cook, i. 237)

The instrument was a 'camp-lamp', British Army issue. It survived the war as a sacred relic, in the possession of Nightingale's friend and co-worker, Mrs Selina Bracebridge.

98 *Charlotte Corday, or Elizabeth of Hungary?*: the Elizabeth of Hungary remark picks up a passing comment by Mrs Gaskell, who said that Night-ingale's character resembled that of the wife of Louis, Landgrave of Thuringia (1207–31), made famous to the British reader by Charles Kingsley's 1848 poem, 'The Saint's Tragedy'. Mrs Gaskell's reference is found in Cook (i. 139). The reference to Corday, the murderess of Marat (in his bath—no ministering angel she), is mischievous.

if it was not a call?: Strachey's repeated stress on 'call' echoes Cook's first chapter on Nightingale and the Crimean War, 'The Call'.

tearing her dolls to pieces . . . into elaborate splints . . . the country house at Embley: this catalogue of Nightingale's neurotic juvenile obsession with the sick and destitute has been much objected to. Cook, for example, plays down the dolls-and-dogs episodes: 'these things are after all but trifles,' he comments: 'Florence Nightingale is not the only girl who has been fond of nursing sick dolls or mending them when broken. Other children have tended wounded animals' (Cook, i. 14). Mark Bostridge further records that 'in the original story, much underplayed by Cook, the dog was not hers but a shepherd's—not a pet then, but a valuable working dog—and Nightingale saved its life by applying ordinary hot water fomentations' (*EVDE* 175–6). Michael Holroyd notes that the 'chief authority' for Nightingale's putting the dog's leg in splints 'appears to have been a Mrs Sarah Tooley, whose popular *Life of*

Nightingale, written in 1904, he very wisely does not include in his bibliography' (Holroyd, i. 287). Embley Park was the Nightingales' country house in Hampshire. The remark about her 'queer imaginations of the country house' as a hospital picks up something reported by Cook: ' "Do you know," said Florence, as she walked with a congenial friend on the lawn in front of the drawing-room, "what I always think when I look at that row of windows? I think how I should turn it into a hospital, and just how I should place the beds" ' (Cook, i. 29). Her remark is less queer when one realizes that the 'congenial friend' was Dr Elizabeth Blackwell (1821–1910), a fellow pioneer in hospital careers for Victorian women.

99 *something like a Protestant Sisterhood*: this is taken from a letter from Nightingale to her cousin Hilary, 11 December 1845, quoted by Cook (i. 44). All Strachey's quotations from, and paraphrases of, Nightingale's correspondence derive from this secondary source.

99 *a Mrs Gamp*: Sairey Gamp, the drunken night-nurse in Dickens's *Martin Chuzzlewit*, whose 'care' almost does for the hero. In addition to becoming a byword for bad nursing, her name gave rise to the Victorian nickname for a 'brolly', or umbrella (a 'gamp').

'It was as if ... I had wanted to be a kitchen maid': see Cook: 'Gentlewomen, it was felt, would be exposed, if not to danger and temptations, at least to undesirable and unfitting conditions. "It was as if I had wanted to be a kitchen-maid," she said in later years. Nothing is more tenacious than social prejudice' (Cook, i. 60). Cook makes it clear that it was not just her parents, but society generally which disapproved of a nursing career for a 'gentlewoman'. Far from 'shuddering' (as Strachey says), her father, Mr Nightingale, is described by Cook as showing 'a degree of broadmindedness with regard to the education and sphere of women which was in advance of the average opinion at the time,' (Cook, i. 60–1).

100 *in ragged schools and workhouses*: see Cook: 'During the next year she found some congenial work in London. She inspected hospitals. She worked in Ragged Schools' (Cook, i. 82). The workhouses are, presumably, a Strachey invention.

the critical event of her life: a slight exaggeration of what Cook says: 'The three months which Miss Nightingale spent at Kaiserswerth in 1851 were a turning point in her career, but they were not immediately effectual in altering the tenor of her life' (Cook, i. 161). Strachey copied this passage out in his notes, but chose—typically—to sharpen it somewhat.

a desirable young man: not named in Cook. Nor by Strachey. He was Richard Monkton Milnes (1809–85).

101 *'I see nothing desirable but death'*: Strachey is weaving together quotations here from Cook (i. 105–6). Cook makes clear (as Strachey does not) that this dramatic exclamation belongs 'eighteen months before' the earlier quotations. Strachey habitually gives no precise dating references, which allows judicious rearrangement for dramatic effect.

101 _We are ducks ... an eagle_: this elaborates a remark (reported by Cook) of Mrs Gaskell's, after a visit to Florence's mother in August 1854: 'Mrs Nightingale says with tears in her eyes (alluding to Andersen's _Fairy Tales_), that they are ducks, and have hatched a wild swan' (Cook, i. 139). Strachey seems to retrodate the remark to 1853.

There follows, crossed out in the manuscript: 'And Florence, happy, busy, free, was not to be lured back into her cage by a little sprinkling of salt. She worked on at Harley Street with all her energy; and she had been there for more than a year when Fate knocked at her door ...' (Add. 54221). Strachey evidently decided at this point to interrupt and start a second section.

The Crimean War broke out: on 14 September (1854) the Allies (principally France and England) invaded the Crimea to liberate it from the Russians. The Battle of Alma was fought on 20 September. On 21 October Florence Nightingale left England. On 24 October, the Battle of Balaclava was fought. Nightingale arrived at Scutari (near Constantinople) on 4 November. Sending Nightingale to the theatre of war was one of the few things the British authorities did effectively and quickly. On 9 October 1854 William Russell Howard in _The Times_ had drawn attention to the woeful inadequacy of arrangements for the British wounded— contrasting it with those for the French (who had sent out fifty sisters of charity). A fund was set up (under the auspices of the newspaper) which significantly reduced delay.

102 _Sidney Herbert_: Herbert (1810–61), statesman, educated at Harrow and Oriel College Oxford. Florence Nightingale met Herbert for the first time in 1847–8, in Rome. He had previously been Secretary for War under Peel, but resigned in 1846. In 1854 he was reappointed by Aberdeen (1852–5), and again by Palmerston (1859–60). It was Herbert who authorized the dispatch of British nurses—at the friendly instigation of Nightingale. Her manipulation of male politicians was, as Strachey stresses, vital to her achievements as a reforming nurse.

the crossing of the letters: see Cook: 'The minds of the Minister and of Miss Nightingale were kindled together. They reached the flash-point of action at almost an identical moment' (Cook, i. 150). Nightingale's letter is dated 14 October, Herbert's a day later.

within a week ... left for Constantinople: Nightingale left England on 21 October with thirty-eight nurses. She was financed principally at this stage by the _Times_ fund of £7,000 (Cook, i. 160) and her own private resources.

... our Divine Lord: Manning's letter is quoted by Cook (not by Purcell) (Cook, i. 161).

The old Duke: the Duke of Wellington (1769–1852), victor of Waterloo (1815) and Commander-of-Chief of the British Army (with its HQ at Horse Guards in London), 1842–52.

103 *at once laughed out of court ... such trifles in the Peninsula*: rather uncharacteristically, Strachey plays down the blimpish scorn poured on Nightingale and described, at indignant length, by Cook. See, for example, the letter of Colonel Sterling, in 1855: 'Miss —— has added herself to the hospital of the 42nd; and will not acknowledge the voice of the Nightingale, who has written an official letter to Lord Raglan on the subject. I suppose he will order a court-martial composed of nurses, who will administer queer justice' (Cook, i. 167). The comment about the Peninsular War (forty-five years earlier) picks up a remark of Sir George Brown—a grizzled veteran who had been thrown into a cart on some straw when shot in the legs in Spain and thought that what was good enough in 1808 was good enough in 1855 (Cook, i. 175).

Dr Hall: Sir John Hall, MD (1795–1866), Inspector of Hospitals in the Crimea. He was appointed to this post while still serving in India—with no first-hand knowledge of the theatre of war he would be operating in. He was not unfriendly in principle to Nightingale but, as Cook says (and Strachey echoes): 'she fought him, and in the end she beat him' (Cook, i. 288).

the 'middle passage': the middle of the voyage for slaves between Africa and America, when casualties among the human cargo ran highest.

104 *Lasciate ... voi ch'entrate*: the inscription over the gates of Hell, in Dante's *Inferno*. See Cook's vivid description of the 'gigantic barrack house', picked up by Strachey:

> North of the General Hospital, and near to the famous Turkish cemetery of Scutari, are the Selimeyeh Barracks—a great yellow building with square towers at each angle. This building was made over to the British for use as a hospital after the Battle of Alma, and by them was always called *The Barrack Hospital*. (Cook, i. 172)

There were, in fact, five British hospitals in the Crimea. Scutari, thanks to Nightingale, would become most notorious.

105 *The structural defects ... candlesticks*: Strachey follows Cook closely in these pages and at this point barely bothers to paraphrase his source, apart from some adjectival embellishment. For example: 'The commonest utensils, for decency as well as for comfort, were lacking. The sheets said Miss Nightingale, "were of canvas, and so coarse that the wounded men begged to be left in their blankets". . . . There was no bedroom furniture of any kind, and only empty beer or wine bottles for candlesticks' (Cook, i. 177).

the miserable band of convalescent soldiers: Michael Holroyd notes, correctively, that 'a good many of them were willing and able-bodied N.C.O.s who, as Florence herself complained, were often sent back to the front after they had been given the bare modicum of hospital training' (Holroyd, ii. 289).

106 *Dr Andrew Smith ... 'nothing was needed'*: Smith (1797–1872) was

Director-General of the Army Medical Department from 1853 to 1858. On 14 October 1854 (seven days before she left England) Nightingale reported to Herbert that 'Dr Smith says nothing is needed' (Cook, i. 157). She was unconvinced.

106 *Lord Stratford de Redcliffe . . . an English Protestant Church at Pera*: this sublimely absurd proposal is found in Cook—with less emphasis (there is, for example, no suggestion that it be a *Protestant* church).

108 *'It would require a new Regulation . . . to bone the meat'*: Nightingale reported this to Herbert in a letter of 5 February 1855—with a shoal of exclamation marks indicating her total amazement at military imbecility.

109 *'I am now clothing the British Army'*: Nightingale made this remark (ironically, and not exactly as Strachey quotes) in a letter (cited by Cook) of 4 January 1855.

who could take the responsibility?: see Cook: ' "It is a current joke here", wrote Miss Nightingale from Scutari, "to offer a prize for the discovery of anyone willing to take responsibility" ' (Cook, i. 207). Her comment is somewhat sharper than Strachey's.

110 *'The strongest will be wanted at the wash-tub'*: quoted by Cook (i. 195), along with an extended description of the total lack of basic sanitary arrangements on which Strachey freely draws (e.g. 'Until Miss Nightingale arrived, the number of shirts washed during a month was six').

after that it was as 'oly as a church: this was in fact from a soldier's letter (and 'holy'). The detail about devout warriors kissing her shadow as it passed comes from the same passage in Cook, and was stored up by Strachey to be used later (Cook, i. 237–8).

111 *had that in it one must fain call master*: Kent's remark to the abdicated Lear, in Shakespeare's tragedy.

112 *with the deadly and unsparing precision of a machine gun*: an anachronism. The first Gatling guns were developed in 1870. Strachey is alluding, bitterly, to the war going on as he writes. He alludes again to the Maxim gun (as the weapon of the future) in his last paragraphs of *Eminent Victorians*.

her vituperations descended on the head of Sidney Herbert himself: Strachey seems to be thinking of a rough patch in their relationship in December 1854 when, as Nightingale thought, Herbert had sent out a party of forty-seven nurses under the separate command of Miss Mary Stanley. Nightingale did not want more nurses—particularly Catholic nurses, as many of Stanley's band were. It is not clear that there was an actual quarrel, or anything more than *froideur* (Cook, i. 188–90).

an aristocratic young gentleman: Mr Jocelyne Percy, as Cook assumes. The sarcastic description of Percy is taken from A. W. Kinglake (Cook, i. 219).

113 *'Let Mrs Herbert know . . . these noble fellows'*: Queen Victoria to Sidney Herbert, 6 December 1854. The Prince referred to is her consort, Albert.

Strachey's notebook (Add. 54219) indicates that he took this episode from Sir Theodore Martin's *Life of the Prince Consort*, 5 vols. (1875–80), iii. 503.

114 *'the British soldier is not a remitting animal'*: written in January 1856 by Lord Panmure (1810–74), Secretary for War after January 1855 until 1858. Strachey echoes Cook very closely: ' "It will do no good," wrote "Mars", convinced against his will; "the soldier is not a remitting animal." But in fact, during the following six months, a sum of £71,000 was sent home' (Cook, i. 279). Strachey's sole addition of the word 'British' (to 'soldier') adds an edge.

inspecting the hospitals in the Crimea itself: Nightingale embarked on this Augean task in spring 1855. She was laid low by 'Crimea fever' on arrival at Balaclava. Her recovery was slow, but she resolutely refused to return to England. She was never entirely well for the remainder of her life.

115 *Mrs Bridgeman . . . the 'Reverend Brickbat'*: Mother Superior of the Kinsale nuns who took over the General Hospital at Balaclava. Nightingale assumed that Hall, by backing Bridgeman, was trying to 'root her out of the Crimea'. It raised her vexation to 'white heat' (Cook, i. 290).

116 *The brooch . . . 'Blessed are the Merciful'*: Strachey suggests the brooch was given with the declaration of peace, signed at Paris, on 30 March 1856. In fact the ornament was sent to Nightingale by her admiring sovereign in November 1855. It was featured in the *Illustrated London News*, 2 February 1856. Nightingale never wore the brooch publicly in England, although she did so when visiting the East.

118 *she visited Balmoral*: Nightingale went to Balmoral on 21 September 1856, having arrived back in England in August. She was not, by Cook's account, as 'shattered' in health as Strachey describes her.

'Sie gefällt uns sehr . . . ist sehr bescheiden': we like her very much . . . she is very modest.

I wish we had her at the War Office: Queen Victoria's enthusiastic remark was made to the Duke of Cambridge.

119 *General Simpson*: Sir James Simpson (1792–1868), successor to Lord Raglan as Commander-in-Chief in the Crimea.

120 *'The Bison' his friends called him*: this somewhat misrepresents Cook, who reports that the nickname was bestowed on 'the burly Scot . . . by Miss Nightingale and *her* friends' (Cook, i. 325).

122 *neither an Aspasia nor an Egeria*: Aspasia was the Greek courtesan who captivated Pericles, the Athenian statesman of the fifth century BC, Egeria was an Italian goddess of fountains and the counsellor and wife of King Numa (successor to Romulus, founder of Rome).

123 *her 'Aunt Mai', her father's sister*: Mrs Samuel Smith. Nightingale called her 'my true mother'. She was with her niece at Scutari. Nightingale, on her return to London, lived until August 1857, at the Burlington Hotel

London and was a frequent visitor to Combe Hurst, the home of her uncle and aunt.

123 *Sir Harry Verney*: he married Florence's sister Parthenope in June 1858.

124 *there were parcels to be done up in brown paper*: this belittling Stracheyan cartoon of Clough was much objected to by the poet's family—particularly the brown paper. Cook (i. 348) merely writes: 'Mr A. H. Clough, then employed in the Education Office, gave her some help, out of office hours with her proofs [i.e. of her *Notes on the British Army*].' Arthur Hugh Clough (1819–61) was the son of a Liverpool cotton merchant, and was educated at Rugby (as a particular favourite of Dr Arnold) and at Balliol College Oxford. He developed religious doubts and gave up the fellowship he had won at Oriel College. As Cook indicates, after a spell at University Hall, London, he took employment with the Education Office. He married Nightingale's cousin, Blanche Smith.

Dr Sutherland, a sanitary expert: Dr John Sutherland (1808–91) was the head of the Sanitary Commission sent to the Crimea, in 1855. He acted as Nightingale's personal physician on her return to England and enlisted himself as an indefatigable supporter of her subsequent efforts for army reform. Sutherland died in July 1891. Among his last words were: 'Give her [Miss Nightingale] my love and blessing.'

125 *a polite official contrivance for exonerating Dr Andrew Smith?*: Nightingale was firmly of the opinion that Smith should have been court-martialled for his derelictions of duty in the Crimea (Cook, i. 354).

Notes affecting the Health . . . the British Army: this report was distributed 'among the most illustrious and influential personages in the land' (Cook, i. 384) in November 1858, but never formally published. It seems unlikely that Strachey read its 'more than 800 closely printed pages'.

126 *only then . . . did he dare tell Dr Smith what he had done*: Strachey extends Cook's more cautious description: 'It throws an interesting side light on the relations of Ministers to their subordinates to know, as appears from Miss Nightingale's papers, that Lord Panmure was careful to have the documents initialled by the Queen before submitting them to Dr Smith' (Cook, i. 354). In Cook's depiction, the politician is canny rather than pusillanimous.

127 *till I say like Xavier de Maistre, Assez, je le sais, je ne le sais que trop*: quoted from a letter of September 1857. Xavier de Maistre (1763–1852) was a French romance writer (the French means: 'Enough! I know it already. I know it only too well'). At this period of her life, as Cook reports, Nightingale was confined to her sofa under the constant superintendence of her Aunt Mai. She none the less offered to go out to India, in November 1857, 'where her friend Lady Canning was at the Viceroy's side during the Mutiny' (Cook, i. 371). Nightingale drew up her will at Malvern, in December 1857, expecting to die soon.

His gout was always handy: Nightingale made this smart comment to Herbert in late 1856 (Cook, i. 335).

128 *Netley Hospital*: the battle over the plans for Netley Military Hospital in Hampshire, especially the layout of its 'pavilions' (based on the design of the latest military hospital at Paris), had raged somewhat earlier, in 1856–7. The Hospital was opened in 1863.

'It seems to me . . . can be duly considered': Palmerston's letter is quoted in Cook (i. 341), followed by the comment: 'But even the most peremptory of Prime Ministers are not all-powerful.'

129 *an Army Medical School*: established in 1859 and formally opened in 1860. It was, Cook notes, 'a scheme to which she attached great importance' (i. 327). The institution later became the Royal Army Medical College, headquarters of the Royal Army Medical Corps.

mortality . . . since the days of the Crimea: this is not quite what Cook says: 'In the three years 1859–61, just one-half of the Englishmen who entered the Army died (at home stations) per annum as formerly died' (i. 397).

The War Office itself—!: in his chapter on the death of Herbert, Cook quotes Nightingale encouraging her failing friend to 'one fight more, the best and last!' (i. 403).

130 *the Nightingale Training School . . . St Thomas's Hospital*: the school was opened on 24 June 1860. It was paid for by £44,000 raised by the Nightingale Fund, after the Crimean War.

Dr Andrew Smith . . . outer darkness: Smith died in 1872. Strachey presumably means 'out of any position of power'; or out of Nightingale's favour.

Sir Benjamin Hawes: Hawes (1797–1862) was, at this point, Permanent Under-Secretary for War.

131 *by gulps of brandy*: Herbert wrote to Nightingale on 7 June 1861: 'On days when the mornings are spent on a sofa drinking gulps of brandy till I am fit to crawl down to the office, I am not very energetic when I get there.' Cook none the less insists that Herbert's 'buoyancy of spirit remained' (i. 404–6). He was not, that is, the complete wreck Strachey describes.

with all the winning cards in your hands!: this is taken by Strachey from a letter written by Nightingale to Harriet Martineau on 21 August 1861 *after* Herbert's death: 'I told him that no man in my day had thrown away so noble a game with all the winning cards in his hands' (Cook, i. 494).

Sidney Herbert beaten!: as Cook records, Herbert declared himself 'beaten' on 7 June 1861 (Cook, i. 404). What Nightingale wrote in response to Sir John McNeill (an old Crimea hand), on 21 June, is somewhat dramatized by Strachey:

What strikes me in this great defeat more painfully even than the loss to the Army is the triumph of bureaucracy over the leaders—the political aristocracy who at least advocate higher principles. A Sidney

> Herbert beaten by a Ben Hawes is a greater humiliation really (as a matter of principle) than the disaster of Scutari. (Cook, i. 405)

132 *Spa*: the health resort in Germany.

Our joint work . . . they could hear no more: Strachey's version dramatizes his source, in Cook:

> He died at Wilton on August 2. 'To the last,' wrote his sister to Miss Nightingale, 'he had the same charm, that dear winning smile, that almost playful, pretty way of saying everything.' But among his last articulate words were these: 'Poor Florence! Poor Florence! Our joint work unfinished.' (i. 406)

If Miss Nightingale had been less ruthless . . . perished: Cook suggests (unlike Strachey) that it was not Nightingale's relentless driving but 'fatal disease' that killed Herbert and that 'Miss Nightingale did not fully realize how ill Lord Herbert was' (i. 402).

Arthur Clough . . . parcels: after a complete breakdown in his health Clough was advised (by Nightingale among others) to go abroad in April 1861. He died at Florence on 12 November.

Aunt Mai . . . left Miss Nightingale: Strachey picks this up from a footnote in Cook (ii. 15–16): 'At this time [December 1861] there was some misunderstanding between them. Mrs Smith's advancing age and home claims brought a cessation of her constant activity in Miss Nightingale's service.'

one of her enormous letters: Strachey is thinking of a letter to Madame Mohl, 13 December 1861, in which Nightingale complains 'my doctrines have taken no hold among women' (Cook, ii. 14). It is in the same letter that Nightingale makes her extravagant declaration about 'widow's caps' which Strachey paraphrases below.

appris à apprendre: learnt to understand.

133 *a sympathetic account of the funeral*: Gladstone wrote his sympathetic account on 10 August 1861. He firmly rejected Nightingale's hint that he take up Herbert's burden in the same letter: 'my duty is to watch and control . . . the Treasury rather than to promote departmental reforms' (Cook, i. 409).

the Poor Law Commission of 1909: this is Cook's observation (ii. 143). He describes the 'remarkable paper' at length.

a small house in South Street: after Sidney Herbert's death Nightingale left Burlington Hotel, where she had been staying some years, for lodgings in Hampstead, where she remained from August to October 1861. In November 1861 her brother-in-law, Sir Harry Verney, lent her his house at 32 South Street.

134 *went out for a drive in the Park*: this paraphrases Cook, freely:

> She seldom went out of doors in London. It was believed that

occasionally, when her heart and nerves were giving her less than the usual sense of weakness, she went out on foot in the Park; but the belief was only whispered: it was a point of honour amongst her circle to respect her house-ridden seclusion. (ii. 309)

137 *what she called the 'germ-fetish'*: Nightingale's controversial views on germs are expressed in her appended comments to Sir J. Clarke Jervoise's pamphlet 'Infection' (1882). As Strachey wrote in his notebook (Add. 54219): 'the object of the pamphlet [is] to show that there is no such thing as infection. The "germ theory" is all rubbish.' In her added notes printed in the pamphlet Nightingale compares the 'germ fetish' to the medieval witch fetish, concluding 'the germ hypothesis, if logically followed out, must stop all human intercourse whatever, on pain or risk of disease or death'. As Cook points out (ii. 172), this inflexible disbelief in micro-organisms had serious consequences in the advice she gave (as Adviser General on Hospitals) to the authorities on the outbreak of cholera in India in 1869.

all hospital windows should be invariably kept open: the doors-versus-windows controversy raged in 1867. Cook writes:

> To Miss Nightingale and the War Office Sanitary Commission the ventilation of barracks or hospitals by open doors was a pestilential heresy; to the Government of India it was the ark of the covenant for salvation in hot weather. Sir John Lawrence in reply to Miss Nightingale's remonstrance told her bluntly that nothing but an imperative order from home would make him close the doors. (ii. 150)

She, of course, was as resolute about windows being thrown open as her opponents were about doors being flung wide.

Lord Lawrence, however, was Viceroy: John Laird Lawrence Mair (1811–79), Viceroy of India, 1863–9.

138 *yellow-fever cases in Panama*: the Panama Canal was opened, officially, on 15 August 1914—a few months before Strachey wrote this essay.

my utter shipwreck: among other blows Nightingale sustained at this period were the death of her father and Mrs Bracebridge. As Cook records: 'Once in the middle of the night she started up and saw pictures on the wall by the night-light lamp. "Am I she who once stood on that Crimean height? . . . The lamp shows me only my utter shipwreck" ' (ii. 240).

Mr Jowett: Benjamin Jowett (1817–93), Master of Balliol College Oxford, 1870–93. He and Nightingale became acquainted through correspondence about her *Suggestions for Thought*—a volume which he wished might be rewritten 'in a more connected form and gentler mood'.

139 *a series of essays for Frazer's Magazine*: Nightingale wrote three pieces in *Fraser's Magazine* (so spelt) between March 1869 and July 1873. Jowett suggested she write them after a total collapse in her health, in December 1867. It would, he thought, divert her from the incessant 'drudgery' of her nursing work. The editor of *Fraser's* was the congenial J. A. Froude.

The subjects Nightingale chose were contemporary 'pauperism' and speculation about 'what will our religion be in 1999?' Carlyle, as Strachey notes, approved the first of the two articles on pauperism (an attack on *laisser faire* offering in its place rational emigration schemes). But he made sarcastic reference ('a lost lamb bleating on the mountains') to the more theological article Nightingale wrote for the magazine in July 1873. A fourth article Nightingale wrote was never printed.

139 *the Dialogues of Plato*: Jowett's commentary on Plato came out in 1871. He immediately began revising it. Nightingale helped. He complimented her as 'the best critic I ever had' (Cook, ii. 222).

  the Bishop of Oxford ... Sir Travers Twiss: Jowett wrote to Nightingale on 16 March 1872: 'The Bishop has disallowed our "Versicles" and some other things on legal grounds—i.e. the opinion of Sir Travers Twiss (poor man!)' (Cook, ii. 228). Cook suggests that Nightingale was drawn to Catholic mysticism at this period of her life. Sir Travers Twiss (1809–97) was a prominent barrister and legal theorist.

  and administer to her the Holy Sacrament?: Jowett did so on 28 October 1862, making the declaration that he would always regard it as 'a solemn event in my life' (Cook, ii. 96).

140 *end her life ... St Thomas's Hospital*: in January 1864 Nightingale sent the following instruction to her friend, Mrs Bracebridge:

> You know that I always believed it to be God's will for me that I should live and die in Hospitals. When this call He has made upon me for other work stops, and I am no longer able to work, I should wish to be taken to St. Thomas's Hospital and to be placed *in a general ward*. (Cook, ii. 103)

  'Do you think you are improving?': according to Cook, what the Aga Khan asked was: 'But are your people better?' (Cook, ii. 248).

141 *Notes on Nursing*: published in 1860.

  a fat old lady: Cook puts it more gallantly: 'the "willowy figure" which distinguished her in earlier years had now become large' (ii. 307).

  Sir Lawrence Alma Tadema and Sir Edward Elgar: distinguished artist and composer, respectively.

142 *and she was not ironical*: Strachey closely follows Cook: 'On December 5, Sir Douglas Dawson, on the King's behalf, brought the Order—then for the first time bestowed upon a woman—to South Street. Miss Nightingale understood that some kindness had been done to her, but hardly more. "Too kind, too kind," she said' (Cook, ii. 418).

DR ARNOLD

STRACHEY'S SOURCES

In this portrait Strachey draws almost exclusively on Stanley's *Life and Correspondence of Thomas Arnold, DD*. Arthur Penrhyn Stanley (1815–81) was educated at Rugby under Arnold and at Balliol College Oxford. He pursued an academic career and became Professor of Ecclesiastical History at Oxford in 1856. He was (like other academics of the period) ordained and went on to become Dean of Westminster in 1864, a post he held until his death. Stanley was Broad Church and wrote—in addition to his pious life of Arnold (published two years after the Doctor's death, in 1844)—numerous works of church history. He was a prominent figure on the late Victorian scene and his wife was a close friend of the Queen. References in the notes that follow are to the one-volume 1852 edition of Stanley's biography of Arnold. As Terence Copley points out (*EVDE* 212), 'Strachey gives no hint of having read any of Arnold's "seventeen volumes" beyond the Stanley letters' (i.e. what Stanley quotes in his biography). In terms of research, the Arnold chapter is the least ambitious of the *Eminent Victorians* quartet. Strachey in fact denied his satirical mill of some valuable grist. He might have made good use, for example, of the so-called 'March scandal'. Arnold flogged a disabled boy to within an inch of his life—under the mistaken impression that the poor wretch had told some unimportant lie (which he hadn't). It made the newspapers but not, of course, Stanley's servile account. More seriously, Strachey fundamentally misunderstood Arnold. Arnold was not, as Copley points out, principally a reformer of schools; his 'great work' (as he called it) was the assimilation of Church and State—the Christianization of England, no less. The public school was merely one engine which would help pull the country in that direction. Here, more powerfully than anywhere else in *Eminent Victorians*, Strachey's motive is 'idoloclasty'—the demolition of the Arnoldian idol created by Thomas Hughes (in *Tom Brown's Schooldays*) and Stanley in his hagiographic *Life*. Strachey worked on his Arnold essay from late 1915 through 1916.

145 *the twelve trustees, noblemen and gentlemen of Warwickshire*: Stanley (p. 42) writes: 'his testimonials were sent into the twelve trustees, noblemen and gentlemen of Warwickshire, in whom the appointment rests.' The decision was made on 10 December. There were fifty candidates and the selection process was less smooth than Strachey's epigrammatic treatment suggests. Arnold had to be persuaded by his Oxford friends to apply. He was worried about interference by the trustees, should he accept the post. And, most anxiously, he did not think he could subscribe wholeheartedly to the Thirty-nine Articles (ordination to the priesthood was a condition of appointment).

 'change the face of education all through the public schools of England': Strachey dramatizes (by making the comment a direct quotation) what Stanley wrote: 'His testimonials were few in number . . . Amongst them was a letter from Dr Hawkins, now Provost of Oriel, in which it was predicted that, if Mr Arnold were elected to the head-mastership of Rugby, he would change the face of education all through the public schools of England' (p. 42).

 that young Thomas might grow up into a prig . . . Smollett's History of England: see Stanley: 'One of the few recollections which he retained of his father was, that he received from him, at three years old, a present of Smollett's *History of England*, as a reward for the accuracy with which he had gone through the stories connected with the portraits and pictures of the successive reigns' (p. 3). The twenty-four volumes dwarfing the toddling prodigy are a Stracheyan embellishment. And of course little Thomas's father did not expect his son to read the book at 3 years old. Stanley attributes the juvenile priggishness ('stiffness and formality') which Strachey dwells on to the child's 'living chiefly in the company of his elders, and reading, or hearing read to him before he could read himself, books suited to a more advanced age' (p. 2).

146 *Mr Justice Coleridge, 'were not low or rationalistic ... textual authority'*: quoted from a 12-page letter from Coleridge to Stanley, written in September 1843, shortly after Arnold's death. Coleridge's remarks are imbued with obituaristic eulogy (Stanley, 15–16). John Taylor Coleridge (1790–1876) was a nephew of the poet and a friend of Arnold's from their time at Corpus. In later life he became Solicitor-General and Attorney-General.

146 *Keble wrote to Coleridge*: the letter is dated February 1819.

'almost to a constitutional infirmity': see Stanley: 'Both as a boy and a young man he was remarkable for a difficulty in early rising, amounting almost to a constitutional infirmity' (p. 2).

He married young: Arnold met Mary Penrose, daughter of the Rector of Fledborough, in January 1819 when he was 24. The young lady was the sister of his school and college friend, Trevenen Penrose. It was, by Victorian standards, a whirlwind affair (at a number of points in his satirical portrait Strachey hints at Arnold's potent sexual drives and energies). The young suitor leased a house at Laleham, by the Thames, in August 1819 and proposed the same month. The couple married a year later, on 11 August 1820. Their first child (of nine) was born a year later.

he began to write a History of Rome: the origins of this great work (as Arnold conceived it) are rather different from what Strachey here suggests. Archdeacon Hare, in 1825, recommended that Arnold read Niebühr's *History of Rome*. He mastered German to do so. What principally interested Arnold was the way in which Niebühr drew lessons from Imperial Rome to apply to the emergent German state. Arnold's fascination with Rome (ancient and modern) was heightened by a visit to the city in 1827, where he met with Chevalier Bunsen (like Niebühr, a German minister at the Papal Court). Bunsen both encouraged and inspired Arnold—in recognition of which his *History of Rome* was dedicated to the German when it was published, in three volumes, between 1838 and 1842. Arnold (more grandly than Niebühr) believed that 'The History of Rome must be in some sort the History of the World' (Stanley, 160). Strachey's implication that the work was written, out of some evangelical spasm, to correct the misapprehensions of England's children, is mischievous.

a serious conversation with Dr Whately: Richard Whately (1787–1863) was a fellow at Oriel when the younger Arnold was an undergraduate. It was Whately who first perceived potential for 'growth' in the not obviously promising Arnold (Stanley, 20). Whately, an academic 'flier', was appointed Professor of Political Economy in 1825 and in 1831 was appointed Archbishop of Dublin. Strachey took the detail of this life-changing 'serious conversation' from Stanley: '[Arnold] used to look back to a visit to Dr Whately, then residing on his cure in Suffolk, as a marked era in the formation of his views, especially as opening to his mind, or impressing upon it more strongly, some of the opinions on which he afterwards laid so much stress with regard to the Christian Priesthood' (p. 35).

147 *and yet, with a feeling of God's help on his side*: this montage of quotations, tendentiously plucked, is taken from Stanley's second chapter, and covers the period from 1822 to 1828. Stanley stresses that it was at this point in his life that Arnold's character took its pronounced turn towards earnestness (p. 36). The quotation about Arnold's 'peculiar love and adoration which he entertained towards our Lord Jesus Christ' is in fact from Stanley himself (p. 24). The last quotation (about battling with the wicked one) which Strachey claims is the report of 'a friend' is specifically said by Stanley to come from 'one who was himself *not* amongst his most intimate friends' (the remark was tinged, that is, with sarcasm).

his legs, perhaps, were shorter than they should have been: it is not clear where Strachey picked up this subversive detail. Terence Copley suggests that Strachey's 'dazzling cartoon' of Arnold might have derived, in large part, from the dazzling cartoonist's own schooldays. The headteacher of the New School at Abbotsholme (where Strachey went), Dr Cecil Reddie, had remarkably short legs (*EVDE* 212).

the flowing robes of a Doctor of Divinity: Arnold was made a Doctor of Divinity, in December 1828, the year he took up headmastership of Rugby. He was always thereafter 'the Doctor' (as in *Tom Brown's School-days*) to his young charges.

a slightly puzzled look: Strachey is thinking of the 1839 portrait by T. Phillips, which pictures Arnold in his Doctor's 'flowing robes'. The 'puzzled expression' is plausibly explained by Michael McCrum in *Thomas Arnold* (1980): Mrs Arnold commented in her journal 'that during the painting of the portrait by Phillips in 1839, Arnold had been so deeply engaged in discussion with Chevalier Bunsen and Crabbe Robinson about Niebühr's *History of Rome* that the artist had called for silence' (p. 140).

Keate was still reigning at Eton: the major public schools—Winchester (where Arnold was educated), Eton, and Rugby were as different from each other in the nineteenth century as they are now. Strachey's exuberantly savage digression about anarchy at Eton is taken, as his notebook indicates, from C. A. Wilkinson, *Eton under Keate* (1887).

148 *'The public schools ... are the very seats and nurseries of vice'*: a lament by Thomas Bowdler (1754–1825, the renowned 'bowdlerizer' of Shakespeare and other English classics). Arnold took Bowdler's jaundiced comment on the public schools as the text for one of his resounding sermons. It is reprinted as the twelfth sermon in his second volume (1829–34).

a place of really Christian education: Strachey subtly exaggerates Stanley's text: 'What was his great object has already appeared from his letters; namely, the *hope* of making the school a place of really Christian education' (p. 84); the word 'hope' suggests something less presumptuous.

149 *first ... thirdly, intellectual ability*: this was the theme of Arnold's regular admonition to his school's Praepostors, or sixth form prefects. He did not speak in this way, as Strachey implies, to *all* his pupils but only to those entrusted with his personally delegated authority. The prefectorial system was one of Arnold's principal innovations at Rugby.

'Shall I tell him ... that's all I want': Tom Brown's Schooldays (1857), chapter 1. Thomas Hughes was, like Stanley, an Old Rugbeian and a fanatic disciple of 'the Doctor'. Arnold features prominently in the novel. With its sequel *Tom Brown at Oxford* (1861) it massively enhanced the cult of 'Arnold of Rugby'.

150 *outside the Sixth Form, no part of the school came into close intercourse with him*: as McCrum points out, Arnold dedicated himself particularly to his sixth form. To the school at large, he was more of a remote preacher rather than a classroom teacher. As Stanley notes, 'lower down the school he was regarded with extreme fear' (p. 58). Arnold only took two classes a week in forms below the sixth. In *Tom Brown's Schooldays* he is described, in one of those classes, giving a 'good box on the ear' to a luckless pupil who makes an egregious mistake in translation from the Latin.

Facciolati's Lexicon, or Pole's synopsis: an eighteenth-century Latin lexicon and nineteenth-century biblical synopsis. This passage, taken from Stanley (p. 109), omits some mitigating details. For example: Arnold's 'courtesy and almost deference to the boys, as to his equals in society, so long as there was nothing to disturb the friendliness of their relations ... the expressions of delight with which, when they had been doing well, he would say that it was a constant pleasure to him to come into the library.'

151 *no theoretical objection to corporal punishment*: Strachey omits Stanley's qualification: 'flogging, therefore, for the younger part, he retained, but it was confined to moral offences, such as lying, drinking and habitual idleness' (p. 91). By 'younger part' Stanley indicates that corporal punishment was appropriate only for 'boys', not the sixth form, whom he treated as adults.

152 *'I assume it ... under any circumstances'*: Arnold wrote this to the chairman of the Rugby trustees. He went on to point out that if his pupils learned to read and write French and German correctly (as 'dead lan-

guages') they would pick them up, orally, quickly enough 'whenever they have any occasion to speak it, as in going abroad for instance' (Stanley, 107).

153 *Greek and Latin languages . . . by which this is to be effected*: Strachey shortens and misquotes: after 'Greek and Latin languages' Arnold continues: 'in themselves so perfect, and at the same time freed from the insuperable difficulty which must attend any attempt to teach boys philology through the medium of their own spoken language, seem the very instruments by which this is to be effected' (Stanley, 106). Stanley points out that his views on this issue hardened during his years of headship.

greatly overrated: Stanley is more judicious: 'the Greek tragedians, though reading them constantly, and portions of them with the liveliest admiration, he thought *on the whole* greatly overrated' (p. 115). Stanley goes on to give a more fair-minded description of Arnold's literary sensibility and prejudices. It is not true, for example, that because of his 'strong moral disapprobation' he 'never' read Juvenal, as Strachey suggests. He disliked what he read.

ἐν παρέργῳ: as a secondary study.

. . . bright blue firmament: Arnold wrote thus to an old pupil, Dr Greenhill, on 9 May 1836.

154 *could only be taught in the school chapel*: Strachey paraphrases Stanley's 'If there is one place at Rugby more than another which was especially the scene of Dr Arnold's labours, both as a teacher and as a master, it is the School-Chapel' (p. 121)—where, of course, his body rests.

would dominate the scene: Strachey colours Stanley's drab description: 'But of him especially it need hardly be said, that his chief interest in that place lay in the three hundred boys who, Sunday after Sunday, were collected, morning and afternoon, within its walls' (p. 122). The rhapsodic description of Arnold in the chapel is drawn, in its details, from Stanley.

the Nicene Creed: see Stanley: 'There was the visible animation with which by force of long association he joined in the musical parts of the service, to which he was by nature wholly indifferent, as in the chanting of the Nicene Creed, which was adopted in accordance with his conviction that creeds in public worship ought to be used as triumphant hymns of thanksgiving' (p. 123).

155 *'The spirit of Elijah . . . the spirit of Christ'*: this is clearer, perhaps, as Stanley puts it: 'When he first began to preach, he felt that his chief duty was to lay bare, in the plainest language that he could use, the sources of the evils of schools, and to contrast them with purity of the moral law of Christianity. "The spirit of Elijah," he said, "must ever precede the spirit of Christ" ' (p. 127). Stanley points out that the severity of Arnold's sermons diminished over the years. Elijah (see 1 Kings 17 ff.) was a

Hebrew prophet in the reign of Ahab. He was, famously, fed by ravens at the Brook Kerith and imperiously confuted the prophets of Baal. It is this last feat that Arnold alludes to.

155 *a kind of awe*: Strachey improves on Stanley's account:

> Even the most careless boys would sometimes during the course of the week, refer almost involuntarily to the sermon of the past Sunday as a condemnation of what they were doing. Some, whilst they wonder how it was that so little practical effect was produced upon themselves at the time, yet retain the recollection (to give the words of one who so describes himself,) that 'I used to listen to them from first to last with a kind of awe'. (Stanley, 131)

The 'old gentleman' and the dramatic decor ('darkened chapel', etc.) are Stracheyan embellishments.

by the Royal hand: in his notebook, Strachey records that these volumes of the third edition of Arnold's sermons, marked by Victoria, were on sale from the bookdealer P. M. Barnard of Tunbridge Wells for four guineas. Quite possibly Strachey bought them.

156 *the fall of Man from Paradise*: see Stanley: 'Conservatism in his mouth was not merely the watchword of an English party, but the symbol of an evil, against which his whole life, public and private, was one continued struggle' (pp. 151–2). Strachey wittily elaborates this prejudice.

. . . the latter part of the seventeenth century: Arnold wrote this in a letter to the Chevalier Bunsen, 6 May 1833. What Arnold indicates is that, in general, he agrees with these sentiments, which were not, originally, *his* but those of his correspondent, Bunsen. He goes on to disagree on various points (Stanley 280).

. . . Botany Bay: a jotting in his notebook indicates that Strachey took this comment from a letter of W. G. Ward to Newman, in 1864, reporting an intemperate remark of Arnold's.

Arnold occasionally visited them, in Rugby: Stanley records that as headmaster Arnold was reluctant to mix town and gown. It was not snobbery, but a sense of the proper place of the school in the community as something apart. He was much happier visiting the local poor in Westmorland (Stanley, 182).

. . . I see no counteracting power: Arnold wrote this in a letter of 29 September 1834. Strachey shortens the quotation considerably, which digresses into the state of affairs in ancient Greece and recent Paris. (Stanley, 311).

the second destruction of Jerusalem: Strachey mangles this quotation (getting the biblical verse references wrong, and altering the general sense) from a letter to Augustus Hare, 24 December, 1830. Any curious reader is referred to Stanley (p. 227). Strachey of course quite reasonably expects none of his readers to follow up Arnold's barrage of instruction.

the gift of tongues had descended on the Irvingites at Glasgow: the Irvingites were founded in the early 1830s by Edward Irving (1792–1834), an excommunicated minister of the Church of Scotland. They adopted quasi-Catholic ritual and liturgy and took the name Catholic Apostolic Church. Arnold read about their talking in tongues at Glasgow in October 1831 and communicated with the Revd F. C. Blackstone about it (Stanley, 241). Strachey quotes him more or less correctly but omits that Arnold was uncertain whether this pentecostalist event was 'a real sign or no'. The Greek means 'ages'.

157 *Jews admitted to Parliament . . . Scripture was not made an obligatory subject at the London University*: the 'Judaizing' lobby, and its 'Jew Bill' (as Arnold offensively called parliamentary initiatives to remove Jewish 'disabilities') much exercised the headmaster of Rugby during the early 1830s. As he told W. W. Hull on 27 April 1836 (not, apparently, ironically), 'I think we might lawfully deal with them on the Liberia system, and remove them to a land where they might live by themselves independent; for England is the land of Englishmen, not of Jews' (Stanley, 373). Arnold was made a fellow of the new University of London (the 'Godless Place in Gower Street') in 1835 but resigned in November 1838 on the grounds, principally, of the University's not making the study of the Bible obligatory for all students. He told the Bishop of Norwich (on 17 February 1838): 'The University has solemnly avowed a principle to which I am totally opposed,—namely, that Education need not be connected with Christianity' (Stanley, 439).

'My great objection . . . it makes Christ virtually dead': quoted from a letter to William Smith, 9 March, 1833. Strachey misses out a clause: '. . . in its present form in England, where it is professed sincerely, is that it makes Christ virtually dead' (Stanley, 278).

. . . in Boston: writing to an American, Jacob Abbott, 1 November 1833, Arnold says: 'I have understood that Unitarianism is becoming very prevalent in Boston, and I am anxious to know what the complexion of Unitarianism amongst you is' (Stanley, 295). It is not known what Abbott replied.

158 *the restoration of the Order of Deacons*: Strachey alludes to a letter by Arnold written to 'an Old Pupil' ('D.') on 20 December 1839, about to become a Deacon, written 'just one and twenty years ago this very day that I was ordained Deacon at Oxford' (Stanley, 492). You are entering, Arnold tells his correspondent, 'an office extinct in all but name. If it could be revived in power, it would be one of the greatest blessings that could be conferred on the Church' (Stanley, 494). Deaconry is the third order of minister, below Bishops and Priests. The name means 'servant'. It was the point of entry into the Anglican priesthood in the nineteenth century and the broad bridge between university and church. Arnold believed that Deacons, as he told A. P. Stanley on 27 February 1839, being 'half laymen' could—as Strachey quotes him here—be the thin

edge of the wedge against Antichrist (Stanley, 471)—principally the Newmanites ('idolaters').

158 ... *their causes and remedies*: Strachey leaves out Arnold's self-deprecating remark, attached to this, that he launched the paper 'more to relieve my own conscience than with any sanguine hope of doing good' (Stanley, 220). He was, of course, as the Reform Bill loomed, neither Tory, Whig, Liberal, nor Radical.

159 *One of his admirers*: the friend was Bonamy Price, writing to Stanley (pp. 168–9). Strachey shortens his source material. Arnold wrote 'unravelling the thread of God's religious education of the human race, from its earliest infancy down the fullness of times, and holding up God's marvellous counsels . . .'

would not end in Socinianism?—nay in Atheism itself?: Socinianism was a sixteenth-century doctrine associated with Lelio Sozzini and his nephew Fausto Sozzini. Its essential tenet denied the divinity of Christ, seeing him merely as a prophet. Arnold was much concerned (as Strachey intimates) by Socinianism in the mid-1830s, but not terribly alarmed. He believed that 'Every great mind must of necessity have the germ of that which, *carried to excess*, becomes Socinianism' (Stanley, 372).

Strauss's 'Leben Jesu' without reading it: this is somewhat unfair. Arnold wrote to Chevalier Bunsen, in October 1836, in passing: 'What a strange work Strauss's Leben Jesu appears to me, judging of it from the notices in the *Studien und Kritiken*' (Stanley, 396).

160 *Finding that the headmaster . . . the next thirty-six hours*: this heroic episode is described in Ward. Strachey came across it, first, in his work on the Manning section and made a memorandum in his notebook.

161 *The longer holidays . . . he declared*: Arnold disliked the flat countryside of Warwickshire, feeling when he was there 'like a potted plant'. In 1832 he bought a family house, Fox How, near Ambleside in the Lake District where he and his family spent blissful vacations. As Stanley reports: 'the wild flowers on the mountain sides . . . were to him, he said, "his music" ' (p. 185).

'Life . . . in themselves so little': Strachey quotes this from Stanley (p. 213). Arnold was, of course, a thoroughgoing Wordsworthian and the act of establishing his country house at Fox How, in Westmorland, in 1832, was a practical expression of discipleship.

164 *a weakness in the ankles*: Strachey's notebook indicates that he took this detail from Thomas Hughes, as quoted in S. Waddington's 1883 *Memoir* of the poet, p. 53 (the source is not cited in Strachey's appended bibliography). Other details about Clough are taken from the same source.

School House: this was the house which Arnold himself took charge of at Rugby. Clough would have been on social terms with the Arnold family as the head boy in the house.

165 ... *I may perhaps not live to finish it*: Strachey transcribes, verbatim, this poignant detail and the following about his pre-mortem diary from Stanley (pp. 606–10). Arnold began keeping the diary some three weeks before his death.

166 *'painful and solemn' reflections*: Strachey artfully leaves out Arnold's qualifying remark: 'I have been just looking over a newspaper, one of the most painful and solemn studies in the world, if it be read thoughtfully. So much of sin and so much of suffering in the world, as are there displayed, and no one seems able to remedy either ...' (Stanley, 610).

the threatening prospect of the moral condition of the United States: Strachey leaves out, again, a moderating afterthought. Arnold pondered: 'the moral condition of the United States,—united on the other hand with their great opportunities for good in "that vast continent" ' (Stanley, 614).

"Vixi": I have lived.

THE END OF GENERAL GORDON

STRACHEY'S SOURCES

As his bibliography indicates, Strachey (who was under some time pressure) read more widely and dipped more eclectically (particularly in newspaper sources) for this section. One cannot, as with the other three portraits, identify a single principal source.

171 *During*: in his notes, Strachey drafted an introduction to this section which in the event he did not use, although he cannibalized some small sections for his conclusion:

In January London, the great clubs and mansions loomed square and solid through the foggy air, while the heavy traffic lumbered along the streets, and politicians briskly passed and repassed, top-hatted, to their offices and luncheons, or discussed the affairs of the nation drawn up in leather chairs about the fire. And in the evening there were parties and concerts, with Signor Piatti playing the violincello, and ladies in looped elaborate dresses coming out of curious hansoms, in a happy atmosphere of middle class and comfortable rococo. The news of the Soudan catastrophe arrived, and there was a great outcry. The public grief vied with the public indignation. The Queen, in a letter to Miss Gordon, expressed her own sentiments and those of the nation. *How* shall I write to you, she exclaimed (Add. 54223)

On reflection, Strachey wrote an emphatic 'No!' under this, and evidently resolved to open with something simpler—Gordon looking for God in the Holy Land.

During the year 1883 ... the neighbourhood of Jerusalem: this opening paragraph is drawn from chapter 12 of Henry William Gordon's *Events in the Life of Charles George Gordon* (1886). See, for example, the chapter 12 summary: 'He lands at Jaffa and goes to Jerusalem—the Altar or Table of the Lord—The Gates of Jerusalem—Skull Hill—the Place of the Crucifixion—The Divisions between the tribes of Judah and Benjamin—the Gibeons of Scripture—The Site of the Garden of Eden—the Ark.'

171 *almost childish sincerity*: this physical description of Gordon is substantially drawn (as notes in Add. 54219 indicate) from the *Revue Politique et Littéraire*, 16 February 1884. M. Joseph Reinach met Gordon on board ship, in January 1880, on a voyage from Alexandria to Naples, and recorded: 'C'était alors un homme d'une quarantaine d'années, de taille moyenne, très maigre, la démarche inquiète, les yeux très doux, vagues, comme perdus dans un monde lointain de pensées, le teint haut en couleur, de ce bronze rouge que donne la "complexion brique" des Anglais quand elle a été dorée par le soleil des tropiques.' (He was a man of about 40, medium height, very thin, with a restless bearing, his eyes gentle, vague, as if lost in a distant world of thoughts, a high colour, that red-bronze taken on by the 'brick complexion' of the English when it has been burnt by the tropical sun.) Strachey also noted in his notes a description of Gordon by Richard Burton, printed in the *Academy*, 11 July 1885: 'those calm benevolent blue eyes and that modest reserved and even shy expression, blent with simple dignity, which, where he was intimate, changed to the sympathetic frankness of a child's face.'

172 *Sir Evelyn Baring and Lord Hartington*: Evelyn Baring, later Earl of Cromer (1841–1917), statesman and diplomatist. His career was to intertwine most fatefully with Gordon's and he is, in Strachey's analysis, the villain of the piece. Like Gordon, Baring began his career as a soldier. Unlike Gordon, he was a classicist and subtle by nature. In 1872 he moved from the army into the diplomatic corps, serving with distinction in India. In April 1876 Egypt, owing to the financial mismanagement of Khedive Ismail, was, effectively, taken into receivership by Britain and France. Baring was appointed British Commissioner and, in 1883, Consul-General. He is generally credited (if that is the word) with sending Gordon to his death, in 1884. Lord Hartington (Spencer Compton Cavendish, 1833–1908) was another distinguished statesman whose career was to connect, disastrously, with Gordon's. He too served in India, before being appointed, in December 1882, as Secretary of State for War. Strachey, at an early point in his thinking about *Eminent Victorians*, contemplated doing a whole essay on Hartington.

was himself a Lieutenant-General: Gordon's father was a major in the Royal Artillery when his son (the fourth boy out of a family of eleven children) was born. Henry William Gordon died, thirty years later, a Lieutenant-General in 1865.

On one occasion . . . a glass door at the bottom: this 'act of insubordination' is taken verbatim from H. W. Gordon, *Events*, 38. The source adds that the captain who predicted Gordon would 'never make an officer' was

Eardley Wilmot—later (as General Wilmot) one of Gordon's closest friends. The clothes-brush incident is similarly taken from *Events*, 38. John Pollock firmly contradicts Strachey's interpretation of this event: 'Gordon did not lose the offer of a commission in the Royal Artillery because of an escapade at Woolwich: he was determined to be a Royal Engineer, and delayed his passing-out in order to achieve the higher marks required' (*EVDE* 308).

Drew: nothing seems known about Drew than that he was a Captain in the 11th Hussars and was a keen amateur archaeologist researching the Welsh Druids. Roy MacGregor-Hastie records in *Never to be taken Alive* (1985): 'Drew was horrified to learn that his young friend seldom went to church . . . Whatever new version of Christianity Drew preached, it was certainly attractive' (p. 31). Shortly after, at Easter 1854, Gordon took his first Communion.

173 *Priceless Diamond . . . Commentaries . . . The Remains of the Rev. R. McCheyne*: *The Priceless Diamond* is an obscure (anonymous) religious tract, published in Birmingham, 1855. The *Commentaries* are those on the Bible by Henry and Scott, condensed by the Revd John McFarlane (1860). The *Remains* are those literary relics of the Scottish divine, Robert Murray McCheyne (1818–43). It is, as Strachey intimates, a dry reading list.

war was declared upon China: the Second Opium War, as it was called, ended in June 1858 on terms deeply humiliating to China. In 1859 four British diplomats, sent to Beijing to collect an indemnity of 4 million taels of silver, were arrested on trumped-up charges and tortured to death. War was declared. Under the command of Lord Elgin, a punitive expedition was launched which resulted in the exemplary destruction of the Summer Palace at Beijing.

the barbarism of the East: MacGregor-Hastie observes: 'Though Lytton Strachey is bitter about "the destruction of the Summer Palace . . ."' everything that could be saved had been saved. Elgin had given orders to this effect and what was eventually blown up was the seat of government, as a warning to the Emperor not to misbehave again. Gordon and other Royal Engineers physically organized the reprisal' (p. 63).

175 *Li Hung Chang*: the introduction of this potentate into his narrative, and reliance on his diaries (of which many passages are copied out in Strachey's notes), constitutes one of the weakest links in Strachey's narrative. He was preparing *Eminent Victorians* for publication in 1917, when serious doubt was cast on the veracity of the source by J. O. P. Bland's *Li Hung Chang* (1917). The diary was exposed as pure fake in 1923. John Pollock comments:

> Strachey may be excused, when describing Gordon's leadership of the Ever Victorious Army in China, for quoting at length from the supposed diary of the mandarin Li Hung Chang, because the book was not exposed as a hoax until five years after the publication of *Eminent*

Victorians: Strachey adds a note to his bibliography that its 'authenticity has been disputed'. He was not to know that the 'diary' had been composed by an American petty criminal in a Honolulu jail. It is worthless as evidence on Gordon. (*EVDE* 308)

178 *is said . . . with a pistol in his hand*: H. W. Gordon records, firmly: 'It is not the fact, as stated by many writers, that Major Gordon sought the Futai [i.e. Li Hung Chang] with the intention of shooting him' (*Events*, 70).

swallowed gold leaf: a Chinese mandarin's preferred (and lavish) mode of suicidal poisoning.

179 *he was particularly fond of boys*: here, and elsewhere, Strachey hints darkly at Gordon's sexuality. MacGregor-Hastie offers the following interpretation:

> Fred Plaut, a London psychiatrist, writing in *Encounter*, June–July 1982, expressed his opinion that 'it seems obvious that Gordon was more homo– than heterosexual [but it] is improbable that he was ever a practising homosexual; in a man who lived so much in the public eye and had many enemies, this could hardly have escaped notice.' Nearly a hundred years after Gordon's death, Plaut's conclusion sums up all the speculation that went on during Gordon's life and after his death. (p. 84)

Gordon told one of his friends, the Revd H. Barnes, in later life that 'I wished I was a eunuch at 14' (MacGregor-Hastie, 150).

the Lancashire famine: the distress in the industrial, textile-producing areas of Lancashire with the cessation of cotton deliveries from the American South during the Civil War.

181 *the apotropaic initials D.V.*: in his notes, Strachey reminded himself to write this instead of what he initially proposed, 'the symbolical letters D. V.' (Add. 54223). DV = 'God willing'.

in such a creed: Strachey could not initially think of the *most juste* and left a blank for what became 'creed' in the proofs.

182 *the Treaty of Paris*: after the Crimean War, in March 1856.

Khedive Ismail: 'khedive' was the title applied to the sovereign leader of Egypt (at this date very much under British superintendence). Beneath the corrupt Ismail were a legion of Pashas and Beys who administered the protectorate, as governors or military commanders. Not all were Egyptian: Nubar Pasha was, for example, Armenian. After the completion of the Suez Canal, in 1869, Egypt was of great strategic importance to England.

183 *Sir Samuel Baker*: Sir Samuel White Baker (1821–93), 'traveller and sportsman', Governor-General of the Equatorial Nile Basin (Equatoria) with the rank of Pasha, 1869–73. He was brother of General Valentine Baker ('Baker Pasha', 1827–87) a general in the Egyptian service and commander of police, 1882–7.

his Italian lieutenant, Gessi: Gordon first met Romolo Gessi, as an officer interpreter, in the Crimea. A polyglot, cosmopolitan soldier (born in Ravenna, half Armenian, but with a claim to British nationality, and a Roman Catholic), Gessi was a year older than Gordon. The two soldiers became firm friends, and their comradely paths crossed again in Egypt, where Gessi died in 1881.

184 *towards stimulants of a more material quality*: the allegation which follows of Gordon's dipsomania is one of the more disputed aspects of Strachey's account. John Pollock writes: 'Gordon was not teetotal, and brandy was the normal social and medical drink in hot countries in his day, although he never touched alcohol in Equatoria. Secret drinking was impossible in a land where everything was quickly known' (*EVDE* 308). Strachey was, however, evidently persuaded by a comment of Richard Burton's, quoted by Colonel Chaillé Long (see the following note) in *L'Égypte et ses provinces perdues* (1892), 183: 'Burton ne le dit pas clairment, mais peut-être bien est-ce dans ce diable de whiskey qu'on pourrait chercher l'origine de ces élucubrations étranges qui ont tant mystifié le public.' (Burton does not say this clearly, but it is perhaps in the demon whisky that we could find the origin of these strange writings that have so mystified the public.)

Colonel Long, the chief of staff: Charles Chaillé Long, whose *My Life in Four Continents* (1912), *The Three Prophets* (1884) and *L'Égypte et ses provinces perdues* (1892) are extensively drawn on in the following pages. Chaillé Long (1842–1917) was, among much else, an American soldier, African explorer and writer. He was commissioned in the Egyptian army, under Gordon. Immediately after this service he explored the Victoria Nile. He was in later life an American diplomat.

a little b. and s. Do you feel up to it?: the actual quotation in Chaillé Long (which Strachey copied out in his notebook) is: 'Gordon came forward to meet me with a quick glide-like step, and seizing my hand, exclaimed: "How are you, old fellow? Come and take a glass of b. and s.—brandy and soda. A peg will help us to talk about Central Africa." ' Although he copied it into his notebook, Strachey did not insert into his text what follows, on p. 28 of *My Life in Four Continents*: 'The b. and s. Gordon took but seldom. Gordon and I generally drank coffee, very black, with a quinine bottle on the table, and from which we took *ad libitum* the quinine instead of sugar.' John Pollock (*EVDE* 309) refutes the whole episode of Gordon retreating to his tent with a brandy bottle 'for days at a time' as apocryphal: 'No such incident took place. Long's account, written forty years later and contradicting his own early accounts, was thoroughly demolished by Bernard Allen [in *Gordon and the Sudan*, 1931; and by Godfrey Elton, *General Gordon*, 1954].'

185 *kick him till he screamed*: Strachey recorded in his notes from *My Life in Four Continents* (pp. 85–6) Chaillé Long's recollection of Gordon slapping the face of his Arab ADC, Hassan, and kicking his Alsatian servant, Kellerman.

186 *the Negus of Abyssinia*: i.e. the emperor.

187 *Lord Lyons*: Richard Lyons (1817–87), the most distinguished British ambassador of the decade, resident in Paris 1867–87.

  Lord Ripon, the new Viceroy of India: George Frederick Samuel Robinson, first Marquis of Ripon (1827–1909), appointed Governor-General of India (after a period of retirement) by Gladstone, in April 1880.

  Lord William Beresford: Admiral (1846–1919). He was, in 1882, a senior officer serving in the bombardment of Alexandria. After retirement, on half pay, he was called back in 1884 to act on the staff of Lord Wolseley during the expedition for the relief of Gordon at Khartoum.

188 *I am glad of it*: Gordon's communications with his sister Augusta, essential to any insight into his state of mind during these great affairs of state, are taken—as the notes indicate—from D. C. Boulger's *Life of General Gordon* (1896).

  Sir Howard Elphinstone: Howard Crawfurd Elphinstone (1829–90), like Gordon a career officer in the Royal Engineers. He won the Victoria Cross in the Crimea.

190 *the Angel Izrail*: one of the four archangels in the Islamic firmament. Izrail is the angel of death.

191 *a second Hegira*: Hegira or Hejira commemorates the departure of the prophet Muhammad from Mecca in September 622.

194 *under Lord Wolseley*: Sir Garnet Wolseley ('Baron Wolseley of Cairo', 1833–1913), commander of the British troops in Egypt. He returned to England just before his friend Gordon left for Egypt in 1884. MacGregor-Hastie comments:

> Just before [i.e. in 1881–2] an Egyptian colonel of peasant origin, Arabi, had led a national revolt against the new Khedive Tewfik and the bankers and businessmen who manipulated him. This was a genuine 'national liberation' movement, perhaps the first of the new imperial era, and was promptly put down by the British Liberal government. Alexandria was bombarded by the British fleet in 1882, and a British army, under Lord Wolseley, defeated Arabi Pasha at Tel-el-Kebir. (p. 149)

  This 'peasant-led revolt' led directly to the Mahdi's uprising which, despite its religious fanaticism, had roots in anti-colonialism.

  Colonel Hicks, a retired English officer: Colonel William Hicks ('Hicks Pasha', 1830–83), served most of his (inconspicuous) career in India, before retiring to Egypt. He was recalled to service and promoted to General and Pasha in February 1883, in order to lead 12,000 Egyptian troops to ignominious defeat and his own destruction at the Battle of Kashgil. The defeat, as Strachey records, threatened the whole rickety power structure of Beys, Pashas, and corrupt satraps in the Egyptian territories.

196 *with Mr Gladstone at their head*: Gladstone had become Prime Minister

in 1880, although (with Egyptian and Irish problems) his hold on office was constantly under threat.

197 *such were General Gordon's prospects on January 7th, 1884*: this is somewhat overstated. The King of the Belgians had, for some time, wanted Gordon to assist with the new Congo state which he had divided up in 'concessionary' regions for the exploitation of rubber and ivory (Gordon might, conceivably, have become a version of Conrad's Kurtz). There was no hurry, however, and in January 1883 Gordon spent a year, as he had longed to, undertaking biblical-archaeological research in Palestine. When in October he returned to Europe, to take up service for the Belgians, he discovered that the British War Office would not give him permission. He was intending to resign his commission, trusting that King Leopold would compensate him. At this point the Egyptian crisis blew up. On 15 January 1884 he was summoned to the War Office by Lord Wolseley.

198 *it is not clear who*: John Pollock is scathing about Strachey's mystification here: 'Strachey says "it is not clear" who in the War Office first suggested Gordon for the Sudan, yet Colonel Bevan Edwards's letter of 22 November 1883 had been printed in a major political biography' (*EVDE* 310).

The Pall Mall Gazette, which, more than any other newspaper interested itself in Egyptian affairs: the *Pall Mall Gazette* had been founded in 1865. Its proprietor, George Smith, had a long-standing commercial interest in the East. W. T. Stead (1849–1912; pioneer of what came to be called 'New Journalism') was appointed Editor in 1883, and made an immediate mark—as Strachey records—with his campaign to save the Sudan (with the help of Gordon). It was a misconceived strategy. Strachey was particularly struck by, and recorded in his notes, a deadly miscalculation in the *PMG* for 27 November 1884 (by Sir Samuel Baker): 'Khartoum . . . must be held at all costs . . . the Sudan can be restored by a determined policy without much fighting.'

199 *Lord Granville*: the 2nd Earl Granville (1815–91), Minister for Foreign Affairs under Gladstone.

While these messages . . . alone again: as his notes indicate, Strachey took this, as he took much else, from Wilfred Blunt's *Gordon at Khartoum* (1911; this passage, and Bishop Temple's amusing comment about polygamy, are both from p. 243). Gordon stayed with his friend, Barnes, for a couple of days after 10 January. In his notes, Strachey records that Barnes administered Holy Communion to Gordon on 11 January 'probably for the last time (with one exception)'. It was the same morning as the carriage ride described here.

201 *less easy to discern*: MacGregor-Hastie notes:

> Fortunately, recent research carried out by members of the American University at Cairo has cleared up much of the mystery. As Sir William Butler has written and Lord Hartington said, Gordon left London to

report on the military situation. He took only hand luggage and little or no money; he was expected back in a month. 'I go to the Soudan tonight to finish a work,' he wrote on 18 January, 'then to the Congo' . . . Nobody will ever know just how the Egyptian government and Sir Evelyn Baring seduced Gordon from his original intention. (pp. 156–7)

201 *a fighter, an enthusiast, a bold adventurer*: John Pollock dissents strongly from Strachey's assessment: 'Strachey's estimate of Gordon as "before all things a fighter, an enthusiast, a bold adventurer", is deeply flawed. Gordon was a man of peace and reconciliation, who only fought to achieve both' (*EVDE* 310).

206 *The train rolled out of the station*: John Pollock notes:

> The celebrated farewell at Charing Cross is somewhat garbled. The 'leather bag' contained Gordon's uniform, brought hurriedly by his nephew; the 'two hundred pounds in gold' had been borrowed by Lord Hartington from friends in his clubs to buy the tickets, as the banks were shut. And the last whispered question, about copies of *Scripture Promises* for Cabinet ministers is an invention by Strachey without any source whatsoever. (*EVDE* 311)

207 *General Gordon was very rude to him*: John Pollock finds this 'a curious interpretation of the incident':

> The insufferable Sultan, produced as a substitute for Zobair, had already been a nuisance before the night railway journey. At Assiout next morning he stepped down from the train in a gorgeous gold-laced uniform. Ignoring the Governor-General he pranced towards the paddle-steamer, followed by his harem . . . [Gordon] ordered him to take off his uniform . . . he would certainly be murdered if he travelled in gold braid; he must not wear his uniform until he had recovered his throne. (*EVDE* 311)

208 *'Il faut être toujours ivre . . . c'est l'unique question'*: 'one must always be drunk. Everything is there: it is the only question.' From 'Enivrez-vous', one of Baudelaire's 'small prose poems'.

'Pour ne pas sentir . . . sans trêve': 'in order not to feel the horrible burden of Time which breaks your back and bends you down to earth, you must be unremittingly intoxicated.'

he tossed off a glass: John Pollock notes: 'General W. A. Scott, who had been on that steamer as General Graham's young ADC, recalled that Gordon had not touched "a drop of spirits" on the Nile voyage' (*EVDE* 312). Strachey, asserts Pollock, has created 'a Gordon of his own imagination'.

210 *Sir Gerald Graham*: (1831–99), the commander sent out after the defeat of General Baker by the local commander, Osman Digna, with the loss of the fortified towns of Sinkat and Tokar. Like Gordon, he was a Royal Engineer.

211 *Mr Power*: Frank Power, of *The Times*. MacGregor-Hastie records the dire consequences of Gordon's indiscretion:

> Power's article immediately aroused the wrath of the Anti-Slavery Society, and Gladstone was forced to announce in the Commons that Zobeir would not be released and, what is more, Sir Gerald Graham and his troops would be withdrawn. The British government would have nothing to do with any scheme which made it appear to be an agent of aggression or repression. The British government could not have done anything worse. (pp. 161–2)

217 *before the wire was cut*: the wire was cut on 16 April.

'He took up the paper ... and was seen no more that morning': as his notes indicate, Strachey took this from an article by George W. Smalley in *Harper's Magazine*, 1898.

218 *His temperament ... eminently unromantic*: Strachey jotted down in his notebook some notes on 'Sir E. B.' for what became this passage: 'cold blue and indecisive eyes. | He could recoil and recoil | Steely bend and bend | The art of giving way. | He gave way and never bent. | Long views, infinite patience, staying power. | Not great enough to be really cynical. | His ambition—to become an institution. | Those powers of misrepresentation. | Eminently correct. | Sh[akespeare] Sonnet. | The East meant nothing to him: it was something to be looked after. | It was also a convenient field for the talents of Sir E. B.'

223 *He seemed to be utterly abandoned*: Strachey jotted down in his notebook: 'After Apr. 21st with a typically convenient unobtrusiveness, Sir E. B. vanishes from the public scene.' See also p. 221.

225 *the large, long, bearded, unimpressionable face*: in the manuscript, Strachey wrote 'the large, red, rough horse face' (Add. 54223). He changed it in proof, presumably so as not to offend Hartington's family more than he already had.

228 *his motives were to be veiled for ever in a tragic obscurity*: John Pollock notes that in the description of the siege of Khartoum Strachey keeps 'reasonably near to the facts' except in this impugning of Stewart's motives: 'These, fortunately for Stewart's memory, were not "to be veiled for ever in tragic obscurity" but could have been found out by Strachey himself. For Stewart only left, against his own wishes, because Gordon begged him to go down river, taking the code-books, to tell the world of Khartoum's desperate condition and prospects. Stewart declined to desert Gordon unless ordered' (*EVDE* 313).

230 *Uriah the Hittite*: the warrior sent by King David into the vanguard of the battle, so that he might be killed and David take possession of his wife, Bathsheba (2 Sam. 11).

232 *'The eye that mocketh ... the young eagles shall eat it'*: Proverbs 30: 17.

235 *'Excellence! ... la verité'*: Excellency! I have sent two letters, without receiving a reply from your excellency. . . . Excellency! I've fought 27

times for the government against the enemy—they've beaten me twice, and I've done nothing dishonourable—nothing that should prevent your excellency from writing me a reply so that I know what to do. . . . *I beg you*, excellency, to honour me with a reply. . . . PS. If your excellency has perhaps heard that I've done something against the honour of an officer and that stops you writing to me, I beg you to give me the chance to defend myself, and judge the truth.

235 *Ernest Renan*: (Joseph) Ernest Renan (1823–1892), French philologist and historian. He was best known for his sceptical *Vie de Jésus* (Life of Jesus, 1863).

236 *Arthur Rimbaud*: (1854–1891), French poet and adventurer. The author, as Strachey indicates, of *Une saison en enfer* (A Season in Hell; 1873) he stopped writing poetry at the age of 21. He was often in Egypt, on various commercial ventures in the 1880s and took an informed interest in the country. The French which Strachey quotes accuses the English of 'typically' behaving like imbeciles in Egypt—they are worse than the Turks, even.

238 *Like Lawrence, I have tried to do my duty*: Sir Henry Montgomery Lawrence (1806–57), killed defending Lucknow (successfully) against mutineers in the Indian Mutiny.

242 *The news of the catastrophe reached England*: Strachey's notes reveal that he was not sure whether the news were received in London on the evening of 11 or 10 February. He prudently omitted any date.

243 *Maxim-Nordenfeldt guns*: in his notes for this passage, Strachey made a closer reference to the current war: 'the future lay with Major Kitchener and the artillery of Messrs. Krupps.'

by a select company of Sudanese buglers: John Pollock comments:

> Strachey ends by mocking the memorial service for Gordon held in the ruins of his Palace thirteen years and seven months later after the Battle of Omdurman. The service, planned carefully by Kitchener, who always looked on Gordon as the hero of his life, was in fact a deeply moving and appropriate farewell. 'Abide with me' was not a 'performance by a select company of Sudanese buglers,' but sung by all present, accompanied by the band of the 11th Sudanese, a battalion of Blacks from the south who had loathed the Mahdi and had shown great valour in the battles. (*EVDE* 313–14).

a step in the Peerage for Sir Evelyn Baring: in a notebook draft for this conclusion, Strachey phrases it slightly differently: 'At any rate, it had all ended very happily—in a vast accession of territory for the British Empire and an Earldom for Sir Evelyn Baring.' In the manuscript, he wrote another slightly different version which concludes: '. . . in a glorious slaughter of fifty thousand Arabs, a vast addition to the British Empire, and an Earldom for Sir Evelyn Baring' (Add. 54219). Strachey evidently gave these final words close attention at the proof stage.

ANTON CHEKHOV

Early Stories
Five Plays
The Princess and Other Stories
The Russian Master and Other Stories
The Steppe and Other Stories
Twelve Plays
Ward Number Six and Other Stories

FYODOR DOSTOEVSKY

Crime and Punishment
Devils
A Gentle Creature and Other Stories
The Idiot
The Karamazov Brothers
Memoirs from the House of the Dead
Notes from the Underground and
    The Gambler

NIKOLAI GOGOL

Dead Souls
Plays and Petersburg Tales

ALEXANDER PUSHKIN

Eugene Onegin
The Queen of Spades and Other Stories

LEO TOLSTOY

Anna Karenina
The Kreutzer Sonata and Other Stories
The Raid and Other Stories
Resurrection
War and Peace

IVAN TURGENEV

Fathers and Sons
First Love and Other Stories
A Month in the Country

ANTHONY TROLLOPE

An Autobiography

The American Senator

Barchester Towers

Can You Forgive Her?

The Claverings

Cousin Henry

Doctor Thorne

The Duke's Children

The Eustace Diamonds

Framley Parsonage

He Knew He Was Right

Lady Anna

The Last Chronicle of Barset

Orley Farm

Phineas Finn

Phineas Redux

The Prime Minister

Rachel Ray

The Small House at Allington

The Warden

The Way We Live Now

	Women's Writing 1778–1838
WILLIAM BECKFORD	Vathek
JAMES BOSWELL	Life of Johnson
FRANCES BURNEY	Camilla
	Cecilia
	Evelina
	The Wanderer
LORD CHESTERFIELD	Lord Chesterfield's Letters
JOHN CLELAND	Memoirs of a Woman of Pleasure
DANIEL DEFOE	A Journal of the Plague Year
	Moll Flanders
	Robinson Crusoe
	Roxana
HENRY FIELDING	Joseph Andrews and Shamela
	A Journey from This World to the Next and The Journal of a Voyage to Lisbon
	Tom Jones
WILLIAM GODWIN	Caleb Williams
OLIVER GOLDSMITH	The Vicar of Wakefield
MARY HAYS	Memoirs of Emma Courtney
ELIZABETH HAYWOOD	The History of Miss Betsy Thoughtless
ELIZABETH INCHBALD	A Simple Story
SAMUEL JOHNSON	The History of Rasselas
	The Major Works
CHARLOTTE LENNOX	The Female Quixote
MATTHEW LEWIS	Journal of a West India Proprietor
	The Monk
HENRY MACKENZIE	The Man of Feeling
ALEXANDER POPE	Selected Poetry

The
Oxford
World's
Classics
Website

www.worldsclassics.co.uk

- Information about new titles
- Explore the full range of Oxford World's Classics
- Links to other literary sites and the main OUP webpage
- Imaginative competitions, with bookish prizes
- Peruse the Oxford World's Classics Magazine
- Articles by editors
- Extracts from Introductions
- A forum for discussion and feedback on the series
- Special information for teachers and lecturers

www.worldsclassics.co.uk

American Literature

British and Irish Literature

Children's Literature

Classics and Ancient Literature

Colonial Literature

Eastern Literature

European Literature

History

Medieval Literature

Oxford English Drama

Poetry

Philosophy

Politics

Religion

The Oxford Shakespeare

A complete list of Oxford Paperbacks, including Oxford World's Classics, Oxford Shakespeare, Oxford Drama, and Oxford Paperback Reference, is available in the UK from the Academic Division Publicity Department, Oxford University Press, Great Clarendon Street, Oxford OX2 6DP.

In the USA, complete lists are available from the Paperbacks Marketing Manager, Oxford University Press, 198 Madison Avenue, New York, NY 10016.

Oxford Paperbacks are available from all good bookshops. In case of difficulty, customers in the UK can order direct from Oxford University Press Bookshop, Freepost, 116 High Street, Oxford OX1 4BR, enclosing full payment. Please add 10 per cent of published price for postage and packing.